MIDNIGHT'S
DESCENDANTS

MIDNIGHT'S DESCENDANTS

A HISTORY *of* SOUTH ASIA
SINCE PARTITION

JOHN KEAY

BASIC BOOKS

A Member of the Perseus Books Group

New York

Published by Basic Books,
A Member of the Perseus Books Group

Designed by Pauline Brown
Typeset in 11 point Sabon by the Perseus Books Group

Library of Congress Cataloging-in-Publication Data

Keay, John.
    Midnight's descendants : a history of South Asia since partition / John Keay.
        pages cm
    Includes bibliographical references and index.
    ISBN 978-0-465-02180-2 (hardcover)—ISBN 978-0-465-08072-4 (e-book) 1. South Asia—History. 2. South Asia—Politics and government. 3. South Asia—Relations. 4. Regionalism—South Asia. 5. Geopolitics—South Asia. 6. South Asia—Social conditions. I. Title.
    DS340.K37 2014
    954.04—dc23

                                                            2013045232

10 9 8 7 6 5 4 3 2 1

In memory of
Julia Keay

CONTENTS

Introduction   *xv*

1   Casting the Die   1

2   Counting the Cost   31

3   "Who Has Not Heard of the Vale of Cashmere?"   65

4   Past Conditional   103

5   Reality Check   133

6   Power to the People   169

7   An Ill-Starred Conjunction   193

8   Two-Way Tickets, Double Standards   223

9   Things Fall Apart   249

10   Outside the Gates   277

11   India Astir   303

    Epilogue   339

Author's Note   *351*
Notes   *353*
Bibliography   *363*
Index   *373*

INDIA			PAKISTAN	
Cong	Jawaharlal NEHRU	1947	M A JINNAH (GG)	ML
		1948	K NAZIMUDDIN (GG)/Liaquat Ali KHAN (PM)	
		1949		
		1950	Ghulam MOHAMED (GG)/K NAZIMUDDIN (PM)	
		1951		
		1952		
		1953	N A BOGRA (PM)	
		1954		
		1955	Iskander MIRZA (GG)/C MOHAMED ALI (PM)	
		1956	Iskander MIRZA(Pres)/H S SUHRAWARDY(PM)	
		1957	CHUNDRIGAR/NOON (PM)	
		1958	AYUB KHAN (CMLA)	
		1959		
		1960		
		1961		
		1962		
Cong	Lal Bahadur SHASTRI	1963	AYUB KHAN(Pres)	
		1964		
Cong	Indira GANDHI	1965		
		1966		
		1967		
		1968		
Cong (R)		1969	YAHYA KHAN (CMLA)	
		1970		
		1971	Z A BHUTTO (Pres/CMLA)	PPP
		1972		
		1973	Z A BHUTTO (PM)	
		1974		
		1975		
	EMERGENCY	1976		
Janata	Morarji DESAI	1977	ZIAUL HAQ (CMLA)	
		1978	ZIAUL HAQ (Pres)	
Janata	Charan SINGH	1979		
Cong (I)	Indira GANDHI	1980		
		1981		
		1982		
		1983		
Cong (I)	Rajiv GANDHI	1984		
		1985	ZIAUL HAQ (Pres)/M K JUNEJO (PM)	PML
		1986		
		1987		
		1988	Benazir BHUTTO (PM)	PPP
NF	V P SINGH	1989		
NF	CHANDRASHEKHAR	1990	Nawaz SHARIF (PM)	PML(N)
Cong (I)	P V Narasimha RAO	1991		
		1992		
		1993	Benazir BHUTTO (PM)	PPP
		1994		
UF	A B VAJPAYEE/	1995		
	H D DEVEGOWDA	1996		
	I K GUJRAL	1997	Nawaz SHARIF (PM)	PML(N)
NDA (BJP)	A B VAJPAYEE	1998		
		1999	Parvez MUSHARRAF (CE/Pres)	
		2000		
		2001		
		2002		
		2003		
UPA/Cong	MANMOHAN SINGH	2004		
		2005		
		2006		
		2007		
		2008	Asif Ali ZARDARI (Pres)/SYR GILANI (PM)	PPP
		2009		
		2010		
		2011		
		2012		
		2013	Nawaz SHARIF (PM)	PML (N)
		2014		

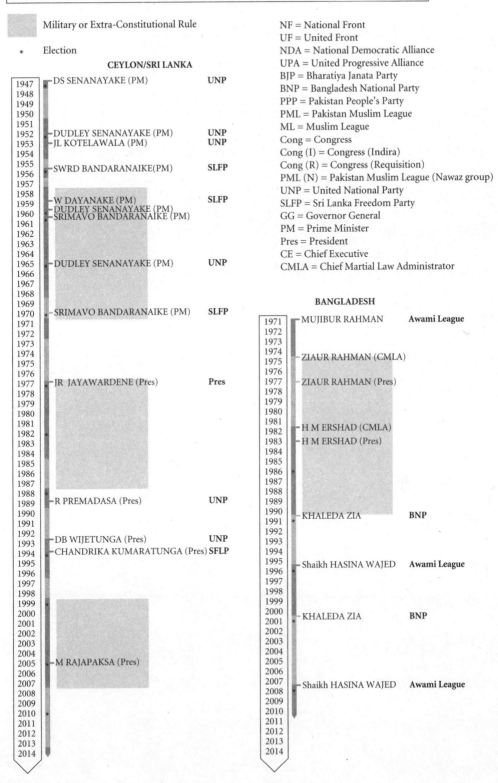

POLITICAL SUCCESSION IN INDIA, PAKISTAN, BANGLADESH AND SRI LANKA

Military or Extra-Constitutional Rule

* Election

NF = National Front
UF = United Front
NDA = National Democratic Alliance
UPA = United Progressive Alliance
BJP = Bharatiya Janata Party
BNP = Bangladesh National Party
PPP = Pakistan People's Party
PML = Pakistan Muslim League
ML = Muslim League
Cong = Congress
Cong (I) = Congress (Indira)
Cong (R) = Congress (Requisition)
PML (N) = Pakistan Muslim League (Nawaz group)
UNP = United National Party
SLFP = Sri Lanka Freedom Party
GG = Governor General
PM = Prime Minister
Pres = President
CE = Chief Executive
CMLA = Chief Martial Law Administrator

CEYLON/SRI LANKA

Year	Leader	Party
1947	DS SENANAYAKE (PM)	UNP
1948		
1949		
1950		
1951		
1952	DUDLEY SENANAYAKE (PM)	UNP
1953	JL KOTELAWALA (PM)	UNP
1954		
1955	SWRD BANDARANAIKE(PM)	SLFP
1956		
1957		
1958		
1959	W DAYANAKE (PM)	SLFP
1960	DUDLEY SENANAYAKE (PM)	
	SRIMAVO BANDARANAIKE (PM)	
1961		
1962		
1963		
1964		
1965	DUDLEY SENANAYAKE (PM)	UNP
1966		
1967		
1968		
1969		
1970	SRIMAVO BANDARANAIKE (PM)	SLFP
1971		
1972		
1973		
1974		
1975		
1976		
1977	JR JAYAWARDENE (Pres)	Pres
1978		
1979		
1980		
1981		
1982		
1983		
1984		
1985		
1986		
1987		
1988		
1989	R PREMADASA (Pres)	UNP
1990		
1991		
1992		
1993	DB WIJETUNGA (Pres)	UNP
1994	CHANDRIKA KUMARATUNGA (Pres)	SFLP
1995		
1996		
1997		
1998		
1999		
2000		
2001		
2002		
2003		
2004		
2005	M RAJAPAKSA (Pres)	
2006		
2007		
2008		
2009		
2010		
2011		
2012		
2013		
2014		

BANGLADESH

1971	MUJIBUR RAHMAN	Awami League
1972		
1973		
1974		
1975	ZIAUR RAHMAN (CMLA)	
1976		
1977	ZIAUR RAHMAN (Pres)	
1978		
1979		
1980		
1981		
1982	H M ERSHAD (CMLA)	
1983	H M ERSHAD (Pres)	
1984		
1985		
1986		
1987		
1988		
1989		
1990	KHALEDA ZIA	BNP
1991		
1992		
1993		
1994		
1995	Shaikh HASINA WAJED	Awami League
1996		
1997		
1998		
1999		
2000	KHALEDA ZIA	BNP
2001		
2002		
2003		
2004		
2005		
2006		
2007	Shaikh HASINA WAJED	Awami League
2008		
2009		
2010		
2011		
2012		
2013		
2014		

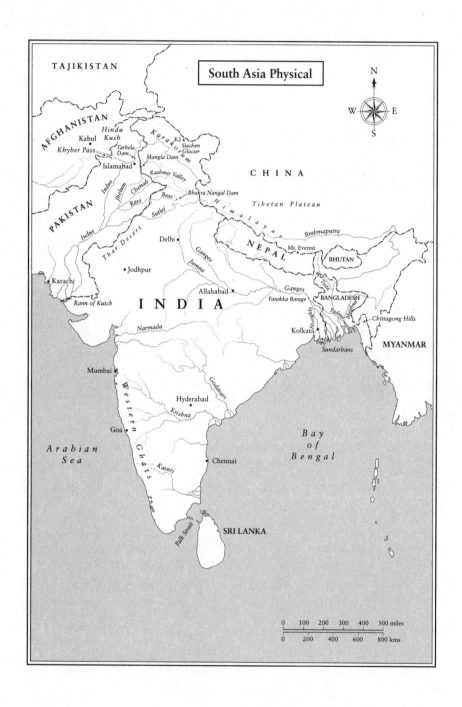

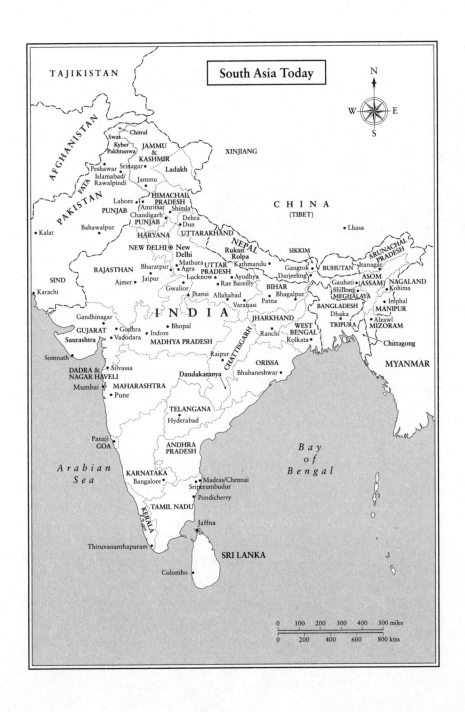

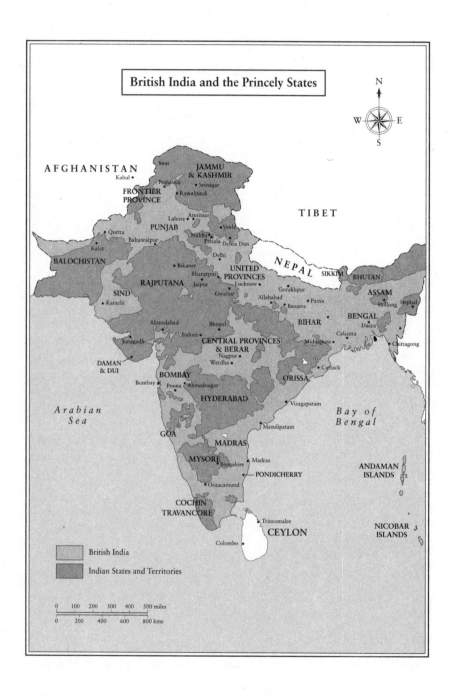

British India and the Princely States

N
W E
S

AFGHANISTAN

Swat

JAMMU
& KASHMIR

Kabul •

Peshawar •   • Srinagar

FRONTIER
PROVINCE   • Rawalpindi

TIBET

Amritsar
Lahore •

PUNJAB   • Simla

Quetta •   Nabha • Patiala • Dehra Dun

Bahawalpur •

Kalat

BALOCHISTAN   • Bikaner   Delhi •

NEPAL   SIKKIM   BHUTAN

Bharatpur   UNITED
PROVINCES

SIND   RAJPUTANA   Jaipur •   Lucknow •   Gorakhpur •   ASSAM

Gwalior •   Allahabad •   • Patna   Shillong •   Imphal •

• Karachi   Benares

Ahmedabad •   BENGAL

Bhopal •   BIHAR   Calcutta •

Junagadh •   Indore •   Dacca •

DAMAN   CENTRAL PROVINCES   Midnapure •   Chittagong •

& DUI   & BERAR
Nagpur •

Wardha •

BOMBAY   ORISSA

Bombay •   Poona • Ahmednagar   • Cuttack

Arabian
Sea   HYDERABAD   Bay of
Bengal

• Vizagapatam

GOA

• Masulipatam   ANDAMAN
ISLANDS

MADRAS

MYSORE   Madras •

Bangalore •   ← PONDICHERRY

• Ootacamund

COCHIN   NICOBAR
ISLANDS

TRAVANCORE

• Trincomalee

CEYLON

Colombo •

British India

Indian States and Territories

0   100   200   300   400   500 miles

0   200   400   600   800 kms

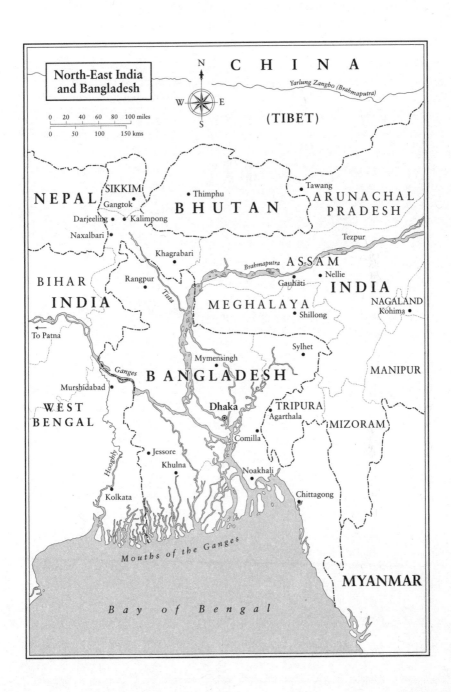

North-East India
and Bangladesh

0   20   40   60   80   100 miles
0   50   100   150 kms

C H I N A

Yarlung Zangbo (Brahmaputra)

(TIBET)

NEPAL   SIKKIM   • Thimphu   • Tawang   ARUNACHAL
         Gangtok •   B H U T A N   PRADESH
Darjeeling • • Kalimpong
Naxalbari •   Tezpur •
                    • Khagrabari
                              Brahmaputra   A S S A M
BIHAR   Rangpur •   • Nellie   INDIA
INDIA   Gauhati •
                          M E G H A L A Y A   NAGALAND
         Tista   • Shillong   Kohima •
To Patna ←
                                        • Sylhet
              • Mymensingh   MANIPUR
         Ganges B A N G L A D E S H
Murshidabad •
WEST   Dhaka   TRIPURA
BENGAL   ⊙   Agarthala •
                                       • Comilla   MIZORAM •
                    • Jessore
         Hooghly   Khulna •   • Noakhali
                                                    • Chittagong
         Kolkata •

                  Mouths of the Ganges

         B a y   o f   B e n g a l   MYANMAR

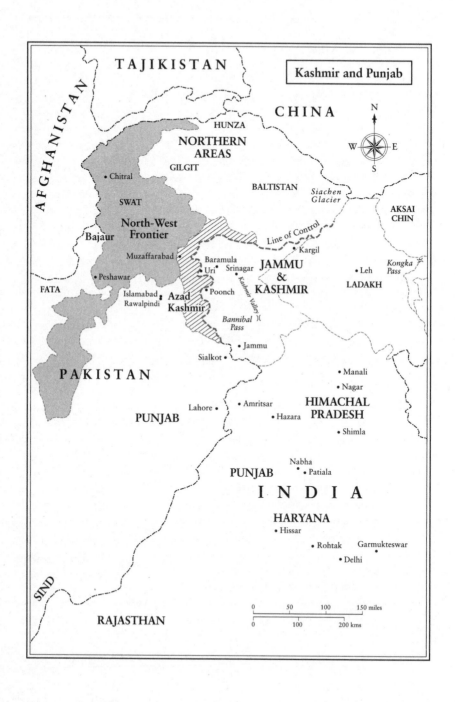

Kashmir and Punjab

INTRODUCTION

APPROACHING BENGAL FROM OPPOSITE DIRECTIONS, the Ganges and the Brahmaputra rivers shy away from a head-on collision and veer south, their braided channels fraying and crisscrossing in a tangle of waterways that rob the parent rivers of their identities. Long before reaching the sea the Ganges has split into the Hooghly and the Pabna, among others, and the Brahmaputra into the Padma and the Meghna. Known as "distributaries," these subrivers then fork some more, creating a maze of broad brown bayous whose combined seaward meanderings define the area known as the Sundarbans. Here, in the world's largest estuarine wilderness, expanses of glossy mangrove and thick muddy water cover an area as big as Belgium. Islands are indistinguishable from mainland; promising channels expire in stagnant creeks. In the several designated wildlife sanctuaries, amphibious adaptation proves the key to survival. Crocodiles loll along the tide line, close-packed like sunbathers. Mudhoppers gawp and glisten in the slime, and the local tigers swim as readily as they prowl.

With roads a rarity, the best way to get around the Sundarbans is by boat, perhaps with a bike aboard for excursions on terra firma. A guide is essential, the trails being few and the landmarks fewer. The rivers tug one way, the incoming tide another. Neither is consistent: saltwater comes down on the ebb, freshwater is backed up by the flow. The logic of the currents is as hard to fathom as that of the international border that here separates India and Bangladesh. Maps show the border as a confident line bisecting islands and slicing through peninsulas as it ricochets from side to side down the broad Raimangal waterway. Its trajectory provides the region with its one feature of human geography. But on the ground—where there is ground—the border is scarcely to be seen. Shifting mud banks and encroaching mangroves are no more conducive to frontier formalities than they are to cartographic precision. Apportioning the Sundarbans between India and what was then part of Pakistan must have been like trying to carve the gravy.

A game warden announces a sighting: "Changeable hawk-eagle." He points to a large raptor lodged in a dead tree. "It's a darker version of the one in peninsular India."

The bird is rooted to its perch and motionless. It could be stuffed, its taloned feet nailed to the branch, except that every now and then it moves its head ever so slightly, as if troubled by indecision. Choosing the behavior appropriate to its species is problematic for a changeable hawk-eagle. Should it quarter low over India's chunk of the Sundarbans or soar high above Bangladesh's? Is this a hawk day or an eagle day? Or just another changeable day? The options make for great uncertainty.

"So is that bit over there India or Bangladesh?" I ask. Nothing seems one thing or another in this gooey wilderness.

"Oh, that's India. Bangladesh is over there. See? But it should be India. Khulna, that whole district, should have come to India at Partition. It had a Hindu majority."

Khulna was not awarded to India because Murshidabad, a Muslim district to the north of Calcutta that straddles the Hooghly River, was preferred by Delhi on the grounds of strategic contiguity and economic convenience. Eastern Pakistan, as Bangladesh then was called, got Khulna by way of exchange. Hence mainly Muslim Murshidabad went to mainly Hindu India, and mainly Hindu Khulna went to mainly Muslim Pakistan. So much for the fundamental principle on which British India was divided by 1947's Great Partition—that contiguous areas where Indian Muslims were in a majority were to constitute Pakistan and areas where they were not in a majority were to constitute the new India.

Dividing the subcontinent had itself been a compromise and proved a heavy price to pay for independence. Flying in the face of fifty years' struggle for a single India and of a shared cultural and historical awareness that stretched back centuries, it had been dictated by three recent developments: Most Indian Muslims had come around to the idea of a Muslim homeland of their own, most Indian nationalists were insisting on a successor state that was strong enough to resist such demands, and the British were desperate for a fast-track exit. Adopted only as a last-minute expedient, Partition was widely regretted at the time. And it has been rued ever since by all who hold life, livelihood, and peace to be dear.

"These people here must be Indian, then," I venture. Fishing boats and a gaggle of schoolchildren hint at a nearby village, but there is no electricity, no road, and no phone line—and all this despite being within ninety miles of downtown Calcutta.

"Well, yes, now they're mostly Indian. But many of them are actually from Bangladesh, some Hindu, some Muslim."

In the Sundarbans the rivers and raptors are not the only changeable things. Decades after British-ruled India was partitioned into the republics of India, Pakistan, and later Bangladesh, national identities in this part of the subcontinent remain as fluid as the wind-ruffled soup that passes for water. So too do patterns of migration and the terminology applied to them. Immediately after the Great Partition of 1947, people who crossed the border were known as "refugees." In the 1960s they became "evacuees," in the 1970s either "optees" or "oustees," in the 1980s "illegal immigrants," and now "potential terrorists." Like the reception afforded them in their chosen destination, their status has been declining. Not, though, their numbers. The exodus into India from the part of Pakistan that in 1971 became Bangladesh has always been difficult to quantify. Some say hundreds of thousands have crossed the border, some say millions. Urban India's twenty-first-century construction boom draws heavily on Bangladeshi labor, much of it illegal. Locally there are migrants who traipse back and forth for seasonal work or even a daily wage. No one is sure who is a migrant worker and who a cross-border commuter. Throughout the delta, people still come and go largely undetected, like the tides and the tigers.

Six hundred miles to the north, where the Bangladeshi border squeezes the Indian state of West Bengal up against the Himalayas, the situation is further complicated by what must be the most eccentric frontier conformation on earth. Here territorial logic veers to the opposite extreme, that of overdefinition. Communities lie trapped in time-warped pockets, their national identity determined by arcane landholding patterns and the inflexible notions of sovereignty so jealously entertained by modern nation-states. With little regard to the religious affinities of the inhabitants, Partition here simply appropriated the piecemeal patterns of cultivation and proprietorship found in the extant land registers and then upgraded them into international borders.

Outside his house a man poses for the camera. In the photo his back is to the wall and his legs are apart. He looks rather pleased with himself. The caption explains that he is standing with one foot in Bangladesh and the other in India, and the wall behind him is part of an extension tacked onto his house so that it too straddles the international border. With a spare room in India, he qualifies as an Indian resident and can avail himself of a connection to the Indian electricity grid. No one else in this bit of Bangladesh has electricity. Providing any social amenities here is problematic because the village is in fact a sovereign enclave.

An enclave is any atoll of territory wholly surrounded by the territory of another sovereign state, in this case India. Elsewhere there are bits of India stranded in Bangladesh. The border picks its way between these enclaves, and such is the complexity of the situation that most maps despair of showing the enclaves at all. But on the ground the formalities of international transfer are faithfully observed. Checkpoints bar the tiniest roads; flags are raised and lowered; papers are stamped, currency changed, SIM cards traded, and bribes disbursed. Cultivators setting off for their fields clutch passports; cross-border shopping trips may be construed as smuggling operations.

Willem van Schendel, professor of modern Asian history in the Netherlands (a country that has enclaves of its own in Belgian territory), estimates that there are 197 such sovereign pockets along this short section of the Indo-Bangladesh border west of the Tista River. Perhaps a hundred thousand people live in the enclaves, which cover a total area of about forty-six square miles. It's hard to be more precise because enclaves may themselves have enclaves. The latter are known as "counter-enclaves" and are, in effect, bits of India that lie within bits of Bangladesh that are themselves within India—or vice versa. In the Bhalapura Khagrabari complex of enclaves, the largest archipelago of Indian territory in Bangladesh, one such Bangladeshi counter-enclave contains a smaller counter-enclave of Indian territory. This is Dahala Khagrabari, which van Schendel calls "the world's only counter-counter-enclave." From here an Indian citizen wishing to reach India proper, a distance of around six miles, has to cross the frontier four times—from India to Bangladesh, Bangladesh to India, India to Bangladesh, and finally Bangladesh to the Indian "mainland." Luckily, Dahala Khagrabari comprises just 17.1 acres and is currently uninhabited, being mostly jute fields. But envy not its farmer.

With their promise of sanctuary, enclaves have attracted unsavory elements. Criminal gangs have tended to take up residence, and smuggling has become a way of life. Under cover of darkness or along paths tunneled through the ten-foot-high jute crop, everything from armaments to cattle, pharmaceuticals, and people is channeled through the enclaves. As of the year 2000 criminal activity has reportedly been on the decline; life, though, remains insecure and social amenities nonexistent. The only obvious advantage of being an enclave dweller is the absence of taxes.[1]

Something similar could be said be of another anomaly of the Indo-Bangladesh border, namely, the *chars*. These are mud banks deposited in the middle of rivers, principally by the flood-prone waters of the wide Brahmaputra. A quarter of a million people live on *chars;* the riverine soil can be very fertile, and the river itself is rich in fish. But people settle there at the risk not only of inundation but also of involuntary migration, for such is the landscaping power of the monsoon-swollen flood that *chars* may shift. If the center of the current happens to be the recognized border—as it is for several hundred miles—a *char* that was in Bangladesh one year may well end up in India the next, or vice versa.

"Most of the islands vehemently either move forward or backward across the . . . international riverine border," complains an observer concerned with the problems of policing these errant landmasses.[2] Though still at the same address, several thousand people may suddenly find themselves unaccredited immigrants in a different country. Border markers get washed away; rivers change course. In some areas the painful business of border negotiation and demarcation, a process that supposedly was concluded soon after Partition in the late 1940s, is still being repeated every year.

In 2006 the Indian authorities, spurred on by the prospect of cross-border infiltrators bent on terrorism, began ring-fencing Bangladesh (not forgetting its enclaves). The new fence has steel stanchions and razor wire and is actually two fences, creating a caged corridor along which laundry can be hung out to dry. The fence stands ten feet high and when completed will be around fifteen hundred miles long. But its march is halted by every river and, as per a previous agreement not to construct contentious facilities on the border itself, it runs several hundred to several thousand feet behind the actual line of demarcation. Thus "a huge quantum of Indian land has fallen in 'no man's zone,'" complains one politician. Within this strip lie villages, farmland, and uncounted residents. One quite short stretch of the fence is reported as having alienated, or "practically disowned," 149 villages and 90,000 people. Indian citizens are being rendered stateless and their property worthless. The issue has been raised in the Indian parliament and aired in the press but without eliciting any promise of compensation or resettlement.[3]

All this is in striking contrast to the nearby open border between India and Nepal. Here there are no fences, no patrols, and minimal formalities. Although Nepal never came under direct British rule and was therefore unaffected by Partition, an agreement had been reached whereby people and goods might cross at will. This agreement still stands, albeit often amended. Immigrants from India already make up a substantial percentage of Nepal's population, while Nepalis settled in India constitute an overall majority in parts of the Indian state of West Bengal. The Gorkha National Liberation Front (GNLF) represents the latter's interests. Demanding the recognition of Gorkhali, Nepal's main language, as one of India's official languages—and so qualifying its speakers for the educational and job opportunities that go with recognition—the GNLF strives, not without occasional violence, for an autonomous enclave within West Bengal or even a separate Nepali state within the Republic of

India. Migration, in other words, is here an accepted phenomenon. National identity, "Nepali-ness," is being officially downgraded to a linguistic identity, "Gorkhali-ness," which is something that can be accommodated within the limits of protest and concession afforded to India's other language groups.

Language remains a contentious issue throughout polyglot South Asia, but in modern India its explosive potential has been steadily tamed by concessions and circumstance. It plays no part in the plight of the enclave dwellers and the migrants along the Indo-Bangladesh border; all of them speak Bengali, whether Indians, Bangladeshis, or not exactly either. The same goes for Tamil-speakers flitting between Sri Lanka and south India. In both cases a shared language in fact serves as a camouflage, making the detection of illegal or undesirable migrants that much more difficult.

Other markers of identity prove less amenable. Beyond the Nepali concentrations in northern West Bengal, and beyond the enclaves and *chars* along the Indo-Bangladesh border, a tendon of Indian territory tugs at a knotted fist of mainly ethnic discontent in the remote hills along the Burmese border. By one reckoning, India's cluster of states in the far northeast is plagued by more than a hundred insurgency groups, most of them pressing their grievances on the grounds of disadvantaged ethnicity: "Manipur tops the list [for the number] of militias with 35, Assam is second with 34 and Tripura has 30, Nagaland has four and Meghalaya checks in with three militias."[4] At any given moment these groups vary greatly in terms of support, objectives, and militancy. But with India, Bangladesh, Burma (now Myanmar), and China all interested parties in the political jigsaw of South Asia's northeastern extremity, ethnic grievances invariably involve territorial disputes, and these readily translate into war-worthy issues involving international sovereignty.

National identities cannot be taken for granted here. Even where the borders are not themselves in dispute, the loyalties of those living on either side of them may be. Like the fickle "distributaries" of the Ganges and the Brahmaputra, the very idea of the nation-state is dissipated and frayed into complex strands of competing allegiances. A Naga, for instance, may subscribe to half a dozen identities:

I am from Khonoma village of the Angami tribe. . . . Now within the village I belong to the Iralu clan. The Iralu clan belongs in turn to the Meyasetsu clan. The Meyasetsu clan in turn belongs to the still wider and larger clan called the Merhuma Khel. The Merhuma Khel is in turn one of three major Khels that make up Khonoma village. The Khonoma village in turn belongs to the Angami tribe and the Angami tribe belongs in turn to the Naga nation. . . . [T]hese ethnic and national identities are precious to me. They in fact define my political existence as a man with a country to call his own. As such, I can never surrender this birth-right to India or any other nation on earth.[5]

Statements such as this, from a Naga nationalist, are dismissed by the Indian authorities as secessionist and totally unacceptable. The Bangladeshi authorities take exactly the same line with their own disaffected Chakma peoples. Both governments classify such communities as "tribal" and attribute their recalcitrance to poor education, misguided leadership, discriminatory policies, and foreign interference. Yet Mahatma Gandhi himself once assured the Nagas that if they did not wish to be part of India, they would not be compelled to integrate with it; India would recognize their independence. To the apostle of nonviolence, forcibly incorporating any disaffected group contradicted the whole idea of free association on which the modern Indian nation was founded.

This all raises a more fundamental question about whether the correlation between a nation and a state is not itself the problem. In South Asia as a whole, and particularly in the chaotic circumstances of the northeast, other cherished affiliations—of kinship, creed, locality, language, tribe, clan, profession, and caste—may need to be factored into considerations of identity. The twinning of sovereignty with territory may need to be "unbundled," and the very notions of political authority and territorial integrity may need reexamination.[6]

By dividing British-ruled South Asia into a mainly Muslim Pakistan and a mainly Hindu India, the Great Partition of 1947 severed—and sometimes pocked—not just the landmass of South Asia but its society, its economy, its infrastructure, and above all its two main religious communities. Religion was indeed the mentor of Partition. It provided the motivation for division, dictated the criteria for realizing it, and underwrote the zealotry that accompanied it. Yet it would be wrong to suppose that Partition was principally about separating two competing belief systems. Doctrinal differences rarely entered into the debate at the time; religious parties, such as the Muslim orthodox Jamaat-e-Islami and the Hindu nationalistic Mahasabha, in fact opposed territorial division. Even the prophets of Pakistan, like the pragmatists of a truncated India, anticipated the presence of religious minorities within the partitioned states. Indeed, they competed in offering guarantees of citizenship and fair treatment to all such confessional enclaves.

When a community is under stress, its sense of itself frequently transcends its attachment to specific tenets. Diversity in matters of faith is trumped by an insistence on communal solidarity that may ignore lesser doctrinal and devotional distinctions. Thus the different traditions of Islam represented by Sunni, Shi'ite, and Sufi practice were no more evident in the rhetoric of Partition than was the rivalry among those cults, disciplines, and doctrines that go to make up Hinduism.

Rather, it was—and is—conduct, culture, and kinship that constitute the markers of confessional identity and the bonds that tie a community together. These may include things such as where and to whom one was born; how one washes and dresses; what one eats and when one fasts; what work one does; when, where, and how (not to mention whom) one worships; whom one consorts with and marries; to what or to whom one looks for justice and redress; whom one idolizes and whom one demonizes; and what songs, verses, and aphorisms one carries around in one's head. Like the tribal layering of Naga identity, all these things define one's existence as a member of a community—though not necessarily of a community with a country to call its own.

In the 1940s, the desire to protect these markers from the perceived threat of Hindu rule on the part of Muslims, and of a privileged Muslim separatism on the part of Hindus, buoyed demands for communal autonomy. The hope was that autonomy would reassure all parties by ring-fencing their interests and preserving their integrity. But in line with the contemporary partition in Palestine, and with almost no debate on the matter, the objective soon underwent a sea change. Areas, not individuals, became the currency of Partition, districts rather than households the unit of exchange. As per the last British viceroy's June 1947 plan to divide the area, "the parties appear to have accepted that communal autonomy was to be realized by the creation of separate territorial sovereignties," writes Joya Chatterji. "There are subtle but significant differences between the notions of communal autonomy and territorial sovereignty. The first emphasizes the rights of the people of a community to self-determination, rights which could in theory be achieved within a single state. The second stresses the bounded space within which a community is sovereign and could be realized only by a territorial separation."[7]

In the last hectic months of British rule, when parts of the country were already beset by sectarian massacres, sovereignty alone seemed to safeguard communal autonomy, with fixed frontiers being its surest guarantee. Yet sixty-five years later, communal discord within and between the post-Partition states of South Asia is more acute than ever. "Whenever there is a riot in India, we suffer here," says a spokesperson for the Hindu minority in Bangladesh.[8] Whenever a Pakistan-trained terrorist opens fire in India, India's Muslims come under suspicion, and whenever India's Hindu nationalists vent their spleen on the Internet, more Pakistani and Bangladeshi Muslims sign up for jihad. Just as the tides, the migrants, and the hawk-eagles come and go unchecked across the Sundarbans, so the tit-for-tat of outrage and retaliation ricochets along the 4,300-mile length of those brave new frontiers ordained by Partition's insistence on a territorial separation.

OVER THE LAST HALF CENTURY the shadows of Partition's brutal dislocation have grown ever longer. They slant across the whole course of events in post-independence South Asia. Some observers liken Partition to a nuclear explosion whose lethal fallout will go on being felt for generations to come. Others see it as a recurring natural phenomenon that, having severed the subcontinent, then (de facto) the disputed state of Jammu and Kashmir, and then the two-part Pakistan, is ever ready to strike again. Nearly all see it as unfinished business. Every war, near war, and insurgency in the subcontinent since the end of British rule owes something to the legacy of Partition. And so long as this sore festers, any normalizing of relations between the partitioned states proves elusive.

Elsewhere in the world various political unions, defense pacts, free trade associations, and hegemonic doctrines (Monroe, Brezhnev, etc.) have lent some coherence to the conduct of international relations. In South Asia, a region where geography, history, economics, and culture all argue strongly in favor of the closest possible association, even modest attempts at regional cooperation flounder. The subcontinent continues to be defined in terms not of shared interests but of past traumas, contested loyalties, and irreconcilable ambitions. Encouraged by governments of every hue, national identity still owes much to an obsessive awareness of the hostile "other" just across the border. Antagonism reigns, officially.

This "othering" extends even to ideology. Each successor nation presents a political profile that seems to challenge its neighbor's. The Republic of India is secular, democratic, internationally respected, and increasingly regarded as an economic success. Pakistan and Bangladesh, on the other hand, are determinedly Islamic, susceptible to military rule, internationally disparaged, and economically struggling. (Nepal and Sri Lanka, the other sizable components of what scholars now prefer to call "South Asia" rather than the "Indian subcontinent," are currently too traumatized by recent civil wars to be easily categorized.) Partition did not just divide most of the region but also launched the successor states on such diametrically opposed trajectories that to this day South Asians commonly prioritize Partition over independence. The second half of the twentieth century is not the "post-independence era" but the "post-Partition era." The euphoria of freedom has been silenced by the shock of division.

The consequences of this division are critical, and not just for South Asia. By 2020 India will have the largest population in the world, and South Asians as a whole will account for a quarter of the people on the planet. Nor, on the grounds of negligible disposable income, can these numbers any longer be discounted as a statistical irrelevance. Already India's middle class is one of the world's most numerous, and its corporate sector includes more multinationals and generates more billionaires than anywhere else in Asia except China. The world's largest market and its largest pool of unskilled labor is rapidly becoming its largest reservoir of innovation and expertise. South Asian excellence now extends to everything from pharmaceuticals and telecoms to finance, information technology, and prize-winning literature.

It also includes rocketry and a terrifying military capability. With both India and Pakistan in possession of nuclear weapons, with neither eager to submit to international controls, and with China's nearby arsenal dwarfing both, the potential for a nuclear conflagration here is all too real. What may be the most promising zone in terms of the world economy is located in what US analysts have dubbed the most dangerous arena on earth.

Worldwide, South Asians account for two out of every five Muslims, and of these nearly as many have their roots in India as in Pakistan or Bangladesh. Through them, Islam's international grievances (over Palestine, Iraq, Afghanistan, and anywhere else within range of a drone) get internalized in South Asia, and through them and other disaffected parties, South Asian grievances (over Balochistan, Nagaland, numerous other hot spots, and above all Kashmir) get externalized in the West. The bloodletting occasioned by a dispute about a mosque in Uttar Pradesh can surface in the British House of Commons. Confrontations in the high Himalayas can bring the world to the brink of armageddon.

Yet to the outside observer South Asia's peoples seem to have a lot more in common than not. In the world's departure lounges they are as ubiquitous and just as hard to allocate to a particular part of the subcontinent as the Chinese. Regardless of nationality, they look not unalike, they often wear similar loose baggy attire, and everyone travels with too much luggage. They are also rather particular about their dietary preferences. Some of the languages they converse in (including English) are mutually comprehensible. They enjoy the same movies and opt for the same music channels. Nearly all admit to regularly engaging in some form of devotional activity, nearly all marry within approved circles, and nearly all take pride in their familial, communal, and regional identities.

Down on the ground, were it not for the border fence, you could still pass from India's West Bengal into Bangladesh without realizing you had changed countries; likewise from the Indian states of Rajasthan and Punjab to the Pakistani provinces of Sind and Punjab (each country has a Punjab because the British province of that name was itself partitioned). The differences between one country and another are much less obvious than those between most adjacent European states. Non-Islamic India is still home to nearly as many Muslims as either Pakistan or Bangladesh. Hindu women may cover their faces like their Muslim sisters, and Pakistani men may wear pajamas like their Indian brothers. Despite its newly trumpeted affluence, India still has more of the malnourished, the unlettered, and the socially deprived than Pakistan and Bangladesh combined. Even the excitement over its growth rate may be deceptive. Only twenty years ago it was Pakistan that was slated to join the Asian periphery's "tiger economies." Thirty years ago it was Sri Lanka. What one economist has called "persistent orderly hunger" is one of the region's shared and all too enduring characteristics.

So too is the confidence born of a deep and incredibly rich matrix of tradition and devotion. Here globalization comes wreathed in garlands and incense. A pudgy Ganesh presides in the boardroom; temple and waqf are quoted on the Mumbai stock exchange. Everywhere matrimonial expenditure chomps into GDP. Pride in the past, an unshakable sense of one's community, and a dazzling array of cultural references are not peculiar to the region. But in South Asia their resilience and centrality are second to none.

Even the constitutional tags are not quite as irreconcilable as they seem. Once in power, democratically chosen leaders have frequently displayed authoritarian tendencies, while autocrats invariably pine for popular endorsement. Military coups have often proved less bloody than elections, and avowedly secular regimes may harbor as much fanaticism and discrimination as avowedly sectarian ones.

Despite Partition and all that followed, South Asians have more in common than they may care to acknowledge. Indeed, Partition itself needs to be seen as a shared experience. By decimating whole provinces, displacing perhaps fifteen million people, and leaving just as many feeling unwelcome in the land of their birth, it everywhere loosened some of those nondoctrinal bonds of community and encouraged a new mobility.

In 1947, the majority of refugees headed for the nearest of the new borders. If they made it to the other side—a big if in the Punjab—they settled down among their co-religionists in India or Pakistan. Some were allocated land that had been vacated by refugees moving in the opposite direction; others swelled the populations of the cities and thereby transformed the parent state's demography. Karachi, the interim capital of Pakistan, attracted so many displaced Muslims from India that these *muhajirs* soon outnumbered the city's native Sindhis. Delhi, if judged by its taxi drivers, became a city of Sikhs, mostly refugees from Lahore; Lahore became a city of Muslims, with scarcely a beturbaned Sikh to be seen; and Calcutta lost its public spaces when parks, gardens, railway stations, and even cricket pitches were turned into makeshift dormitories by the displaced from all over eastern Bengal.

A few migrants quickly changed their minds and went back, some doing so several times. Others had their minds changed for them. When, in 1971, East Pakistan became Bangladesh, refugees from India who had been welcomed into East Pakistan as Muslims in 1947 found themselves interned as non-Bengalis in a now proudly Bengali Bangladesh. Perhaps a hundred thousand of these so-called Biharis are still there, eking out a pitiful existence in Bangladesh's refugee camps; others have been shunted across India to Pakistan, and a lucky few have since obtained visas to reside overseas.

In this they are not alone. Emigration was as much a by-product of Partition as was urbanization. Over the three decades immediately after 1947 an estimated two million South Asians, many of them already displaced by Partition, exited the subcontinent altogether. Better prospects and wages undoubtedly tempted them, but it was the push factor of dislocation and enforced mobility that proved crucial. Thanks to Partition, what might have been a modest trickle of economic migrants turned into the flood of expatriates, now over twenty million strong, known as the South Asian diaspora.

Applying the term "diaspora" to the South Asian exodus remains controversial, although reasonable enough. South Asia's Partition and the Nazi Holocaust often have been bracketed together, with comparisons being drawn between the apparently chaotic and unpremeditated nature of the one and the systematic, state-directed nature of the other. But more to the point, just as in some unspeakable way the Holocaust made the need for a Jewish homeland manifest and thus reversed one diaspora, so did Partition yank at the bonds of kinship, locality, and community and unleash another great exodus of peoples.

Few in the India and Pakistan of the 1950s and 1960s considered the spectacle of mass emigration as grounds for congratulation. Plucked from villages in unfancied districts such as Sylhet (east Pakistan), Mirpur (Azad Kashmir), and Jalandhar (India), then penned, tagged, and bused to an international airport, the huddles of all-male migrants hunkered down beside the check-in desks seemed a sad commentary on the lofty hopes of independence. Their minders brandished wads of tickets and newly minted documentation, seldom allowing the passport holders to hold their own passports; most of the migrants could barely sign their name or pronounce their destination. Their identities, like their paychecks, were in hock to their gang masters.

In the 1960s these emigrants were destined principally for low-paid jobs in the United Kingdom and North America, thereafter and more substantially for the Gulf states. Others followed well-trodden trails to eastern and southern Africa, the Caribbean, Southeast Asia, and the Pacific. These were the destinations to which bonded workers recruited for labor elsewhere in the British Empire had traditionally been dispatched. The new migrants looked no more go-getting or better-prepared than their nineteenth-century antecedents. A hookah might be passed among them in the airport forecourt; betel-stained saliva betrayed their presence in the departure lounge. The white-shirted businessmen and briefcase-clutching bureaucrats brushed past with eyes averted.

Yet in retrospect this unpromising stream of exiles heralded a new respect for the region's international profile and added an important new dimension to the fraught relationships between its post-Partition states. By the 1980s cash remittances sent home from places as far apart as Dubai and British Columbia were critical in sustaining the economies of all the South Asian states. They also transformed the built landscape in the emigrants' Bangladeshi, Indian, and Pakistani areas of origin. At about the same time second-generation South Asians in the West were being joined by a second wave of emigrants from the subcontinent. Young and ambitious, both were more interested in professional qualifications and internships than in hourly rates. History sanctioned their quest for advancement. Without exception, all the architects of independence, from Gandhi to Nehru, Jinnah, Ambedkar, and Patel, had acquired their legal training in Britain. Political freedom had come courtesy of diasporic passport holders; economic betterment would follow suit.

For now it was US degrees, corporate experience, entrepreneurial skills, and silicon technology that were the attractions. And unlike being a bus conductor, cooking curries, or spouting courtroom rhetoric, these were qualifications in high demand back in South Asia. The massive back-transfer of skills and then investment that resulted would dramatically empower the Republic of India and to a lesser extent its neighbors. From it sprang the great transnational community of South Asian origin that would be so ideally placed to prosper in a globalized century. The despised diaspora was metamorphosing into the most desirable of elites. In short, and by some delicious quirk of fate, peoples so keen to equate community with nation, nation with state, and identity with a bounded territory were proving the most adept at transcending such obstacles.

Regrettably, this also has a downside. Ensconced nowadays in the airport's premium business lounges, the Asian knights of the global economy are not encouraged to transcend the febrile frontiers of South Asia itself. Once reviled as deserters by patriotic nationalists, those emigrants who return are now embraced and feted. Originally a term of contempt, "non-resident Indian" (NRI) has become an accolade. New Delhi—and Islamabad and Dhaka with regard to their Pakistani and Bangladeshi equivalents—not only woos its NRIs but most emphatically claims them. Their US, Canadian, and EU passports carry Delhi's endorsement of their status as "persons of Indian origin" (PIOs) or "overseas citizens of India" (OCIs). Residential options, tax breaks, and investment incentives await the prodigals; receptions and conferences are organized specifically for them; whole government ministries pander to their needs; homegrown CEOs and rupee billionaires flock to join them.

The diaspora's inward investment has powered up domestic economies throughout South Asia. But the start-ups and the statistics are not the only things to benefit from diasporic largesse. Numerous nongovernmental agencies and charities, among them organizations commonly blamed for the abiding level of communal strife, are also handsomely supported by this overseas citizenry. A classic example was provided by Sri Lanka's Liberation Tigers of Tamil Eelam (LTTE), otherwise known as the "Tamil Tigers." For thirty years the LTTE obtained arms and training in India and found sanctuary there while being heavily bankrolled by the donations of Tamils and Tamil sympathizers resident in the West. Kashmiris, principally in Britain, funded the Jammu and Kashmir National Liberation Front; Sikhs, many in Canada, helped sustain the Khalistan movement for an independent Sikh state. Likewise, Saudi dinars are channeled through diasporic Muslims to the Islamist madrassas of Pakistan; and US dollars raised by diasporic Hindus finance the temple building and social and educational programs of extremist outfits such as the Shiv Sena and the RSS. For longer than anyone can remember, Naga nationalists have been funding their open insurgency from overseas.

Where funds can be transferred, often undeclared and undetected, so can ideas. Through social networks, blogs, and SMS, and through the distribution of CDs, DVDs, and print, the diaspora exerts an influence on opinion in South Asia that is commensurate with its hefty financial donations. For the bonds of kinship and community, however attenuated, still apply. The status of diasporic families in the land of their settlement often depends on the approval of their caste or community back home; so do their chances of extending their family landholdings in South Asia and of securing suitable marriage partners. By supporting communal interests and disseminating exclusionist views, the diaspora validates both itself and its affiliates in South Asia. Diasporic endorsement of, say, the 1992 demolition of Ayodhya's Babri Mosque emboldened the zealots responsible and lent a veneer of international respectability to the interminable debate that followed.

Activists sustained by diasporic support are carried along on the ebb and flow of migration. A. Z. Phizo, for many years the charismatic leader of the Naga National Council, directed operations almost entirely from the safety of a UK residence. So did, and do, the leaderships of the Muttahida Qaumi Movement (MQM, representing the voluble *muhajir* community in southern Pakistan), the Sikh separatist Khalistan movement, the Kashmir government in exile, and the Baloch separatists of Pakistan's western extremity. They are in good company. At one time or another, sanctuary in the West has been the choice of many of Pakistan's and Bangladesh's political leaders, including several Bhuttos. A host of lesser dissidents at odds with the regimes of South Asia also avails itself of the immunity of exile. And in the opposite direction come diasporic "tourists," sometimes with misguided convictions and terrorist assignments.

The globalization of protest is not a peculiarly Muslim phenomenon. Worldwide, the first to blow up a jumbo jet in midflight were not Palestinian activists but members of a Sikh separatist group; they then took the life of an Indian prime minister. Tamils assassinated the next prime minister and made suicide bombing their specialty. Earlier it had been a Hindu supremacist who gunned down Mahatma Gandhi. More recently, Indian Maoist (Naxalite) revolutionaries have blown up nearly as many police officers as the Pakistani Taliban.

In what follows, the notice taken of the influence and agency of the diaspora may seem disproportionate. It can, for instance, hardly compare with the death and dislocation that were directly occasioned by Partition, nor with the decades of mutual hostility and misery inflicted by the unending strife over Kashmir. The story of postcolonial South Asia is seldom inspirational. Among those I call Midnight's Descendants, the body count of those who have succumbed to wars, civil strife, natural disasters, and unalleviated poverty has yet to be exceeded by the number of those so enriched as to qualify as middle-class.

Other regional commonalities are more striking. For the first decade and a half, both India and Pakistan concentrated on nation building. Constitutions were drafted, dissent confronted, and sovereignty asserted. India absorbed its princely states, snapped up the colonial enclaves of Pondicherry and Goa, did a smash-and-grab-style takeover of the kingdom of Sikkim, and received a bloody nose from the Chinese in the Himalayas. In like manner Pakistan cowed its separatists in Balochistan, wrestled with dissent in East Bengal and in the North-West Frontier Province's Tribal Areas, and snapped up what it could of Jammu and Kashmir state.

This nation-building phase was followed in the 1970s by a wave of rank populism. Indira Gandhi in India, Zulfikar Ali Bhutto in Pakistan, and Mujibur Rahman in Bangladesh chalked up massive electoral victories. With the exception of Nepal, all of South Asia basked under democratic rule. But it was short-lived. Economic woes and popular adulation tempted all three leaders into autocratic ways, which were then emphatically rejected. Gandhi was toppled by the electorate that had empowered her; Bhutto and Mujibur Rahman were overthrown and eliminated by the military. A people-powered era subsided into one of edgy accommodation in which confessional values thrived.

The 1980s marked the rise of the religious right. Pakistan under Zia ul-Haq and Bangladesh under Ziaur Rahman warmed to their Islamic brethren in the Gulf and conciliated Islamic opinion at home. For Pakistan, "liberating" Kashmir still topped the agenda, but the Soviet occupation of Afghanistan ensured sympathy, support, and a steady militarization of Islamic sentiment. In India, on the other hand, it was among right-wing Hindu and Sikh parties that zealotry prospered. A series of devotional spectaculars saw the Hindu nationalist Bharatiya Janata Party (BJP) garnering ever more support. To meet this long-term challenge, the Nehru-Gandhi Congress Party tarnished its own secular credentials and paid a heavy price. Sikhs, Assamese, Sri Lankans, and Kashmiris were fatally antagonized. Two Gandhis were assassinated, Indira in 1984 and her son Rajiv in 1991.

On this fraught scenario dawned the era of globalization in the last years of the century. India and to a lesser extent all the other countries of South Asia have undoubtedly benefited. Democracy has been given a second chance in Pakistan, Bangladesh, and Nepal. Pluralist politics and coalition governments have become the norm in India. Despite glaring examples of neglect in education and health services, living standards are rising. But these economic and political dividends have been offset by a challenging level of expectation, appalling examples of corruption, and little in the way of normalized state-to-state relations. The globalization of protest, militancy, and criminality has yet to be successfully addressed by any South Asian state.

There are, of course, other ways of periodizing the post-Partition era. It could, for instance, be characterized in international terms. The first generation of Midnight's Descendants was born in awe of British rule. The second looked to Moscow, Washington, or both, and the third looks increasingly to Beijing. In varying degrees Pakistan, Sri Lanka, Nepal, and Bangladesh now see China as their best safe-guard against India's regional hegemonism (which is often perceived as bullying). India is more ambivalent, with respect for the post-Mao achievements of the People's Republic tempered by suspicion of Chi-na's authoritarianism and apprehension over its intentions along the Himalayan frontier and in the Indian Ocean.

To many Indians, China is the superpower that India might have become but for Partition. When in the late 1940s South Asians were opting for the division of their subcontinent, China's leader-ship brusquely demolished the divisions within its own subconti-nent. Manchuria and Tibet were reclaimed, central Asian borders reaffirmed, Hong Kong put on notice, and Taiwan's defection vigor-ously contested. The indivisible nature of the People's Republic has since come to be seen as one of its strengths, while the fissiparous nature of South Asia's republics remains their greatest weakness. Yet Partition, by sundering the region and dictating so much of what followed, lends to their story an essential cohesion of its own. United in ferment, Midnight's Descendants have no difficulty with such con-tradictions. And of all these paradoxes, not the least—and a good place to begin—is surely the most easily forgotten: that, given cooler heads and a bit more time, Partition might well have been avoided altogether.

I

CASTING
THE DIE

I N THE EARLY AFTERNOON OF MARCH 24, 1946, THREE members of the British cabinet, plus their staff, were driven from Delhi's makeshift airport to the monumental residence built for the viceroy of what was still British India. The traffic was light—it was a Sunday—and along the capital's leafy avenues the cars were outnumbered by carts, some of them high-sided hay wains drawn by enormous white oxen, others rubber-tired flatbeds hauled by wispy-haired water buffalo whose languid pace allowed for a snatched bite at the herbaceous bounty provided by the municipal groundsmen.

New Delhi, the garden city laid out as the capital of British India only twenty years earlier, dozed in the afternoon heat, unroused by the visiting cabinet ministers, untrodden by policemen or postmen—both were on strike—and unbothered by the postwar turmoil beyond India's distant frontiers. It was just eight months since the British Labour Party had taken office in London and seven since Japan's surrender had brought an end to the Second World War. Half the world was still in uniform. A blitzed and rationed Britain faced the biggest reconstruction crisis in its history. Yet in London, Prime Minister Clement Attlee had reconciled himself to dispensing with three of his most senior colleagues for what would turn out to be a hundred-day absence. Their mission was that important.

Of the three cabinet ministers, Lord Pethick-Lawrence was there as of right; as secretary of state for India, he headed a branch of the London government whose personnel and budget exceeded those of both the Foreign Office and the Colonial Office. Another of the delegates, Albert Victor Alexander, later Earl Alexander, had responsibility for safeguarding the British empire's maritime links as First Lord of the Admiralty. The third, Sir Stafford Cripps, had led an earlier mission to India, was the prime mover in the present one, and was currently president of the Board of Trade. All were men of high principle. Pethick-Lawrence had once received a custodial sentence for encouraging suffragette defiance; Cripps, a vegetarian and a teetotaler, had once been expelled from the Labour Party as too left-wing; and Alexander, a blacksmith's son, had been known to double as a lay preacher. All sympathized with India's national aspirations and shared its leadership's socialist values. Their integrity, their seniority, and their extended leave from cabinet duties bespoke their government's intent. Britain's Labour Party had already committed itself to "freedom and self-determination" for the peoples of India; now it must deliver. As per its instructions, the delegation's task was "to work out in cooperation [with India's political leaders] the means by which Indians can themselves decide the form of their new institutions with the minimum of disturbance and the maximum of speed." Thus would be consummated what the mission's statement called "the transfer of responsibility" and what the delegates themselves called "the transfer of power."[1]

The cabinet delegates, all of them around sixty years of age, reeking of tobacco, and unaccustomed to the ease of light linen suiting, were immediately dubbed "the Magi" by Lord Wavell, the current viceroy. The Indian press preferred to call them "the Three Wise Men." They might have come from the West and arrived by plane, but the treasure they bore was indeed priceless. India was at last being proffered the means of securing full and unconditional independence. After decades of sacrifice and disappointment, repression and obfuscation, protest and imprisonment, *azadi* (freedom, independence) was within the grasp of the subcontinent's four hundred million.

In the history books this first postwar initiative in the endgame of British rule is known simply as "the 1946 Cabinet Mission," an impersonal phrasing that has deterred scrutiny and obscured its importance. Within a year the new viceroy, Lord Mountbatten, would force through a very different handover of power that would relegate the Cabinet Mission and all its doings to the India Office's bulging archive of begrudged concessions and aborted proposals. Yet, for all this, the mission deserves recognition as one of the twentieth century's milestones. It marked the beginning of the end for the British Empire in India; it was the first such overture to offer independence on a plate, to India or anywhere else; and it was the last to provide any real hope of staving off a division of the South Asian subcontinent.

Only in retrospect was it a failure. Both of the main contenders for power in India—the Indian National Congress, guided by Jawaharlal Nehru, and the Muslim League, headed by Mahomed Ali Jinnah—would in fact accept a mission proposal that emphatically rejected any division of the country; the demand for a sovereign state of Pakistan was so hopelessly impractical, declared the proposal, as "not to be an acceptable solution." Even Jinnah, the man who epitomized the demand for a separate Muslim homeland called Pakistan, would not demur over what he called merely these "injudicious words." Fitfully and faintly, a hint of consensus arced across India's dark horizon of sectarian rivalry. The rainbow would soon fade, but throughout 1946 the country lay within a whisker of attaining full independence as a single sovereign state. Partition, in other words, was no more a foregone conclusion in the run-up to independence than was the genocidal mayhem of its aftermath.

Rolling up their shirtsleeves of Sea Island cotton, the cabinet ministers got down to work in the hermetically air-conditioned offices of a wing of the viceregal palace (one of the world's largest residential buildings, it is now Rashtrapati Bhawan, the official home of the Republic of India's president).[2] For two weeks they listened—to the views of the viceroy and his Executive Council, to the governors of British India's fourteen constituent provinces, the representatives of its several hundred quasi-sovereign princely states, and the spokesmen of its main political parties and communal groupings; in all, they would interview "472 people on 181 separate occasions."[3] Then for four weeks they drafted—first an outline of the likely constitutional options (a large two-tier federal India versus two or more smaller one-tier Indias), followed, when the Muslim League rejected both, by a statement of their own that proposed a large three-tier federal India. This too was unacceptable, but in the hope that common ground would emerge through direct Congress-League contact, the Cabinet Mission invited the interested parties to send representatives to a conference.

By now it was early May. The thermometer on the terrace outside the viceregal palace hovered around a hundred degrees. Tarmac bubbled like porridge, and it was the turn of the railways to be paralyzed by strike action. A suggestion that the delegates repair to Simla, 220 miles to the north and 6,500 feet higher, promised some welcome relief plus a tantalizing glimpse of the Himalayan snow line. It was approved in a rare show of unanimity; elevation was just what the discussions needed. With the railways at a standstill, the mission flew to Simla's nearest airstrip, at Ambala, before addressing the hairpin bends of the nearly perpendicular ascent to the town by car.

But the "Queen of Hill Stations," as so often, disappointed. The change of scene brought no change of heart. Simla's pine-scented zephyrs neither cooled heads nor cleared the air. The conference lasted more than a week and served only to highlight League-Congress differences. Consultation degenerated into altercation. By May 13 the delegates were trailing back empty-handed to the inferno that was Delhi. Pethick-Lawrence was getting tetchy; Cripps, the mission's intellectual heavyweight, was wilting with diarrhea, which might have been dysentery; and Alexander had discovered an urgent need to visit a British naval base in Sri Lanka (then Ceylon).

Nevertheless, three days later, the mission came up with its own solution. All its "proposals" having been shot down by either Congress, the League, or both, the mission had decided to stop inviting comment and instead to offer a "recommendation." This favored another three-tier, one-state constitution. Of the three tiers, the first would comprise British India's fourteen directly administered provinces. Their recently elected legislatures would then take their provinces into three predetermined regional groupings roughly corresponding to the northwest, the northeast, and the remainder of the country; this was the second tier. The groups would then arrogate to the central government—the topmost tier—certain all-India responsibilities, including foreign affairs, defense, communications, and some revenue-raising powers. The groups might award to the center other responsibilities. They might also determine their own constitutions. Although a cumbersome device, the importance of the groups lay in the fact that two of them, those in the northwest and northeast, corresponded to the Muslim-majority regions earmarked by the Muslim League for its putative Pakistan. The League could thus reassure itself that the substance of a Muslim homeland had not been entirely precluded, while the Congress could reassure itself that the principle of an undivided India remained intact.

Overall the structure was essentially a graduated federal pyramid, with the fourteen provinces tapering to the three groups and then the one center. Residual sovereignty would lie with the provinces and the groups, while the central government was comparatively weak. But provision was also made for an all-India constitution-making body, or Constituent Assembly, to give effect to the whole plan. The Constituent Assembly's members would be selected by the provincial legislatures on a religious basis: Muslims would choose Muslim members and Sikhs Sikh members, and the great majority would choose "general members," a term designed to avoid identifying the supporters of the determinedly secular Congress as overwhelmingly Hindu.

All the recommendations contained in this May 16 statement had been worked out in advance with London and anticipated by some of the earlier proposals. It was a longish document and a particularly taxing one, with more than the odd devil in its considerable detail. In fact, the detail was so complicated that it required weeks of clarification by the mission, then exhaustive debate within the two main parties. Yet, not without grave misgivings and reservations, on June 6 Jinnah and the Muslim League accepted it; so too, though anxious over the interpretation of some clauses and in the face of Mahatma Gandhi's disapproval of the confessionally based groups, did Congress on June 25.

For the moment Partition was ruled out, as was a sovereign Pakistan; from Afghanistan to Burma, an independent India would have the same dimensions as British India. On this happy note the members of the Cabinet Mission began packing their bags. Exhausted, they flew back to London on June 29.

"We ask the Indian people to give this statement calm and careful consideration," Cripps had pleaded at a press conference. "I believe that the happiness of their future depends on what they do now. . . . But if the plan is not accepted, no one can say how great will be the disturbance, or how acute and long the suffering that will be self-inflicted by the Indian people."[4]

THE DISTURBANCE AND SUFFERING began within a matter of weeks, for the Cabinet Mission, despite its apparent success on the constitutional front, had inadvertently made things worse. A constitutional framework had been agreed upon, but an actual constitution would have to wait on the deliberations of the Constituent Assembly. These could take months—as indeed they would (or, as in the eventual case of Pakistan, decades). In the meantime, Congress insisted that an interim government composed of Indian nationals should take over the reins of power. In Nehru's view and in that of Gandhi, a constitution must be the product of an independent nation; freedom, if it meant anything, must include the freedom to formulate one's own institutions. De facto independence must therefore precede the constitution-making process. The League took the opposite view; as Jinnah saw it, an interim government that inherited the paramount powers and patronage of the British Raj would be at liberty to influence the Constituent Assembly's interpretation of the May 16 statement, even overrule it. If there had to be an interim government, therefore, Jinnah demanded a safeguard: half the interim government's members must be Muslims nominated by his Muslim League, negating any hostile intervention by the other half, consisting mainly of Congress "general members."

"Now happened one of those unfortunate events which change the course of history," noted Maulana Azad, a scholarly and emollient Muslim who, unlike Jinnah, rejected the idea of Pakistan and was at the time president of the Congress Party. At a press conference Nehru was asked whether Congress accepted the May 16 plan in toto. Off the cuff Nehru replied that Congress would indeed enter the Constituent Assembly but then added that it would do so "completely unfettered by agreements and free to meet all situations as they arise." In effect, concluded Azad, Nehru was claiming for Congress the right to "change or modify the Cabinet Mission Plan as it thought best." This "astonishing statement" called into question the good faith of one of the main signatories and so undermined the whole agreement. Maulana Azad, as a Congress Muslim from a Muslim-minority province that was never likely to be part of any Pakistan, had a vested interest in an undivided India; he was horrified. Jinnah was perhaps less so; in Nehru's casual admission that he did not consider the agreement binding, Jinnah saw his often-aired fears confirmed. If the other signatory reserved the right to change or modify the agreement "as it thought best," the League wanted nothing to do with it. It therefore withdrew its earlier acceptance.[5]

Meanwhile, Congress had decided to withhold support for the proposed interim government. This time it was not Nehru who was responsible but Gandhi. No longer a Congress officeholder but still very much the party's conscience, the seventy-six-year-old Mahatma balked at the parity between Muslims (accounting for roughly 30 percent of India's population) and non-Muslims (70 percent) implied by the proposed makeup of the interim government, and he took particular exception to Jinnah's insistence that only the Muslim League was entitled to nominate Muslim members.

Thus, within days of the Cabinet Mission emplaning for London, the Constituent Assembly was being boycotted by the League, while the interim government was being boycotted by the Congress. Of the two representative institutions set up under the mission's plan to expedite the handover of power, neither was left with more than a single rickety leg to stand on.

Landed with this tottering structure, Wavell, the viceroy, would do his best. Nehru would revise his position and Jinnah would be credited, wrongly, with second thoughts; a Constituent Assembly would indeed assemble and an interim government would be formed. Though the transactions of neither would induce a spirit of collaboration, well into 1947 all the interested parties remained engaged in a constitution-making process based on the Cabinet Mission's recommendations—including its insistence that the territories constituting British India should continue as a single sovereign state.

It was events rather than debates that poisoned this uncertain process, then rendered it redundant. Back in 1942 Congress had severely embarrassed the British with the Quit India movement, designed to sabotage their war effort and persuade them to leave India immediately. The movement had been suppressed, but only with great violence and thanks to some draconian wartime regulations. Now, according to the League, in the dog days of 1946 the British were fearful of a new wave of Congress noncooperation that would be impossible to contain without the troop levels that had pertained in war and that must therefore lead to the ignominy of forced eviction. It was this consideration that had led the Cabinet Mission to overlook Nehru's ambivalence about constitution making and to indulge Gandhi's intransigence over Muslim representation in the interim government. In other words, the Muslim community was being "betrayed," as Jinnah put it, by a British government reluctant to risk Congress retaliation. A record of mass menace was evidently more persuasive than one of reasoned argument; taking this lesson to heart, on July 29 Jinnah announced that "this day we bid goodbye to constitutional methods."[6] In the first all-India protest it had ever organized, the Muslim League called on its supporters to stage their own brand of "direct action." It also named the day: Friday (the Muslim day of prayer), August 16.

The League's protest was to be framed as a demand for "Pakistan," a term that was already understood to mean an independent homeland for the League's Muslim constituency or what Jinnah called the "Muslim nation." But what this Pakistan would actually mean with respect to territory, population transfers, and relations with the rest of India was far from clear. Jinnah preferred it that way: the vaguer the term, the more elastic its scope and the more electric its appeal. Yet despite the pro-Pakistan banners and posters (there was as yet no Pakistani flag or anthem), and despite the vast crowds of demonstrators, and the usual scuffles, Direct Action Day on August 16 occasioned no major confrontations in the great northwestern centers of Muslim India—Delhi, Lahore, the Punjab—that would witness the worst atrocities of an eventual Partition. Instead it was Calcutta, then India's largest conurbation and business capital, that exploded.

As in Dhaka, where lesser disturbances had been ongoing for weeks, the explosion was triggered by a minor local issue that, magnified in a prism of economic grievances, industrial disputes, and confrontational party politics, assumed the black-and-white, them-or-us terms of the city's already endemic Hindu-Muslim animosity. In the gory press reports of the "Great Calcutta Killing" that ensued, the word "Pakistan" received scarcely a mention, nor was it prominent among the declared demands and anxieties of the combatants. Partition and its implications for Calcutta, a city that had a Hindu majority but was the capital of a province (Bengal) with a Muslim majority, was little understood; likewise, the niceties of constitution making and government formation in far-off Delhi were irrelevant. Rather, the spark that ignited the explosion of violence was an innocuous and apparently commendable resolution by Bengal's provincial assembly. Passed on a show of hands by its incumbent Muslim League ministry, it simply ordained that, to minimize the inevitable friction if non-Muslims worked while Muslims marched, Direct Action Day should be observed by all as a public holiday.

"Calcutta in Grip of Insane Lust for Fratricidal Blood," ran the August 17, 1946, headline in the *People's Age,* the nation's Communist (and so confessionally neutral) mouthpiece. The riots amounted to "a communal orgy the like of which had never been seen before." Indeed, the Muslim League's Direct Action Day on the sixteenth had "turned into an open civil war between Hindus and Muslims."[7] Thousands were being killed, the streets were strewn with corpses, the hospitals were overflowing with wounded, fires raged unchecked, and whole districts were being looted. One witness told of corpses being roped together like sporting trophies, another of babies being hurled from balconies, children clubbed to death, and mothers and daughters abused and butchered. Only the British, usually the butt of Bengali protests, had been left unmolested, and only the police had been of a mind to observe the declared holiday.

Politicians on both sides had to bear much of the responsibility. Congress members, after walking out of the Bengal Assembly in protest over the holiday resolution, had publicly denounced the League in the most intemperate terms. The League had responded with equally inflammatory sentiments. Both had welcomed the support of known criminal elements whose actions they had subsequently declined to condemn. The League government had at first delayed recalling the police and then deployed them less than evenhandedly, and, when the situation was clearly beyond its control, it had failed to call on Bengal's British governor to send in the army. The governor, in turn, should have acted sooner, whether asked to or not. As it was, the killing went on unopposed for two days and unquelled for four. Four thousand died, and eleven thousand survived serious injuries.

In retrospect, the Great Calcutta Killing would come to be seen as the turning point in South Asian relations. For decades nationalists of every hue had concentrated their fire on British imperialism; a common enemy cemented a common sense of purpose. Now, with independence as good as won, nationalists turned on nationalists in a civil war between the country's two main communities. It was Gandhi's worst nightmare and Nehru's idea of madness, and it seemed unstoppable. Rightly or wrongly, the outbreak in Calcutta would be construed as the first eruption in a chain reaction of communal atrocities that, spreading erratically, gained in intensity until a year later they climaxed in the mass genocide of Partition.

Calcutta certainly set the pattern of savagery. No one knew who started the killing. Rumor raced ahead of verifiable report. The gangs responsible, whether Hindu or Muslim, invariably claimed to be avenging prior atrocities or acting in self-defense. Street talk of "massacres" no more captured the full horror than did the official designation of the disturbances as "riots." Even "civil war" was something of a misnomer. Some parts of the city were unaffected, with the Communist *People's Age* smugly noting that "reports from the working-class belt indicate that the hysterical frenzy has not contaminated the workers." The combatants were divided along purely communal lines, their object being not to expel or detain their opponents but to terrorize, desecrate, and exterminate them. Age went unrespected and innocence unacknowledged; just to be of the wrong community was provocation enough. Votive objects—a domestic deity here, a treasured Quran there—were trashed and fouled. Mosques were defaced, shrines burned. Women, the embodiment of every community's exclusivity, were a particular target. Some had been raped or abducted, while the dead had been physically incised with the religious hallmarks of their murderers. Either way, the objective was the appropriation of all that the other community held sacred.

As with the later massacres, the scale and the intensity of the Calcutta killings took both British and Indians by surprise. No Indian political leader, "neither the [Bengal] government nor the opposition nor the press," anticipated the magnitude of the tragedy. As later too, the national politicians in Delhi seemed more obsessed with the squabble for power than with its consequences for the febrile communities they represented. Like the frailest of firefighters, Gandhi alone would track the flames of violence, touring the stricken areas—Dhaka, Noakhali (both in eastern Bengal), and then Bihar, all before the end of 1946—as he fasted, marched, and painfully practiced the communal harmony that he so tirelessly preached. His colleagues preferred to accuse their political opponents either of starting the troubles or of failing to suppress them, both of which only stoked the fires of hatred for the next round of atrocities. No one seemed capable of comprehending the scale and obscenity of the killing. In the midst of forming the interim government, Nehru breezily declared that his arrangements must "not be upset because a few persons misbehave in Calcutta"; Jinnah similarly refused to believe that any member of the Muslim League "would have taken part in using any violence." A joint inquiry might have cleared the air. Neither party would agree to it. Instead, both conducted their own inquiries. Each duly found against the other.[8]

Ironically, the effect on the British was wholly counterproductive. Direct Action Day, though conceived by Jinnah as a way of demonstrating that the League could bite as well as bark and must therefore be taken seriously, merely impressed the British with the urgency of disengaging. The viceroy and his advisers were convinced that the situation was getting out of control. An all-India civil war seemed imminent, with the British ill-equipped to prevent it and in danger of being caught in the crossfire. Not for the first time, Wavell wavered over the prospects for a peaceful transfer of power and began drawing up a plan B. The *B* stood for "breakdown"—a breakdown in the constitutional process and a breakdown in law and order. To a military man who had presided over the Allies' wartime retreats in both North Africa and Southeast Asia, a carefully phased withdrawal was the obvious answer, first from the comparatively peaceful south of India to the Gangetic plain, then to the strategic redoubt of the Punjab and the northwest. In this scenario, Jinnah's Pakistan, if it ever materialized, would come piecemeal, later rather than sooner, and by agreement with Westminster regardless of Congress. The Calcutta killings had neither advanced the League's cause nor made Pakistan inevitable. What they did make inevitable was an early British departure and the near certainty of constitution making being sacrificed to the exigencies of the moment while the apprehensions of undivided India's four hundred million citizens were left to fester.

"PAKISTAN? WHAT GOOD IS THAT TO US? We want oil, cloth, sugar, wheat. And we want justice—that is all."

Such were the sentiments expressed by a couple of Qureshi Muslims when, in March 1947, they were asked how they felt about a Pakistan that was looming larger with every communal massacre and constitutional impasse. Qureshis claim descent from the Arab invaders who first brought Islam to India in the eighth century; these ones had bicycles and were heading for a building site near the Narmada River in what is now Madhya Pradesh. Famed for speaking their mind, Qureshis might have been expected to welcome the idea of Pakistan. But in this case their response was wholly negative, and it was not untypical. It echoed that of sundry Pathans, Punjabis, Jats, Mewatis, and Rajputs—Muslims and Sikhs as well as Hindus—whose opinions had been quietly canvassed over the previous four months by the inquisitive Malcolm Lyall Darling.

An aging Quixote on a small gray horse, Darling had ridden out of Peshawar one raw November morning in 1946. From a start within sight of the Khyber Pass, he had been ambling east and south ever since. By March 1947 he was in what was roughly the center of India, nearing the end of his epic ride. Dressed in creaky leather boots, tweeds of many pockets, and an outsize sola topi to protect his hairless pate, he looked exactly what he was: ex-Eton, ex-Cambridge, and ex-ICS (Britain's elite Indian Civil Service). But not for him the face-saving constitutional conundrums of Delhi or the peacekeeping anxieties of Calcutta. Darling was controversial. A gentle critic of many aspects of British policy, he had turned to Nehru when planning his itinerary and would report to Gandhi on the findings of his trip. During thirty-six years' service his specialty had been setting up agricultural cooperatives and encouraging "the Punjab peasant in prosperity and debt" (as per the title of one of his books). Rural life remained his passion. An hour or two spent chatting with agriculturalists under the village pipal tree he accounted well spent and entirely pleasurable. The diary of his eighteen-hundred-mile ride from the Indus to the Narmada during what would be north India's last winter as an undivided land affords the most comprehensive investigation on record of rural opinion at this critical moment. Ministers in limousines might be deciding the subcontinent's future, but it was the threadbare figures aboard the ox carts, whether in the boulevards of New Delhi or in the back of beyond, who would have to live with the consequences—or die because of them.

Oddly, Partition and Pakistan, though hotly debated and now only a matter of months away, were not yet, according to Darling, at the top of the villager's agenda. Mention of *azadi* did occasion excitement— and more especially so after February 1947, when the British finally announced a deadline for their departure. At the time Darling was trotting through a yellow sea of oilseed rape between Gwalior and Jhansi. He approved of the deadline. He had in fact been urging commitment to a cutoff date for years, if only to concentrate the minds of the constitution makers. Now, though, the announcement hinted as much at necessity as at tactics. Despairing of the Congress-League negotiations (or the lack of them), desperate to depart ahead of any communal bloodbath, and highly doubtful of Wavell's step-by-step "breakdown plan," the London government had decreed that, agreement or not, it would pull out of India by June 1948.

Yet however imminent, even *azadi* was seen by the toiling masses less as a national triumph than as an economic panacea, for with self-government there would surely come the oil, cloth, sugar, wheat, and justice that were everywhere in such desperately short supply. Oil for lamps and cooking, cotton cloth for clothing (a single man's outfit of turban, trousers, shirt, and shawl took twenty yards, "and women require considerably more"), sugar for sweets and treacly tea, and wheat (or rice) as the staple of subsistence—without these things life was barely supportable. Yet rationing, a wartime necessity in India as in Britain, had slashed their availability, while the combination of inflation and distributive corruption had pushed the prices of the little that was available way beyond the set rates. Incomes had roughly doubled in the previous five years, but "even the controlled price [of wheat]—Rs 10 a maund—is four times what it was before the war, and 'in the black' [i.e., on the black market] it is Rs 14 to 16," reported Darling.

> As we rode, we were waylaid again and again by officers, other ranks, headmen and peasants, drawn up by the roadside in long lines headed by some medaled veteran. They all had the same complaint—the complaint that has run like a telegraph wire all along our road for the last sixty or seventy miles. "We have nothing to eat, we are dying of hunger, there is no sugar, no cloth, no matches. Look at our children, how ragged they are! Our lot is unbearable!" No one of course was dying of hunger, and many were tolerably well dressed. But . . . in ten to fifteen days 80% of the people . . . [will] have to buy their food and most of them will have to do this "in the black" . . . All agree that, if sufficient grain is not imported in the course of the next fortnight, there will be sheer starvation.[9]

This was the situation in the extreme west of the Punjab, which was generally reckoned the most productive province in the country. Darling found the same in what is now Haryana, and the refrain, echoed by those Qureshi contractors, continued right down into Madhya Pradesh. Even in the cities, where the fixed-rate allowances of cloth and foodstuffs were on a more generous scale, the poor were feeling the bite. The widespread protests—the endless strikes, shut-ins, shut-outs, and often bloody confrontations—were more about the cost of living than about the iniquities of foreign rule. "It was a time," notes the editor of a recent collection of contemporary reports, "of remarkable, indeed unprecedented, labour unrest and it saw the beginnings of several powerful peasant movements." If Calcutta's "working-class belt" had really resisted the frenzy of the August killings, it may have been because, while celebrating solidarity with the striking postal workers, the laboring classes were readying themselves for upcoming strikes in the docks and on the tramways. "The range of participation [in the unrest] . . . extend[ed] from sweepers through miners and railwaymen to white collar employees in post offices, banks and military establishments. Even policemen [were] affected, and that across several provinces . . . Taken together these [outbreaks] illuminate certain alternative possibilities that have been almost forgotten today."[10]

Rather more than a "possibility" is the inference that sectarian bigotry was by no means the only cause of civil strife in 1946–47. The Communists were as active as the "communalists" (India-speak for religious zealots). The waves of protest that had until lately buffeted British imperialism now pounded the ramparts of capitalism just as much as they undermined the breakwaters of secularism. A strike in a railway workshop in far-off Madras province had turned violent almost as readily, and at about the same time, as had Direct Action Day in Calcutta. Nehru and Jinnah might paint glossy word pictures of "the great future that beckons us," but their roseate visions were often lost on a hungry and fearful public. In rural areas, starvation was no idle threat. Only three years earlier millions had died in the great Bengal famine of 1943. Though blamed primarily on the British and their world war, it was common knowledge that the famine had been exacerbated by the Bengal government's inadequate relief effort and by the hoarding and profiteering of Bengal's grain contractors. The province's government had been that of the Muslim League, giving Congress a ready scapegoat, and the contractors were mostly Hindus, providing the same for the Muslim

League. All too easily, distress of any sort could be translated into the confrontational rhetoric of Congress-League rivalry and so, by extension, into the incendiary terms of sectarian hatred.

Darling found the same thing happening along the line of his epic ride across northwest India. Power and responsibility in the provinces had been handed over to elected governments back in 1937. It was they—Congress-run in most provinces, League-run in a few—who had imposed the rationing, who had lately tightened it, and who were responsible for administering it. Hence, just as the incumbent League ministry in Bengal bore the brunt of the blame for the Calcutta killings, so the Congress ministries in three of the five provinces through which Darling rode were being blamed for the economic hardship. The accolade of "most corrupt [department] in a very corrupt province . . . is now universally accorded to the Food Supply [Civil Supplies] Department and its satellite traders who, controlling the very basis of life, exploit their neighbours to the full, as they once did with their money-lending."[11] This was apropos of North-West Frontier Province (NWFP), where a Congress ministry presided over a largely Muslim population, but it applied equally to the Punjab and the United Provinces (UP). Congress governments stood accused of rewarding their supporters with lucrative posts in the Food Supply Department, from where, abetted by Hindu contractors and moneylenders, their largesse was channeled exclusively to Hindu recipients and Congress voters. According to one of Darling's informants, it was this situation rather than the prospect of Pakistan that accounted for the growing popularity of the League among Punjabi Muslims: "The chief spur is the fear of Hindu domination, deriving from the domination of the Hindu money-lender and trader which . . . has taken a new lease of life with the control of supplies. The fear is widespread and the bloody doings in Bengal [the killings in Calcutta and Noakhali] and Bihar have created, to quote the Assistant Registrar, some hatred in their hearts."[12]

As yet the hatred was only a presentiment, continued Darling's informant; the relationship between the different communities in this particular Punjabi village was "still a happy one." But by March, when Darling was reaching the end of his ride, it was not at all happy. From Calcutta and Bihar the intercommunal killing had spread to

Garhmukteshwar in UP, then to the villages of western Punjab. As Darling closed his diary on the Narmada, his first informants back beside the Indus were already succumbing to the madness. As victims, perpetrators, or both, many more would follow them before his diary was published in 1949.

WHEN TRAVERSING THE NORTHWEST, including its several princely states, it was impossible for the wayfarer not to be reminded of the complexity of the subcontinent. Preserving the unity that both British administrators and Indian nationalists so cherished was all very well on government letterhead, but, on the ground, amid the heat and the dust, an undivided India, *bharat khand,* could look to be wishful thinking. The four hundred million now hammering "at Freedom's Door," as Darling put it, were converging from all points of a finely calibrated social, religious, and political compass. Beneath the village pipal tree literally dozens of conflicting identities awaited the visitor, some so subtle as to be scarcely discernible, others starkly distinct. Counterposing just Muslims and Hindus—a practice long favored by the British and now championed by Jinnah, endorsed by the Cabinet Mission Plan, and fitfully contested by Congress—woefully oversimplified the situation.

For one thing, it ignored the Sikhs. Though statistically irrelevant in the rest of India, in the Punjab the followers of the Ten Gurus and the Granth Sahib made up around a quarter of the population and were, reported Darling, as evenly distributed about the province's Muslim and Hindu majority areas "as the ingredients of a well-made pilau." This was the problem. Muslims and Hindus enjoyed majority status in numerous provinces; if sovereignty was to reside in the provinces and groups as per the Cabinet Mission Plan, each was ensured a share of power. But it was not so with the Sikhs. A minority in their Punjab homeland, they were, like the tidbits of mutton in the pilau, so nicely spread about the plate as to be minorities even in most of that province's districts and subdistricts.

The Cabinet Mission had been made aware of this problem. Sikh spokesmen had lobbied for a settlement that would afford them some guarantee of local autonomy and religious freedom and that would not further fragment them by dividing the pilau—the Punjab—between a Muslim Pakistan and a non-Muslim Hindustan. (At the time it was assumed that an India without its Muslim-majority areas would call itself "Hindustan," the land of the Hindu, rather than lay claim to the term "India.") Partition would, of course, produce precisely this disastrous bisection of the Sikh community. But the Cabinet Mission's master plan for a united India was equally objectionable in that it consigned the Sikhs to demographic inconsequence within a Muslim-dominated Punjab that would itself be attached to the Muslim-dominated northwestern group of provinces. "We have been thrown into a pit," moaned a young Sikh to Darling.[13]

In making almost no provision for the Sikhs, the plan ignored a community that was arguably the most distinctive and assertive in the whole country. Uncut hair, billowing beards, and tightly tied turbans positively trumpeted the identity of all Sikh sardars; their neat fields and thriving agricultural cooperatives brought a special glow to Darling's heart; and their disproportionate representation in British India's regiments, not to mention their familiarity with firearms and their attachment to costume weaponry (dirks and swords), left little doubt that they would defend their interests. These interests were not purely doctrinal. Muslims were sometimes accused of embracing independence as a chance to put the clock back to a pre-British India when the Muslim Mughals ruled most of the subcontinent. Sikhs felt somewhat the same about their province. The Punjab had been British for less than a hundred years. Before the 1840s it had been the heart of an independent Sikh kingdom—or sometimes empire—extending from the Khyber Pass to Tibet. As champions of the Punjabi language and as the region's erstwhile rulers, the Sikhs effectively defined the province. Their empire's political capital, Lahore, was still the administrative capital, and their spiritual capital, Amritsar, was still its only rival. Sites associated with the triumphs and tribulations of early Sikhism were scattered right across the province, as were Sikh shrines, places of pilgrimage, and centers of worship. Whatever the electoral mathematics, the sardars felt entitled to special consideration. Their dream of an independent Khalistan, like the Muslims' dream of Pakistan, was as yet more a battle cry than a realistic proposition, but, as the Punjab began to shatter along its Hindu-Muslim fault line, the idea of an autonomous Sikh homeland was becoming ever more attractive.

Another casualty of the constitution makers' tendency to polarize Hindus and Muslims (and indeed Sikhs) was the rich matrix of customs and values that both communities shared. In the villages of central Punjab even the experienced Darling sometimes had difficulty telling who was a Muslim and who a Hindu. They were hard to distinguish because Muslims (and Sikhs) were often descended from converts whose caste or tribe was still that of their Hindu neighbors. There were thus Hindu Gujars and Muslim Gujars, and Hindu Jats, Muslim Jats, and Sikh Jats. It was the same with Rajputs. Wrote Darling, "Riding along this morning, I asked a Muslim Inspector [or zaildar] . . . whether Muslims ever have their horoscopes read. 'Yes,' he replied, and added, 'all Bhatti Rajput Muslims have this done by the family Brahmin.' The Naib-Tehsildar [deputy officer], a Hindu, joining in, said: 'The Zaildar and I are of the same tribe. He is a [Muslim] Bhatti and I am a [Hindu] Bhatia; our origin is the same.'"[14]

Further on, Darling heard tell of some fifty Rajput villages that had converted to Islam around 1700. Recently they had offered to "return to the Hindu fold on the one condition that their Hindu kinsfolk would give them their daughters in marriage." This was refused and they remained Muslims, "but they still interchange civilities at marriage, inviting mullah or Brahmin, as the case may be, to share in the feasting." Such communal harmony was by no means unusual. Oral testimony has amply confirmed that even in Bengal and Bihar, the scene of the first great killings, Muslims commonly participated in Hindu festivals and Hindus in Muslim festivals. Each might also consult the other's holy men, share their myths, mimic their greetings, and in some cases partake of their food. Conduct might be no more reliable in deciding who was a Hindu or a Muslim than ethnicity.

South of Delhi, Darling's route lay among the Meos of a region known as Mewat. "Clanny and feckless," he thought, the Meos were once reputed a criminal tribe who lived by highway robbery. Few outsiders entered their often scruffy villages (one of which, Gurgaon, now challenges Delhi with its shopping malls and call centers), and here, for a change, Darling found the tables turned: It was the villagers who were quizzing him about his own caste: "No, I am not a Muslim." "Then are you a Hindu?" The Meos had a particular interest in the matter because their own identity was problematic. Officially they were regarded as Muslims and, according to Darling, they already favored the League. But fellow Muslims were not always anxious to acknowledge them as such nor to intermarry with them. This was because they combined irregular attendance at the mosque and erratic performance of *namaz* (the Muslim prayers) with a passionate devotion to Lords Krishna and Rama.

Sadly, according to Shail Mayaram, a latter-day champion of the Meos, such bi-confessionalism was being eroded from two sides. On one hand, the tract-distributing Tablighi mission was actively promoting Islamic orthodoxy among the Meos, and, on the other, zealots of the Mahasabha, the Hindu triumphalist party, were actively promoting anti-Muslim sentiment among the Meos' Hindu neighbors. Willy-nilly the Meos were coming to think of themselves as Muslim because that was how others saw them. In an increasingly polarized society there was no place for a cross-communal community. Come Partition, the Meos would pay dearly for their heterodoxy, experiencing death and dispossession at the hands of their Hindu neighbors, then rebuff and rejection at the hands of their Muslim "brethren."[15]

Most of the Meos' neighbors in that part of the Punjab that is now the Indian state of Haryana were Hindu Jats. Relations between the two communities had been cordial until the 1930s. Then population pressures had led to a period of agrarian unrest as the Jats coveted the Meos' land. There were armed affrays and the troops had to be called in. But religion had not been an issue at the time. It became so only when Congress and the League squared off against each other in the 1940s. And in the country south of Delhi—all the way to Agra and Jaipur, in fact—this politicization of communal sentiment had especially dire consequences. For here agrarian, ethnic, and religious tensions were exacerbated by what was undoubtedly the greatest anomaly of all in a supposedly "united India"—namely, that much of it was far from united in that it was not actually ruled by the British. Indeed, it never had been, for this was princely India.

Long before he reached Mewat, Darling's equestrian odyssey had repeatedly taken him into territories whose administration owed nothing to his former fellows in the Indian Civil Service and everything to the good sense (or otherwise) of one of India's innumerable princes. In the Punjab the princely states of Patiala and Nabha, both ruled by Sikh maharajahs, had yielded a rather frosty welcome, and Bahawalpur state, ruled by a Muslim nawab, was beset by poor harvests. Villages in the princely states were less likely to have a school than those in British-ruled India, noted Darling, and the people were therefore less well informed.

There was, though, he thought, something to be said for princely rule. Justice—a commodity that his Qureshi informants found as scarce as cloth, sugar, and wheat—tended to be abundant there. It was swifter, cheaper, and more effective than under the British dispensation. As a result, crime was rarer and the roads safer. The classic case was Swat, a long sub-Himalayan valley that debouched into North-West Frontier Province and that Darling had skirted in the first week of his ride. In Swat's alpine setting, holidaymakers pitched their tents and anglers cast their lines without a care for the notoriously unruly Pathan clans of the valley. It was all thanks, explained one of Darling's informants, to the wali (ruler) of Swat rigidly enforcing "the *Shariat*, the Law of God." "[In Swat] a man commits a murder and in twelve hours he will be arrested, tried and shot. Here [i.e., in the British-run NWFP] it may take a year or two and as likely as not, when tried, he will get off, and then a blood feud starts." On the whole, Darling thought this "a sad reflexion on our [i.e., British] rule."[16]

Sixty-three years later, when sharia was reintroduced into Swat by Taliban zealots, it would receive no such endorsement. The government in Islamabad at first prevaricated, then panicked. Mobile-phone footage of a convicted adulteress being publicly flogged brought howls of protest from Benazir Bhutto's Western backers and prompted a massive military intervention by the Pakistan army. Thousands died, and in scenes reminiscent of Partition's aftermath, hundreds of thousands streamed out of the valley to avoid the carnage. Almost no one recalled that sharia had a long pedigree in Swat and might not be entirely distasteful to the Swatis. Though rough and gender-biased, it slashed the crime rate, ensured the security of property and persons, and was a more effective deterrent than the slow, corrupt, and painfully overloaded judicial system operating in the rest of Pakistan.

In early 1947, along the sandy trails south of Delhi, Darling found justice less of an issue than religion. Mewat (the name simply means "Meo country") extended from British-administered Gurgaon deep into the territories of three princely states, two of which (Bharatpur and Dholpur) had Hindu Jat maharajahs. Entering Bharatpur, Darling noted how the traffic tailed off and the wayside murmurings became a veritable "cataract of complaints." Here the export of grain was forbidden and that of cattle taxed, the land revenue was higher and the corruption worse, "and of course no one had any sugar or cloth." The Meos were reduced to rags, with not a garment that was free of holes. (Darling suggested darning, then remembered the state of his socks.)

For these woes, Meos and Jats were united in blaming the maharajah of Bharatpur's administration, but they did so for different reasons. "There is a good deal of political agitation going on in the State," explained Darling, "sponsored, if not engineered, by supporters of Congress, and doubtless this [cataract of complaints] was an echo of it."[17] But while the Meos blamed the Congress agitators for turning the administration against them as Muslims, the Jats took exception to the Congress supporters as godless secularists who were indifferent to Hindu rights and were antimonarchist republicans to boot. Their maharajah, Brijendra Singh, was himself in no way to blame. On the contrary, the Jats looked to him as their savior. They saw no contradiction between nationalism and princely absolutism because the nation to which by preference they subscribed was Jat, not Indian, and their maharajah epitomized it.

The prospect of a Jatistan along the lines of the Muslim Pakistan or the Sikh Khalistan was already being bandied about. Just six weeks after Darling passed through the Jat country, it would surface in a pithy slogan: "With *biri* in hand and *pan* in mouth we are busy making Jatistan." *Biri*, the peasant's smoke, and *pan*, his betel-leaf digestif, were markers of Hindu identity. The Jats' subnationalism thus announced its Hindu credentials. In this it had the full backing of the maharajah. As a patron of the ultra-Hindu Mahasabha, His Highness's Hindu supremacism was as far to the right on India's religious spectrum as his monarchist convictions were on its constitutional spectrum.

Fatally, if rather desperately, in the spring of 1947 the Meos met this Jat challenge with calls for their own Meoistan. While accommodating their unorthodox beliefs, Meoistan was to be an agrarian republic informed by both the Communist class struggle and consensual village custom. It was thus "both a radical and a traditional [alternative] based on a vision of intercommunal solidarity and a decentring of power." But come the summer, continues Shail Mayaram, "what it elicited was a mass extermination campaign"—one in which the campaigning was done mainly by the Bharatpur Jats and the extermination was suffered mainly by the luckless Meos.[18] Many thousands would be massacred and many thousands more "converted," and hundreds of thousands would swell the flood of refugees. Within the context of Partition all of them would be seen, and counted, simply as casualties of the great Hindu-Muslim conflagration. As elsewhere, subnational agrarian, economic, and governmental anxieties went largely unrecorded.

The know-it-alls in the newsrooms and the corridors of power who simply counterposed Hindu and Muslim when agonizing over the partitioning of a "united India" ignored a host of other identities and relevant factors. In reality, the rising tide of communalism was obliterating existing communities as readily as it fashioned new ones. The polarization of Muslim and Hindu, while providing the impetus for the Pakistan movement, was also the product of that movement.

ALTHOUGH THE CABINET MISSION PLAN took no account of all these subnational identities, its failure to clarify the future status of the princely states themselves was surprising. By leaving open the question of what was to become of the states, the plan not only generated unrealistic expectations (such as that for Jatistan) but also ensured that the princely issue would loom large in the final run-up to independence. Thereafter it would dog Indo-Pakistan relations, and in the case of Kashmir rankle to this day. All of which was also somewhat ironic—in fact, doubly so, for while the existence of the princely states belied the notion of pre-independence India being a single entity, it was the terms of their accession that would ensure that post-independence India was not a single entity either. Indeed, the new India would remain pretty much the same size as the old, since "the combined area and population [of the princely states] nearly matched that of the districts claimed by the [Muslim] League for Pakistan."[19]

In total, the princely states accounted for about 40 percent of India's territory and 25 percent of its population. Their number is usually put at around six hundred, though most were quite insignificant, being little more than fragmented land holdings, perhaps embracing a village or two. In Saurashtra (now in Gujarat but then an intricate tapestry of mini-states), the nicely named principality of Veja-no-ness extended to under an acre "and had a population, in 1921, of 184."[20] Another was apparently little more than a well. Once traded as jagirs—revenue-yielding fiefs—among rulers and their allies, such holdings had been frozen in time at the moment of British conquest. Their incumbents (assuming they had either assisted the British or not opposed them) had been recognized as rightful rulers in return for their own recognition of the British crown as the paramount power. This involved surrendering the right to conduct their external relations and accepting a degree of British supervision with respect to their internal affairs.

But in practice such arrangements involved all manner of different relationships. Smaller states such as Veja-no-ness had no jurisdictional powers and could scarcely claim even a residual sovereignty; the larger ones were effectively self-governing, maintained their own forces, and jealously clung to all the trappings of a sovereignty that was freely acknowledged by the paramount power.

Of these larger princely states, more than a hundred were accounted "salute states," their rulers being entitled to proclaim their sovereignty on ceremonial occasions with a gun salute of up to twenty-one salvos. About a dozen of them were vast, their territories, populations, or both exceeding those of most member states in the newly founded United Nations. The composite state of Jammu and Kashmir, a Himalayan spin-off of the former Sikh empire, claimed a land area bigger than France; Hyderabad, in the south, had a population equivalent to that of Italy. Nor were they all cesspits of reaction and feudal privilege. Travancore, on the Kerala coast, boasted a literacy rate far above that of directly ruled India; others had developed an industrial capacity or were richly endowed with mineral resources, and several had endorsed some form of popular representation and set up consultative or legislative bodies.

Although many of the smallest states were concentrated in western India, the rest were scattered fairly evenly about the subcontinent and often were not contiguous. Maps thus gave the impression of British India's fabric being as perilously holed as a Meo's outworn kurta. Yet this was only half the story. Their variety was as challenging as their distribution. Some were ruled by Muslim nawabs (including Hyderabad's Nizam and Swat's Wali), others by maharajahs, rajahs, or lesser variants of the same who might be either Hindu or Sikh. Whatever the ruler's faith, it was not uncommon for the faith of the majority of his subjects to be different. Famously, the greatest princes commanded immense wealth and built ever more fanciful palaces; less famously, the least were hopelessly in debt and lived in shabby obscurity. And not even the mapmakers of the Survey of India had been able to do justice to the unconsolidated nature of princely holdings. Erratic boundaries and isolated enclaves and counter-enclaves abounded. Communications suffered accordingly. As Darling had discovered, road transport was stifled by innumerable state customs barriers where duties were levied, bribes were extorted, and some goods could not pass at all. It was the same with the railways and the postal service. Fifty years later Indian Railways would still be grappling with the illogic of state-centered networks and the numerous different rail gauges bequeathed by princely whim.

All this rendered the states highly vulnerable. Making a case for hereditary monarchy in the mid-twentieth century was difficult enough, and it was not helped by the reluctance of many rulers to welcome reform. Inevitably it was the princes' outrageous eccentricities and their lavish expenditure on foreign travel, luxury cars, and well-stocked zenanas that made the headlines. All, great or small, recognized that their best chance of retaining their rights lay in presenting a united front, yet their wildly different circumstances seldom admitted of their sustaining it. The smaller states resisted federating with the larger, and the larger resented their claims to special treatment being muddied by the unrealistic expectations of the smaller.

Of course national sentiment, not to mention common sense, demanded that they throw in their lot with either Congress or the League. It would dispel the suspicion that they were British puppets and be welcomed by most of their subjects. It would also deserve a generous response from the political parties, for Congress and the League badly needed the states. Without them, an independent India would be denied the territorial uniformity expected of a modern nation-state and be incapable of planning an integrated economy. The same went for a possible Pakistan; without the states and some semiautonomous tribal areas, its territory would be even more perforated than the moth-eaten periphery for which Jinnah would eventually have to settle.

On the other hand, and much to British relief, individually the states were still less viable. All of them depended to some extent on the directly administered provinces not just for oil, cloth, sugar, and wheat but also for coal, power, and even water. Moreover, not one of them was readily defensible. A few had written treaties that obliged the British to afford them indefinite protection, but in the absence of British troops this would scarcely be practicable, and Westminster therefore had no intention of honoring the treaties. According to Cripps, "the efflux of time and change of circumstances" had rendered the treaties no longer "appropriate to the conditions of the modern world." With the departure of the paramount power, "paramountcy"—one of those barely definable terms, like "suzerainty" and "dependency," with which empires disguise their dominion—would lapse. Although Congress demanded that all such obligations pass to the new paramount power as part of the transfer of responsibility, the Cabinet Mission had demurred. In a rare reference to the matter, it reiterated the British contention that "all rights surrendered . . . to the paramount power will return to the states." At a press conference Cripps went even further, opining that the states would thus "become wholly independent."

This was music to princely ears. Hyderabad and Travancore immediately gave serious thought to joining the world's concourse of sovereign nations by dispatching ambassadors and applying for UN membership. They and many other states expected to retain their links with the British crown by negotiating their individual or collective entry into the British Commonwealth. And all recognized that the retraction of paramountcy did at least improve their bargaining position vis-à-vis the new political leadership represented by Congress and the League.

The League was generally supportive of the states; its desired Pakistan would contain comparatively few, of which only Kashmir was a possible contender for independence. But it was otherwise with Congress. As the voice of all India's peoples, it claimed to represent the subjects of the princely states as well as those of British India. In the Chamber of Princes (the princely forum), Congress was thus confronted by a second grouping of potential secessionists who, though less vociferous than the League, could be just as unaccommodating.

While insisting that paramountcy must lapse, the British government had urged the princes to negotiate their future status with the nationalist leadership. Indeed, the Cabinet Mission Plan had envisaged the princes participating in both the Constituent Assembly and the interim government. But, like the League, the Chamber of Princes had prevaricated. It too insisted on disproportionate representation in the Constituent Assembly while demanding numerous concessions regarding the legitimacy of monarchical government and autonomy in the states' internal affairs. In early 1947, Nehru, whose centrist, socialist, and democratic sentiments were no secret, steeled himself to offer sufficient safeguards to split the princely chamber into pro- and anti-accessionists. But there still remained the problem of how to win over the latter, and anyway the Constituent Assembly had been prorogued in the face of Jinnah's refusal to participate. Meanwhile, the British government's February announcement of a deadline for independence had left the future status of the princes unchanged.

What did change was the viceroy. In March 1947, just as Malcolm Darling was completing his long ride, Lord Louis Mountbatten arrived as Wavell's replacement. Unlike Wavell, the new viceroy enjoyed Whitehall's utmost confidence plus the luxury of having drafted his own brief. With numerous other advantages—a royal connection, an open mind, an attractive wife, and an infectious sense of urgency—Mountbatten would plunge straight into the constitutional impasse between Congress and the League. The princes would therefore have to wait.

In May 1947, a year after it had been presented, the Cabinet Mission Plan was finally ditched along with the all-party Constituent Assembly. The demands of Congress and the League remained irreconcilable, but an uneasy lull in the massacres in the Punjab offered some hope. June brought the critical turnaround when Mountbatten endorsed Partition and quickly followed this by announcing an earlier deadline for its enaction. Only in July, as the days ticked away and Congress agonized over the loss of Pakistan, did it dawn on Mountbatten that it was the princely states that "held the key to a negotiated settlement."

V. P. Menon, Mountbatten's "political reforms commissioner" and the unofficial intermediary between Congress and the viceroy, has been credited with coming up with the terms of the deal, which had something for everyone. Mountbatten would dragoon the states into signing Instruments of Accession to the new India (and in a few cases to Pakistan). Congress, in return, would accept Partition and the loss of Pakistan; the princes would be mollified by having to hand over their powers only with respect to defense, foreign affairs, and communications—in effect, no more than they had surrendered under the system of paramountcy. Moreover, by way of further reassuring them with a residual British connection, India and Pakistan would join the British Commonwealth, giving Mountbatten something to crow about and saving British blushes with a face-saving formula that was of some strategic value in an increasingly bipolar world.

Given the urgency of the situation, it was a persuasive package. But as with Partition itself, the self-imposed haste so concentrated ministerial minds that the wider issues of implementation received little attention. The princes would not all sign on the dotted line, Congress would honor the terms of their Instruments of Accession only for a matter of weeks, the Muslim League would do its utmost to render India as moth-eaten as Pakistan by encouraging princely defections, and Mountbatten would wash his hands of the whole business as quickly as he could. In short, the power brokers seemed oblivious to the anxious faces under the countless village pipal trees in the back of beyond. Chauffeur-driven negotiators sped down the Delhi boulevards without sparing a thought for the dark mustachioed drivers in their undarned cotton rags atop the creaking bullock carts.

2

COUNTING
THE COST

IT HAS OFTEN BEEN ASKED WHY NO ONE SEEMS TO HAVE FORESEEN the hell that Partition was about to unleash. The Calcutta killings of 1946 and those elsewhere in Bengal and Bihar gave ample warning, as did the atrocities perpetrated in western Punjab in early 1947. A few officials, both Indian and British, did anticipate trouble and called for reinforcements. But in Delhi the excitement over independence claimed the moment to the exclusion of all else. Victory in the freedom struggle was not to be gainsaid. It was assumed that the entire nation shared in the rejoicings and that, in the prevailing spirit of goodwill, Partition could be effected without bloodshed. The haste with which it had been adopted might actually help. Instead of laborious consultations and the tensions that must result from them, most of the people affected were to be presented with a fait accompli. Territory would be allocated to India or Pakistan on the basis of the majority community; minorities, whether Hindu, Muslim, or Sikh, were to be reassured with soothing words and the glorious prospect of freedom.

Aside from an arrogance born of bureaucratic habit and indifference to the plight of the lower castes, this attitude overlooked the considerable novelty of communities being equated with territories and nations with sovereign states. It also ignored the fact that a British

India riddled with princely states had never been the uniform entity that partitioning implied. And it took no account of South Asia's prior acquaintance with political division and the concept of sovereignty as something layered rather than absolute. Nehru insisted that a sense of all-Indian nationhood could be traced back into the mists of antiquity; but for most of its interminable past the Indian subcontinent had not been governed as one. Fragmentation was in fact the norm and a strong, centralized polity as championed by Congress very much the exception. Despite claims to the contrary, history was on the side of Partition.

In yet another paradox, it has been argued that it was not Jinnah but Nehru himself who was ultimately responsible for Partition and so, indirectly, for the imminent holocaust. The demand for Pakistan, say the protagonists of this view, need not have meant separation.[1] Jinnah wanted guarantees for his Muslim nation in the form of a Pakistan composed of all the existing Muslim-majority provinces of British India—so including the whole of Bengal (with Calcutta) and the whole of the Punjab (possibly with Delhi). The result in terms of population would have been something much nearer parity between this so-called greater Pakistan and a rump India composed solely of the non-Muslim majority provinces. Such an arrangement should have sufficed to preclude mass migration and the killings that would accompany it because Muslim opinion within the unpartitioned subcontinent would be well represented in the Constituent Assembly and could be decisive in the formation of a central government. Nothing if not consistent, Jinnah in 1946 had demanded a similar parity with respect to the interim government; indeed, the Cabinet Mission's grouping of provinces could be read as foreshadowing this greater Pakistan.

Jinnah's somewhat excessive demands were informed by past experience. In the 1930s, Congress ministries in provinces with a vociferous Muslim minority, notably UP, had been accused of ignoring the sensibilities of Muslim constituents and shunning the Muslim League's claims to office. Arguably, this could now be prevented; the League had emerged from recent elections much stronger, and the possibility of its retaliating in its own Muslim-majority provinces could be expected to act as a deterrent to Congress exclusivity.

Moreover, a Pakistan within India might be more manageable than one outside it. The anomalies and inconveniences of Pakistan's two halves being themselves partitioned by more than six hundred miles of potentially hostile territory would be largely negated. A Pakistan within India might be less vulnerable to internal ethnic and linguistic contradictions than it would be if left to its own devices. Also, the League would be well placed to forge alliances with other non-Congress parties, including those representing the lower-caste and no-caste communities or less numerous minorities such as the mixed-race Anglo-Indians. Such an alliance might even contest power with Congress in the central government. Thus Jinnah, provided that his greater Pakistan was forthcoming, had much to gain by not insisting on Partition. Some loose form of federation, or just a treaty that preserved a façade of unity, might suffice. It would be a small price to pay in terms of diminished sovereignty, and anyway the arrangement was to be subject to revision after ten years.

But if this was indeed what Jinnah wanted, he never actually said so. Adamant about what he would reject, he could be remarkably reticent about what he would accept. Nor was it what he was offered, for to Nehru an India hobbled by a subordinate Pakistan had begun to look like a worse option than an India relieved of a sovereign Pakistan. Only a strong central government could tackle India's massive social problems, oversee the incorporation of the princely states, root out feudal and colonial attitudes, plan the framework of a modern economy, and set a proud example for the world. A weak federal center, as posited by Jinnah, would paralyze the state-building process and play into the hands of other possible separatists, for instance in the northeast and the south of the country. New Delhi therefore would do better if it wrote off Pakistan completely and bade good riddance to the unbending adversary who claimed to be its sole spokesman.

This did not, though, mean giving Jinnah the greater Pakistan he wanted. The quid pro quo of conceding sovereignty was that the new Pakistan must be pared down to its Islamic heartland. With non-Muslims (Sikhs and Hindus) outnumbering Muslims in both the eastern half of the Punjab and the western half of Bengal, there was some logic to these two great provinces being themselves partitioned.

In effect, instead of a greater Pakistan, albeit within India, Jinnah was obliged to settle for a lesser Pakistan, albeit outside India. "Maimed, mutilated, and moth-eaten" was his own description of the new construct; he would never accept it, he had declared. But in 1947, with his supposed bluff over separation called, that was precisely what he did have to accept. And hence as the countdown to independence proceeded, it was Nehru who readily endorsed Mountbatten's Partition plan and Jinnah who, when asked to do so, merely hung his head. The gesture seemed to signify despair as much as assent.

AUGUST, THOUGH IN THE MIDDLE OF THE MONSOON, is not an unpleasant month in Delhi. Cloudbursts douse the heat and clearing skies excite the vegetation. Trees erupt into flower, puddles shrink into sward. Were the subcontinent's New Year timed for the growth cycle instead of the daylight cycle, it would surely fall in August. In 1947, as midmonth approached, there was much optimism along with some understandable self-congratulation. Mountbatten had chosen the date for the handover of power: August 15. He thought it propitious, being the second anniversary of Japan's surrender at the end of World War II, an event in which his own part as commander of Allied forces in Southeast Asia would of course be noted. India's astrologers also deemed it propitious, and Pakistan's leadership contented itself with insisting on just a twenty-four-hour precedence. By opting for August 14, Pakistan would be winning independence ahead of India and so from the hands of the British government in London rather than from the Congress government in Delhi.

Incredibly, as it now seemed, both nations had wrested their freedom through largely nonviolent pressure, and, although the final round of negotiations had been conducted at breakneck speed, relations with London had never been better. In fact, the restraint shown by both sides had set a valuable precedent for future decolonizations elsewhere. The majority of erstwhile India remained intact. And even Pakistan, the two-part exception, looked to have secured the resources—military, diplomatic, and economic—to defy the odds stacked against it. Bisection, though regrettable, had to be better than dissection, and, if that was the price of liberation, then so be it. The delights of independence would quickly allay the pangs of Partition.

Yet when addressing New Delhi's Constituent Assembly on the eve of independence, Nehru invited the people to reflect as much as to celebrate. The tone of his famous oration was more messianic than triumphant, its twin themes of redemption and destiny sounding positively Churchillian.

> Long years ago we made a tryst with destiny, and now the time comes when we shall redeem our pledge, not wholly or in full measure, but very substantially. . . . [The] future is not one of ease or resting but of incessant striving so that we may fulfil the pledges. . . . The day has come—the day appointed by destiny—and India stands forth again. . . . We have much to do before we redeem the pledges . . . no resting for any one of us until we redeem our pledge in full.[2]

The rhetoric lost nothing by repetition; a moment so solemn positively invited a rambling retrospective. The pledge he spoke of was to "the service of India and her people and to the still larger cause of humanity," while the quaint idea of a tryst, a prearranged meeting at an appointed hour, was intended to evoke a sense of common progression. History had ordained it, and struggle had confirmed it. For Nehru, a formidable intellect and an ardent socialist whose moods could be attributed to his excessive workload, August 15, 1947, marked the nation's longed-for epiphany. "At the stroke of the midnight hour, when the world sleeps, India will awake to life and freedom," he intoned. Out with the old, in with the new.

Jinnah, a minaret of a man compared to Nehru, erect and impeccable with corbel-like cheekbones and a cupola of coiffed silver hair, was both more cautious and more cautionary. Addressing Pakistan's Constituent Assembly in Karachi on August 11, he seemed scarcely able to believe that his call for a sovereign Muslim nation was being realized. Only what he called "an unprecedented cyclonic revolution" could have brought about the birth of Pakistan; it was the consummation of a scheme so "titanic," so "unknown," that it had "no parallel in the history of the world." Yet for Pakistan to function, grievances such as those voiced by Malcolm Darling's anxious informants must be quickly addressed. Bribery and corruption would be put down "with an iron hand," he warned, jobbery and nepotism would never be tolerated, and black-marketing in foodstuffs was the greatest crime of all.

No less important was the suppression of what Jinnah now called "the angularities of the majority and minority communities." In an outspoken assertion of cross-communal equality—one that would come to haunt the new nation—the man already hailed as Quaid-i-Azam, supreme leader, announced to the Pakistan Assembly:

> You are free; you are free to go to your temples, you are free to go to your mosques or to any other place of worship in this State of Pakistan. You may belong to any religion or caste or creed; that has nothing to do with the business of the State. . . . We are starting in the days where there is no discrimination, no distinction between one community and another, no discrimination between one caste or creed and another. . . . [If] we keep that in front of us as our ideal . . . you will find that in the course of time Hindus . . . cease to be Hindus, and Muslims . . . cease to be Muslims, not in the religious sense, because that is the personal faith of each individual, but in the political sense as citizens of the State.[3]

Nehru, the champion of secularism, could not have put it better. For Jinnah as well, freedom meant casting off not just the bonds of foreign rule but those of communal rivalry. The Muslim nation must be all-inclusive. To a state predicated and won on the uncompromising basis of a shared religion he now offered as its guiding principles "justice and complete impartiality." The success of the Pakistan movement was dependent on "an evolution of the greatest possible character," plus those vaguely "cyclonic" forces. In keeping with this unspecified agency, Pakistan might "become one of the greatest nations of the world" provided it demonstrated neither "prejudice or ill will," "partiality or favouritism." Islam received not a single mention in the speech. Its unacknowledged presence was like that of a no longer welcome guest. Evidently the advent of nationhood heralded a new departure in national definition.

Mountbatten too milked the moment for all it was worth. Where so many of his countrymen had floundered over the last three decades, he had triumphed in a matter of weeks. The nettle of Congress-League distrust had been grasped, the Gordian knot of irreconcilable claims and counterclaims summarily severed. Not a single British life had been lost in the act of disengagement, and the bisection of the sub-continent, though about to be anything but peaceful, was deemed to be unmarred by actual war. In British eyes, Mountbatten made the loss of empire almost palatable. The manner of its surrender was portrayed as a credit to all concerned, and the abiding friendship of the successor states was construed as a benediction on the whole two-hundred-year Raj. Each of the successor states had opted to join the British Commonwealth, and each was pledged to liberal values and democratic government; neither felt inclined to humiliate the ex-imperialists, and both retained the services of some senior British personnel. It was a more amicable parting of the ways than had seemed possible during the previous decades of acrimonious struggle.

Like the monsoonal cloudbursts, the plaudits rained down on the beaming Mountbatten from all sides. New Delhi invited him to stay on as governor-general. Prime Minister Clement Attlee noted that "broadly speaking the thing went off well" and "we left behind so much good will." Churchill, defender of the empire and inveterate opponent of Indian independence, was greatly reassured by India's and Pakistan's willingness to join the Commonwealth. And to the already impressive royal connections of his last-ever viceroy, King George VI added an earldom. While modestly deflecting the praise, Mountbatten yet lapped it up. His showmanship had paid off; a career that might so easily have been tarnished by failure or tarred by the shame of retreat had in fact been burnished. Yet, looking back many years later, he would be less sanguine about his achievement and a lot less delicate. "I fucked it up," he told John Osman, a BBC journalist, in 1965.[4]

Wrong-footing critics with outrageous volte-faces was all part of the famous Mountbatten charm, yet this disclaimer was not insincere. At the time his main regret had been his failure to secure an invitation to become governor-general of Pakistan as well as India; much to his fury, Jinnah insisted that he himself would be governor-general of Pakistan. Jinnah was deeply suspicious of the cozy relationship between Nehru and the Mountbattens—especially that between Nehru and Lady Edwina Mountbatten—and he didn't trust the ex-viceroy to act as an impartial arbitrator in the division of the spoils between the two dominions, principal among these being the army. Nor, unlike Nehru, could Jinnah afford to relinquish even the trappings of his authority to a post-imperial pawnbroker. From the Chittagong Hills to the North-West Frontier, fissiparous tendencies already menaced the bipolar Pakistan. The new India could be expected to exploit them.

> To share a common Governor-General with Hindustan [i.e., the new India] would have given Congress an excuse to use this joint office to make terms separately with the Muslim areas [i.e., Pakistan] in the event that the Pakistan constituent assembly fell to pieces. It was to avoid this disaster that Jinnah had to exercise the powers of a Governor-General himself and in the process consolidate the [Muslim] League's authority over the Muslim [majority] areas.[5]

Mountbatten blamed himself for not having secured a prior understanding. As he told his daughter at the time, "Your poor old Daddy has finally and irretrievably 'boobed' . . . made a mess of things through over-confidence and over-tiredness."[6] He ought to have foreseen Jinnah's move, and he thought he would have but for the pressure of his own deadline. But much later he seems to have had second thoughts not about the governor-generalship but about the deadline itself. In retrospect it was this more than anything else that had "fucked it up."

Bringing forward Attlee's cutoff date of June 1948 to his own of August 1947 has often been considered Mountbatten's masterstroke. Yet at the time it appalled his staff and confounded those who had habitually complained of Britain's procrastination. Nehru had thought the new timetable "too much of a rush," the princes needed all the time that they could possibly get (and more), and the Muslim League doubted whether such a schedule, however agreeable to the prospects of Pakistan, was actually feasible.[7] Announcing his plan on June 3, 1947, Mountbatten allowed just over ten weeks for its implementation. There was to be no time for second thoughts and precious little for negotiation. That was the point. As he advised London, speed—one might almost say panic—was of the essence.

For Mountbatten, this urgency was tactical; it would concentrate minds, demonstrate good faith, and narrow the options. It was not a sine qua non of the terms of transfer. It was not even an immediate imperative. The threat of civil war had in fact receded. Calcutta still simmered, but since April the communal outbreaks in the Punjab had subsided and, but for the plight of the Meos in and around the princely states south of Delhi, there had been nothing on a comparable scale elsewhere. Those, therefore, who professed to hold the unity of India so dear, like Nehru, might reasonably have challenged a deadline that, while making Partition virtually inevitable, allowed almost no time to prepare for it. That they did not object was significant. Gandhi had famously declared, "You shall have to divide my body before you divide India." But Gandhi, now seventy-seven and sidelined by Congress, was devoting his remaining energies to dousing the embers of communal violence wherever they smoldered. Jinnah continued to be adamant about a Pakistan of some sort, and Nehru did nothing. Persuaded by the realization that India would be stronger without Pakistan, and mindful of that viceregal promise to stampede the princely states into accession, he let it stand. Thus the responsibility for Partition may be said to have itself been partitioned—not perhaps "wholly or in full measure, but very substantially."

DIVIDING THE ASSETS OF AN EMPIRE between two deeply suspicious heritors called for wisdom and an ongoing spirit of compromise. Neither was much in evidence. Nehru had brains and breadth of vision, Jinnah tenacity and stature, and Mountbatten bravado plus breeding. But none had the time, the inclination, or the skills needed to apportion sundry budgets, deconstruct entire ministries, allocate all manner of weaponry and aircraft, crunch numbers on everything from pipe bands to pencil sharpeners, manage the logistics of cross-border transfer, and delineate the actual frontier. All this was dependent on the attributes of their lieutenants—the hard-nosed pragmatism of the burly Sardar Patel plus the mandarin mind of V. P. Menon (for India) and the resourcefulness of the dependable Liaquat Ali Khan (for Pakistan).

In this exercise India had a head start, not least because it was still called India, becoming the Union of India at independence in 1947 (and in 1950, after the adoption of the Constituent Assembly's new constitution, the Republic of India). The term "Hindustan" (meaning "Hindu-land"), though hitherto applied to India minus the Muslim-majority provinces and preferred by many Pakistanis to this day, was allowed to lapse. "It is nevertheless significant that until the bitter end the [Muslim] League continued to protest against Hindustan adopting the title 'Union of India,'" reports Ayesha Jalal.[8] Jinnah objected to both the "Union" and the "India" and is said to have seen the rebuff of his protest as further evidence of collusion between Mountbatten and the Congress leadership.

Etymologically "India" might actually have suited Pakistan better; it derives from "Indus" and originally indicated just those lands beside the Indus River that today constitute Pakistan. But "Pakistan" had been preferred by the Muslim League ever since the 1930s, when the term had been coined in Cambridge as an acronym for the Muslim-majority regions of the northwest: *P* for the Punjab, *A* for Afghania (a contentious name for the North-West Frontier), *K* for Kashmir, *S* for Sind, and an unconvincing -*TAN* for Balochistan. (There was no *B* for Bengal, a telling omission at the time and one fraught with the potential for further partition, notably in 1971.) By a happy coincidence, another reading of the name "Pakistan" had it meaning "land of the pure." Either reading would do. Jinnah relished it and had no designs on the word "India" himself. But he had sound reasons for objecting to New Delhi's co-opting it. On the strength of it, the new India would claim the old India's seat at the United Nations. It also arrogated to the new India what Jinnah regarded as a spurious continuity and a provocative precedence.

Others objected on the grounds that the word "India" did not convey *enough* continuity and precedence—indeed, that it was tainted because it was of foreign origin. Ceylon, a British colony but never a part of British India, would gain its independence in 1948 and redesignate itself Sri Lanka in 1972, thus reviving an ancient indigenous name, shedding a Greco-Roman and colonial one, and appeasing nationalist sentiment. India nearly did the same. The term "Bharata-varsha," or simply "Bharat," figured in the Sanskrit epics and was strongly urged by those who thought a primordial name hallowed by Hindu tradition more appropriate. Although Nehru, the arch-secularist, would have none of it, "Bharat" still features in the writings of Sanskrit-minded apologists for Hindu nationalism. It appears on numerous maps, occasionally resurfaces in national debate, and could yet be officially preferred.

If antiquity was ambivalent about India's identity, recent history offered ample compensation. New Delhi's Congress government had the advantage of stepping into the capacious shoes of the British Raj. The ruddy imperial edifices that reared above the capital's leafy canopy needed only to be renamed. The rotunda that had been the Legislative Assembly building became the Parliament building; the monumental Government House, the residence of the viceroys, became Rashtra-pati Bhawan, the residence of the presidents. Kingsway was renamed Rajpath (Government's Way) and Queensway Janpath (People's Way). Within the colonnades of the central government's sandstone secretariat buildings, the peons and the pigeons were joined by flocks of *khadi*-clad freedom fighters, now with ministerial portfolios. What with inheriting the lion's share of the erstwhile Indian Civil Service (soon renamed the Indian Administrative Service) along with the archives, the high court, various other national institutions and surveys, and an abundance of both state offices and office stationery—including the pins used as paper clips—India's new government took possession of a capital already equipped with all the paraphernalia of power.

Pakistan came off less well. Entire ministries had to be improvised in tin sheds, and quite senior clerks took up residence in a railway station. Packing cases were converted into desks, meals were often served in alfresco canteens, and long thorns were gathered from roadside shrubbery because the supply of paper pins had failed to arrive.

Lahore, the Mughal city that had been the capital of the undivided Punjab province, would have been the obvious choice as the home of the new government but was ruled out on the grounds that it was too close for strategic comfort to the new border with India. A safer haven might have been afforded by Dhaka (then spelled Dacca) in East Bengal. As the onetime capital of Bengal's nawabs, it had some fine buildings and lay at the heart of what was now Pakistan's most populous province. Yet such was the bias—social, linguistic, cultural, military, and strategic—in favor of Pakistan's western provinces that Dhaka's claims were barely entertained. Instead Karachi, a fetid port city near the mouth of the Indus that doubled as the administrative headquarters of the lately formed province of Sind, had been chosen.

Karachi was declared merely the interim capital. Like much else in Pakistan, it was a makeshift arrangement. For while the new India inherited a functioning state plus its majestic capital, the new Pakistan was having to improvise everything from scratch—and do so under the direst national emergency imaginable. Already thousands, rising to millions, were on the move. Already the chain reaction of atrocities had resumed. Ahead loomed a crescendo of killing unlike anything ever witnessed elsewhere in so-called peacetime. Pakistan, which was itself, in Jinnah's words, the product of an "unprecedented cyclonic revolution," was about to occasion a second "titanic" convulsion with "no parallel in the history of the world."

WAR, EVEN CIVIL WAR, might have been more manageable than the internecine strife that engulfed large parts of both India and Pakistan in the latter half of 1947. It had begun in early August in the Amritsar district of east Punjab when gangs of armed Sikhs started exacting revenge for the atrocities of the previous March in west Punjab. Muslims were massacred and their villages set on fire. The pogrom then spread to Lahore as Muslims retaliated against both Hindus and Sikhs. *Gurudwaras* (Sikh temples) were trashed, Hindu temples desecrated, infidels butchered. And the mayhem continued fiercer than ever, even as far away as in Delhi and Karachi, the high-flown rhetoric poured forth and the two nations deliriously hailed their independence. "Rejoicings; Happy Augury for the Future" read a headline in the *Times of India* on August 18. "The jeremiahs who foresaw trouble" had been utterly confounded, the newspaper reported. In doing so, the *Times* not only belied the idea that "trouble" of some sort was wholly unexpected but lulled its readership into a dangerously blinkered complacency about the conflagration in the neighboring Punjab.

There, dawn on August 15—Independence Day in Delhi but the day after in Pakistan—found a memorably named British official, one Penderel Moon, being driven into Lahore from his post as minister and adviser to the nawab of Bahawalpur. A Muslim princely state contiguous to Muslim west Punjab, Bahawalpur was about to join Pakistan. Confident that the transition would be peaceful, the nawab was sojourning comfortably in Surrey and Moon was heading for the hills and a fortnight's holiday. Bahawalpur itself was quiet. The Punjab, give or take a few roadblocks, seemed much as usual. Not until Moon reached Lahore itself did he notice anything untoward.

> As we approached the built-up area, we overtook a military lorry in the back of which there was a soldier with a rifle and two or three bloodstained corpses bouncing about on the floor. A little farther on five or six men were lined up along the side of the road with their hands up and a soldier covering them with his rifle. Two hundred yards beyond there was a corpse lying on a charpoy . . . and to the left, from the city proper, numerous dense columns of smoke were rising into the air.[9]

Lahore, in short, was not celebrating. It was burning. Over lunch at Faletti's Hotel, Moon learned that the city's largely Muslim police, in a pattern that would be emulated by both sides, were siding with the killers and even affording them covering fire. Under the circumstances he was strongly discouraged from proceeding to Simla by car. Instead he sallied forth for the railway station and a nonexistent train.

At exactly the same time, Nehru and the Mountbattens were forcing their way through the flag-waving crowds along Delhi's Rajpath. They had just attended the Independence Day ceremonies at India Gate. King George VI had assured India that freedom-loving people everywhere would want to share in their celebrations, but such was the press of freedom-savoring Indians that the formalities had had to be curtailed. Mountbatten could barely salute the Indian tricolor from the safety of his carriage. His daughter had managed to reach the podium only after removing her high heels and—helped by, among others, Nehru—clambering over the densely packed masses. "An enormous picnic of almost a million people, all of them having more fun than they'd ever had in their lives" was how Mountbatten described the gathering.[10] It was fun all around. The musicians couldn't reach their bandstand, and the gun salutes were drowned out by the cheering. Nehru found himself thrust into the viceregal carriage by well-wishers, there to be joined by some sari-clad matrons scooped up by Lady Edwina Mountbatten lest they be trampled underfoot. "The rest of the day was taken up with parties, speeches and almost impossible progressions through the undiminishing throngs in the streets."[11]

Lahore, on the other hand, was silent. Even the railway station, reportedly "a veritable death trap" at the time—indeed, "a scene of wholesale carnage . . . under a continuous rain of bullets"—was in fact almost deserted.[12] Penderel Moon found only twenty Sikh policemen, all cowering behind a barbed-wire barricade for their own protection, plus a displaced and distraught stationmaster. The stationmaster had just arrived, having escaped from his charge at the nearby Mughalpura depot by requisitioning a locomotive. Two days previously, forty-three non-Muslims, many of them Sikhs, had been massacred there; now their brethren were retaliating. "We were attacked by 8,000 Sikhs," he reported. "They have killed several hundred. I have been telephoning for help for thirteen hours."[13]

Moon, a goggle-eyed administrator with progressive views, supposed this estimate of the carnage an exaggeration, but he admitted that cross-border trains were already being targeted. A week earlier, one carrying Muslim clerks to staff the new Pakistani government in Karachi had been scheduled to pass through Bahawalpur en route from Delhi. It never arrived; a bomb had derailed it near Ferozepur, leaving three dead and numerous wounded. "This was one of the first train outrages and the first incident to make any noticeable impression on the Muslims of Bahawalpur," noted Moon. In the same week several hundred terrified refugees had detrained in the state unannounced. They claimed to have been driven out of their homes in the Indian princely states of Alwar and Bharatpur (near Delhi). Lucky to be escaping imminent genocide, they were in fact the first of a mass migration of Meos. But they were no more welcome as refugees in Bahawalpur than as residents in Bharatpur. The authorities "told them that if they were seeking the promised land of Pakistan they had come to the wrong place and better go on to Punjab or Sind. Gradually they drifted away."[14] Educated Muslims were badly needed in Pakistan; threadbare peasants with lax ideas about Islam it could do without.

Giving up on the trains, Moon traveled on to Simla in a military convoy that was escorting members of the British administration in the Punjab on the first leg of their long journey home. They were leaving the province, he noted, in much the same state as they had found it a hundred years earlier: blood-soaked and in chaos. Yet this was only the beginning. Within hours the situation would worsen dramatically. Partition, in principle so reasonable, was in practice anything but.

At the time, much of the precise border between the two new nations was still uncertain. While the flags of the successor states were being saluted all over the subcontinent, in the vicinity of the expected border it was unclear which flag should be flying. The broad terms of one partition, that of India and Pakistan, had been agreed on, but the precise alignment of the subsidiary partitions in Bengal and the Punjab had been entrusted to a third party and then kept under wraps. Several million people thus greeted independence, if they greeted it at all, not knowing for sure to which country they belonged. Only when the boundary was awarded and published would they discover their fate, make plans accordingly, and so open the floodgates to the twentieth century's greatest transfer of population.

In the hectic last days of British rule, boundary commissions for both Bengal and the Punjab had been set up. Maps had been hastily consulted, opinions sought, and red lines drawn. Sir Cyril Radcliffe, a British judge who had never before visited the subcontinent, had been entrusted with this heavy responsibility and assured of complete independence. He had also been told to finish his work ahead of the transfer of power. This he did, but without the luxury of being able to inspect the actual terrain, acquaint himself with its peculiarities (such as those errant rivers in Bengal), or derive much support from his commissioners, two Muslim League appointees and two Congress appointees, who invariably upheld the interests of their political patrons and divided accordingly. It was Radcliffe's vote that was decisive.

"Nobody in India will love me for my award," he wrote. They would not. The sealed documents were delivered to Mountbatten two days before independence but were only made public two days after. By then Radcliffe had emplaned for London, never to set foot in South Asia again. All parties had agreed to respect his findings, and it was accepted that implementation would be the responsibility of the successor governments. Mountbatten, heading for the hills like Moon, considered his work done. British hands, already washed and ready for congratulatory shaking, were not to be soiled by any last-minute bloodletting.

The only exception was a British-commanded Boundary Force, supposedly fifty thousand strong, that was to keep the peace in the Punjab and oversee its partition. Though active enough, it failed to do either. No more than about twenty-five thousand troops materialized, meaning that there were fewer than two men for each square mile.[15] And instead of operating under a unified command, the force was itself quickly partitioned. Suspicious of its impartiality, on August 29, at the height of the massacres, the successor governments opted to exercise distinct commands, disband the force, and deploy the troops intended for peacekeeping to protect and succor their co-religionists.

The mutual suspicion was made worse by the terms of Radcliffe's actual award. Dividing erstwhile India into its Muslim- and non-Muslim-majority provinces had been comparatively straightforward, but the lesser territorial units to be parceled out when dividing up the Punjab and Bengal posed a trickier challenge. These lesser elements had been specified merely as "areas"; they might be districts, subdistricts, or even smaller units. And although the twin principles of partitioning—division on the basis of the religious majority plus contiguity to areas of a like complexion—were generally paramount, other factors such as local traditions, irrigation networks, and strategic necessity might be taken into account. There was thus scope for exceptions and still greater scope for suspicions about exceptions. Well-founded rumors would circulate that Radcliffe had been "influenced." India's expectations with regard to the Punjab border, especially where it afforded an access route to Kashmir, seem to have found favor with him. So did Indian demands with regard to a northern corridor, or "chicken neck," linking West Bengal and Assam; concessions to Pakistan in the Chittagong and Khulna areas of East Bengal were supposedly made in return.

In Karachi and New Delhi these matters were warmly debated. But to the toiling masses for whom the border's various corridors, salients, irrigation headworks, and enclaves were home—and had been since time immemorial—the announcement of the new border was positively incendiary. Being "awarded" to what was considered a hostile state, or excluded from what was considered a supportive one, amounted to an existential threat. As Indian Muslims seeking Pakistan, and Pakistani Sikhs and Hindus fleeing from it, began pouring across the border, Punjabis on either side of the delimited but still undemarcated line were swept along by the tide.

Whole villages, clans, subcastes, and kinship groups moved house—sometimes literally, detaching the roof joists of their homes to cart them away in the hope of reusing them. In early September, Penderel Moon, back in Bahawalpur after curtailing his holiday, recorded the arrival there of a disheveled and unwashed gentleman called Bagh Ali. "He arrived on foot . . . along with 5000 members of the Sakhera tribe, many of whom were his tenants"; after a week on the road, "one could hardly imagine that he was a wealthy Muslim landowner and a MLA [member of the Punjab Legislative Assembly]," recalled Moon. Bagh Ali and his people hailed from Ferozepur, a place that had been expected to go to Pakistan but which in fact was awarded to India. But what most distressed Moon was the news that this throng, along with their bullocks, carts, and farm implements, had been officially ordered to migrate. It was not the feared Sikh paramilitaries who had forced them out but a government directive from Ferozepur's subdivisional officer. Unbeknown to Moon, Delhi and Karachi had just agreed on an exchange of population between the two halves of the partitioned Punjab. The arrangement was intended to reduce the violence, which both governments roundly condemned. But forcible migration was a different matter. In the Punjab it was state-sponsored.

Over the long border between western India and the western wing of Pakistan some ten to twenty million people are thought to have crossed, some going east, others west, during the months of August, September, and October. Additionally, anywhere between two hundred thousand and one million people were massacred—in their homes, in their fields, on the road, in the trains—or left to die by the wayside. In a sandy tract near Fazilpur in Bahawalpur, Penderel Moon spied what he thought were some piles of manure. Closer inspection revealed them as piles of bodies.

> In two and threes and sixes and tens, more and more came into view as we rounded the curve of the village . . . till they lay "Thick as autumnal leaves that strew the vale of Vallambrosa." Men, women and children, there they all were jumbled up together, their arms and legs akimbo in all sorts of attitudes and postures, some of them so life-like that one could hardly believe that they were really dead.[16]

It reminded Moon of pictures he remembered from his childhood of the Napoleonic battlefields. Three hundred and fifty Hindus had been mowed down by Pathan rifle fire in this one incident.

Hundreds of thousands more were plundered of their chattels, a term that was taken to include their womenfolk and children. Girls and young mothers were perceived as embodiments of all that the other community held most sacred and were picked off accordingly. Abducted, exposed, traded, raped, mutilated, or forcibly appropriated, most would never know justice and many would prefer suicide. Those who would later be "recovered" and repatriated fared little better. Dishonored and perhaps traumatized, they might find themselves unwanted or even locked away by their former loved ones.

The horror lay as much in the obscenity of the atrocities as the scale, and to these atrocities, as to all the other massacres and burnings, there was often a pattern. Though characterized as "lunacy," the mayhem was madness with a method. On both sides the perpetrators were invariably male, well armed, and often ex-soldiers or paramilitaries. Incitement came in the form of pamphlets, partisan press reports, and pronouncements from political and religious leaders; premeditation was evident in both the planning and the execution of the attacks; and guns as much as knives were the weapons of choice. As historian Yasmin Khan notes, "This was not haphazard, frantic killing but, at its worst, routine, timetabled and systematic ethnic cleansing. Large groups of men, with their own codes of honour and often with a sense of warlike righteousness, set out day after day in August and September to eliminate the other."[17]

Of the few things that disqualified the conflict as "war," the near absence of battles was the most obvious. The aggressors, instead of engaging one another—something that respect for the border largely precluded—directed their attacks exclusively at the innocent and the defenseless. Conversion was occasionally an option for the victims, mere surrender rarely so. For the assailants, the objectives were simply expropriation and maximum slaughter.

Most refugees traveled on foot, with or without livestock and sometimes accompanied by wagons bearing their possessions. The caravans stretched as far as the eye could see, converging at river crossings. An airborne Nehru following the line of a cross-border road in east Punjab would recall overflying the same massed column for ten miles. He put its human component at more than a hundred thousand souls. Another caravan, tracked in west Punjab, was thought to number four hundred thousand. In September Penderel Moon recorded an influx into Bahawalpur of forty to fifty thousand Muslims from Rohtak and Hissar (west of Delhi); they were so severely undernourished that "some two thousand of them died within a few days of their arrival."[18] As late as November an official from the British High Commission in Delhi, while driving through Mewat, encountered a ten-mile column of Meos still on the move.[19]

Exposure, debilitation, dehydration, starvation, disease, and drowning (the monsoon had returned with a fury in September) may have caused as many fatalities as the knife and the bullet. Yet the subsequent figures would seldom distinguish deaths from natural causes, nor would they attempt to define what causes might be considered natural. All that can be said with confidence is that the scale of the tragedy was such as to frustrate accurate assessment at the time—and ever since.

"Estimates of casualties are largely a matter of guesswork," noted Moon, who nevertheless gave his own calculation of the number killed: it was "unlikely to have been more than two hundred thousand" and was probably rather less. This was based on "fairly precise figures for about half the districts of West Punjab and . . . intelligent guesses regarding the remainder"; in this total, on the basis of reports from across the border, he had included twice as many fatalities for India's east Punjab plus much fewer for the neighboring states of Rajasthan, Sind, and Balochistan.[20] Moon was writing only of the border between India and West Pakistan and did not include deaths in Bengal or elsewhere in India, nor apparently those in the princely state of Jammu and Kashmir. But his guesswork deserves some respect. As a onetime member of the British Indian Civil Service, a current member of the Pakistan Administrative Service (Bahawalpur formally joined Pakistan in early October), and a soon-to-be member of the Indian Administrative Service, he straddled the divide and had no particular axe to grind.

Nor, having witnessed some of the attacks and collected descriptions of many more—indeed, having accepted responsibility for not having prevented some of them—could Moon be accused of generalizing about them. It has been suggested that any consensus around higher estimates of half a million to a million or even two million fatalities may be a means of "distancing ourselves from the specificity and details of those killings even as we seek to underline their enormity and consequence."[21] This recourse to rounded-up figures is thought to be especially common practice with respect to the atrocities suffered by those classed as "others" rather than "ours"; "their" losses could be approximately quantified, "ours" tended to be recorded in gruesome and specific detail.

Into this error falls the account produced by Gopal Das Khosla in 1989. An avuncular figure, Cambridge-educated, Justice Khosla was much respected in Indian government circles as "a safe pair of hands" and would head several government-sponsored investigations. By the 1980s he was semiretired and often in Manali (Himachal Pradesh), there with walking stick to pace the hill paths and write his *Stern Reckoning*. Using the records of a 1948 Government of India "fact-finding organisation," he came up with a total for non-Muslim fatalities of "between 200,000 and 250,000," to which he believed that an equal number of Muslims who "perished in the riots in India" might be added. Hence the figure of half a million, which more than doubled Moon's estimate. Khosla further ignored Moon's careful calculation of the fatalities in Pakistan's west Punjab (Moon had given 60,000 instead of Khosla's 200,000–250,000) and contradicted Moon's contention that the killings in India's east Punjab might be twice as many. Yet by combining these two assessments—Khosla's 200,000–250,000 in the west and Moon's "twice as many" in the east—the total could be, and was, further conflated to three-quarters of a million.

To substantiate his findings, Khosla compiled a tabulated appendix listing more than five hundred places where mass killings, conversions, and conflagrations had taken place. Each entry included a note on the nature of the atrocities ("Murder, arson, mass conversion and loot," "Murder, rape, loot and abduction," etc.) together with an estimate of the numbers killed, injured, forcibly converted, or expelled. Yet on examination, all his listed incidents occurred in Pakistan, the victims being Sikhs and Hindus, as were Khosla's informants. Of the Muslims who died in the massacres in the new India—or "the riots," as he preferred to call them in this case—there is no listing at all. Nor does it appear that the figures given for any of the listed incidents were corroborated by Pakistani witnesses. Yet this was crucial, as a British relief worker at the time discovered. In the Sialkot district of Pakistan, Richard Symonds was informed by the Indian liaison officer that in a recent assault "1500 were killed," yet "the Pakistan account said only thirty." Or again, two weeks after an attack at Mianwali, "estimates of the number of Hindus killed varied between 400 and 2000."[22] In the face of such flagrant misrepresentation, probably by both parties, extreme caution is in order. Without it, "otherizing" becomes just as partial as the blatant propaganda that has marred, indeed disfigured, nearly all such later calculations.[23]

A FURTHER EXPLANATION for the wildly divergent assessments of Partition's casualties lies in the uncertainty over the figures for the other province to be partitioned, Bengal. While some calculations, including Moon's and Khosla's, ignore Bengal altogether, a few go to the opposite extreme and infer a casualty rate comparable to that in the Punjab. This is absurdly pessimistic, and the guesswork here is even more conjectural. Much depends on how Partition—a flimsy term when stripped of its more horrific associations—is defined and on what is taken to be its time frame.

With more than sixty million inhabitants, Bengal had been easily British India's most populous province (pre-Partition Punjab had about twenty-eight million). It was also its most volatile. The potential for sectarian strife had already been demonstrated in the Calcutta Killings of August 1946 and in the subsequent massacres in Noakhali and Tripura (Tipperah). Here, the violence that seems to have taken so many by surprise in the Punjab was expected. In anticipation of it, Gandhi had already reestablished himself in Noakhali, from where he transferred to Calcutta two days ahead of independence. He needed to be at the likely epicenter when the seismic shift of August 15 occurred.

Now frailer and seemingly smaller than ever, the Mahatma was trundled round the city in an ancient Chevrolet. As he toured the trouble spots and drew massive crowds to his evening prayer meetings, his reputation transcended the religious divide. He talked up a spirit of mutual regard and inspired a sense of brotherly achievement in maintaining the peace. Mountbatten called him his "one-man boundary force." For three critical weeks he remained there, preaching communal harmony, praying for it, and fasting to exact pledges of it. He also promoted it by example, cohabiting with Husayn Shaheed Suhrawardy, the bon viveur barrister "with a nimble brain but an irritating habit" who led the Muslim League in Bengal. Lately chief minister of the province, it was Suhrawardy who had been widely blamed for inciting the earlier killings.[24]

Notwithstanding their incompatibility, such was the influence of the two men—the sticklike Mahatma and the rotund Muslim Leaguer—and such was the military presence prompted by fear of another bloodbath that the tactic worked. Observing the near absence of sectarian massacres in the subcontinent's greatest metropolis, first Gandhi and then the press dubbed it the "miracle of Calcutta." Optimists noted "a spectacle of friendship and fraternity between Hindus and Muslims," Communists detected a comradeship born of working-class solidarity, and intellectuals rejoiced in what they took to be evidence of the Bengalis' cultural superiority. The normally dyspeptic general who headed the Eastern Command went further. "The love in Calcutta was impressive above all other places," he recalled. But he ascribed it less to Gandhi's nonviolence than to a combination of the Muslim community's "depression," the non-Muslim community's exultation, and his own increased troop levels.[25]

The euphoria in Calcutta lasted throughout the crisis months immediately after independence and dissolved only when the city reverted to its usual levels of industrial strife, social upheaval, and chronic politicization in 1948. Overall, when compared to Lahore and the Punjab, Calcutta and Bengal seemed to have gotten off lightly. The death toll could almost be described as bearable, while the atrocities were largely localized. On the other hand, the population transfer was here more destabilizing than in the Punjab, much more protracted, and ultimately perhaps greater.

Dispersal being a lesser evil than death, this raises the question of why the Partition experience in Bengal differed so from that in the Punjab and whether the precautions taken in Bengal could have proved equally effective in the Punjab. The answer to the last is probably no. In the Punjab there were more guns, for one thing. There, and in the neighboring North-West Frontier Province, society prided itself on its decidedly military ethos. The northwest had long been the British Indian army's main recruiting ground and accounted for around half its intake; service families, military colonies, and paramilitary fraternities abounded. Come the end of the war, many thousands of Punjabi Sikh, Muslim, Hindu (Dogra and Jat), and Pathan servicemen had been demobilized, but not all surrendered their arms, and, of those who did, many were emboldened to reacquire them or obtain equivalents of local manufacture. In championing the anxieties of their co-religionists and avenging the massacres reported from across the border, Punjabi ex-servicemen of every persuasion found employment in a cause that was lucrative, congenial to their traditions, and applauded by their kinsmen.

This was not the case in Bengal. Generally Bengalis, whether Hindu or Muslim, were supposed to disdain the military arts. The province was thus underrepresented in the army's ranks and almost devoid of officers. When he arrived in Dhaka in late 1947 as East Bengal's first general officer commanding, Brigadier Ayub Khan, Pakistan's future ruler, found "there was no army," just two half battalions, and "no office, no table, no chair, no stationery—virtually nothing at all."[26] Firepower had played little part in the earlier "riots" in Bengal, and there had been even less evidence of tactical planning. The killing sprees had often seemed spontaneous and unpredictable, and in west Bengal the heavy, and usually heavy-handed, presence of the largely Muslim police had already been depleted by migration. In short, Gandhian pressure plus greater official awareness here stood a chance. Conversely, against the professionals orchestrating the carnage in the Punjab such intervention probably would have failed.

Other factors were also important. Given the deltaic terrain, communications in Bengal were notoriously slow and depended more on waterborne transport than on roads and railways. In the monsoon conditions of August and September whole districts were temporarily submerged, distracting the inhabitants from mutual hostilities and severely restricting their mobility. In addition, the governments of India and Pakistan, though in the Punjab officially sponsoring an exchange of population, here actively discouraged it. It was supposed that mass migrations might destabilize the delicate political arithmetic on which both the Congress in West Bengal and the League in East Bengal based their prospects of retaining power. If conducted on any scale, migration could easily deplete one-half of the province while overwhelming the other; and both prime ministers, Nehru and Liaquat Ali Khan, were dead set against it. "I have been quite certain, right from the beginning," Nehru wrote, "that everything should be done to prevent Hindus in East Bengal from migrating to West

Bengal . . . even if there is a war."[27] Throughout the period 1949–52, when a further two million Hindus from East Bengal joined the million or so who had migrated in 1947–48, Nehru remained firm. But twenty years later Indira Gandhi, when faced with precisely the war scenario that her father had envisaged, would take a very different line. East Pakistan's Bengalis, now calling themselves Bangladeshis, would be admitted to India whatever their religion, so furnishing the justification for another Partition, this time of Pakistan.

Discouraging migration did not, of course, prevent it. In 1947 the new border had yet to be marked and was impossible to police since it wandered across existing roads and railways as capriciously as the annual floods. Wags quipped that Radcliffe could not have been sober when he wielded his red marker. Until new roads and rail tracks could be laid, India's West Bengal was cut in two and its northeastern extremity in Assam (and beyond) was little better than an enclave, reachable only by air or by obtaining authorization to cross Pakistani territory. Such authorization was not impossible to obtain and refugee trains continued to operate between Dhaka and Calcutta until 1965. Calcutta's Sealdah station turned into a vast dormitory for displaced persons; public spaces throughout the city, and even private gardens, were similarly commandeered. Yet to many Bengalis this may not have been entirely alarming. Refugees often considered their displacement temporary and expected to return to the homes and lands they had left behind as soon as circumstances permitted. At the time it seemed quite inconceivable that the economic, cultural, and social links that bound the commercial and manufacturing center of Calcutta to its productive eastern hinterland could simply be severed by constitutional diktat.

Hence, instead of the fraught and one-off mass migrations typical of the Punjab, in Bengal in 1947 "there was no immediate interchange of population, nor even panic." In fact, in India's West Bengal "it was not till December 1949 that it became obvious that an influx of refugees from East Pakistan had started."[28] Thereafter the millions of comings and goings, sometimes by the same people, would extend over a period of years and eventually decades. How many crossed or recrossed, whether permanently or temporarily and whether under coercion or voluntarily, it is impossible to say. In India such "refugees" were quickly downgraded as "evacuees" or "optees." They might thereby be entitled to some minimal relief, but they were not, as in the Punjab, afforded compensation in the form of land grants or rehabilitation expenses; such favorable treatment might have acted as an incentive and increased the flow. As a result, many incomers went unrecorded and the surviving tallies are far from complete.

Yet they kept on coming. A million or so Muslims crossed out of West Bengal and Assam to East Bengal in the first five years, many being originally from Bihar, from where they had earlier fled to Calcutta during the 1946–47 massacre in their homeland. It was thus their second such migration, though by no means their last; in the case of these Muslim Biharis the nightmare of dispossession would continue on down the generations. In the same period anything from four to ten million Hindus from East Bengal crossed into the Indian states of West Bengal, Assam, and Tripura. The largest of these migrations took place in the 1950s and 1960s, prompted by the persecution of Hindus in East Bengal (early 1950s) and Muslim outrage over events in Kashmir (1963–65). Later disturbances, including the birth pangs of Bangladesh in 1971, that country's first military coup in 1975, and the communal disturbances in India after the 1992 demolition of Ayodhya's Babri Mosque, would precipitate still other dramatic exoduses.

The introduction of frontier formalities to some extent regulated this ebb and flow. Passports became mandatory in 1952, immigration certificates in 1956, and visas after 1965. Yet such obstacles also served to divert the tide of migrants away from the regulated crossing points to the seventeen hundred miles of poorly patrolled frontier in between. The real number of migrants thus became more incalculable than ever. Pocked with enclaves and punctured by waterways, the border in the east remained decidedly soft and, in the eyes of many, only quasi-legitimate. As late as 1950 no less a figure than former chief minister Husayn Shaheed Suhrawardy saw nothing odd about attending Pakistan's Constituent Assembly in Karachi while continuing to make his main place of residence in India's West Bengal, in fact in a salubrious part of Calcutta. Similarly, Nurul Amin, then chief minister of East Bengal, continued to rely on his old physician in West Bengal for medicine. The latter was none other than Dr. B. C. Roy, the Congress chief minister of West Bengal; "and would you believe it, when Nurul Amin's gout was very bad, he came to Calcutta just for an hour by plane for a consultation," reported an East Bengali informant. "Despite the riots [of 1950], the two are still good friends."[29]

If "Partition is both ever-present in South Asia's public, political terrain and continually evaded," this may in part be because, in the east as in Kashmir, it is still being enacted.[30] Indeed, in Bengal a degree of population movement appears to be endemic. Once somewhat unfairly described as a "rural slum," East Bengal in 1947 had no industrial base; even its cash crop of jute was dependent on West Bengal's processing mills. Its population stood at around forty-two million, of whom about eleven million (26 percent) were Hindus, mostly lower-caste agriculturalists and artisans but with an influential landowning and commercial elite. On the other hand, across the border, India's West Bengal along with Assam had just six million Muslims, about 16 percent of the total population, most of these being landless laborers or urban poor. Additionally, West Bengal embraced Calcutta, India's largest industrial and commercial center, while the tea plantations in the Darjeeling hills and Assam afforded a further source of employment. In Bengal as a whole, therefore, the post-1947 movement of people was overwhelmingly one-way, from east to west, Pakistan to India; although triggered by sectarian killings or the fear of such violence, it was often lubricated by more practical considerations such as economic advancement, employment opportunities, educational advantage, or marital ties.

This was nothing new. The east-west flow, the rural-urban drift, and the quest for improved livelihoods may be rated permanent features of the Bengali economy. As a result of the 1943 famine, Calcutta already hosted a large refugee population before Partition. Floods and agrarian distress in East Bengal/Bangladesh would replenish the resettlement camps of both Calcutta and Dhaka with depressing regularity. Distinguishing between political refugees and economic migrants is here problematic.

How to cope with the influx of often destitute and traumatized millions taxed both successor governments, so detracting from their ability to conduct the business of administration. In the Punjab, on both sides of the border, the problem had been somewhat eased by the availability of land. Since most migrants were agriculturalists, land holdings vacated by uprooted Punjabi emigrants were hastily reallocated to grateful Punjabi immigrants. This ensured continuity of food production and warded off famine. It also created tenacious settler communities whose intransigent attitudes toward their former country of residence would bedevil future Indo-Pak relations and be compared to those of Israeli settlers on the West Bank. But in West Bengal it was different. There was almost no available land. The smallest of the new India's provinces, West Bengal was also much the most densely populated and had the highest rate of unemployment. Prospects for the incoming flood of refugees were grim.

In the immediate aftermath of Partition it was Delhi that had been convulsed by the levels of violence and displacement expected of Calcutta. Refugees from Lahore and other cities in West Pakistan, many of them Sikhs, poured into the capital, there to spread horrific tales of the violence they had either suffered or witnessed at the hands of Muslims in what was now Pakistan. Naturally this excited hostility toward the city's large Muslim community and brought calls for revenge. The patriotic crowds that had hailed independence on August 15 were baying for blood by the end of the month. Muslims, regardless of whether they supported Pakistan or had any intention of moving there, found themselves liable to be massacred in the streets; their homes were appropriated, their womenfolk molested, their businesses plundered and torched.

As the mayhem extended from Old Delhi to New, some sixty thousand Muslims sought refuge behind the high walls of the craggy Purana Qila (the name means "old fort"), which supposedly complemented Rashtrapati Bhawan at the opposite extremity of Rajpath; others encamped round the Taj Mahal–like tomb of the Mughal emperor Humayun or barricaded themselves in quarries on the Ridge, located northwest of the city. Until mid-September "the Indian government regarded these camps as the responsibility of the Pakistan High Commissioner." He, however, was "hardly in a position to move out of his house," noted the British relief worker Richard Symonds, who was a witness to the events. In "places that could not properly be called camps but rather areas in which humanity was dumped," eminent families squatted side by side with once-prosperous shopkeepers from Old Delhi and never-rich Meos from nearby villages such as Gurgaon.[31] There was no sanitation, few tents, little food, and only a skeleton guard to man the gates. Wrote Symonds, "You might meet anyone from a nawab to a professor. Rich men offered thousands of rupees if we could hire them an aeroplane to Karachi. It seemed possible to buy anything from a taxi to a hawker's box of matches."[32]

Taxis did change hands. As of September 1947 turbaned Sikhs replaced hennaed Muslims at the wheel of most of the capital's public conveyances. The burning, looting, and lynching lasted the best part of a month; as with the next pogrom to overtake the capital—that of 1984, in which Sikhs would be the target—some officials were accused of connivance and numerous political hotheads of incitement. On both occasions, adequate troops failed to materialize, with the peacekeeping burden in 1947 being assumed by a variety of volunteer organizations.

On one occasion Nehru himself joined the volunteers. Leaping from his official car, he laid into a Hindu trundling a handcart piled high with stolen goods and demanded that they be returned. The man refused, whereupon the prime minister seized him by the throat and shook him. The offender did not strike back. "If I must die, it is an honour to do so at your hands," he croaked. Nehru then relented.[33]

In the camp at Humayun's Tomb, which backs onto railway tracks, Taya Zinkin, a young volunteer and later a reporter, welcomed the news that some of the refugees were to be moved out by train to Pakistan. They, however, refused to budge without a military escort and an assurance that she would hold herself personally responsible for their safety. Both safeguards were forthcoming, and "7,500 men, women and children piled into the train, onto it, under it and in between it."

It was an incredible sight. They were riding to safety and a new life.
In the setting sun they waved at me from the roofs, the windows,

the footboards. I stood on the platform waving back. . . . My train was the biggest train to Pakistan. For a long time it would be the last. It was ambushed in Patiala by the Sikhs. The military escort did its duty to the last man; not one survived; they were Gurkhas. Five hundred refugees reached Lahore safely but as the train pulled up in the Lahore station there were 3000 dead and 4000 so severely wounded as to be left for dead.[34]

By the time calm had been restored in Delhi, the city could no longer be described as having India's largest urban concentration of Muslims. Not all were evacuated to Pakistan, but the incoming tide of Hindus and Sikhs so swamped their numbers as to transform the city's demography and geography and launch its population's inexorable growth from around a million in 1950 to nearly twenty million by the century's end. The same tragic scenes and the same dramatic growth were witnessed in Lahore, which became a wholly Muslim city when its sizable Hindu-Sikh population virtually disappeared overnight. Other cities on both sides of the new border were similarly affected. Karachi, though comparatively calm, lost its large Hindu mercantile community to Bombay. In their stead, it absorbed the bulk of those Muslims from cities in central and northern India (principally Lucknow, Allahabad, Bhopal, etc.) who had opted for Pakistan. Mostly Urdu-speakers and once prime movers in the demand for a Muslim homeland, these *muhajirs* (a term, cognate with *haj/hijra,* that sanctified their flight from India by associating it with that of the Prophet from Mecca) would jealously retain their identity in their promised land and contribute a clamorous new element to Pakistan's ethnic mix. As *muhajirs* competed with Sindhis, Pathans, and Balochis for jobs and housing in what was Pakistan's commercial as well as administrative capital, Karachi underwent a transformation into Pakistan's Calcutta.

Even places in the extreme south of the subcontinent were affected when the Indian government in Delhi urged constituent provinces/states, such as Madras, to take such refugees as they could handle. But the response was not always favorable, mainly because it was unclear whether the control and expense of relief and rehabilitation should be borne by the states affected or by the central government. Friction and delays resulted. Nor were the refugees themselves always keen on resettlement in distant lands. The rains there might fall at the wrong time of year, the crops might be new to them and the language unknown. Just as Punjabis preferred to be accommodated in the Punjab, Bengalis expressed a preference for staying in Bengal.

This was bad news for Calcutta. As East Bengali refugees poured into the city after 1948, the numbers living on the streets or sleeping on the railway platforms could be counted in the hundreds of thousands and those corralled into shantytowns and squatter camps in the millions. The camps spread to the west bank of the river Hooghly and to all the city's surrounding districts; "what was once a rural hinterland was transformed in less than two decades into a huge urban sprawl."[35] By the 1990s it was estimated that there were two thousand bustees, or shantytowns, on the east bank of the river and a further fifteen hundred on the west bank. Three million people lived in them, representing 49 percent of the city's total population; of these, 87 percent were classed as immigrants, mostly from East Bengal.

Among the immigrants themselves there was a sense that they had a right to be in Calcutta. Mostly Hindus and all Bengali-speakers, they felt safe among other Hindu Bengalis and, though now in India, were consoled to be still in their native Bengal. Conditions might be appalling, but they were reluctant to embrace onward resettlement in some totally alien corner of the subcontinent. A lucky few thousand were squeezed into vacant lands either within West Bengal itself or in neighboring Bihar. And some of the urban colonies actually prospered as employment initiatives blossomed and the tents gave way to mud and thatch, then clapboards, corrugated metal, and a semblance of permanence. For most, though, a sheet offered the only shelter and minimal government relief the only sustenance. Laid out like sardines on roadsides and railway platforms, they blocked the thoroughfares and fouled the amenities. Cholera became rife. The city was choking to death on a surfeit of people.

To address the situation, an ambitious scheme was launched in the late 1950s. A substantial part of West Bengal's East Bengali intake was to be resettled three hundred miles away in sparsely populated forest uplands along the borders of Orissa and what is now Chattisgarh. The seventy-seven thousand square miles allocated for this exercise in pioneering was known as Dandakaranya, a term that translates as either "forest of Dandak" or "forest of punishment." Trees and scrub were cleared, plots laid out, loans offered, wells dug, and roads cut, and by 1973 some twenty-five thousand families had removed there. But they had often done so reluctantly, and already they were drifting back to Bengal. By 1979 nearly half had left. To riverine rice farmers, getting crops to grow in the thin and moisture-unretentive soil was worse than punishment; dams had failed to materialize, crop yields were dismal, there was no alternative employment, and the indigenous tribal people deeply resented the newcomers. The settlers, in short, were far from settled. "They say that their love for West Bengal is alive as their hope about Dandakaranya is dead," ran a 1978 news report on the new exodus, "that all their Dandakaranya days were dark and dreary . . . 'because of the humiliating conditions in which they lived.'"[36]

But returning to Bengal was not that easy. By now the whole issue of the East Bengali refugees had been heavily politicized. To the astute politicians of West Bengal, the grievances of a vast and heavily concentrated community had initially represented a desirable vote bank. Leftist parties, especially the Communist Party of India, had espoused the refugee cause and had duly fought the Dandakaranya plan on their behalf. Congress, happy to see the Communist vote depleted, had supported it. But by the time the Dandakaranya settlers began drifting back, the Communists were in power in West Bengal as part of a Left Front government. The votes of the returnees were no longer a priority. Re-rehabilitating them could only alienate existing supporters and damage the prospects of reconstruction. Tens of thousands were therefore turned back. Thousands more were forcibly evicted from an island they had nevertheless illegally occupied amid the mangroves of the Sundarbans.

Exiles four times over—from East Bengal, West Bengal, Dandakaranya, and then the Sundarbans—this pathetic band typified the tragedy of Bengal's "long Partition." What became of them is unclear, but it may be no coincidence that in the wake of their wanderings there would spread what in 2010 Manmohan Singh, India's prime minister, would call the nation's "gravest internal security challenge." He was referring to the so-called Naxalite or Maoist revolutionaries, whose armed insurrection was terrorizing large parts of eastern and central India. In one of several attacks, seventy-six members of the Central Reserve Police Force had just been ambushed and killed by a Naxalite group calling itself the Dandakaranya Special Zonal Committee. Dandakaranya itself, according to the *Times of India*, was now the "den" of the Naxalites; their supporters, many of them indigenous tribal people, candidly traced both their grievances and their political indoctrination to the unwelcome influx of Bengali settlers in the wake of Partition.

Sixty-five years after the event, the impact of the Great Partition is still being felt—and not just in Bengal and the Punjab. In Karachi the influx of Muslim *muhajirs* from India was on a scale comparable with that of East Bengalis into Calcutta. Literate and industrious, the *muhajirs* would stay put and through the MQM become a thorn in the flesh to successive regimes in Islamabad. Not without bloodshed, they still control much of Pakistan's largest metropolis. Parts of Hyderabad, the south Indian city that was the scene of another Partition-related crisis, are periodically devastated by motorbike bombers keen to incite their large Muslim component. Markets in Delhi and suburban trains in Bombay have also been targeted.

But, sporadic and essentially domestic, these outrages pale into insignificance compared to the horrors witnessed in Kashmir. In this former princely state, Partition's business has yet to be concluded. Compounded by the excesses of the military and paramilitaries, the same atrocities prevailed at the end of the century as in 1947. The same arguments over the state's status were being replayed and the same colossal troop levels maintained. More than anywhere else in South Asia, Kashmir was set to ensure that the legacy of Partition would not be forgotten.

3

"WHO HAS NOT HEARD OF THE VALE OF CASHMERE?"

BUT SAHIB, WE ARE KASHMIRIS, SEE. WE ARE NOT INDIANS."
The year was 1967, but the sentiments were those of 1947. My question to Ghulam Mohamed, a houseboat proprietor, had been about why he was refusing to take bookings from Indians. His answer came from twenty years back. To a young would-be correspondent with not much to report, Kashmir seemed trapped in a time warp. On the leaf-strewn terrace outside Ahdoo's bakery in Srinagar the cups were chipped, the coffee came in electroplated pots, and the conversation was thick with dogma. Two decades of what Ghulam Mohamed called "Indian occupation" had changed very little. Removing his lambskin fez, from which most of the wool had long since been rubbed, Ghulam Mohamed would listen, scratch his head with long bony fingers, then grin mischievously.

"See, Kashmir is not India. India begins at Jammu—over there, across the Bannihal Pass. Here, this is not India."

His English was excellent, though marred by a delivery as monotonous as that of a bumblebee, and whatever the subject it invariably conveyed a litany of complaints. These ranged from the price of mutton to Hindu toilet habits, bad manners in general, the iniquities of the British Labour Party, and the supposed plight of the tourist trade. In Ghulam Mohamed's conversational repertoire, bemoaning the ways of the world served as a default setting. It was how many Kashmiris dealt with their unhappy situation as South Asia's bloodiest bone of contention.

By 1967 most of the Kashmir Valley had been under New Delhi's rule for nineteen summers. Another Pakistani attempt to wrest it from India had just failed, and the Bannihal Pass, beneath whose summit the only access road now burrowed through a dripping tunnel, had been reopened. The tourists were returning; the political mudslinging had resumed. Ahead loomed a spell of what Kashmiris liked best: business as usual. An engineering college was under construction, new emporia were opening, and the powder-blue berets of the United Nations Military Observer Group in India and Pakistan (UNMOGIP) offered some assurance that Kashmir's problems had not been forgotten by the world at large. Natives of the valley, including Ghulam Mohamed, might be loath to admit it, but there was much to be said for Indian rule.

And yet the place remained palpably un-Indian. Uniquely, here English and Urdu were the official languages, with Hindi not much heard or written. Islam was the prevailing faith, tweed the preferred textile, and shawls and carpets the main trade. Instead of the shady banyan and mango of the plains, sprightly willow and poplar lined the roadsides. The year had recognizable seasons that came in the right order, and, judging by the umbrellas and the galvanized roofing, rain could be expected in all of them. The tea was sometimes pink; the meat was cooked in milk. Kingfishers piped among the sedge, dahlias and marigolds bedecked the gardens, and timbered bridges cantilevered crazily over the waterways. In Srinagar, the capital, the puddled alleyways and the higgledy-piggledy houses with their latticed shutters reminded V. S. Naipaul, then writing *An Area of Darkness,* of a dank medieval Europe. Instead of India's heat and dust, here there was water everywhere, snow on the peaks, and scarcely a sari to be seen. Of all the erstwhile princely states, Kashmir alone neither fitted the image of India nor felt like India.

Back in July 1947, when Mountbatten had undertaken to dragoon the princely states of British India into joining the new India, he had caviled over their exact number. Likening the possibly 565 states to apples, he had inquired whether having, say, 560 "in the basket" by the time of independence would be good enough. Sardar Patel, the Congress leader who was home minister in the interim government with responsibility for the princely states, acquiesced. With less than a month in which to fill the basket, Patel and the ubiquitous V. P. Menon did the arm-twisting, Mountbatten turned on the charm, and the signed Instruments of Accession came rolling in.

Although historians, both South Asian and British, have found much to criticize in Mountbatten's viceroyalty, his handling of the princely states, with the possible exception of Kashmir, has scarcely been faulted. The integration of the states has been called "a revolutionary, watershed event," even "the world's biggest bloodless revolution."[1] Mountbatten himself reckoned that by sweet-talking the princes into acceding to India he had "brought off a coup second only to the 3rd June plan"—that is, his master plan for independence cum Partition.[2] "Mountbatten's talk to the Chamber of Princes [of July 25, 1947] was a *tour de force*," writes historian Ramachandra Guha. "In my opinion it ranks as the most significant of all his acts in India. It finally persuaded the princes that the British would no longer protect or patronise them and that independence for them was a mirage."[3]

Asked merely to relinquish responsibility for the defense, foreign relations, and cross-border communications of their states, the princes were surrendering nothing they had not previously surrendered to the British; in return, they were being offered generous pensions, tax concessions, official postings, and many lifetime privileges (including immunity from private prosecution, free electricity and medical care, exemption from customs duties, and a state funeral at the end). Mountbatten's imprimatur merely added further reassurance by giving some imperial respectability to the horse trading. His task was not onerous and he conducted it with his customary conviction.

Yet by August 15 considerably more than five of the pro forma Instruments of Accession remained unsigned. Indore and Jodhpur were engaging in brinkmanship, Bhopal was prevaricating, some minor states in Saurashtra (Gujarat) were toying with accession to Pakistan, and, on the distant border with Burma, Manipur was holding out for independence, which, if secured, would gouge a substantial chunk out of India's already eccentric eastern profile.

Much more ominous, though, was the obduracy of Hyderabad in peninsular India and of Jammu and Kashmir in the extreme north. Together these two accounted for around half the total territory of princely India and about a third of its population. Additionally, both were considered of enormous strategic and psychological value. Hyderabad had been negotiating for a lease of lands that would give it access to the west coast, thus almost cutting off the extreme south of India from the rest of the country. And the composite state of Jammu and Kashmir not only adjoined both Pakistan and India but also shared a long and mostly undemarcated frontier with Chinese-claimed Tibet and Soviet-friendly Afghanistan; the possibility of its making common cause with either of these formidable neighbors was viewed with alarm. Without Hyderabad, the new India would look nearly as "maimed and moth-eaten" as Pakistan, and, without the lake-strewn "Vale of Cashmere" made famous in the West by poet Thomas Moore, it would be shorn of what, by common consent, was reckoned the subcontinent's outstanding natural attraction. Moreover, the Nehru family originally hailed from the Kashmir Valley. "[It] affects me in a peculiar way," the Indian prime minister would confess. Like "a mild kind of intoxication . . . the very air of Kashmir has something mysterious and compelling about it."[4] The Nehrus vacationed there, considered the place as peculiarly their own, and would make it a point of honor to claim it for India.

Sardar Patel and V. P. Menon felt just as proprietorial about the princely states in general. What Menon embarrassingly termed "the final solution" to the princely problem was regarded as a purely Indian affair and of no concern to anyone else. Others begged to differ. In particular, the Pakistan government in Karachi would follow events in Hyderabad and Kashmir with mounting alarm. Many in India, including Nehru, still regarded Pakistan as an experiment that could well be doomed to failure. Possibly to them, and certainly to most Pakistanis, India's speedy absorption of the otherwise independent princely states looked to be the prelude to a bid to reclaim parts, if not all, of Pakistan itself.

The British too retained an interest in the matter through the Commonwealth. Mountbatten had assured one reluctant princeling that "if you accede now [i.e., before August 15] you will be joining a Dominion [India] with the King as Head . . . [and] if they change the Constitution to a republic and leave the Commonwealth, the Instrument of Accession does not bind you in any way to remain with the republic."[5] By implication, if the Indian government reneged on the terms of princely accession by abolishing hereditary rights, the princes might expect London's moral support in any bid to reassert their sovereignty.

Other interested parties included those European powers, notably Portugal and France, that still clung to colonial toeholds on the subcontinent, the Portuguese principally in Goa, the French in Pondicherry. The Portuguese had been around since before the Mughals, and the French were entertaining the possibility of supporting Hyderabad's claim to independence. Both could expect a rough ride from a Congress government that was sworn to eradicate all colonialisms, claimed to represent India's peoples en masse, and insisted on the integration of their territories in toto.

Similar concerns troubled the Himalayan kingdoms of Sikkim, Bhutan, and Nepal. Technically sovereign states, none of these had been numbered among the princely states of British India, although each had entered into treaty arrangements with the British. Now feeling exposed by the British withdrawal, their monarchs were wary of New Delhi's offers to reinstate the treaties and were especially sensitive to the antimonarchist policies being promoted by India's democratic and determinedly populist Congress.

Nor were any of these concerned parties much reassured by the tactics on display. In Travancore (Kerala) the state's respected dewan, or chief minister, resisted Mountbatten's blandishments and asserted his maharajah's right to independence; for doing so, he was waylaid in the street and severely stabbed. He survived, though not so his state; Travancore's cowed maharajah promptly signed on the dotted line. The nawab of Bhopal, a personal friend of Mountbatten's, preferred exile to the ignominy of puppet status. The ruler of Manipur was reportedly locked in a Shillong hotel until such time as he would sign away his inheritance.

Most of these incidents occurred prior to the handover of power. Afterward, as the bloodletting of Partition subsided in October 1947, attention switched to the fate of the three princely states whose future was still contested. In the case of one, Junagadh, in what is now Gujarat, its nawab had already pronounced in favor of Pakistan, but Junagadh was not contiguous to Pakistan, and New Delhi had objected. In all three cases a much greater anomaly underlay the indecision: in Junagadh and Hyderabad, a Muslim ruler presided over a largely Hindu population, while in Jammu and Kashmir it was the other way round, with a Hindu maharajah ruling over a Muslim majority. Each was thus impaled on the horns of a dilemma, for the ruler's personal preference was likely to be at variance with that of his subjects as well as being inconsistent with the twin principles of Partition (the religion of the majority and contiguity to territory of a similar complexion).

All that could be said for sure was that, whatever the requirements for princely accession—whether a decision by the ruler, a preference clearly expressed by his subjects, or a combination of both—it stood to reason that the Muslim-ruled states of Junagadh and Hyderabad would join one successor nation and that Hindu-ruled Jammu and Kashmir would join the other. The possibility that all three might end up in the same successor state could logically be discounted—or so it seemed. With the three coming under pressure at the same time, it could scarcely be argued that circumstances had changed; likewise, with princely independence having been declared an unacceptable "mirage" by Mountbatten, fudging the issue by going it alone seemed out of the question.

In August all three had signed standstill agreements pending further negotiation. Though Delhi declined signing with regard to Kashmir, it was generally understood that India and Pakistan would refrain from active interference, while the states themselves were supposed to make no unilateral moves. But the standstill quickly broke down in Junagadh. Encouraged by Sardar Patel, two of Junagadh's subsidiary statelets disavowed the nawab and opted for India. Although the legality of this move was questionable, the nawab could hardly be described as popular—11 percent of Junagadh's revenue went to the maintenance of about eight hundred dogs in the royal kennels, which featured luxury unavailable to most of the state's other subjects.[6] In support of Junagadh's dissident statelets, a Junagadh government in exile headed by a nephew of Mahatma Gandhi's was set up in Bombay. Pro-India troops massed along the state's uncertain borders, and Congress-supported rabble-rousers were busy within. In late October, under considerable pressure, the nawab boarded a plane and fled to Karachi with four wives and a like number of tail-wagging companions.

That left his dewan, one Shah Nawaz Bhutto, to pick up the pieces. Dewan Bhutto had originally encouraged the nawab to join Pakistan. As one of Sind's great feudal landowners—and the founder of Pakistan's best-known political dynasty—he had nothing against hereditary rule. But as a scion of the Muslim League, Bhutto deferred to Jinnah, who read the situation differently.

For it so happened that just as the nawab and his entourage were leaving Junagadh, Jammu and Kashmir's maharajah, along with an impressive convoy of motor vehicles, was decamping over the Bannihal Pass from Srinagar. The two crises, hitherto unrelated, had coincided, and therein lay Pakistan's great opportunity. Like a chessboard pawn, Junagadh might be sacrificed provided that, come the next move, Kashmir could be taken. Jinnah, and now Dewan Bhutto, therefore backtracked. By accepting an Indian proposal that in Junagadh the nawab's decision should be contingent on the outcome of a popular vote, they were establishing a precedent of vital relevance to the future of the Muslim-majority state of Jammu and Kashmir.

Though it was not mandatory that a prince's accession should be endorsed by his subjects, the idea had been urged by both Mountbatten and the Congress leadership. Outside princely India, referenda on whether to join India or Pakistan had already been held in the North-West Frontier Province and in the Sylhet district of Assam. In both cases the vote had gone in favor of Pakistan. Sylhet had been detached from Indian Assam and awarded to neighboring East

Pakistan; the North-West Frontier Province had been confirmed as a constituent part of West Pakistan. Though the Muslim League, unlike Congress, did not concede the need for popular endorsement, the League soon came to recognize its value.

In Junagadh such a plebiscite was sure to overturn the nawab's earlier decision in favor of Pakistan, as it overwhelmingly would in February 1948; Bhutto would follow the nawab and his dogs to Pakistan, and, despite further objections from Karachi, the state was taken to have allocated itself to India. But by extension, applying the same principle to Jammu and Kashmir must mean there was every chance that it would fall on Pakistan's side of the fence. In Kashmir too the ruler was unpopular, both as a feudal autocrat and as a non-Muslim presiding over a Muslim majority. A plebiscite would therefore probably go against him. Indeed, the mere threat of it should have been enough to dissuade him from opting for India. In short, by effectively abandoning Junagadh, Pakistan sought to secure Jammu and Kashmir. But for the Kashmiris themselves, it was not quite as straightforward as that. Twenty years later a self-appointed spokesman such as Ghulam Mohamed—"But Kashmir is not Pakistan and it is not India"—could still be decidedly ambivalent about whether the state should have joined Pakistan in 1947 and, indeed, about whether, then or since, it would have so voted. By 1967 Pakistan had been exposed as a poor advertisement for democratic sovereignty, while Kashmir's predicament never lent itself to simple solutions. There had been other considerations as well back in 1947. For one thing, the situation had already deteriorated into the first Indo-Pakistan war; for another, there was Hyderabad. The war betrayed the depth of feeling over Kashmir in both India and Pakistan, while Hyderabad was relevant because it hinted at the possibility of Kashmir scorning both suitors and going it alone.

As Pakistani eyes were being lifted unto the hills, India had kept one eye fixed firmly on the peninsula. There Hyderabad's situation was directly analogous to that of Junagadh: a Muslim ruler, the immensely rich Nizam Mir Usman Ali, lorded it over a vast population, four-fifths of which was non-Muslim. His sprawling state was around fifty times the size of Junagadh and about as far from

Pakistan as could be. It was contiguous only with India, indeed surrounded by it. But to the nizam this was neither here nor there. A miserly skinflint where most princes were conspicuous spendthrifts, he was no keener on conferring his state on Pakistan than he was on giving it to India. His preference was for playing off one nation against the other while cultivating his British and European contacts and hoarding his sovereignty as jealously as he did his diamonds. In effect, he would prefer to sign not an Instrument of Accession to either state but sovereign treaties with both.

An autonomous Usmanistan (a more nationlike name for Hyderabad) had been touted in some of the Muslim League's pre-Partition propaganda. With a population of sixteen million—about the same as that of Sri Lanka and Nepal combined—with a division-sized army and an illustrious history dating back to Mughal times, Hyderabad had as good a claim to independence as anywhere. To realize it, the nizam was prepared to defy New Delhi and even dip into his bottomless coffers. At great expense he enlisted the legal services of a king's counsel from the English bar, plus that bar's favorite tactic of aggressive procrastination.

In Hyderabad, however, as in Kashmir, the ruler's authority was already being challenged. Hyderabad was no peripheral backwater like Junagadh. A local Congress-affiliated party was demanding full democratic representation plus an end to hereditary rule; a socialist party chimed in by urging outright accession to India. Communist cadres were dismantling the larger landholdings in the turbulent Telengana region of the state, and in the main cities Islamist paramilitaries (Razakars), with or without the tacit support of the nizam's government, were terrorizing pro-India communities, most of them Hindu. Thus as Muslim refugees poured into the state from central India in the aftermath of Partition, Hindu refugees flooded into the neighboring Madras and Bombay provinces. As in the Punjab and Bengal, though on a smaller scale, powerful constituencies were being created by the crude expedient of repositioning people.

In this exercise, time might be thought to favor the nizam. Accordingly, in October 1947 the nizam's legal counsel, backed by Mountbatten, began to lobby Nehru and Patel for a one-year extension of

Hyderabad's standstill agreement. The Congress leaders reluctantly concurred, and Mountbatten chalked up another triumph. No longer viceroy but a decidedly hands-on governor-general, in the same month Mountbatten enjoyed the satisfaction of seeing his nephew and protégé, Philip of Greece, preparing to wed Princess Elizabeth, the heir presumptive to the British throne. As one who was about to be even more closely related to the House of Windsor, Mountbatten was confident that by playing on the nizam's regard for the British monarchy he could get him to sign a document that, though neither an Instrument of Accession nor a treaty, combined enough of both to satisfy all parties.

There matters stood—with the Indian and Hyderabadi governments supposedly sworn to avoid provoking each other, the nizam and his supporters still nursing hopes of independence, and Mountbatten as buoyant as ever—when in late October reports came from the other end of India that truckloads of ragtag soldiers were advancing up through the apple-laden orchards on the hillsides of the outer Himalayas with the intention of taking a large bite out of the juiciest fruit of all. Kashmir, it seemed, was being invaded. Homesteads were aflame, villages were subject to pillage, and bridges were being captured. In less than a week, with his outposts fallen, his army on the run, and his state in peril, the maharajah of Kashmir would be propelled into India's arms. And so, as if from nowhere, there began a conflict that would rumble on into the next century and comfortably outlast even Ghulam Mohamed's drone of woe.

"It was a case of retaliation," Ghulam Mohamed always claimed. "See, Kashmiris had nothing to do with it. These people with guns, they were Pathans from Yaghistan. We were the victims."

Launched on October 22, 1947, what Indians regard as an unprovoked Pakistani-backed invasion of the Kashmir Valley and what Pakistanis regard as a spontaneous expression of Muslim solidarity in the face of the maharajah's oppression rapidly escalated into open warfare. The invaders would overrun about a third of the entire state, threaten Srinagar itself, and bring India's army and air force rushing to the rescue. Thousands died, tens of thousands were displaced, and for generations to come millions would pay the price. Because of Kashmir, Indo-Pakistan hostility would become the defining motif in South Asian relations. A new generation, Midnight's Children, and then another, Midnight's Grandchildren, would imbibe the mythologies constructed around the Kashmir crisis and grow up in its atmosphere of irreconcilable claims and counterclaims. This near-existential enmity would spawn its own national heroes in succession to the freedom fighters of old and induce a myopia that is as puzzling to foreigners as it is troubling to neighbors. The policies subsequently pursued by India and Pakistan with regard to Sri Lanka, Nepal, Bangladesh, and especially Afghanistan were, and still are, heavily influenced by the unfinished business over Kashmir.

The so-called Kashmir problem also necessitated massive troop deployments, hasty weapons purchases, and an incipient arms race. Defense spending would in turn devour slender budgets, frustrate much-needed social reform programs, stunt economic growth, and discredit not just the Mahatma's legacy of nonviolence but also Nehru's lofty boast of international nonalignment and Jinnah's pledge of sectarian inclusiveness. As if the post-Partition slaughter of the previous two months had not been enough, in late 1947 India and Pakistan hovered so close to all-out war as to put Partition itself in jeopardy. But whether this opened a new chapter in South Asian relations or simply prolonged an old one is open to debate.

THE BRITISH-DRAWN MAPS must bear some of the responsibility. Jammu and Kashmir state was not, and never had been, the confident entity that it appeared on paper. It was a more arbitrary, complex, and disparate creation than even its composite name suggests. Most of the state was within the high Himalayas or beyond, and so arguably not part of the South Asian subcontinent at all. Nor was it simply a combination of mountain valley (Kashmir) and submontane glacis (Jammu). Scholars tend to divide the state into four or five distinct sociogeographic regions, each having little in common with the others apart from the maharajah's overarching claim to sovereignty.

Jammu, in the plains, is indistinguishable from the neighboring Punjab. At the time its considerable population included slightly more Hindus and Sikhs than Muslims, and had the area not been part of a princely state, Radcliffe's red pen surely would have awarded it to New Delhi. Yet Jammu was not just some appendage of the Jammu and Kashmir state that could be quietly lopped off. It was in fact integral to it. The Hindu Dogra maharajahs originally hailed from Jammu, and Jammu City still served them as the state's winter capital.

The more populous Kashmir Valley, on the other hand, lies 6,500 feet higher, is hemmed in by snowcapped mountains, and feels a world away from the Punjab and the Indian subcontinent. Though largely Muslim, it had seldom been aggressively so. Indeed, it accommodated an influential class of Brahmin landowners and intellectuals, otherwise known as pandits (including the Nehrus' ancestors), who had prospered under Dogra rule. With its own language, cuisine, and costume, plus a reputation for fine crafts and outrageous salesmanship, the valley boasted a distinctive culture, called Kashmiriyat, and an enviable tradition of communal harmony.

Before its incorporation into the Mughal empire in the late seventeenth century the valley had often been an independent kingdom. It had come under the rule of its Hindu Dogra maharajahs only in the 1840s when the British, in cynical mode, had chosen not to administer directly such a far-flung and indeterminate territory. Instead, and in return for their allegiance and a large cash indemnity, the Dogra maharajahs had been confirmed in their lately won inheritance. Their often unsavory rule was thus prolonged, and, though the British frequently had occasion to regret Dogra excesses, they found compensation in adopting the valley as a vacation spot where, sallying forth from Henley-style houseboats, they might embrace the alpine scenery with rods, guns, cameras, and picnic baskets.

To the south of the valley, and to the west of the Bannihal Pass and Jammu, lesser valleys and pine-clad ridges border the plains of what is now Pakistan. Comprising several onetime fiefs, this third segment of Jammu and Kashmir state was loosely referred to as Poonch (or sometimes "Punch"), that being the main administrative center. Comparatively well populated and, like the valley, largely Muslim, Poonch had a claim to autonomy under a related Dogra dynasty, plus a history of resistance to rule from Srinagar/Jammu.

Notoriously turbulent and an important recruiting ground for the British Indian army, Poonch was where the trouble started.

Such were the three core regions of the state—Jammu, the Kashmir Valley, and Poonch. But north and northwest of the valley, among and beyond the glaciers of the Karakorum range, were numerous lesser chiefdoms and statelets. These had been lumped together by the British as the Gilgit Agency and had even less in common with the valley and its Dogra rulers, who were here heartily detested. Sparsely populated and again Muslim, though more Shi'ite than Sunni, the Gilgit region had been attached to the Jammu and Kashmir state purely for British strategic convenience. In 1935, for the same reason, much of it had been leased back by the British. Accessible from the valley for only part of the year, and then not without considerable effort, the Gilgit region's status in the wake of the British withdrawal could best be described as uncertain.

Finally, to the northeast and east of the Kashmir Valley, beyond even snowier passes, the valley of the upper Indus opened out into the arid wastes of Baltistan and Ladakh. The former was once Buddhist, the latter still so, and both were more Tibetan in aspect than Indian. But they had been under Dogra rule for over a century, and, although they contained a negligible fraction of the state's population, they accounted for about three-quarters of its land area as well as almost its entire border with Tibet and Chinese Xinjiang. Ladakh's social, cultural, and commercial ties were as much with this Inner Asian world as with South Asia, and, prior to the Chinese intervention in Tibet in 1950, Ladakh showed more interest in an association with Lhasa than with New Delhi or Karachi.

In sum, here was a highly artificial state but one that, when taken as a whole, was of great geostrategic interest to both India and Pakistan and that, fringing the two, might go either way. Its religious complexion argued for its joining Pakistan, but New Delhi had expectations that its maharajah, the sole embodiment of its tenuous unity, would prefer India. Yet its composition lent itself to dismemberment, and its history and general ambivalence, no less than its contested status, argued for some form of autonomy, particularly with respect to its core southern regions.

Two other factors were relevant. In the valley the maharajah's authority had long been under threat from populist political parties, and in Poonch it was contested by a junior claimant to the maharajah's throne backed by one or more of Poonch's militaristic clans. Among the valley's several political parties, the most effective was the National Conference under the leadership of Sheikh Mohamed Abdullah. The term "sheikh" was in this case one of popular respect rather than religious orthodoxy. A commanding figure, son of a shawl merchant and educated at the prestigious Aligarh Muslim University in UP, the sheikh espoused radical socialism, not Islamism. His National Conference had been so named when in 1938 it had broken with its parent Muslim Conference, a party that subsequently allied itself with Jinnah's Muslim League and was generally in favor of Pakistan. In contrast, the sheikh's National Conference, while spearheading the grievances of the valley's Muslims against their Dogra rulers, adopted a less sectarian stance more in tune with that of India's Congress Party.

"They say that Sheikh Sahib was Nehru's friend," Ghulam Mohamed told me in 1967, using a doubly respectful moniker for Abdullah. "What kind of friend? What did Nehru do for Kashmir? Nothing, see, nothing." But with the passage of time Kashmiris such as he had conveniently forgotten that in 1947 Sheikh Abdullah owed his pivotal role, indeed his lionization ("the Lion of Kashmir" being another of his sobriquets), almost entirely to Nehru. In fact, it was his regard for Nehru, and Nehru's for the sheikh, that would undermine any chance of the state going it alone. The two men had much in common. "There can be no doubt that Jawaharlal Nehru saw Sheikh Abdullah as his political twin," writes Alastair Lamb, an authority on Kashmir, adding cryptically that the relationship "may well have involved more than shared political opinions."[7] With the six-foot-four sheikh towering over his Indian counterpart, they made an ill-assorted pair, but both were secular in outlook, both were socialists and democrats by conviction, and both were immensely proud of their Kashmiri heritage and had nothing but contempt for the blatantly discriminatory regime of the thoroughbred-loving maharajah in his Savile Row suits.

In May 1946, not for the first time, the sheikh had faced trial for sedition. He had demanded that the maharajah leave Kashmir, thus spurring the Quit Kashmir movement, and followed this up by advocating a redistribution of landholdings and more jobs for Muslims. Riots had followed, with protesters killed and Srinagar put under curfew. Greatly alarmed for his friend, Nehru had absented himself from the Cabinet Mission's deliberations and rushed up to Kashmir to defend the sheikh in court, though on this occasion he was turned back at the border (on a later occasion he was hauled back by Mountbatten and Patel). The sheikh had been duly convicted and imprisoned, and he was still in Srinagar's jail when the momentous events of August 14 and 15, 1947, came and went. In the valley the Pakistani flag was raised, then hastily removed; in parts of Poonch it flew longer, as did the Indian flag in Jammu.

With Maharajah Hari Singh apparently following the nizam of Hyderabad's lead and holding out for some form of independence, Nehru looked to his old friend for a more pro-India pronouncement. Sheikh Abdullah obliged. At the time he said nothing about autonomy or independence but was adamant about "freedom." This he defined as freedom from Dogra rule, freedom for himself and his followers from their Srinagar detention, and freedom for the Kashmiri people, rather than the maharajah, to decide between India and Pakistan. Abdullah's "Quit Kashmir" call echoed that of the 1942 "Quit India" movement, and similarly his freedom struggle against the maharajah mimicked that of the Congress leadership against the British—in Kashmir too, detention merely increased the detainees' popularity and raised the stakes. Nehru was probably right in supposing the sheikh to be the nearest thing to the voice of the Kashmiri people, although the sheikh's popularity scarcely extended beyond the valley into Jammu and Poonch, let alone Gilgit or Ladakh. Nehru was also confident that the sheikh's inclinations—democratic, socially radical, confessionally neutral, and distinctly personal vis-à-vis the pro-Pakistan Muslim Conference—would be best served by opting for India.

Meanwhile, the Punjab erupted in the horrors of Partition. In east Punjab, and throughout the rest of India, Muslims who were reluctant to decamp to Pakistan lived in fear for their livelihoods if not their lives. They badly needed reassurance about their future prospects in India, and, to Nehru's way of thinking, nothing would comfort them more than the spectacle of a Muslim-majority state such as Jammu and Kashmir endorsing New Delhi's noncommunal stance by freely acceding to India. It would also bolster India's secular credentials, while, according to Nehru, "any weakening in Kashmir by us would create a far more difficult communal situation."[8]

Unfortunately, this far more difficult communal situation was already evident in Jammu and Poonch. In Jammu, hard by the blood-soaked Punjab, some sectarian contagion was probably inevitable. The resultant killings and expulsions replicated those in the Punjab, with the maharajah's Dogra troops here participating in the atrocities committed by Jammu's non-Muslim majority on its Muslim minority. As reported by Richard Symonds, whose role as a refugee monitor now took him from the Punjab to Kashmir, the Jammu killings preceded the October 22 "invasion" of Kashmir and were partly responsible for it. "From about 17 October," he wrote, "Muslims in villages near Jammu were rounded up [by the maharajah's officials], told that Pakistan had asked them to leave, and sent on foot towards the Pakistan border. On the way they were slaughtered by civilian Sikhs and the Dogra Kashmir troops, sometimes assisted by some Rajputs and depressed classes."[9]

News of these killings, plus a trickle of survivors, soon reached Poonch, greatly inflaming an already volatile situation there. According to Symonds, ongoing resistance to some punitive taxes levied by the maharajah on the Muslims of Poonch had already provoked open rebellion, and it was these rebellious and now confessionally incensed anti-Dogra Muslims of Poonch who turned increasingly to their co-religionists in neighboring Pakistan for arms and assistance.

In other words—and most notably those preferred by Pakistanis—the ragtag invaders who were about to enter Kashmir territory were merely responding to a call for help from fellow Muslims under threat from their Hindu overlord. The incursion was therefore spontaneous; it owed nothing to the government of Pakistan and had no designs on the Kashmir Valley itself. All of this would appear somewhat implausible in the light of subsequent events—although no more so than India's adamant disclaimers of the prior support afforded to the maharajah by elements of the government in New Delhi.

Such Indian support was needed because the maharajah's forces were no match for the Poonch rebels, most of whom had battle-field experience. "Of the 71,667 citizens of the state of Jammu and Kashmir who served in the British Indian forces during World War II, 60,402 were Muslims from the traditional recruiting ground of Poonch and Mirpur [i.e., southern Poonch]," notes historian Victoria Schofield.[10] Like the Muslim, Sikh, and Dogra ex-servicemen who were responsible for the worst killings in the Punjab, Poonch's military veterans were a force to be reckoned with. They so tested the maharajah's troops that, according to sources cited by Alastair Lamb, well before the Pakistani incursion into Kashmir the maharajah was receiving covert logistical and technical assistance from India plus the services of "at least one infantry battalion and a battery of mountain artillery." Both of the latter were drawn from what had been the army of the Sikh state of Patiala but was now, since Patiala's accession to India, part of India's forces.[11]

There was nothing particularly sinister about this. The Patiala auxiliaries were intended not for deployment against Pakistan but to uphold the maharajah's authority within his own state. Their presence nevertheless represented, if not a prior incursion, then certainly a provocative escalation. The uprising within the Poonch district of the still technically independent state of Jammu and Kashmir was being surreptitiously internationalized, and, by the same logic that prompted the maharajah to look to India, the Poonchi rebels looked to Pakistan.

For rifles, mortars, and explosives, the Poonchis—or Azad Kashmiris (Free Kashmiris), as they now preferred to be called—sought out Pakistani intermediaries willing to supply their needs from official arsenals and from the roadside showrooms of the Pathan (Pashtun) gunsmiths of the North-West Frontier Province. Additionally, several thousand Pathans volunteered their services as fighters. Most came from the tribal areas of Hazara, Dir, Bajaur, and Kurram, which, though attached to the NWFP, had been largely abandoned to their own devices following the British withdrawal. It was these redoubtable warriors from the frontier's tribal areas whom Ghulam Mohamed always called "Yaghis," "Yaghistan" being a pejorative term for anywhere that was habitually ungovernable.

Pathans also provided the necessary transport and fuel; their haulers, then as now, had a monopoly on the cross-border trucking business between Afghanistan and the plains. And as was ever the case in frontier affairs, the tribesmen's Islamic zealotry barely disguised an inveterate rapacity. To the irregulars who headed off into the Hazara hills en route for Kashmir, the news of Muslims being massacred in Jammu excited calls for revenge and promised the sanction of jihad. But no less enticing was the promise of plunder afforded by Kashmir's abiding reputation as a terrestrial paradise of pulchritude and plenty.

To what extent the Pakistan government was aware of all this activity is unclear. Intelligence was scarce, and there was as yet no such thing as an Inter-Services Intelligence (ISI) directorate. The obvious parallels with Pakistani disclaimers of official support for subsequent cross-border interventions—whether in Kashmir or Afghanistan—are nevertheless striking. Then as later, Pakistani officials cited tribal autonomy as an excuse for their impotence, and then as later they nevertheless cultivated a nexus of informal contacts with both the tribes and their Poonchi/Azad Kashmiri sponsors.

Retired and absconding officers from the Pakistan army were certainly involved in the Kashmir incursion, although regular troops at first were not. And while Liaquat Ali Khan, the prime minister, seems to have had some early knowledge of what was going on, Jinnah himself may have been kept in ignorance of it, either because he did not wish to be informed or because he was already suffering from the ill health that would soon end his life and it was thought best not to inform him. Government ministers in Karachi may also have been poorly apprised of the situation. Still living out of packing cases as they grappled with the refugee problem and the mechanics of government, they had little time for studying conditions on the far northern frontier and were in no position to influence them.

Pakistan's acting commander in chief, in Rawalpindi, and the governor of the North-West Frontier Province, in Peshawar, were better placed. Both were British and both nursed some sympathy for Pakistan's claim to Kashmir. But under orders from their British superiors to resign rather than become involved in hostilities, they trod carefully and urged caution. Pakistan's army was still being pieced together from elements of undivided India's; indeed, its share of the latter's military hardware had yet to materialize. It was in no position to mount its own invasion of Kashmir. Nor, since this could well lead to a disastrous civil war, was it keen to oppose those tribesmen intent on such an invasion. Thus the most that can be said with any confidence is that the Pakistani authorities, while not entirely ignorant of the Kashmir adventure, declined publicly to authorize it and failed signally to impede it.

ONCE ACROSS THE PAKISTAN-KASHMIR BORDER, the first wave of eighty-odd trucks crammed with tribesmen and their Azad Kashmiri sponsors found their progress up the Jhelum Valley eased by the desertion of Muslim troops within the maharajah's forces. Bridges had been left unblown, towns undefended. Muzaffarabad fell and was looted, then Uri. From there a side road led over the hills to Poonch, while ahead lay the valley itself. The greater prize proved the stronger temptation; instead of heading off to eject the maharajah's forces from Poonch, the raiders pushed on for Baramula, gateway to the Vale of Cashmere. Nearing that town, the brigadier commanding the maharajah's retreating forces was badly wounded. Having vowed that the enemy would enter the valley over his dead body, he was as good as his word and took his own life. His forces looked to be in hopeless disarray. An ill-organized incursion in support of an obscure rebellion suddenly had the valley at its mercy.

Baramula is only thirty-seven miles from Srinagar. From there an attack on the capital itself was clearly on the cards; this being manifest to the panic-stricken maharajah, he too changed tack. On October 24 he sent an urgent appeal for military assistance to New Delhi. He was aware that the quid pro quo might be that he sign a pro forma Instrument of Accession, and he indicated his willingness to do so "subject to the condition that the terms of accession will be the same as would be settled with H[is] E[xalted] H[ighness] the Nizam of Hyderabad."[12] An airlift of Indian troops followed on October 27. Srinagar airport was secured, and from there Indian Air Force planes launched sorties down the valley, strafing the invaders, attacking their transport, and bombing their supply lines. Although Baramula was put to the sword in a final act of wanton attrition, the main enemy advance was halted there. Meanwhile, the maharajah had duly signed the Instrument of Accession.

Despite sharing a religion with the invaders, the valley's civilian population had shown themselves largely indifferent to the incursion. They welcomed neither their Azad brethren nor their Pathan colleagues and often suffered from their depredations. As yet they showed no inclination to fight for the right to decide their future, and they were soon skeptical about the invaders' claim to be doing it for them, for if the invaders' intent was to preempt India's designs on the state, it had spectacularly misfired. Instead it was precipitating the Indian action.

New Delhi had prepared the ground well. Both Gandhi and more recently Mountbatten had paid personal visits to Srinagar. At the time they had failed to get a pro-India decision out of the maharajah, but they had at least prevailed on him to sack his independence-minded prime minister and release Sheikh Abdullah from detention. In fact, the sheikh was now rallying his Srinagar supporters to resist the invaders.

On October 25, within hours of the maharajah's appeal to India, V. P. Menon arrived in the valley. He clarified the terms of Indian military intervention, namely, temporary accession of the state pending confirmation by a plebiscite, plus the installation of Sheikh Abdullah as a minister in the maharajah's government. He also persuaded the maharajah and his family to leave Srinagar immediately. They did so in convoy soon after midnight on October 26, heading over the Bannihal Pass for Jammu. Ostensibly this was for the maharajah's safety. From an Indian point of view it would also ensure that, should the city fall to the raiders, its ruler would not. But in Pakistani eyes the maharajah's departure was tantamount to flight and so constituted an abrogation of his authority, contravening the standstill agreement; thus whatever he signed thereafter was deemed irrelevant.

It has also been questioned whether the signing of the Instrument of Accession took place before the airlift of Indian troops began or whether the official record was simply doctored to make it seem so.[13] Mountbatten, as India's governor-general, had been invited to chair the top-level Defence Committee that considered the maharajah's appeal. Eager to include Jammu and Kashmir in his basket of princely states and so notch another triumph before his governor-generalship ended, Mountbatten had supported the Indian action, although with reservations. It was he who insisted that the act of accession must precede the movement of troops and that a plebiscite must follow it. With British army officers still serving in both Pakistan and India, his "major concern was to prevent an inter-Dominion war."[14] The legal niceties were therefore critical; India's case for intervention had to be cast iron. Yet even Mountbatten's official biographer concedes that attaching so much importance to the accession was a grave mistake: "If there had been no accession, the Indian presence in Kashmir would have been more evidently temporary, the possibility of a properly constituted referendum have become more real. By exaggerated legalism the Governor-General helped bring about the result he most feared: the protracted occupation of Kashmir by India with no attempt to show that it enjoyed popular support."[15]

Critics of hereditary rule, including Nehru and Sheikh Abdullah, also accepted that some form of popular endorsement was desirable. The problem was, and would long remain, how to make it convincing. That a formal plebiscite would, in fact, never be held was less because New Delhi resisted it than because, with its troops in permanent occupation, no such vote would be deemed free and fair. In effect, Mountbatten's insistence on formal accession as a prerequisite for intervention precluded his other condition of a democratic vote to endorse accession.

Twenty years later, even Ghulam Mohamed could see little merit in the idea of a plebiscite. Sucking smoke from a clenched fist out of which protruded a perpendicular cigarette—he claimed this made it more like a hookah—he tended to see things in personal terms: "We trust Sheikh Sahib, see. He is Kashmiri. We vote for him, not for India or Pakistan. Kashmir is for Kashmiris. What need to vote for someone else?"

At the time Sheikh Abdullah welcomed the Indian intervention. As the state's emergency administrator and soon to be prime minister, he would bestride the valley's politics and waste no time in introducing a radical redistribution of landholdings and other populist reforms. Given his appeal, his apparent approval of the accession could be taken to signify the attitude of most Kashmiris. What need, then, for a plebiscite? Nehru's confidence in the sheikh seemed to have paid off. Delhi had cause to rejoice.

KARACHI, OF COURSE, DID NOT REJOICE. News of the Indian airlift and of the state's official accession brought howls of protest plus a demand from Jinnah that the Pakistani army be immediately sent into the Kashmir Valley. Seemingly Pakistan was no sooner born than it was confronted with the prospect of a lobotomy. For if Nehru valued Jammu and Kashmir's accession as corroboration of India's secular stance, no less did Jinnah contest that same accession as contravening the two-nation principle on which Partition had been based. Moreover, without the K of Kashmir, Pakistan would be not just unpronounceable but indefensible, and its claim to be a homeland for all South Asia's Muslim majorities would be compromised. Worse still, the addition of Jammu and Kashmir so expanded India's territory that on paper it now encircled northern Pakistan and abutted both the unruly tribal areas and an unpredictable Afghanistan. Pakistan's security was hopelessly compromised. In the face of what amounted to an existential threat, Jinnah had little choice but to order the army to respond.

But his British commander in chief objected. The army wasn't ready, he claimed, and anyway all those British officers on whom its formation depended would have to stand down if Pakistan invaded what India now held to be its own territory. War was risky and potentially prejudicial to any favorable settlement. Under the circumstances, therefore, the most that could be done was to consolidate the gains already made by the Azad Kashmiris and their Pathan accomplices. Arms, ammunition, supplies, and advisers would be made available to them and reinforcements allowed to reach them;

meanwhile, the government in Karachi would explore a variety of diplomatic options on their behalf.

Six months later, in May 1948, by which time Pakistan's army was in better shape, the commander in chief did authorize a deployment of forces. But it was on the understanding that they were to avoid direct contact with Indian troops and simply deter any Indian encroachments into Pakistan itself. That might still involve their entering Kashmiri territory, and it gave them no immunity from Indian air attack. Willy-nilly, India and Pakistan were now engaged in mutual hostilities that amounted to war in all but name.

To Pakistan's frustration over the uncooperative attitude of its British officers there was one notable exception. High in the valleys of the far northwest of Jammu and Kashmir, in what had been the British-leased Gilgit Agency, news of the state's accession to India had gone down badly. The Gilgit Scouts, a British-officered frontier corps of battalion strength and mostly Pathan in composition, had already shown itself averse to being transferred from British command to that of the Dogra maharajah. The threat that, following the maharajah's accession to India, it might now be incorporated into the Indian army was the final straw. Having ascertained that both the local population and the assorted *mirs* (rulers) of the neighboring statelets— Hunza, Nagar, and so forth—felt much the same way about Indian rule, the Scouts resolved to take matters into their own hands.

With the active encouragement of their twenty-four-year-old commanding officer, a lanky Scots major called William Brown, on the night of October 31 they staged what Brown called a coup d'état. Claiming the support of all the region's scattered peoples, the Scouts relieved Gilgit's Dogra governor of his authority, cut the telephone line to Srinagar, picketed all the main passes, found safekeeping for the region's few non-Muslims, and announced the formation of a provisional government. In a breathless telegram to the chief minister of Pakistan's North-West Frontier Province, Brown relayed the news: "Entire pro-Pakistan populace have overthrown Dogra regime." But this was misleading; according to the historian of the Scouts, Brown himself was "the only person in authority who had unequivocally declared in favour of Pakistan."[16] Others were toying with the idea of an independent confederation of Karakorum states, while most were just happy to have cast off the maharajah's claim to sovereignty and forestalled that of India.

For two weeks the fate of the region hung in the balance. Hunza and Nagar (north of Gilgit on the Chinese border) offered to accede to Pakistan, while Brown doggedly prepared the ground for the accession of Gilgit itself. India naturally suspected premeditation; it was claimed that, using Pakistan as a proxy, the British were up to their old game of geostrategic management by reserving for themselves a vantage point on the so-called roof of the world. But this scarcely tallied with Pakistan's dilatory response to Brown's appeals. Karachi was in a quandary. It was one thing to lend support to native Kashmiris in their struggle for a free Kashmir, quite another to endorse an outright renunciation of Jammu and Kashmir's integrity and accept the cession of a vast chunk of what was widely supposed to be its territory. The Gilgit populace might indeed be pro-Pakistan, but Karachi based its case on a still intact and unoccupied Jammu and Kashmir exercising its right to decide its future free of outside interference. A Pakistani acceptance of the cession of the Gilgit region would seem to undermine this. It would look as much like a piecemeal grab at the Dogra state as did the Indian occupation of the valley that Karachi was so bitterly contesting.

On November 16 a Pakistani representative finally flew into Gilgit to oversee the administration; two months later Brown was replaced as commander of the Gilgit Scouts by an Azad Kashmiri major. The status of the region continued unclear. Its peoples, having rejected Kashmir's rule, were not willing to be tucked under the wing of the fledgling Azad Kashmir state (i.e., the "liberated" areas of Poonch, Muzaffarabad, and the eastern end of the valley). They preferred Pakistan and would accept whatever temporary tutelage it felt able to offer pending a general settlement of Jammu and Kashmir's future. Anyway, winter was closing the passes and military operations were being wound down. According to Alastair Lamb, the forensic champion of the Pakistan case and bête noire of the Indian defense establishment, "The nature of the Kashmir war had, however, been changed fundamentally . . . it was impossible now to deny with any conviction that Pakistan had a legitimate interest in the Kashmir conflict which directly involved sectors of its sovereign territory."[17]

More obviously, a new and extremely challenging northern front had been opened in the Indo-Pak war; no longer was the conflict confined to just Poonch and the valley. In May 1948, as the snows receded, the Scouts marched out of Gilgit and, joining with Azad Kashmiri and tribal forces, turned left up the Indus River. Baltistan was taken and the only road from Srinagar to the Ladakhi capital, Leh, was severed. Ladakh itself looked doomed. Its monastic authorities, horrified at the prospect of being "liberated" by fanatically Muslim Pathans, consulted their oracles but were ill equipped to offer other than token resistance.

Happily, the lamas' resolve went untested. In the nick of time Ladakh was reinforced by another airlift of Indian troops, many of them Nepali Gurkhas. The conflict was taking on a pan-Himalayan complexion. After further heroics and heavy losses, in October and November 1948 Indian forces reclaimed the road from Leh down to the valley, although not Baltistan nor an inhospitable corner of northern Ladakh. These remained outside Indian control and, posing an ongoing threat to Ladakh's lifeline with the outside world, necessitated a heavy Indian troop presence along the length of the optimistically named Srinagar-Leh Highway.

By the end of 1948 an estimated ninety thousand Indian troops were stationed in Jammu and Kashmir. The numbers opposing them must also have been in five figures. And already the climate was taking as heavy a toll as the fighting. With altitudes of ten to thirteen thousand feet, temperatures that plunged below zero all year round, and a length of more than three hundred miles, the new front taxed the stamina and resources of both sides. Their respective tasks had become both harder and less certain. No longer was it just a question of expelling raiders from the valley or abetting freedom fighters in Poonch. The defection of the Gilgit region—what Pakistan was now vaguely calling "the Northern Areas" (of Pakistan? of Kashmir?)— had effectively split the state. It was not exactly a stalemate. The fighting continued throughout 1948 as the pro-Pakistan forces, augmented by regular troops, planned an offensive into Jammu, and the

Indians hammered away at Poonch and reclaimed the road to Leh. But neither side was prepared for the massive offensive now needed to dislodge the other completely. It was time, high time, to talk.

BACK IN OCTOBER 1947 when news of India's intervention had first broken, not the least of Jinnah's complaints had centered on New Delhi's reluctance to communicate. The Indian government had failed to inform Pakistan of the maharajah's accession until after it had been accepted, and had failed to give warning of the airlift of Indian troops until after it was under way. Both accession and intervention contravened the terms of Pakistan's standstill agreement with the maharajah, and neglecting to inform Pakistan of its proposed action was not how a fellow member of the Commonwealth was supposed to behave. Moreover, India's silence looked to Pakistan like duplicity. For if New Delhi was so certain that Pakistan was responsible for the tribal incursion—the reason given for both the accession and the intervention—why had it not cautioned Pakistan that intervention was imminent unless the raiders were recalled? Why too, after the intervention, was Nehru so reluctant to accept the advice of those who urged him to meet with Liaquat Ali Khan, his opposite number, to explain India's position and bring an end to the fighting?

With Nehru unwilling to make a move, it had fallen to India's governor-general to break the logjam. On November 1, 1947, Mountbatten flew to Lahore for talks with Jinnah. Mountbatten explained that the maharajah's appeal and India's lightning response had constituted an emergency situation. Srinagar had been under threat, its airport might at any minute have fallen to the raiders; the airlift of troops therefore had to go ahead immediately, with no time for consultation with Pakistan. Nehru had, though, found the time to alert the prime minister of Britain. In a communication dated October 25 (after the maharajah's appeal but before the airlift) he had told Attlee that India was actively considering military intervention but that such a move was not "designed in any way to influence the state to accede to India."[18] Evidently the accession, far from being a prerequisite for intervention, as Mountbatten maintained, was for

Nehru just the icing on the cake. It could, then, have been deferred and Pakistan could have been alerted.

Jinnah did not mince his words. He called the Indian fait accompli a clear case of "fraud and violence" and insisted that only a complete withdrawal of Indian troops could now redeem the situation. He also indicated that Pakistan would not object to a referendum in Junagadh if a similar poll could be held throughout Jammu and Kashmir—but not while Indian forces were in occupation of the valley and not while Sheikh Abdullah, supposedly India's quisling, was in the government. Only if both were removed would a free and fair plebiscite be possible.

Jinnah also objected to Mountbatten's suggestion that the whole matter be referred to the United Nations. The UN was something of an unknown quantity at the time. It was barely two years old, having celebrated its second anniversary on the day the maharajah issued his appeal to Delhi. It had no permanent headquarters and no track record in such disputes. Mountbatten nevertheless persevered. With neither India nor Pakistan prepared to compromise, a third party's involvement seemed to offer the only hope. Over several meetings in December 1947 he formulated an ingenious—possibly too ingenious—plan whereby both sides would embrace UN involvement, though for quite different reasons.

He convinced Liaquat Ali Khan that a plebiscite might indeed be the only way forward and that some form of UN supervision would be the best guarantee of it being conducted fairly. In assessing the prospects for such a plebiscite, the UN likely would also look into the status of Kashmir, the validity of the accession, and the role of the Indian military. Meanwhile, Mountbatten encouraged Nehru to refer the matter formally to the UN. This was to take the congenial (to India) form of a complaint about Pakistan's support for the "tribal invasion" and would be submitted under the terms of Article 35 of the UN's charter. The article entitled members to alert the Security Council to any situation "likely to endanger the maintenance of international peace," yet it gave the Council no right to impose a solution; all the Council could do was examine the situation and make suggestions for defusing it. India might thus register its plight as the injured party without exposing itself to any mandatory directives and with a fair chance that its complaint would be upheld. This might also deflect attention from the disputed nature of the accession, the proportionality or otherwise of India's intervention, and any other contentious matters that Pakistan might raise.

If this was indeed the gist of Mountbatten's scheme, it was well received. Alastair Lamb has likened it to the sort of arrangement favored by divorcing couples when, to satisfy the requirements of the law, one party agrees to be portrayed as the transgressor and the other as the aggrieved.[19] It was therefore not without an element of collusion that on January 1, 1948, an India seeking condemnation of Pakistan plus the withdrawal of its surrogate troops made a submission to the UN, and a Pakistan seeking the withdrawal of Indian troops as the prerequisite for a plebiscite coyly concurred.

Each side duly presented its case before the Security Council later in January 1948. But there events took an unexpected turn. The indictment of Pakistan's interference as delivered by India's spokesman was politely received but elicited no demand for a Pakistani withdrawal until three months later. On the other hand, with Britain and the United States as suspicious of Nehru's relations with the Soviets as of his actions in Kashmir, the Pakistani spokesman's five-hour denunciation of the maharajah's rule and of India's perfidy was received more favorably. A commission of inquiry, the UN Commission for India and Pakistan (UNCIP), was quickly set up and immediately got down to work. It would spend the next six months touring the region, verifying the facts of the dispute, offering advice, and exploring a variety of possible solutions. "Not only has the dispute been prolonged," complained India's Sardar Patel, "but the merits of our case have been completely lost in the interaction of power politics."[20]

It was not just the Cold War that was responsible for the frosty attitude toward New Delhi's case. In the course of 1948, events in Delhi had a significant bearing on international attitudes. On January 13, in the midst of the discussions at the UN, the ailing Mahatma Gandhi embarked on another fast. This, his last great protest, had nothing to do with the rights and wrongs of the Kashmir situation but everything to do with the ongoing plight of Muslims in India and of Hindus and Sikhs in Pakistan. With the two countries now as near to war as made no difference, rabid nationalists were more suspicious than ever of the loyalties of these minorities. In India and especially Delhi, the Rashtriya Swayamsevak Sangh (RSS), a youth "army" with a Hindu supremacist agenda and operating on what Nehru called "the strictest Nazi lines," denounced the Muslim "enemy within" and found enthusiastic support among the more embittered of the city's post-Partition refugees.[21]

The Congress Party responded with a resolution in which it reaffirmed its commitment to a secular India of "many religions and many races." But its current hostility toward Pakistan did not exactly bear this out. In retaliation for the Kashmir incursion, India was currently withholding Karachi's share of undivided India's military hardware plus some half a billion rupees owing to Pakistan from undivided India's sterling balance (that is, funds accumulated by India in the United Kingdom for services rendered during the world war). Feelings ran high, and the RSS zealots were placated neither by the anti-Pakistan statements of a Muslim such as Sheikh Abdullah nor by lofty talk from Nehru about Kashmir being an exemplar of India's multifaith credentials. In Delhi, Ajmer, and elsewhere, Muslims continued to be attacked, their mosques trashed, and their property appropriated. The Mahatma's fast was thus a plea for religious tolerance, for an end to the victimization of Muslims in India, and for fair treatment with regard to the resources owed to Pakistan.

If Nehru's secularism was of the head, Gandhi's was of the heart. The nonreligious Nehru opposed sectarian sentiment on principle, while the intensely devout Gandhi condemned it by example as incompatible with that spirit of humanity he believed common to all faiths. And as usual, Gandhi's tactic worked: The frail embodiment of India's freedom struggle got his way. Already perilously weak, after just five days he extracted the reassurances needed to end his fast; neither the government nor the nation could risk having the death of the country's redeemer on its hands. The government capitulated over the sterling funds owed to Pakistan, and even the RSS signed the all-party declaration promising that Muslims and their property would henceforth be respected.

Not everyone, though, was reconciled. Rogue elements connected to the RSS made no secret of their belief that Gandhi had "blackmailed" the government into "pandering to Muslims" and so betrayed the nation. By "nation" they actually meant the Hindu nation, and this at a time of war with Muslim Pakistan. Such evident "treachery" could not go unavenged. Within hours of ending his fast the apostle of nonviolence narrowly escaped the attentions of an inept bomber, and within days he was dead, shot at point-blank range by a Brahmin assassin called Nathuram Godse. A onetime member of the RSS, Godse was neither an impressionable underling nor a crazed maverick. Until the day of his execution he would insist that by his "patriotic" action he had rid the nation of a dangerous traitor.

The death of the Mahatma on January 30, 1948, shocked the world. When over the radio Nehru noted how "the light has gone out of our lives and there is darkness everywhere," he seemed to speak for all humanity. In the twentieth century perhaps only the shooting of President John F. Kennedy would attract more universal condemnation. In both cases, tributes to the man and grief at his loss were matched by horror over his death at the hands of a fellow countryman. Independence was supposed to consolidate nations; democratic accountability and liberal values were supposed to forestall violence. How could it have happened?

As the subcontinent's first postcolonial political assassination— the first in what would become a dismal record of such outrages—it particularly appalled South Asians. Pakistanis, though noting how the "Hindu nation" rhetoric of the RSS echoed the "Muslim nation" thesis beloved of the Muslim League, regretted the loss of Gandhi's bridge-building efforts and drew their own conclusions about India's commitment to sectarian equality. Indian revulsion went deeper. It reunited both government and people in condemnation and brought a strong reassertion of secular values. The RSS was banned and its leadership arrested; political parties that were sympathetic to it, including the Hindu Mahasabha, were discredited; and Nehru and Patel, whose differences over policy and tactics often mirrored those of Congress and the Mahasabha, were reconciled.

But the triumph of moderation was short-lived. A year later the ban on the RSS was lifted and its leaders released; its political affiliates eagerly reentered the electoral fray. Meanwhile, in Kashmir the fighting had resumed. At the UN the point scoring went on, and in the far-off but not forgotten princely state of Hyderabad matters edged toward a new crisis.

There the Islamist paramilitary Razakars, on one hand, and the Indian government, on the other, ratcheted up the pressure on the reclusive nizam. His existing standstill agreement with Delhi was little respected. The nizam's advisers toyed with referring the matter to the UN. Indians blockaded the delivery of essential supplies to the state; arms were nevertheless alleged to be reaching it.

Perhaps more crucially, in June 1948 Mountbatten stood down as India's governor-general. With both Kashmir and Hyderabad in turmoil, he departed the scene of his earlier triumphs with a brace of resounding failures and breathing a sigh of good riddance; the fate of the two most hotly contested of the princely states still rested in the balance. But as a result of Mountbatten's resignation, New Delhi was relieved of the cautionary counsels of another respected architect of independence, and by the same token the nizam's hopes of sympathy and support from Windsor, if not Whitehall, were effectively dashed. "With Mountbatten gone, it became easier for [Sardar] Patel to take decisive action," notes Ramachandra Guha. This Patel did on September 13, 1948. Following violent Congress-led demonstrations within the state and a draconian crackdown by the nizam's security forces, regular units of the Indian army rolled across the border heading for Hyderabad city. Euphemized as a "police action," the Indian offensive lasted just four days and was accounted a total success: the Razakars were routed and the nizam acceded to India. Several thousand, both combatants and noncombatants, lost their lives in the fighting, though far worse was the sectarian violence that followed. According to the official but never publicized Sunderlal Report, somewhere between twenty-seven thousand and forty thousand Muslims were massacred by their Hindu neighbors in retaliation for the earlier excesses of the Razakars.

Pakistan, though ignorant of these atrocities, would of course protest the accession. It claimed, not unreasonably, that the nizam had signed the Instrument of Accession under duress and that the document was therefore invalid, just like that signed by the maharajah of

Kashmir. Lest anyone think differently, for decades thereafter maps printed in Pakistan would show a gaping hole in the middle of peninsular India where the erstwhile state had been. But in reality the nizam had been no more enthusiastic about joining Pakistan than Kashmir's maharajah had been. Indian spokesmen had magnified Hyderabad's contacts with Karachi for their own purposes, and Jinnah had unwisely responded with occasional overtures designed principally to antagonize India. On one occasion he had famously declared that should Congress lay hands on the state, one hundred million Muslims "would rise as one man to defend the oldest Muslim dynasty in India." It was more bluster than threat; they had no interest in doing so, and they didn't.

Nor, as it happened, was Jinnah able to raise his own howl of protest over the "police action" in Hyderabad. Indeed, the Pakistani reaction in general was muted, as the whole nation was in mourning. This was not because of Hyderabad's fall but because of a far greater loss, for even as Indian troops crossed the border into Hyderabad, Jinnah lay dead in his Karachi residence, felled by a combination of cancer, pneumonia, and nicotine.

A Pakistan without its Quaid-i-Azam was even more bereft than an India without its Mahatma. Jinnah's reputation was unassailable, though his legacy was far from certain. While credited with having fathered a nation, created a state, and carved out a country, the Great Leader had exercised control of its affairs for little over a year. A constitution had still to be drawn up, a capital chosen, and policy directives determined. He can scarcely be blamed if the nation he fathered proved so prone to fragmentation, if the state he founded would so nearly fail, and if the country he carved out would so soon be carved up.

Jinnah had died in the night of September 11, 1948, less than two days before the Indian assault on Hyderabad began. Insofar as Karachi's incontrovertible tragedy deflected attention from New Delhi's controversial triumph, the news was not unwelcome in India. But whether the near coincidence of the two events was in fact pure chance has yet to be revealed. India's contingency plans for a military intervention in Hyderabad had been hatched as early as the previous March, although it seems unlikely that the actual invasion could have been mounted on just thirty-six hours' notice. On the other hand, Jinnah's worsening condition had been public knowledge since September 1, on which day he had been rushed from his hill station retreat to the gubernatorial residence in Karachi. This news of an impending crisis in Pakistan, if not the crisis itself, may well have triggered the buildup to the Indian takeover of Hyderabad.

THE MOVE ON HYDERABAD, though immensely popular in India, did nothing to bolster New Delhi's international bona fides with regard to Kashmir. UNCIP had now completed its inquiries and was flitting back and forth across the Atlantic while drawing up its proposals. A cease-fire was the obvious priority, and a resolution to that effect was adopted in August 1948. But with both sides intent on last-minute gains in the field, Liaquat Ali Khan prevaricated over guarantees regarding the plebiscite, while Nehru toyed with the idea of partitioning the state. Not until January 1, 1949, did the cease-fire become operative. The UNMOGIP was set up to monitor it, and the plebiscite was supposed to follow, although no date was set and no agreement reached about the removal of troops prior to its implementation.

Meanwhile, in Indian parlance the former princely state of Jammu and Kashmir became the Indian state of Jammu and Kashmir, with Azad Kashmir and the Pakistan-controlled Northern Areas being treated merely as temporarily alienated territories. All the former princely states that had opted for India were being absorbed into the constituent provinces (now known as states) of the Indian Union. Jammu and Kashmir's status was thus brought into conformity with them, despite the fact that its accession had yet to be endorsed by the plebiscite to which all were supposedly committed.

Nehru was still counting on the sheikh's popularity as India's best guarantee of a favorable plebiscite. He therefore stood by the sheikh when the latter's radical land reforms alienated Hindu opinion, especially in Jammu, and when his populist rhetoric further riled the maharajah. Though named *sadr-i-riyasat* (nominal head of state),

Maharajah Hari Singh was being so blatantly sidelined by both Nehru and the sheikh that he was beginning to regret his hasty accession. He therefore reminded Patel that the accession had in fact been provisional and that it was high time to negotiate a permanent settlement with all options on the table, including that of independence. This threatened the entire Indian position in Kashmir and at the UN, which was quite unacceptable; the maharajah must go. In May 1949 Sardar Patel advised him to take a holiday and, while away, to relinquish his role as Kashmir's head of state in favor of his eighteen-year-old son. Hari Singh took the hint and never again set foot in the state. His son, Karan Singh, also got the message. Thereafter he would prefer life as a Congress stalwart and avid student of Hindu scripture to that of a gadfly in Kashmir's constitutional ointment.

No sooner was one separatist tendency silenced, though, than another piped up in the formidable shape of Sheikh Sahib. To Nehru's dismay, the sheikh too seemed to be having second thoughts, and this despite recent concessions. For without giving an inch on the legitimacy of the maharajah's accession (and therefore India's sovereignty in Jammu and Kashmir), Nehru had accepted the sheikh's contention that Kashmiri opinion must be mollified by some recognition of the state's special status. Article 370 of India's 1950 constitution did just that. Jammu and Kashmir being as yet "not in a position to merge with India" (as the proposer of the article put it), the state was to have its own Constituent Assembly, its own flag, its own prime minister (other states had only chief ministers), and its own commercial tariffs. And though its people were to enjoy the rights of Indian citizens, it was not necessarily to be subject to the jurisdiction of India's supreme court. In effect, the state was being granted semi-autonomy. Its prime minister, the redoubtable sheikh himself as of 1949, had a free hand, and he had begun to play it.

In October 1951 the sheikh's popularity won him a thumping majority in elections to the state's constituent assembly. This should have been gratifying to Nehru, vindicating his long-standing confidence in his "twin." But it was not. For already the sheikh was, as Nehru saw it, "behaving in a most irresponsible manner." In fact, the Indian prime minister was becoming so exasperated with his Kashmiri counterpart as to complain that "the most difficult thing in life is what to do with one's friends." While on a visit to Washington back in 1948 the sheikh had apparently sounded out US representatives as to a possible declaration of Kashmiri independence. Nothing had come of this, nor of some desultory contacts with the leadership of Azad Kashmir. But when addressing the state's new constituent assembly, the sheikh revived these options, declaring that it was the assembly alone—not New Delhi—that would determine Jammu and Kashmir's relationships, whether with India, Pakistan, or neither. On the whole he still favored India, he said, but only if it remained true to Gandhi's legacy of sectarian harmony and the even-handed treatment of India's Muslims.

This emphasis on nondiscrimination was in part prompted by divisions within Jammu and Kashmir state. In Jammu the Praja Parishad, a party representing Jammu's Hindu majority, opposed the sheikh's socialist policies as much as it distrusted his Muslim sympathies. It looked back to the good old days of its Dogra rulers and, finding no champion in young Karan Singh, turned increasingly to Hindu sympathizers in the rest of India. Foremost among these was the Jan Sangh, an emphatically Hindu party newly formed by Dr. Shyama Prasad Mookherjee in the wake of Gandhi's assassination and the disgrace of the RSS. Mookherjee, a venerable Bengali and once of the Hindu Mahasabha, needed an emotive issue over which to improve his party's electoral standing. Kashmir provided it. He took Nehru to task over the Indian military's failure to secure all of Jammu and Kashmir and over the constitutional indulgence that left the state virtually autonomous under Sheikh Abdullah as its "king of kings." Jammu wanted only to be integrated with the rest of India. How could any Indian patriot not sympathize?

Rising to his theme, and with his supporters now taking to the streets in Delhi as well as Jammu, Mookherjee visited the state in 1952 and then again in 1953. On the first occasion he condemned the sheikh's National Conference, praised the loyalty of the Praja Parishad, and vowed to secure the release of those of its activists who had been arrested. On the second visit he was himself arrested and detained in a Srinagar jail. There, not helped by the conditions, he died of a heart attack and pleurisy. The Hindu cause had its first distinguished martyr. Vast processions accompanied his obsequies. Threats like those leveled at Gandhi during his final fast were made against both the sheikh and Nehru. Clearly the noncommunal India that Abdullah had made a prerequisite for Jammu and Kashmir's full accession had yet to materialize.

Coincidentally, in April 1953, the sheikh welcomed to the valley Adlai Stevenson, governor of Illinois and US presidential candidate. Stevenson was on vacation but nevertheless spent several hours closeted with the sheikh. It was assumed that Kashmir's future was discussed, though no explanation was forthcoming. Nehru again wrung his hands and wished himself rid of his troublesome friend.

Relief came three months later when the post-Mookherjee disturbances were at their peak. On August 8 the sheikh was ousted, apparently by a pro-India faction within his own party, and then immediately arrested. Nehru claimed to know nothing about it, but neither did he go rushing to his old friend's rescue this time. Save for brief tastes of freedom in 1958 and 1964, the sheikh would remain in detention for the next twenty-two years. And though the charges against him varied, none was ever proven.

To Kashmiris, the plight of the sheikh seemed analogous to their own. They too were India's captives and the valley was their prison. Makeshift arguments advanced by Indian spokesmen were treated with scorn. With the maharajah now persona non grata and the sheikh behind bars, the twin pillars on which the Indian case for incorporation rested lay at the bottom of Srinagar's Dal Lake. The contention that the need for a plebiscite had been eliminated by a subsequent vote of the Jammu and Kashmir constituent assembly in favor of integration was laughable. In Kashmiri eyes its supporters were little better than traitors. The occupying Indian troops remained in the valley, Pakistan clung to Azad Kashmir and the Northern Areas, the imprisoned sheikh was as popular as ever, the UN proposals lay gathering dust, and UNMOGIP merely monitored violations of the cease-fire line. "Few UN forces can have spent so much effort over so many years to so little purpose," writes journalist Andrew Whitehead.[22] Even as the tourists kept coming and investment trickled in, Kashmir festered.

In India and Pakistan the issue refused to go away. But with both countries facing formidable obstacles to national integration elsewhere, efforts to resolve the conflict were sporadic and often hostage to domestic affairs. From the nation building of the 1950s and early 1960s India and Pakistan would emerge as two very different states, and it was these differences—constitutional, international, and psychological—that would propel Kashmir back to the top of the South Asian agenda and set both nations on a new collision course.

4

PAST
CONDITIONAL

HISTORICAL JUDGMENTS ARE NOTORIOUSLY UNRELIABLE; often they say more about the time in which they are made than about the past. By the 1980s the period in India known as the Nehru years (1947–64) was reckoned to have been a nation-building success, while the Ayub Khan years in Pakistan (1958–69) were accounted a calamitous precedent. Yet by the end of the century it was the other way around: Nehru's "years of hope and achievement" were being portrayed instead as "wasted years," and the Ayub era was hailed as Pakistan's "golden decade." A "shining India" poised to dazzle the world with its economic performance was wondering why it had taken half a century to get there, while a guttering Pakistan looked back with near nostalgia to the promise and comparative prosperity that had illuminated its adolescence.

Contemporary history, with its reliance on prolific comment but restricted-access documentation, can be made to say pretty much what one wants. All that can be safely ventured with respect to the Nehru and Ayub years is that, at the time, it is likely that neither matched up to any of the above characterizations. Wafts of doubt obscured their wider import. Images of the period convey as much uncertainty as confidence; their never-bright shades of Pakistani green

103

and Indian vermillion have been touched up by posterity's preference for hard acrylic glosses.

In Pakistan, despite the fervor engendered by statehood, there were grounds for gloom right from the start. In fact, the country's first crisis of confidence came almost immediately and, by furnishing a pretext for the Ayub era, contributed to the later contest over that era's significance. Few if any new nations can have found the odds so heavily stacked against them. To the obvious challenges—those of agreeing on a constitution, forging an administration, accommodating a deluge of refugees, bridging the more than nine hundred miles that divided the two halves of the country, integrating peoples sharing neither ethnicity nor language, conciliating elites unaccustomed to accountability, planning a modern economy, balancing a hopelessly lopsided budget, and conducting a war with India—was added the still greater conundrum of defining what the new nation actually stood for.

Even Jinnah seems to have had no clear vision of what sort of state Pakistan should aspire to be. Proclaimed as a haven and homeland for South Asia's "Muslim nation," the country would have been swamped had all sixty million of India's Muslims moved there. Hence no appeal for such an exodus had been issued. On the contrary, in 1950 a pact with India was belatedly signed that discouraged migration, both of Muslims into Pakistan and of non-Muslims out of Pakistan. Luckily, in the immediate aftermath of Partition only a fraction of India's Muslims had actually crossed the border. But of Pakistan's slightly smaller non-Muslim community nearly all of those in its western wing had removed to India.

Since its eastern wing (in which Hindus still made up around 18 percent of the population) was habitually discounted by Pakistan's leadership, this rather upset the equilibrium whereby one country would treat its main minority—Muslims in India, Hindus in Pakistan— as "hostages" for the fair treatment of its outnumbered brethren in the other. It also raised a question mark over what Jinnah had intended in his much quoted speech on the eve of independence about religion having "nothing to do with the business of the state" ("You are free to go to your temples . . . your mosques or to any other place of worship . . . we are all citizens and equal citizens of one State"). Was he indicating that an inclusive Pakistan was to be as doctrinally neutral as Nehru's India? Or was he simply responding to the needs of the moment by reassuring the Hindu community that there was no need for them to leave? In later speeches he took a more partisan line, praising the Quran as a comprehensive guide to all human activity and referring to Pakistan's future as that of "a truly great Islamic state." He may have experienced a change of heart; more probably he was just glossing the obvious—that, Pakistanis being mostly Muslims, the Quran must be honored, and that the state could be described as Islamic in the general sense in which the British Isles, say, were Christian. And even supposing he had finally come around to the idea that the state must actually privilege Islam, what form should an Islam-based state take?

Jinnah himself, a Shi'ite by birth but decidedly Westernized in his tastes and "famously ambivalent about his understanding of the relationship between Islam and politics," offered no answer to this question.[1] Nor, seemingly, did anyone else. According to Mazar Ali Khan, a distinguished Pakistani journalist (and the father of another, Tariq Ali), sometime in the late 1960s the question received a public airing. A. K. Brohi, the lawyer who would become the "midnight counselor" to President Zia ul-Haq, placed an advertisement in the Pakistan press: "To anyone who could derive from the teachings of Quran a pattern for a constitution for Pakistan he would give a prize of rupees 5,000. This was when 5,000 meant something—that is before heroin [fueled inflation]. But nobody did. I'm no scholar of Islam but this much I know: Islamic teachings offer nothing which could be read as a constitutional blueprint or a pattern for the government of a country."[2]

If anything, Quranic exegesis suggests that an Islamic nation-state is a contradiction in terms. Sovereignty lies with Allah; laws are preordained by the sharia, the interpretation of which rests with the scholarly ulama. If there is to be a role for the masses and their legislating representatives, this sovereignty would have to have been devolved to the people by some divine dispensation, and, even then, the recipient of this sovereignty is said to be the *umma* of *dar-ul-Islam,* or the worldwide Muslim community, a supranational entity that transcends all lesser ethnic, territorial, and political loyalties.[3] "[The] uncertainties that stemmed from conflicting perceptions of Pakistan's identity as a nation-state defined by territorial borders and as a Muslim state created in opposition to territorial nationalism" were not about to go away, as Farzana Shaikh notes.[4] Islam, instead of cementing Pakistan's integration, would prove highly divisive.

Jinnah and the Muslim League had certainly established a state for over half of British India's Muslims, yet Muslim doctrine, when not undermining that state's legitimacy, directed its subjects to look beyond national frontiers and to engage in the struggles of the wider *dar-ul-Islam* in a spirit of brotherhood. Hence intervention in Kashmir, whether by warlike volunteers or the government, was as much about fulfilling a religious duty as about securing more territory for Pakistan; the same goes with respect to confrontation with India over any perceived injustices inflicted on its Muslim minority. It is such contradictions between the universal Islam of Quranic orthodoxy and the Islamic nationalism of the Muslim League that led Shaikh, writing in 2009, to identify the search for a consensus about the meaning of Islam as "the cancer that threatens Pakistan's body politic."[5]

The problem had surfaced within weeks of Partition when in 1947 Pakistan's Constituent Assembly had met to formulate a constitution. Quranic reasoning with its emphasis on the influential role of the scholarly ulama and its ambivalence about democratic sovereignty had previously persuaded doctrinally based parties such as the Jamaat-e-Islami to oppose the League's demand for a sovereign Pakistan. They were nevertheless keen to be consulted now that Pakistan was a reality. Well represented within the provincial assemblies and the Constituent Assembly, they would press hard for constitutional acknowledgment of Islam's role and for the ulama's right to advise on government policy.

The Muslim League, on the other hand, was at a considerable disadvantage. Unlike the Congress Party in India, it lacked organizational and ideological cohesion and had been an effective force for barely a decade. At the provincial level, it had swept to power only in 1946, when the prospect of imminent independence had brought well-entrenched power brokers in Punjab, Sind, the NWFP, and East Bengal flocking to its standard. To them, the League was essentially a single-issue party, and once that issue—that is, Pakistan—had been won, there was little to hold them together. Particularisms of language, ethnicity, and social organization, plus competition for jobs and investment, reasserted themselves. The League found itself with formidable opponents within its own ranks.

The League's national leadership was at a further disadvantage in that it lacked an obvious power base in Pakistan. The arena in which Jinnah, Liaquat Ali Khan, and most of the League's other leading lights had come to prominence had been the All-India Muslim League, whose roots lay not in those regions in the northwest and Bengal that now constituted Pakistan but in India itself, especially UP, the Central Provinces, Bombay, and Calcutta. To command support within Pakistan's Constituent Assembly and the administration, the League's central leadership was therefore obliged to conciliate not only the Islamic parties and various regional parties but also its own provincial leaderships.

Had Jinnah lived, his vision for Pakistan might have crystallized. His stature might then have ensured nationwide acceptance for whatever he ordained. As it was, his legacy was sufficiently ambiguous merely to fuel contention. As prime minister and, after Jinnah's death, in effect president, Liaquat Ali Khan assumed the reins of power and the role of executor for the Quaid-i-Azam's legacy. He too, while acknowledging the supremacy of Islam, continued to insist that the constitution be based on the delegation of sovereignty to the people. This "naturally eliminates any danger of the establishment of a theocracy," according to the Basic Objectives Resolution, adopted in 1949 as a framework for the constitution. But the objectives included no mention of secularism as such and declared that the state should be Islamic, democratic, and federal (the last being a reassertion of Jinnah's pre-Partition preference for provincial autonomy). The secular-minded therefore saw the objectives as a victory for the Islamic parties, and the resolution was passed only on the understanding that new elections to the provincial assemblies would be held. These took place in 1952 and, though based on a restricted franchise, did nothing either to ease the central government's worries or to diminish the legitimacy of the new provincial assemblies as against that of the unchanged national Constituent Assembly.

To succeed Pakistan's last British commander in chief, Liaquat appointed a like-minded general, the pipe-smoking Ayub Khan. Both men cultivated friendly relations with the United States, whose interest in Pakistan as a front-line state on the periphery of the Soviet Union promised more substantial dividends than anything on offer from the cash-strapped United Kingdom. Washington, though, was slow to respond, and barely two years into his rule, on October 16, 1951, while addressing a public meeting in Rawalpindi, Liaquat Ali Khan, like Jinnah, was lost to the cause, assassinated by a hired gunman who was himself killed in the hail of bullets that followed. The Martyr of the Nation duly joined the Great Leader in Pakistan's founding mythology, but it was a measure of the country's insecurity that the assassin's paymasters were never identified. Possibly they objected to Liaquat's US bias, possibly they feared that he was about to reverse it, or just as possibly they were serving some domestic interest that no one cared to probe too deeply.

Twice orphaned, still without a constitution, still without most of Jammu and Kashmir, and with trouble already brewing in its eastern wing, by 1952 the infant dominion looked doomed to the disillusionment predicted for it by India's skeptics. In New Delhi, Nehru's Congress, buoyed by a resounding victory in the first national elections, ruled unchallenged, but in Karachi factionalism and corruption discredited the League's leadership and undermined the administration. As a historian wrote, "It is not surprising that Pakistan had six prime ministers and one commander-in-chief in eight years (1950–58) whereas in the same period India had one prime minister and six commanders-in-chief."[6] The institutional balance of power was already shifting decisively north, away from the political maneuvering in Karachi to the shady swards of the military cantonments in Rawalpindi. In 1951 a bureaucrat with military connections took over as governor-general, and in 1953 another, the former ambassador to the United States, was installed as prime minister. Although neither had ever stood for election, their representative credentials were not that much worse than those of Constituent Assembly members who had been indirectly chosen by the provincial assemblies, themselves elected on a limited franchise back in 1946 when Pakistan was just an exciting slogan. The Constituent Assembly, no more representative than it was sovereign, thus was doubly vulnerable.[7]

Democratic representation, however tenuous, nevertheless offered the best avenue for the redress of regional disputes. These were many and ranged from open revolt in Balochistan and resentment of the immigrant *muhajirs* from India who were swamping Sind to a mischievous pogrom in Punjab (it was directed at members of the Ahmadi community, followers of a nineteenth-century quasi-prophet whom the orthodox regarded as heretical). No grievances, though, were more acute than those being voiced amid the tangled rivers and the teeming fields of distant East Bengal.

WITH A POPULATION EQUAL TO that of all Pakistan's other provinces combined, East Bengal ought to have been calling the shots. Additionally, its jute industry was Pakistan's main source of foreign earnings; indeed, in the early 1950s the industry was enjoying something of a bonanza thanks to the high demand for hessian by the Western allies fighting in Korea (it was used, among other things, for sandbags). Yet East Bengalis were enjoying none of the benefits. They barely figured in Pakistan's armed forces or its civil service, and in the administration and judiciary they were represented by Westernized luminaries such as the mercurial Calcutta politician Husayn Shaheed Suhrawardy and Khwaja Nazimuddin, a relative of the former nawab of Dhaka who had succeeded Jinnah as governor-general. Public services were almost nonexistent, and any investment, notably in jute processing, came in the form of concessions to foreign firms. The typically poor farmers and sharecroppers of the province were no better off under West Pakistan's colonial-style rule than they had been in their rural slum under the British. Their only strength lay in their superior numbers and their marked politicization, which various parties, Islamist, peasant, and Communist, strove to mobilize.

In 1950 this simmering resentment found a soft target in East Bengal's still substantial Hindu community. Some Hindus—landowners, shopkeepers, moneylenders, and professionals—had decided to stay put in 1947, and their example had been followed by the larger and more widely dispersed underclass of low-caste and casteless Hindus. Heightened in part by communal tension over Kashmir, popular hostility toward the Hindu elite now turned into resentment of all Hindus. East Bengali Hindus of any class were seen as scapegoats for the province's essentially social and industrial grievances. Official sanction for this anti-Hindu sentiment came in the form of legislation over the size of landholdings and the criteria for public employment, both of which discriminated against Hindus. Harassment and the looting of Hindu properties followed, engendering widespread fear and the first major exodus across the still ill-defined frontier into India.

The effect was instantly apparent in Calcutta, India's largest city. Taya Zinkin, now a reporter working for the *Manchester Guardian,* watched as, "suddenly, inexplicably, at the beginning of 1950, what had been a slow and steady trickle of refugees from East Bengal began to swell into a stream. They were coming from Khulna across the delta, a district in East Bengal with a Hindu majority, only twenty-five miles from Calcutta and as difficult to cordon off as one Berlin from another."[8] The Indian sense of outrage was heightened when a visit to East Bengal by the chief minister of West Bengal prompted a general riot in Dhaka. More Hindu properties were ransacked and some four hundred people lost their lives. Retribution came swiftly. In West Bengal several thousand Muslim men, women, and children, many of whom had fled to Calcutta from riot-torn Bihar in 1946, were massacred by Mahasabha-led zealots. "I had seen horror in plenty, in Spain at the beginning of the civil war, above all in Delhi at Partition, but never before had I seen such bestiality," wrote Zinkin after picking her way through the mangled corpses in the killing yards of Howrah.[9] It was Partition's madness all over again. So much for the hostage theory, whereby fair treatment of one nation's minority would be seen as a safeguard for fair treatment of the other nation's minority. On both sides of the border, the vernacular press carried demands for war. United in shock, Nehru and Liaquat Ali Khan promised inquiries and confidence-building measures.

Such conciliatory gestures from Pakistan's power brokers in Karachi did nothing to endear them to their East Bengali subjects. Nor did their centralizing tendencies, which were displayed over the matter of a national language. More than relations with India or contortions over Islam, it was this purely domestic issue that would expose the fragility of Pakistan. Bengalis spoke Bengali, a medium with a cultural pedigree second to none and that, given East Bengal's numerical superiority, was spoken by more Pakistanis than any other language. It was, though, incomprehensible to speakers of Punjabi, Sindi, Pashtu, and the other tongues of West Pakistan. It was therefore deemed unsuitable as the national language. Jinnah had said as much himself when in 1948 he had decreed that Pakistan's official language must be Urdu. Protesters had immediately taken to the streets in Dhaka; for once the Quaid-i-Azam had been happy to leave the final decision to the deadlocked Constituent Assembly.

Urdu was scarcely any more popular in the provinces of Pakistan's western wing. Originally the hybrid lingua franca of the Mughal army, it was written in a suitably Islamic script and had since been enriched by writers and poets. But in pre-Partition India it had been the native tongue principally of the urban Muslim elite. Its adoption for national purposes of education and administration would therefore empower those *muhajirs* who had migrated from such rarefied milieux, a group that included most of the League's leadership.

Beloved of the Karachi bureaucrats, Urdu was further resented in East Bengal on account of its association with the court of Dhaka's erstwhile nawabs. Typical of this conservative East Bengali elite was the urbane Khwaja Nazimuddin, who, having swapped the governor-generalship for the prime ministership, in 1952 confirmed in Dhaka that Urdu was indeed to be the national language. The news sparked a furor. Dhaka's students called a general strike, which was supported by various popular groups including the newly formed Awami League. When the demonstrations threatened to get out of hand, the government panicked and the police were ordered to open fire. Four students were killed in the fracas, many were injured, and the army had to be called in to restore normality. It was a harbinger of things to come. "The Dhaka killings"—a label denied to the earlier slaughter of Hindus and reserved exclusively for this comparatively modest affair involving Bengali nationalism—"sealed the League's fate in east Bengal."[10] The killings also signaled the beginning of the province's second freedom struggle and would provide the future Bangladesh with its first martyrs.

Provincial elections in East Bengal, postponed in 1952 because of the language riots, were eventually held in 1954. The results were no less dramatic for being wholly predictable. A variety of left-leaning parties dominated by the Awami League swept to power, while the Muslim League limped away with just ten seats out of more than three hundred. Among the losers were the entire Bengali contingent in the Constituent Assembly in Karachi. The victors then formed a United Front government and immediately demanded the resignation of these Constituent Assembly members, a move that would end the League's dominance in the highest institution in the land.

If a state without a constitution can be said to face a constitutional crisis, this was it. East Bengal was finally throwing its demographic weight onto the scales. More than half of Pakistan's citizens, living in its most inaccessible province, were opposed to the priorities, policies, and constitutional proposals of the central government. Dhaka and Karachi were on a collision course.[11]

The collision was averted only by the suspension of East Bengal's new government and the imposition of direct rule. Serious ethnic conflict in the jute mills provided a pretext, as did the indiscreet comments of Fazul Huq, the United Front's octogenarian leader, who had confided to eager Indian listeners his regrets over the partitioning of Bengal and his hopes for East Bengal's independence. This was treason in Pakistani eyes. With the approval of Commander in Chief Ayub Khan, General Iskander Mirza, a hard-line former army defense secretary, was dispatched to Dhaka as governor. Mirza immediately prorogued the new assembly and placed the province under governor's rule, an expedient available under the British-legislated Government of India Act of 1935, which, in the absence of a new constitution, still applied. More than a thousand people were arrested, including the young Awami League activist Mujibur Rahman. Public debate was quashed. What Bengalis ridiculed as West Pakistan's "chocolate Raj" was adopting the strong-arm tactics of its pale-skinned predecessor.

In the light of these events, politicians of every hue began to fear for their authority, and none more so than those in the Constituent Assembly in Karachi. Exposed as less representative than ever, the assembly sought to forestall its own suspension by reining in the powers of the governor-general. This merely precipitated the inevitable. Plotted in a London hotel room, the decisive coup of October 1954 was consummated in another bedroom, that of the ailing governor-general. Apparently in an agony of backache at the time, the governor-general lay wrapped in a sheet and rolling on the floor. "He was bursting with rage, emitting volleys of abuse, which, luckily, no one understood," Ayub Khan wrote later.[12] Mirza and Ayub, acting in concert, urged a reconciliation between the governor-general and the fearful prime minister. But this, it transpired, could be achieved only by the dissolution of the assembly. According to Ayub, he was then invited to take over the reins of state himself. He refused. The assembly was dissolved regardless. An emergency government was formed with both Mirza and Ayub in its cabinet, and a new Constituent Assembly was swiftly selected by the lately installed provincial assemblies. Under orders to expedite the long-awaited constitution, it got down to business immediately.

In 1955, Mirza, who had by now relinquished the governorship of East Bengal, himself replaced the ailing governor-general. To accommodate the demands of the East Bengalis he announced the formation of a bipartite Pakistan: East Bengal would constitute one unit, as East Pakistan, and all the remaining provinces would be grouped together in another unit, as West Pakistan. Known as the "one-unit scheme," it won the support of influential Bengalis such as Suhrawardy, who in 1956 served as prime minister. But it encountered strong opposition from the downgraded provinces of West Pakistan and in particular from Punjab, which was much the largest and most assertive of these.

Meanwhile, goaded into action by the junta of bureaucrats and generals, the new Constituent Assembly produced in nine months what its predecessor had failed to deliver in nine years. The country's first constitution, promulgated in 1956, declared Pakistan "an Islamic republic" yet did little to substantiate its Islamic credentials. The governor-general was replaced by a president, which meant that Mirza merely changed his ceremonial dress. National elections were promised, though never held. And the Constituent Assembly simply became the National Assembly. Prime ministers appointed by it came and went. There were four in as many years, most of them nominees of President Mirza and his associates. "The whole situation was becoming curiouser and curiouser," recalled Ayub Khan, pretending to be as bemused as Alice in Wonderland.[13]

In West Pakistan, squabbles between remnants of the Muslim League and various other parties over control of their "one unit" turned first vicious and then violent, as each formed their own militias. In Karachi the cavalcade of prime ministers meant that a third of the assembly's members now held cabinet rank, and in Dhaka governors were being dismissed and administrations toppled with a rapidity that even contemporaries found confusing. Matters there reached a climax when in September 1958, during a second brawl in the East Bengal provincial assembly, the deputy speaker was felled by a missile, said to have been either a desktop or a chair. He died as a result. The province's military authorities thereupon recommended armed intervention; otherwise, it was claimed, the province would dissolve into chaos. Meanwhile, a similar request had come from Balochistan, at the opposite extremity of the country, where the khan of Kalat, a hereditary leader, had hoisted his ancestral standard in an apparent bid for autonomy. "The hour had struck," recalled Ayub Khan. "The responsibility could no longer be put off." It was time for what he liked to call "the revolution."[14]

When the trouble erupted, the commander in chief happened to be enjoying a spot of fishing in Nagar, one of the mountain statelets that made up the Northern Areas. He returned to Rawalpindi and then took the train for Karachi. President Mirza, he would later claim, had already decided that the political chaos must be ended. Pakistan was demonstrably unready for democracy. Assailed from within and without, and with even the armed forces in danger of being infected by the strife, the country's very survival was in jeopardy. A period of stability was needed, and the army alone could guarantee it. Of all the institutions of state only the army had emerged from the aftermath of Partition in a functional form. It was a source of stability and pride in the western provinces, from which it was recruited, and it was as yet untainted by the political chaos. To many it seemed more responsible and no less representative than the politicians.

On October 7, 1958, after another round of ministerial musical chairs in Karachi, it was not the hour that struck, as per Ayub Khan's diagnosis, but the generals. President Mirza and Commander in Chief Ayub abrogated the two-year-old constitution, proclaimed martial law throughout both units of the country, dismissed all the assemblies, and named Ayub himself as chief martial law administrator. Troops moved into Balochistan. More took over the nation's seaports and airports, radio and telegraph stations. Political parties were banned, the press was muzzled, and the judiciary washed its hands of responsibility under a recently formulated doctrine of necessity—"that which otherwise is not lawful, necessity makes lawful," according to the courts. There was almost no opposition. Relief was more in evidence than outrage. The country's first flirtation with representative government was over, "and thus began [its] long experiment with autocracy and oligarchy, with democratic tendencies bursting through from time to time."[15]

In a matter of weeks it appeared that the responsibility that could no longer be put off could not amicably be shared either: the hatchet-faced Mirza was put on a plane to London for a long and comfortable retirement. To this happy dumping ground, others—presidents, prime ministers, generals, and dissidents—would follow him over the years. According to Ayub, Mirza had been intriguing behind his back and had "got cold feet"; he favored a speedier return to civilian rule than Ayub thought advisable. One man was thinking in terms of days, while the other's time frame was years. The years won.[16] Surrounded by a group of more amenable associates, among them a still floppy-haired Zulfikar Ali Bhutto (the son of Junagadh's last dewan), Ayub Khan began his controversial decade in power.

COME THE FIFTIETH ANNIVERSARY of independence in 1997, the Indian political scientist Sunil Khilnani would mark the occasion with an incisive retrospective entitled *The Idea of India*. Seven years later Stephen Philip Cohen, an American specialist, followed suit with *The Idea of Pakistan*. Both works reexamine the formative eras of, respectively, Nehru and Ayub Khan, and both have been highly acclaimed. Neither is a comparative study, but they may perhaps be juxtaposed. It might, for instance, be thought significant that while an Indian academic took on India, it fell to an American academic to dissect Pakistan. Of more immediate relevance is the revisionist rigor of the India book compared to the alarmist tone of the Pakistan book. Khilnani kicks off with fifty pages on the novelty and importance of Indian democracy, followed by chapters on the economy, urbanization, and Indian identity. The nature of this Indian identity is found to be contentious, but there is no doubting its centrality, nor that of the state as the keel of India's stability. The country's trajectory is revealed as a steady, if ponderous, progression.

Cohen is much more cautious. His chapter titles—"The Army's Pakistan," "Political Pakistan," "Islamic Pakistan," "Regionalism and Separatism"— read like a checklist of unresolved issues. They hint at repetitious crises and profound uncertainty about the very concept of Pakistan. Though no doomsaying Jeremiah, Cohen addresses the proposition that Pakistan, "the first post–World War II state to break up," is now slated to become the next "failed state."[17] Five types of failure are offered; Pakistan is found to conform to four of them. Even while Cohen was writing the book, he says, Pakistan "was thought to be on the verge of collapse or rogue status."[18] Thus while India's ailments invite forensic diagnosis, Pakistan's plight cries out for the defibrillator. It was ever so. Beset by a bipartite configuration, an assertive military tradition, ambivalence over the role of Islam, and a persecution complex with respect to its Indian sibling, Karachi was struggling from infancy. Partition had been no more even-handed in doling out the prospective health risks than it had been in divvying up the princely states.

Back in 1958 nowhere was Pakistan's conspicuous failure as an operational democracy more cruelly exposed than in neighboring

India. Both new nations had had to face identical challenges. Constitutions had to be drawn up, social injustices of caste/class and gender redressed, nationwide elections held on a universal franchise, economic plans formulated, international postures adopted, and fissiparous tendencies contained. Yet while Pakistan had failed on nearly all counts, India, despite its far more daunting scale, could claim a reasonable degree of success.

The credit for this is rightly given to the vision, energy, and political skills of a Westernized intellectual in long coat and tight cotton leggings, Jawaharlal Nehru. Pakistan had lost both Jinnah and Liaquat in its first five years. India had lost Mahatma Gandhi and then Sardar Patel (the latter to natural causes in 1950). Nehru alone remained. An unassailable symbol of the freedom struggle, he came to embody the Indian nation's ambitious transformation. Unlike Jinnah, from both instinct and study he knew the sort of country he wanted and insisted that it was this "idea of India" that would prevail. Gandhi and Patel were widely mourned, but their deaths had simplified matters by removing two focal figures whose visions had often conflicted with Nehru's. Gandhi's utopian dream of a self-sufficient village-based economy had led him to suggest dispensing with all instruments of state power and disbanding even the Congress Party. Conversely, Patel had had little patience with particularist sensibilities and seemed to favor an India that was authoritarian, conservative, and unapologetically Hindu, not far removed from that promoted by the ultranationalists of the Mahasabha and Jan Sangh. Neither man was without disciples and their legacies would linger on, but they would have to contend with Nehru's vision of a centralized, egalitarian, secular, and socialist republic.

These properties were enshrined in the Indian constitution, which Ramachandra Guha, in a chapter entitled "Ideas of India," reckons "probably the longest in the world."[19] Drafted by numerous committees and debated at length in a Constituent Assembly that was no more representative than that in Pakistan, the constitution's 395 articles and eight schedules passed into law on January 26, 1950. Nehru's championship, Patel's negotiating skills, and the well-drilled

Congress majority in the assembly had ensured a smooth passage. The Indian Union had become the Republic of India and the princely states had been swept under its multicolored carpet.

In a land with little in the way of indigenous constitutional precedents, such an elaborate document was both a novelty and a source of pride. It was not, though, without inconsistency. "Democracy in India is only a top dressing on an Indian soil, which is essentially undemocratic," warned Dr. B. R. Ambedkar, the leader of India's Dalits (then known as untouchables or *harijans*), who was also the legal brain that had undertaken much of the constitution's actual drafting.[20] Drawing on the constitutions of western Europe and North America, it guaranteed equal rights to every individual—but this in a society that traditionally discounted individualism and was about as unequal as could be.

Other contradictions followed from this. Khilnani notes two. One was a tension over citizenship. All Indians were equal in theory, but because in practice so many were victims of the rankest discrimination, a special schedule stipulated affirmative action for the most disadvantaged castes and communities. This was entirely laudable, yet by reserving a quota of educational places and public service jobs exclusively for, say, Dalits, the constitution empowered an entire community rather than its individual members. To qualify, therefore, communities were well advised to stress their solidarity, which led to fierce intercommunity competition and bloc votes being traded for promises of "scheduled status." "The Constitution, and the politics it sanctioned, thus reinforced community identities rather than sustaining a sense of common citizenship based on individual rights."[21]

The other tension noted by Khilnani was that between the powers awarded to the central government and those awarded to the provincial (now state) governments. Naturally, certain specified subjects were reserved to each; defense, for instance, was the responsibility of the center and sales taxes the responsibility of the states. A few areas, such as education, agriculture, and land redistribution, were shared, the center having directive powers but the states being responsible for implementation. This led to the well-founded suspicion that landowning interests might piously uphold redistributive measures in Parliament confident in the knowledge that they would be diluted or deferred at the state level.

But more so than in other federal constitutions, the authority of the center was to be paramount. Tucked away as Article 365, the central government reserved to itself in the person of the republic's president the right to suspend any state government on the advice of its governor, himself a central appointee. This decidedly authoritarian provision, though appropriate enough to the British Raj, which had formulated it, would be much resented when invoked to browbeat or topple democratically mandated state governments that declined to toe the central government's line. In practice federalism seemed more a sop to regional sentiment than a brake on the exercise of central authority.

Arming the state with more powers than seemed strictly necessary was thought essential if the redress of inequalities and the radical reform of the economy were not to be stalled. It was no less vital in terms of containing dissent and promoting the integration of what was surely the world's most excessively compartmentalized nation. Such was the agglomeration of different religions, castes, tribes, cultures, language groups, and colonial enclaves that many international observers doubted the feasibility of an Indian nation. The franchise gave to all a say, but to very few did it give a taste of power. The recalcitrant and the disenchanted would readily resort to force, and the government would respond in kind. More political strife was experienced, and far more lives lost, in Nehru's India than in Ayub's Pakistan. Integration was not for the fainthearted.

In the case of religion, divisive rivalries were supposed to have been blunted by Nehru's insistence on secularism. The state was not anti-religion but doctrinally neutral. Sikhs, Muslims, animists, Christians, Parsees, Jews, and so on were to enjoy the same religious freedoms as the more than 80 percent of the population who considered themselves Hindus. But with Hindus and Muslims on both sides of the Bengal border massacring each other even as the constitution came into force in 1950, and with the Kashmir issue still far from resolved, many non-Muslims demanded a more partisan attitude from their leaders. Parties such as the (Hindu) Jan Sangh and the (Sikh) Akali Dal would pander to such sentiments and show scant respect for the secular sensibilities of Nehru's Congress. From Kashmir to Kerala, Bengal to Gujarat, outbreaks of so-called communal violence would be a constant.

Dealing with the princely states was less controversial. If Sardar Patel's greatest service had been that of securing their accession, his last had been that of integrating them. Riding roughshod over previous pledges about noninterference in the states' internal affairs, he pressured all but the largest states (e.g., Jammu and Kashmir, Hyderabad) into forming confederations. Such confederations were then either incorporated into India's existing provinces/states or—as in the case of Rajasthan—made provinces/states in their own right. Either way, any notion of the princes continuing to exercise their sovereign rights as per Mountbatten's reassurances was summarily dismissed.

Even shorter shrift was given to non-princely opponents of national integration. Glorying in the nation's diversity—New Delhi's default position whenever separatists reared their heads—assumed a uniform acquiescence by all of India's peoples. The British Raj had been characterized by gradations in rule that took account of local circumstance, historical happenstance, and imperial convenience. Such inconsistency was anathema in a modern nation-state. When in 1947 Gandhi had told a deputation from the Naga peoples of the far northeast that if they preferred to be independent no one could force them to be part of India, they had taken him at his word. But Nehru and Patel would have none of it. The Nagas' demands were "absurd," according to Nehru; their mist-shrouded hills were as much part of Mother India as neighboring Assam was. In recognition of their distinctive ethnicity (Mongoloid), social configuration (clan-based), and confessional allegiance (largely Christian), the most the Nagas could hope for was a degree of preferential autonomy within the Indian republic.

This, however, was unacceptable to those in the Naga National Council who were already pledged to secure full independence. Though they had taken no part in India's long freedom struggle, many Nagas were quite prepared to die in their own. Incidents of violence quickly multiplied, much of the Naga country became a no-go area, and by 1954 the longest-running of India's "forgotten wars" was under way. It went largely unreported in the rest of India and was little noticed outside. International goodwill toward the subcontinent's newly enfranchised millions discouraged scrutiny of an obscure conflict in its remotest extremity. Meanwhile, Indians tended to dismiss the Nagas as feather-wearing primitives with a propensity for head-hunting and heavy drinking. They were, in short, "tribals," just like the various *adivasi* (aboriginal) peoples who eked out a slash-and-burn existence in the less favored margins of Bihar, Orissa, and peninsular India. The constitution afforded to these other "tribals" various safeguards and integrational incentives, to which they responded by forming political parties and participating in the electoral process. Eventually some would win federal status for areas in which they were concentrated, such as Jharkhand and Chattisgarh.

The Nagas, though suspect on account of their nostalgia for British rule and their attachment to the American-run Baptist missions, could have had a similar deal. In fact, in the early 1960s they got one: Nehru responded to approaches from a moderate section of the Naga National Council by declaring Nagaland the latest and smallest of India's constituent states. But it made little difference. Against the elusive "insurgents" New Delhi had already seen fit to deploy "one regiment of mountain artillery, seventeen battalions of infantry and fifty platoons of Assam Rifles."[22] Villages had been burned and atrocities committed by both sides. Meanwhile, Angami Zapu Phizo, the Nagas' inspirational but intractable leader, had escaped into East Pakistan. From there he traveled to London and finally won some press coverage for what he called the "racial extermination" to which his "Christian nation" was being subjected. A cease-fire in 1964 was at last followed by peace talks. Phizo seemed willing to settle for the sovereignty and qualified independence claimed by nearby Bhutan and Sikkim. Delhi would have none of it. By 1966 the killing, burning, and abductions had resumed.

Naga intransigence was sustained by a sense of ethnic, confessional, and social distinction. Language was not a major bone of contention, partly because many Nagas had been schooled by the Baptist missionaries and spoke English. But elsewhere language— and the role, if any, to be awarded to English—was highly divisive.

The constitution was itself a battlefield. It recognized sixteen major languages in India and acknowledged several hundred others, but since many of the concepts it aired could not easily be expressed in any of them, it was actually written in English. This was regretted. English was not considered an Indian language and was tainted with imperialist associations. As in Pakistan, administrative convenience plus the need for democratic transparency demanded that there be one officially sanctioned national language, and patriotic sentiment demanded that it be an Indian one.

Nehru favored Hindustani. A hybrid of Hindi and Urdu, it was confessionally neutral and widely understood in the north, although it was the first language of few and was not richly endowed with abstract nouns. Hindi itself had no subtler a vocabulary, but its deficiencies could be rectified. The philologists got to work and soon Nehru was complaining that All India Radio had introduced so many Sanskritic neologisms that he couldn't recognize reports of his own speeches. Hindi was nevertheless spoken by more Indians than any other language. The "Hindi belt" stretched right across northern and central India from Rajasthan to Bengal. It was therefore the obvious choice as the official link language, and the constitution did indeed say as much, but not unequivocally. There was first to be an official inquiry and a fifteen-year moratorium while Hindi won wider acceptance and refined its vocabulary of legal, constitutional, and scientific terms. And during this switchover period English might continue to be used as an alternative official language.

This reprieve owed as much to politics as to linguistics. In the non-Hindi-speaking south the elevation of Hindi was encountering intense hostility. Hindi and most other north Indian languages derive from Sanskrit, but, in what would emerge as the southern states of Tamil Nadu, Kerala, Karnataka, and Andhra Pradesh, the languages (respectively Tamil, Malayalam, Kannada, and Telugu) were of Dravidian origin. With their own scripts and grammatical structures, they differed as much from Hindi as did Japanese. Those who spoke them would thus be at a major disadvantage when Hindi became the language of government, administration, and higher education. Ready access to qualifications, government service, and public sector jobs, plus a sense of privileged identity, awaited the chosen language group; the lot of all the others would be hard study, perpetual disparagement, and a marginalized heritage.[23]

The south's preference was for English. It was already more widely used there than in the north and, as an alien tongue, posed a lesser threat to the primacy of the native languages. "Hindi never; English ever" became the popular chant as Tamils took to the streets. Delhi's committee of inquiry upheld the decision in favor of Hindi, further offending the south, but Nehru pledged that English would be retained for as long as the south insisted, which greatly upset the north. As the fifteen-year deadline of 1965 approached, feelings ran high. Hindi-speakers, championed by the Jan Sangh and other parties, defaced English signs, burned vehicles with number plates using the Roman alphabet and Arabic numerals, and terrorized tourist cities such as Varanasi (Benares). It was worse in the south. There the Dravida Munnetra Kazagham (DMK), a Dravidian party that was pledged to all things Tamil, happily added the language issue to its secessionist portfolio of grievances. Strikes crippled the Congress-led administration. From books to billboards and timetables, anything in Hindi was torched. When Tamil youths, four of them students, publicly torched themselves, the scenario closely resembled that of the 1952 language riots in East Bengal. The police opened fire; more than sixty were killed.

With the death of Nehru in May 1964 it would be left to his successors to quell the troubles and reappraise the policy. In 1967 what Guha calls "a virtual indefinite policy of bilingualism" was adopted. Hindi was confirmed as India's official language but English was to be retained as an "associate official language" for as long as the non-Hindi-speaking states cared to exercise a veto over its phasing out. With respect to education, the package was presented as a three-language formula: schools were to teach a regional language (say, Tamil), the official language (Hindi), plus one other (almost invariably English). Thus was calm restored at the cost of a formula that bore rather heavily on young minds.

Happily, though, childhood dedication would be vindicated. As Nehru had foreseen, the retention of English would bequeath to India a new generation of educated English-speakers well placed to cash in on the intellectual and scientific advances of an increasingly anglophone world. In the silicon economy at the turn of the twenty-first century, what swept India into global currents was as much its ability to send talented people outward as its ability to attract call centers inward. English made all things possible, easing the path of emigrating Indians and reassuring incoming tourists. The literary heights were there to be stormed and the multinational corporations to be wooed. Midnight's business-class offspring would owe a rarely acknowledged debt to the "Tamil martyrs" and the linguistic fudging of Nehru's "wasted years."

WHILE THE NEHRU GOVERNMENT agonized over the official language, another language-related issue of equally explosive potential had somewhat confusingly interposed itself. The provinces of British India had developed from the so-called presidencies of Madras, Bombay, and Calcutta. Often they embraced more than one main language group, and just as often their geographical boundaries bisected language groups. Congress, on the other hand, had long since opted to base its regional organization on the country's linguistic divisions. This proclaimed respect for local cultures made them easier to mobilize and, come independence, would facilitate the imposition of this linguistic geography on the political geography of the British. Thus, for example, instead of a vast polyglot Bombay province, there might be two smaller states corresponding to its main ethnolinguistic components, notably Gujarati-speakers in the north and Marathi-speakers in the south. (Sind, now in Pakistan, had been detached from Bombay on the grounds of both religion and language in the 1930s.)

There was no question that this linguistic "states reorganization" would be implemented. All parties were in favor. It was just a question of when. Nehru was in no hurry. After the upheavals of independence, a wholesale reorganization of the country's constituent states could hardly be considered a high priority; nor, in the fallout from Partition, could the creation of a host of new and potentially disruptive regional entities. He therefore temporized. The constitution ignored the question, and Congress consigned its consideration to a committee. This, by endorsing both the principle and the need for patience, merely fired up linguistic nationalists throughout the country. In the north, Sikhs demanded the division of India's slice of the Punjab into Punjabi-speaking and Hindi-speaking states; it was no coincidence that the former would for once give the Sikhs a narrow majority. In the west, both Gujarati- and Marathi-speakers laid voluble claim not just to their majority areas but to Bombay itself. And in the south speakers of all four Dravidian languages sallied forth in support of their prospective states, with none mobilizing more energetically than the speakers of Telugu.

Second only to Hindi-speakers in numerical terms, Telugu-speakers were divided between Hyderabad state and the northern part of Madras province. Their identity was thus imperiled and their voting strength split by the Tamil majority in Madras and by minorities speaking Urdu and other languages in Hyderabad. A Telugu state, which was to be named Andhra after an ancient Telugu dynasty, would rectify this. And its champions were not prepared to wait. Backed by parties ranging from the Mahasabha to the Communists, Telugu leaders organized strikes and fasts and rattled even Congress by enticing defectors from its ranks. The final straw came in 1952 when the fifty-eight-day fast of a Telugu-speaking Gandhian called Potti Sriramulu ended in his death. Incensed supporters brought the state to a standstill and clashed with police. Several were killed, government buildings were attacked, and trains and buses were halted. Though painfully aware that conceding one linguistic state would only encourage other demands, Nehru capitulated. A Telugu-speaking Andhra Pradesh came into being in October 1953.

The clamor for further adjustments elsewhere was met by the setting up of a States Reorganisation Commission. Reporting in 1955, this recommended various changes: the remaining three language groups in the south were to be given their own states (Tamil Nadu, Karnataka, and Kerala), and several changes were made to the Hindi-belt states. But the Sikh demand in the Punjab was put on hold, and a suggestion that an inland Marathi-speaking state be carved from Bombay, leaving the rest of the state bilingual, satisfied no one. In Bombay the report was met with massive riots and more deaths, as were several attempts to revise it. The trouble rumbled on till 1960. By then the electoral consequences of alienating such an important Congress stronghold had become as apparent as the discontent. Once again it was time to bow to popular pressure and the constraints of the ballot box. Bombay was divided into Gujarat and Maharashtra, the former being augmented with the addition of the princely states of Saurashtra (Junagadh among them) and the latter being awarded the prize of metropolitan Bombay. Once again pragmatism had come to the rescue of principle.

In retrospect the linguistic reorganization would be reckoned a success. Far from encouraging separatist tendencies, it removed a major source of conflict and, as political scientist Rajni Kothari noted, "resulted in rationalising the political map of India without weakening its unity."[24] But in the state capitals it did encourage a more assertive federalism. The fourteen linguistically constituted states of 1960 would soon double in number as more groups adopted similar tactics. State governments would grow more confident in taking on the central government, and by the 1980s state parties based on particular language or caste groups would be well enough represented in the Delhi parliament to be critical components in the coalitions that increasingly held power at the national level.

IF TAMIL NADU HAD LED the agitation against Hindi as the official language and Andhra the demand for the linguistic reorganization of the states, it was another southern state, Kerala, that posed the nearest thing to an ideological challenge. More to the international community's surprise than India's, in 1957 Kerala's voters returned to the state assembly the world's first-ever freely elected Communist government. At the same elections (state and national elections were being held simultaneously), the Communist Party won twenty-seven seats in the Lok Sabha, the national Parliament's lower house, consolidating its nationwide position as the largest opposition party. These gains were thought highly significant at the time. The Cold War was at its height, the Hungarian uprising had just been ruthlessly suppressed, and Maoist China was gearing up for its Great

Leap Forward. In the previous months China's Chou Enlai had twice been to India, while Russia's Bulganin and Khrushchev had just been rapturously fêted during a state visit.

Nehru himself, though critical of Stalinist methods, greatly admired the social and industrial achievements of the Soviet bloc. To emulate them, he personally chaired the influential National Planning Commission, which in 1956 rolled out the second and most ambitious of India's five-year plans. Modeled on Soviet practice, this committed the government to a socialist pattern of development that prioritized the creation of an industrial base and insisted that strategic industries must be under state ownership. Manufacturing capacity backed by a revamped infrastructure would also reduce the country's dependence on imports, so reinforcing political sovereignty with the steel mesh of economic self-sufficiency. Expectations duly soared. Economists were consulted and foreign experts, many of them from eastern Europe, abandoned their wives to the tropical sun and the hotel poolside as they fanned out across the country. Technical appraisals were drawn up for everything from engineering colleges to steel mills and hydroelectric dams.

"India in the 1950s fell in love with the idea of concrete," as Khilnani puts it. Liquid mix was apparently poured at the rate of ten tons a minute, sixteen hours a day, for three years just for the Bhakra-Nangal dams on the Beas River. Producing more coal, more power, more fertilizer, more steel sheet and tube became a national obsession. The front pages were an inky blur of production graphs and statistics, while what remained of the day's heavily rationed newsprint seemed reserved for government tenders. Research institutes and technical colleges proliferated. Between 1950 and 1965 the number of students studying engineering and technology at diploma or degree level shot up by 750 percent, and it seemed that an inquisitive M.Sc. lurked in every railway compartment. Industry, science, and technology were hailed as the new temples of progress, with proficiency in English as the key to admittance. "That India can even think of participating in the globalisation process in today's [1999's] world of high technology," declares a standard text, "is largely due to the spadework done since independence, particularly the great emphasis laid on human resource development in the sphere of science and technology."[25] Intended to provide India with the wherewithal for instant Soviet-style liftoff as one of Asia's industrial giants, this massive investment would take three decades to manifest a return, and then in the form of a joyful embrace of global capitalism.

But none of this was enough for the Communists of Kerala. With no industry to speak of, only glaring inequalities and high unemployment, Keralans were more concerned about workers' rights, agricultural incentives, and the promised redistribution of landholdings. Unfortunately, it was these that were being starved of funding and commitment by the planners' preference for rapid industrialization. Thus the Communist Party of India, though lately a champion of armed insurrection and still suspected of taking its orders from Moscow, could honestly agree to work within the constitution. The reforms it desired to enact were already national policy; they just weren't being effectively enforced. Kerala would show the way.

To win power in a state with a mind-boggling mix of castes and religions, the Communist Party needed first to cultivate its own constituency. This it did with conspicuous success by becoming the mouthpiece and tool of the Ezhava caste. Originally tappers of the toddy palm on which Kerala's connoisseurs depend for their hooch, the low-caste Ezhavas were no exception to the state's high rate of literacy. They were readily politicized. "The Christians tend to vote for Congress," reported Taya Zinkin on one of several visits, "the Muslims usually vote for the [Indian] Muslim League, the [Ezhava] Toddy Tappers are the heart of the Communist party, [and] the [upper-caste] Nairs are split."[26]

There was nothing exceptional in all this. Its assertive castes and large Christian and Muslim minorities made Kerala something of a maverick state, but the affiliation of political parties with particular communities was standard practice. It was how democracy in India (and sporadically Pakistan) worked. Electoral politics were played out on a board whose counters represented entire communities. A party's job was simply to advance the interests of the community that had endorsed it—or forfeit that community's support. Communists, no less than Congress, had to play by these rules. As events would demonstrate, it was not India's susceptibility to Communist ideology that was being tested in Kerala but the subordination of ideological principle to the exigencies of Indian electoral practice.

The Communist Party's 1957 victory was followed by a brief honeymoon. Death sentences were commuted, cases against political sympathizers were dismissed, and a modest land reform was introduced to give tenants security of tenure. But the state's large tea and coffee plantations were not nationalized, nor was private enterprise penalized. The new government showed a marked respect for the constitution, with E. M. S. Namboodiripad, its diminutive chief minister (a Stalinist with "a dash of Khrushchevian common sense"), doing nothing to incur New Delhi's wrath.[27] The criticism, muted at first but soon deafening, came from opposition parties within the state, and it focused less on policy than on moves they themselves would expect to take when in power, namely, advancing issues dear to their main supporters.

Of these, the most critical touched on the matter of education. Far more children, both male and female, attended school in Kerala than in any other state. Indeed, so great was the consequent appetite for reading material that some 140 Malayalam newspaper titles were published daily to assuage it. Many of the schools were denominational, and naturally they served to induct children into the traditions of their particular communities. The Nair Service Society was no different in this respect from the Catholic Church or the Muslim educational foundations. All received state grants, appointed and dismissed their own teachers, and, within the constraints of national policy, chose their own curricula. Unwisely, the Communist government sought to change this by introducing an Education Bill. The bill, which was supposed to improve the security of teaching jobs, would oblige schools to select their teachers from a list drawn up by the Public Service Commission; such a list must, of course, conform to constitutional principle, with at least half its named teachers being drawn from those backward castes entitled to preferential public service access.

That meant prestigious jobs for the toddy-tapping Ezhavas and, through them, a chance to insinuate Communist-written textbooks.

But as Zinkin put it, "non–Toddy Tapper parents in Kerala did not want Toddy Tapper Communists to teach their children."[28] On this most sensitive issue, Christians and Muslims of every persuasion, plus most Hindus who were not of scheduled caste status, were as one. The government had foolishly stumbled on the single issue around which all its opponents could unite.

Throughout 1958 the tension mounted. While in Pakistan the parliamentary brickbats were flying and Generals Mirza and Ayub Khan were readying themselves for "the revolution," in Kerala the revolutionaries were already on the run. The state's Congress Party led the charge, cynically savaging the Communist government for implementing reforms approved by Congress's own national leadership. Strikes were orchestrated and demonstrations held. In one such protest the demoralized police shot dead six Congress Party members, so adding misuse of power to an anti-Communist charge sheet that already included corruption, incompetence, maladministration, and intimidation.

Meanwhile the Supreme Court in Delhi was considering an appeal claiming that the Education Bill was unconstitutional. The appeal was rejected, and the bill became law in early 1959. This brought forth Mannathu Padmanabhan, a Nair leader and revered disciple of the Mahatma whose eighty-one years had been spent in exemplary service to the community. Stomping the state in the best Gandhian tradition, the untouchable Padmanabhan (he was actually a Brahmin) urged mass civil disobedience and ensured that the schools remained closed for business. Pickets blocked the roads and strikers shut down all manner of public buildings; massive protest marches demanded the government's resignation. When the police broke up the demonstrations, more died and the jails overflowed,

Were the government to resign, it would mean another election, and against a united opposition, the Communists could only lose—not just office but also face. Accordingly, in an unlikely move for a party dedicated to overthrowing the bourgeois Congress, they turned to New Delhi. Nehru had been partly responsible for legalizing the Communist Party. He had just entertained the Soviet leadership and was known to disapprove of the tactics employed by the Kerala Congress Party. He was now invited to visit Kerala and did so in June 1959, preempting a massive march on Trivandrum, the capital. But he could neither persuade the Communists to resign nor convince himself to recommend their dismissal. In a taste of things to come, it was his daughter, Indira, then president of the Congress Party, who made his mind up for him. The big march had been rescheduled for early August. Even as it converged on Trivandrum, word came that the government had been dismissed and the assembly dissolved under Article 365. President's rule administered by a directly appointed governor would take over until such time as new elections could be held.

In early 1960, the new elections duly returned to power the Congress-led coalition of non-Communist parties. But it was not the end of the road for Communism in Kerala. Though split by the rift between Moscow and Beijing, the Communists would be back in power after the following election, and thereafter Communist coalitions would continue to alternate with Congress coalitions indefinitely. The party's secretary had complained in 1957 that "Communism within a democratic constitution is like capitalism without private enterprise." But it was not the democratic provisions of the constitution that were the party's biggest problem. Rather, it was the constitution's interventionist provisions, plus the community-based peculiarities of Indian electoral practice. The Communists had learned their lesson. "Twenty-eight months of rule in Kerala has made them a party like any other," concluded Taya Zinkin.[29]

Taming ideological tigers was as integral to the process of nation building as accommodating South Asia's many ethnic, linguistic, and confessional separatisms. In general, India was far more successful at this than its neighbors. Sri Lanka would be crippled by both ethno-linguistic and ideological challenges. So would Nepal. And Pakistan's failure to assuage mainly regional dissent, most notably in Bengal, would prove fatal. But India too had its failures.

When in 1967 the Communist Party (Marxist), or CPM, came to power in a United Front coalition in West Bengal, many feared the worst. They need not have worried. West Bengal's Communists took to electoral politics as readily as Kerala's. For the next thirty years, under the frequent leadership of the CPM's charismatic Jyoti Basu, the most volatile of India's states enjoyed a consistency of redistributive radicalism, if not much stability. But it came at a price. Just as the CPM had splintered from the Communist Party of India (CPI) over the latter's allegiance to Moscow, so the Communist Party Marxist-Leninist (CPM-L) had splintered from the CPM over the latter's willingness to accept office. Instead, the CPM-L tore a leaf out of Chairman Mao's Little Red Book and withdrew from democratic politics to concentrate on grassroots revolution.

The party's baptism of blood came in Naxalbari in the north of the state; lands were grabbed, landlords were beheaded, and the police retaliated. Now known as Maoists or Naxalites, the revolutionaries found support wherever social iniquities were most acute. Although eventually contained in West Bengal, the movement thrived in other deprived areas and, come the end of the century, would resurface with a vengeance. Vast tracts of Andhra Pradesh, Chattisgarh, and Orissa (including Dandakaranya) became no-go areas for the security forces. Meanwhile, just across the border from Naxalbari, a Maoist sister movement would bring the troubled kingdom of Nepal to its knees.

5

REALITY CHECK

BREAKING RECORDS BECAME A COMPETITIVE OBSESSION IN the 1950s and 1960s. In 1961 the Russian Yuri Gagarin was the first into space, and eight years after that the Americans Neil Armstrong and Buzz Aldrin first walked on the moon. But *The Guinness Book of World Records,* issued annually starting in 1955 and itself a publication that broke all records, featured a photograph of an earlier record-breaking feat that set the standard. Against a cobalt sky it showed a hooded figure in heroic pose scaling a hump of snow while brandishing aloft an ice axe tied with flags. Unrecognizable behind snow goggles and oxygen mask, this was Tenzing Norgay, a resident of Darjeeling in West Bengal. Along with the New Zealander Edmund Hillary (who took the photo) on May 29, 1953, Tenzing became the first man to bestride the top of the world. The achievement had no political relevance, which made it all the more psychologically uplifting. India had something to crow about.

The conquest of Everest was as proudly claimed by Nehru's India as it was by the expedition's British organizers. From Tenzing's ice axe there fluttered, between the ensigns of Britain, Nepal, and the UN, a just-visible Indian tricolor. Much as in the United Kingdom the feat was taken as a benediction on the coronation of Elizabeth II, so in the Republic of India it was seen as complementing what empire diehards such as Winston Churchill had pooh-poohed as impossible—the successful conduct of an all-India general election.

In 1952, on a universal franchise, a creditable 60 percent of the 176 million Indians entitled to vote had gone to the polls, setting a world record. With another world first coming so soon after, independent India was standing tall.

Yet it could have been very different. Prior to Partition, Tenzing Norgay had been living in Chitral, a princely state in the skirts of the Hindu Kush on Pakistan's side of the border between the Northern Areas and Afghanistan. Of the maybe seven million non-Muslims who had opted to leave Pakistan and make the dangerous journey into India, Tenzing had been one; otherwise it might have been Pakistan that was celebrating in 1953.

India, however, was not alone in claiming Tenzing's feat as its own. The mountain itself, though named and trigonometrically measured by surveyors operating from the Indian foothills, stands far beyond the Indian frontier, not to mention above it. It is in fact in the Great Himalaya range that constitutes the borderland between Nepal and Tibet. But the mountains here being more than sixty miles deep and the watershed by no means corresponding to the main range, it was as yet unclear in whose territory Everest actually stood. The Chinese said Tibet's, and so China's; the Nepalis said Nepal's. Everest was thus of interest to others, and so, in the same straddling way, was Tenzing. As a Sherpa who was supposedly born in Tibet, he could be regarded as Tibetan and hence an adopted Chinese. And following a childhood spent mainly in Nepal, that country too laid claim to his achievement. Moreover, it was from Nepal that the successful 1953 expedition had been launched; it relied heavily on Nepali support and porters and could not have been undertaken without Kathmandu's permission.

This was a new development. Before World War II all attempts to climb Everest had been launched from Tibet with the sometimes reluctant blessing of Lhasa's Dalai Lama. Meanwhile, the kingdom of Nepal had remained firmly closed to climbers, as it had to most other visitors for over a century. It was Indian independence, followed two years later by the proclamation of the People's Republic of China, that isolated Tibet from its southern neighbors, opened up Nepal, and so ushered in a new era in sub-Himalayan relationships. Additionally, it would be as a spin-off of these events that the Nepal-

Tibet border was settled and the ownership of Mount Everest finally clarified.

In November 1950, a month after Maoist China's People's Liberation Army (PLA) moved in to reclaim (or "liberate") Tibet, King Tribhuvan of Nepal had deserted his capital, Kathmandu, and fled to India. The king was little more than a figurehead; power in Nepal had long rested with the Rana family of hereditary prime ministers. But the Ranas now faced serious opposition. In imitation of Congress in India, popular movements were challenging Rana rule and demanding a more representative form of government. Parties such as the Nepali Congress (founded in India in 1947) derived their ideas and much support from Indian sympathizers, while Nepalis whose political horizons had been broadened by service in the India-based Gurkha regiments of the British Indian army gave to the struggle something of a diasporic dimension.

Indeed, the Gurkhas might be claimed as the first of South Asia's transnational communities. Defeated in the Anglo-Nepal war of 1814–16, the Gurkha kingdom had been effectively partitioned by British retention of its western districts (Garhwal, Kumaon, Dehra Dun, etc.). At the same time the Gurkhas' aptitude for warfare, their limited domestic prospects, and their flexibility with regard to caste (though Hindus, they were agreeable to service overseas) had recommended their recruitment into British India's forces. In the first half of the twentieth century around two hundred thousand had served with distinction in various theaters of World War I and more than a quarter of a million in World War II. But as in the Punjab and in Jammu and Kashmir, demobilization saw many returning to their hills with poor prospects of employment allied to a sense of entitlement and notions of popular sovereignty. At the time of India's independence, many Gurkhas transferred to the British army and some would eventually secure residence rights in the United Kingdom. But more than half of the Gurkha regiments that remained under arms opted to join India. In Kashmir and elsewhere along India's mountain frontier, their abilities at altitude proved invaluable and their loyalty to India went unquestioned. Not surprisingly, many Gurkhas reasoned that if a Congress government could unite the Indian nation, then so it could the Nepali nation.

When in 1950 the popular unrest within Nepal turned to revolt, the king had seen his chance. Instead of opposing demands for representative government, as the nizam of Hyderabad had, he aligned himself with them, hoping thereby to discredit the Ranas and regain some vestige of his dynasty's lost authority. King Tribhuvan's exile, a ploy to distance himself from the Ranas, was short; he stayed in India for only three months. But it was long enough for the insurgents in Nepal, aided by some volunteers from India and Burma, to force the Ranas to compromise. Under a power-sharing agreement between them and the Nepali Congress, the king returned.

Nine months later the Ranas were elbowed aside, ushering in a decade of parliamentary-style government under a constitutional monarchy. New Delhi applauded, most Nepalis celebrated, and so did the mountaineering fraternity. Nepal's relations with India had just been regularized under the 1950 Treaty of Peace and Friendship. This confirmed that landlocked Nepal's border with India would be open to both trade and unregulated migration; in an arrangement fraught with difficulties for the future, Indians might settle in Nepal and Nepalis in India without let or hindrance. Under the new dispensation foreigners might also seek entry and their diplomatic representatives might apply for climbing permits. The race for Everest, stalled by World War II, resumed.

Possibly influenced by the king of Nepal's flight, just a month later, in December 1950, the fifteen-year-old Dalai Lama also fled his capital, in this case before the advancing troops of the Chinese People's Liberation Army. From Lhasa he too headed south for the Indian border, but there he was persuaded to turn back. India in the person of Nehru, though sympathetic to the democratic forces in Nepal, was not prepared to uphold an obscurantist theocracy in Tibet. Moreover, any condemnation of Chinese aggression in Tibet would prejudice India's fraternal relations with the new Communist regime in Beijing. Commitments to Tibetan autonomy inherited from the British were accordingly downplayed, and India declined to support a Tibetan appeal to the UN. Under the circumstances His Holiness had little choice but to turn around and make the best terms he could with Beijing. These meant abandoning any notion of Tibetan sovereignty, "returning to the big family of the Motherland—the People's Republic of China," and cooperating to "drive out imperialist aggressive forces."[1] The chances of imperialist mountaineers being admitted to Tibet were now zero. In effect, Tibet's Himalayan portal had slammed shut just as Nepal's swung ajar.

An approach route to Mount Everest from the Nepal side had been reconnoitered in 1951. Then in 1952 two Swiss expeditions nearly made it. Tenzing Norgay accompanied both of them as sirdar in charge of the other Sherpas and as a full member of the assault team. In the same dual role he was recruited by the British-led expedition of 1953. He was emphatically not a mere support member. His experience by then was second to none, and it was wholly appropriate that he shared the ultimate prize.

Everest put Nepal on the international map. Expeditions to the mountain itself and to other peaks in the Nepali Himalaya became an annual event. By 1960 four Swiss climbers had also attained Everest's summit and three Chinese climbers had made the ascent from Tibet. Tourists and trekkers followed in ever greater numbers, providing a much-needed boost to the Nepali economy and taking a heavy toll on the mountain environment. By the end of the century an average year saw several hundred thousand backpackers streaming through Kathmandu, several thousand attempts on Everest itself, and several hundred breathless pioneers actually jostling for position on the icy hump where Tenzing and Hillary had first stood.

But down in Kathmandu, Nepal's new age of international engagement was doing nothing for the political process. As in Pakistan, the politicians struggled to meet the expectations of a widely dispersed and extremely diverse population and were sorely challenged by autocratic tendencies, here represented principally by the monarchy. King Tribhuvan's death in 1955 brought his son, King Mahendra, to the throne. An interim constitution, the second of many, had already been fatally diluted by amendments, and the promised elections had failed to materialize. In 1959 Mahendra promulgated a new constitution, albeit one that reserved considerable powers to the monarchy. He then called the first national elections. These were conducted successfully and were handsomely won by the Nepali Congress under B. P. Koirala.

Educated in India during his family's long exile there—indeed, a onetime member of the Indian Congress—Koirala was the second of several brothers, three of whom would occupy the prime minister's office. But his tenure lasted less than a year. Like Sheikh Abdullah in Jammu and Kashmir, he introduced radical land reforms that excited popular expectations but encountered strong opposition from vested interests. In 1960 King Mahendra broke the resultant stalemate by staging what was becoming a Nepali specialty: a royal coup. He repealed his own constitution, arrested B. P. Koirala, banned all political parties, and declared directly elected parliaments unsuited to Nepal's barely literate people. A new constitution better suited to such conditions was proclaimed in 1962.

This introduced a partyless system based on elected village councils, or panchayats. The panchayats in turn elected district councils, which in turn chose representatives for the National Panchayat or parliament. The panchayati raj, with its bottom-up structure and its supposedly ancient credentials, carried the imprimatur of India's revered Mahatma, but it also bore a close resemblance to the system then being pioneered in Pakistan under the banner of "basic democracy." And like basic democracy, it left ample scope at every level of the electoral hierarchy for the exercise of the prerogative and influence reserved to the sovereign or president. With amendments, the system would nevertheless survive the release of B.P. Koirala in 1968, the death of King Mahendra in 1972, the succession of King Birendra, and a somewhat dubious referendum on its retention in 1980.

Only in the course of the 1980s would it come under heavy fire as Koirala's successors in the Nepali Congress Party secured positions in the National Panchayat. King Birendra offered a concession in the form of direct elections to the national body. Yet the protests continued. Finally Birendra relented. The panchayat constitution of 1962 was abrogated, and, after countless false starts, in 1990 Nepal got yet another constitution. This restored parliamentary democracy, but again it would not last. In remote parts of the country Naxalite Maoists were already offering a radical alternative.

More even than Pakistan, Nepal was handicapped by an identity defined by its relationship with India. Pinioned against the Great

Himalaya with Indian territory on its other three sides, it had little choice. The country was one of the least developed in the world. Overland transport between its extremities involved loops into India. Though imports came mostly from India and exports went mostly to India, all other trade also had to pass through Indian territory. And the gross national product relied heavily on remittances from Nepalis employed in India (including Gurkha servicemen). An outreach of the Indian economy, then, Nepal's political options were few.

It nevertheless did its utmost to assert its individuality. Proclaimed as the world's only Hindu kingdom, it adopted the world's only five-sided flag (an elision of two triangular pennons) and set its clocks for the world's only quarter-hour time zone (fifteen minutes behind Indian Standard Time). Heedless of visitor convenience, the value of its rupee also lagged behind that of India. UN membership and obligations to international donors and aid agencies afforded some leverage in relationships with Delhi; so did Nepal's command of the hydroelectric and irrigational potential of several major tributaries of the Ganges. But it was China in Tibet, its only other neighbor, that was of most concern to India.

Historically Nepal and Tibet had enjoyed a checkered relationship marked by incursions and counter-incursions interspersed with tributary exchanges. That a now Communist China might renew its interest in Nepal seemed unlikely so long as New Delhi and Beijing were on the best of terms. But as of the late 1950s this changed. In 1960 Kathmandu, having previously had diplomatic relations only with Delhi, exchanged representatives with Beijing. Tension between its two colossal neighbors was introducing Nepal to the gentle art of playing one off against the other. It made good sense, but only so long as the possibility of India and China actually coming to blows over their Himalayan hinterland could be discounted.

INDIA'S SUPPOSEDLY "WASTED YEARS" under Nehru are usually taken to refer to the patchy performance of the economy rather than the conduct of external affairs. Between 1950 and 1965 the country's GNP grew by a respectable, if not sensational, 4 percent a year, thanks largely to the Planning Commission's prioritization of heavy

industries and power generation. But even these favored sectors seldom realized the potential that had been forecast for them: siltation
choked the turbines, and the big new steel plants proved woefully in-
efficient. Elsewhere the main blockage was bureaucratic. A labyrinth
of licenses and quotas (the "permit raj"), designed to protect indigenous production, so hobbled the private sector that basic industries
such as textiles, consumer goods, and agriculture languished. In a
nation proudly committed to self-sufficiency through import substi-
tution, the ability to feed itself was an obvious priority. Yet, though
agricultural yields did increase, they failed to keep pace with the
growth in population. Despite more irrigation, ambitious agrarian
development schemes, and some land redistribution, by 1965 cereal
imports from the United States under a public loan program would
top forty million tons a year. Begging bowls, even when cast in an
Indian blast furnace, were still begging bowls.

External affairs, on the other hand, looked to be a much less controversial field. Initially they were handled with intellectual panache
by Nehru himself, and by the late 1950s India's standing with the
rest of the world could hardly have been higher. Having dedicated his
country to the "still larger cause of humanity" in his independence
oration, Nehru had wasted no time in championing the freedom
struggles of other peoples suffering under colonial rule. Already in
early 1947 an Asian Relations Conference had brought to Delhi representatives from all over South and Southeast Asia, including Nepal,
Tibet, Ceylon, and Afghanistan. The Asian continent was awakening,
Nehru declared; India stood ready to listen and help.

By 1954 it was prepared to lead. In talks with China designed to
normalize relations following the Chinese retrieval of Tibet, Nehru
and Zhou Enlai jointly invoked the hallowed Five Principles of
Peaceful Coexistence, or *panchshila*—namely, equality, nonaggression, noninterference in each other's internal affairs, respect for each
other's borders, and respect for each other's sovereignty. Soon after, at
a meeting of Asian heads of government in Colombo, Nehru boldly
insisted that universal acceptance of these principles would ensure
that "there would hardly be any conflict and certainly no war."[2]

The "hardly any conflict" might have been a reference to Pondicherry. In this still-French enclave south of Madras, demonstrators

backed by most of India's political parties were demanding an end to French rule and integration with India. Noninterference notwithstanding, Nehru too pressed their cause throughout 1954. His timing was impeccable. With France reeling from defeat at Dien Bien Phu, then smarting over the Geneva partition of Vietnam and facing another colonial revolt in Algeria, capitulation over Pondicherry was a near certainty. Better, reasoned Paris, to sell Mirage fighter jets to India than to deploy them in defense of a worthless outpost. Without as much as a show of force by either side, the seafront colony and its satellite enclaves were duly handed over in November 1954. From the colonial past that left just Goa and its Portuguese satellites. Abetted by New Delhi, Goans too were agitating for an end to colonial rule. But Lisbon under the dictatorial rule of President Antonio Salazar stood firm.

The Five Principles of Peaceful Coexistence resurfaced at the epochal Asia-Africa Conference convened in Bandung by President Sukarno of Indonesia in the following year. Here Nehru, long a champion of Indonesian independence, positioned himself at the helm of what was becoming the Non-Aligned Movement. Heads of state and senior representatives from twenty-nine anti-imperialist and recently independent nations attended the conference, including Egypt's Gamal Nasser, Cyprus's Archbishop Makarios, Zhou Enlai from China, Pham Van Dong from North Vietnam, U Nu from Burma, and Prince Sihanouk from Cambodia. South Asia was well represented with deputations from Pakistan, Nepal, and Ceylon. But in this galaxy of midcentury luminaries, it was the *pandit* Nehru, accompanied by his daughter Indira, who set the pace. The Five Principles, fleshed out into twelve, were duly adopted in the final communiqué and incorporated into the charter of the budding Non-Aligned Movement.

Nonalignment meant being open to both the capitalist West and the Communist Soviet bloc yet dependent on neither. The movement was presented as a haven of consensus in an otherwise bipolar world of nuclear-armed and ideologically confrontational power blocs. That was the theory—a peace-loving third bloc dedicated to challenging all forms of imperialism and defusing Cold War tensions. No doubt it appealed to Nehru's superior intellect in the same way as did neutrality in the choice of a national language, a mixed economy with both public and private ownership, and a lofty secularism between competing belief systems.

But if nonalignment meant anything, it ought also to have meant that the subscribers were themselves unaligned. This was not the case. At the time China, for instance, a key member of the Non-Aligned Movement, was still bound to the Soviet bloc in ideological comradeship and to the USSR by a treaty of Friendship, Alliance, and Mutual Assistance. Others, including Pakistan, were already incorporated into the Anglo-American framework of "containing" Communism as members of the Southeast Asia Treaty Organization (SEATO) and/or its Middle Eastern counterpart, the Baghdad Pact (later the Central Treaty Organization or CENTO). As critics gleefully noted, the Non-Aligned Movement's neutrality was compromised from birth.

Nehru preferred to overlook such inconsistency and to talk up the Five Principles of Peaceful Coexistence. But these too were not without flaws. Pledging noninterference and respect for one another's sovereignty presumed that the signatories' sovereignty enjoyed popular legitimacy, as evidenced by respect for human rights, the rule of law, and accountable government; yet all too often these safeguards were being flouted, while the parliamentary democracy so dear to Nehru and so central to India's self-image was notably absent. Similarly, respect for one another's borders rested on the assumption that they were not in dispute. Yet as creations of the discredited colonial powers, many international borders were little better than the optimistic projections of imperial strategists. They might ignore social factors, historical precedents, and natural features, and they seldom conformed to the highest standards of international jurisprudence. As India was about to discover, endorsing such frontiers could prove just as contentious as contesting them.

Among the frigid passes of the Himalayas, almost no section of international frontier had been approved and ratified (let alone demarcated) by all those parties whose authorization was deemed essential by the present regimes. Strung along the mountain glacis, Afghanistan, Jammu and Kashmir, Nepal, Sikkim, and Bhutan had been preserved by the British to form a defensive buffer zone between their jealously ruled Indian Raj and the sometimes expansive empires of the Russian tsars and the (Manchu) Qing emperors. The Republic of India inherited these arrangements and gratefully adopted them. But the borders of the buffer states were themselves open to question, there were gaps between these states, and beyond them in the east there was a long tail of hitherto unadministered and largely unpenetrated territory. (In India it was designated the North-East Frontier Agency—NEFA—and later Arunachal Pradesh.) Moreover, with Jammu and Kashmir now subject to a de facto division, the Ladakh region's inhospitable borderland with western Tibet had become an Indian responsibility, while the glacier-choked declivities of the Northern Areas' border with Chinese Xinjiang now pertained to Pakistan.

Almost none of these borderlands was of any value. Extremely remote, rising from thirteen thousand to twenty-six thousand feet above sea level, seldom frost-free, and largely uninhabited, they were strategically more a liability than an asset. The maps, although far from consistent, nonetheless showed them as someone's sovereign territory, and, as such, they could not easily be relinquished. "The first and almost instinctive reaction of every new government was to hold fast to the territory bequeathed to it," noted Gunnar Myrdal.[3] "What the colonial power had ruled, the new power must rule"—and especially so if it was answerable to a chamber of disputatious parliamentarians and a nationalistic press for any failure on this score.

Thus the news, confirmed in Delhi in 1958, that across 100 miles of howling wilderness in what Indian maps showed as eastern Ladakh the Chinese had unilaterally constructed a motorable road did not go down well. Known as the Aksai Chin, the region was in fact a salient of high-altitude desert to which the British had once laid claim as a possible trade corridor and bargaining counter but had never actually used for either purpose. The area was, however, vital to the Chinese as offering the most practicable alignment for a direct road link between their Xinjiang Province and the western end of a reclaimed Tibet. Several thousand workers had toiled for nineteen months in appalling conditions to build the road, and not once had they come across any evidence of an Indian interest in the region.

That of course proved nothing. The maps told their own stories, and Beijing seems to have been as aware of the Indian claim as Delhi was of the Chinese counterclaim. But opportunities to discuss this discrepancy were let slip, most notably in 1954 when Sino-Indian talks had amicably confirmed the Chinese reclamation of Tibet. A complacent Nehru accepted without question the wishful British incorporation of the Aksai Chin and insisted that there was nothing to discuss. Conversely, a confident Zhou Enlai took the lack of any Indian presence there as evidence of Delhi's having written off what all peace-loving anticolonialists must consider an imperialist impertinence.

Indian protests and Chinese repudiations followed—and then Chinese protests and Indian repudiations when an Indian patrol, belatedly directed to the area, was detected by the Chinese and detained. Meanwhile, within Tibet the Chinese were ruthlessly suppressing a revolt spearheaded by the Khampa people in the east of the country. The brutality of the People's Liberation Army (PLA) amounted to genocide and prompted some Khampas to flee to India. Others extended their resistance west. By March 1959 Lhasa itself was in turmoil. Outraged by the treatment of the Khampas, the Tibetan government was defying its Chinese mentors, and the PLA was preparing to bombard the city. Partly to save Lhasa, partly to keep alive the spirit of resistance, it was agreed that the Dalai Lama should again be smuggled out of the country. Traveling this time under the protection of the Khampa guerrillas, the fugitive party headed for Tawang, a monastic complex east of Bhutan in what had been a Tibetan salient but was now claimed by India. Over the next few years a hundred thousand Tibetan refugees would follow their leader's example and flee south. The long exile had begun.

Under pressure—from right-wing elements in India, from the international outcry, and from his own conscience—Nehru offered the Dalai Lama political asylum. Beijing did not object provided that India and its guest did nothing to inflame the situation. But in fact His Holiness spoke out about conditions in Tibet. His utterances were relayed by the Indian press, exciting anti-Chinese demonstrations in many Indian cities. Moreover, "it [was] evident that support and direction for the Tibetan rebels came through Kalimpong [a West Bengal "nest of spies," according to Nehru], and that the Government of India connived at this."[4]

So much for nonaggression, noninterference, and mutual respect for one another's borders. In the space of just four years, Sino-Indian talk of nonalignment and peaceful coexistence had been horribly compromised. The Indian crowds that had hailed the post-Bandung era of Asian solidarity with the slogan "Hindi-Chini bhai-bhai" ("India and China are brothers") now hurled abuse at Beijing and aimed rotten eggs at Chairman Mao's portrait. Nehru, acting as his own foreign minister throughout, bore the main responsibility and valiantly tried to reconcile his internationalist principles with the hard-line nationalism expected of a leader defending his people's homeland and dignity. But as the diplomatic exchanges were overtaken by more deadly exchanges along the disputed frontier itself, it was his defense chiefs and especially their minister, the waspish Krishna Menon, who would be found lacking.

THE FIRST MAJOR INCIDENT came late in 1959, and not in Ladakh but at Longju, at the other end of the Himalayas in NEFA. In this remote sector India insisted that a 1914 boundary alignment proposed by Henry McMahon (the British diplomat better known for the series of contentious letters that would trigger the Arab Revolt against Ottoman rule in Arabia) enjoyed the same map-delineated and so unchallengeable authority as that which included the Aksai Chin. By way of substantiating this claim, outposts were being established along the supposed line, one of which at Longju came under heavy fire and had to be withdrawn; it was unclear whether it was on the Indian side of the McMahon Line or not. But here in the east the Chinese had earlier indicated a willingness to consider the Indian contention and to accept the McMahon Line, at least temporarily. They continued to hint as much until 1961, the implied quid pro quo being that India should relinquish its claim to the Aksai Chin.

Such a straight swap had everything to recommend it except the strength of Indian public opinion against any territorial derogation anywhere. Things such as official transparency, accountable government, and a written constitution had their drawbacks. The Chinese leadership might be unfamiliar with, say, freedom of expression, but Nehru endeavored to explain. Additionally, his hands appeared tied by a preamble to the constitution that made any surrender of India's presumed territory problematic. The issue had first surfaced over a possible exchange between New Delhi and Karachi of some of those anomalous enclaves and counter-enclaves on either side of the line of Partition in Bengal. With implications for Kashmir as much as for the McMahon Line or the enclaves, in 1960 the Supreme Court ruled that an amendment to the constitution would be required for any alienation of Indian territory. This would not have been impossible (it required a two-thirds majority) and anyway the ruling was subsequently challenged, but at the time it served to bolster Nehru's case for intransigence. Zhou Enlai, of course, wrote it off as eyewash.

Later in 1959 a more serious clash occurred at the Kongka Pass in Ladakh. An Indian patrol exchanged fire with a Chinese unit and suffered nine fatalities. The pass was on the southern approaches to the Aksai Chin, suggesting further forward movement from the Chinese side. Coming soon after Longju, this "brutal massacre of an Indian policy party," as the *Times of India* put it, prompted a redeployment of Indian firepower.[5] From the dusty and tank-friendly plains of Punjab an ill-prepared division was transferred to the leech-infested ravines of NEFA.

Against a background of acrimonious talks and increasingly bellicose threats, the military buildup on both sides continued through 1960 and accelerated in 1961. So did the standoff in Ladakh and NEFA as India attempted to effect occupation of the territory it claimed. Defense Minister Krishna Menon, a prickly leftist who had spent more of his life in Bloomsbury than along the Himalayas, quarreled with his defense chief, alienated most of his Congress colleagues, and seemed unwilling to credit his Chinese comrades with hostile intent. Nehru stood by him for old times' sake. Rattled and now looking all of his seventy-one years, the prime minister derided his critics as "infantile and childish." He treated parliament to rambling discourses on China's impropriety and stressed his own willingness to discuss the geographical minutiae nevertheless: "Whether this hill is there, or whether this little bit is on this side or that side, on the facts, on the maps, on the evidence available—that I am prepared to discuss. . . . But the broad McMahon Line has to be accepted and so far as we are concerned, it is there and we accept it."[6]

In early 1960 Zhou Enlai reiterated his offer to discuss the crisis in person. Nehru, despite reservations and widespread accusations of appeasement from parliamentary critics and the press, finally agreed. In April the Chinese prime minister flew in to a frigid reception. Arriving by way of Burma, he returned by way of Nepal. In Rangoon and Kathmandu, Zhou was notably reasonable. Treaties of friendship were signed with both countries. Subject to minor adjustments, China also accepted a section of the McMahon Line that affected Burma and agreed on a joint demarcation of the Nepal-Tibet frontier. The alignment of the latter finally settled the status of Mount Everest: it was agreed that the frontier bisected the summit, so permitting access from both Nepal and Tibet.

All this Delhi took to be an elaborate charm offensive aimed at demonstrating Chinese flexibility and so exposing Indian intransigence. For at the Delhi talks nothing at all was achieved. Zhou, coming from a position of strength in the Aksai Chin, wanted to negotiate. Nehru, coming from one of weakness, would only discuss. As over Kashmir, he insisted that negotiations could be opened only after all foreign—in this case Chinese—troops had been withdrawn from within what India considered its frontiers. This meant the Chinese pulling out of the Aksai Chin altogether and abandoning their new road. Loss of face, no less than loss of access to western Tibet, made it unthinkable.

The Chinese nevertheless proposed a temporary withdrawal by both sides from the actual lines of occupation. India rejected it, preferring low-level discussions that bought time for a glacial buildup of its forces and for the edging forward of its outposts. Critics, within the army as well as in parliament, remained unconvinced. A more forceful approach was urged. Yet the army was ill-equipped to take on the battle-hardened PLA, and its supply chains were hopelessly overstretched.

Moreover, the country's third general election was imminent. Due in early 1962, it could not be coming at a worse moment. Assailed by deepening economic difficulties, the Congress government was also facing riots in Bombay over the bifurcation of Maharashtra state, ongoing troubles in Punjab and Nagaland, and above all doubts over its defense minister at a time when the loss of Himalayan chunks of the motherland remained unredressed. A distraction was badly needed, and preferably one that would unite the nation behind Congress. It was thus hardly coincidental that in late 1961, after more than a decade of restraint and with the army already overstretched, a division of troops was somehow found for an irresistible three-pronged advance not across the treeless wastes of the Aksai Chin but into the sleepy backwater of rustling palms and bell-ringing churches that was Portuguese Goa.

The Portuguese authorities offered protests but put up no resistance. The capital of their once mighty Estado da India fell with scarcely a shot being fired. New Delhi's intention of absorbing all of Portugal's enclaves had long been taken for granted, and Goans for the most part welcomed the intervention. The Indian public was ecstatic. "Our Finest Hour," trilled a headline in one English-language daily. Absurdly it was supposed that the victorious "commandos" who could so easily terminate a colonial anachronism in peninsular India could surely tackle a Himalayan intrusion. Krishna Menon was forgiven. Docile as a dove in the face of the Chinese, he had swooped like a hawk on the Portuguese. He had ignored Nehru's misgivings about the use of force and, without in any way embarrassing his Chinese friends, had sent Beijing a powerful message.

Naturally, there was some international disquiet. Pakistan ridiculed India's oft-avowed renunciation of force in the settling of international disputes, as did many in the West. Fifteen years later, for an almost identical swoop on the Portuguese colony of East Timor, the Indonesia of General Suharto would be internationally pilloried and its troops ejected by a UN force. The difference lay in the principals rather than the principle. In Goa it was the dictatorial rule of Salazar that was ousted, while Nehru's impeccably democratic credentials triumphed. Conversely, in East Timor the aggression came from an Indonesian dictator and it was the aggrieved East Timorese who espoused democracy. India, as a flag bearer in the East for Western-style democracy, could count on a degree of indulgence from the "free world," plus the gratitude of the Goan people, who had at last been given a say in their future.

As an electoral ploy, the seizure of Goa had the desired effect. Criticism of Indian inaction in the Himalayas was suddenly muffled, Menon's failings were forgiven, opinions on the unpreparedness of the army were revised, and in the elections of early 1962 Congress romped home with another massive majority. Emboldened by Goa, the strategists now turned to a "forward policy" with respect to the Aksai Chin and the McMahon Line. Patrols were stepped up and pickets established deeper inside the disputed territories. By the summer they overlapped those of the enemy on the Ladakh front. From PLA posts, loudspeaker appeals were directed at the Indian army's Gurkhas, reminding them of the new Sino-Nepal alliance. The Gurkhas stood firm, and to New Delhi's pleasant surprise it was the Chinese who backed off.

The same forward policy in NEFA had less happy results. On Thagla Ridge east of Tawang, which the Chinese took to be on their side of McMahon's rather thick line, the eyeballing continued for weeks and the PLA's loudspeaker offensive grew ever shriller. A change of command on the Indian side brought up two new battalions on September 9, plus orders for another strategic advance prior to removing a Chinese redoubt on the ridge. Better armed and acclimated, the Chinese anticipated the move; the next day they attacked the advance post in force. Both sides suffered some twenty to thirty casualties, but the PLA prevailed. The Indians pulled back.

This incident was either the final blow in the crescendo of Indian provocation or the opening salvo of the Chinese offensive. "For the first time the Chinese had forcefully resisted an Indian forward move," writes the China-sympathetic Neville Maxwell, then of the London *Times*.[7] "In the event," glosses Ramachandra Guha for the Indian side, "it was the enemy who acted first."[8] Neither side did anything immediately. The Chinese did not follow up their success by crossing what they took to be the McMahon Line, and the Indians did not withdraw from behind it. Rather, Nehru made it clear that, despite the obvious supply difficulties faced by the Indians, force would, if necessary, again be applied to reverse the setback and "regain" the Thagla Ridge; talks were out of the question, he said, until such time as "instructions to free our territory" were satisfactorily met. Meant to quell the domestic outcry, this was taken by the international press as tantamount to an ultimatum, if not a declaration of war. The Chinese too read it as such and made no secret of their preparations for a preemptive strike.

On October 20, six weeks after the earlier affray, Chinese mortars opened fire on the Indian positions, and the PLA advanced in both NEFA and Ladakh. What Indians dubbed China's "blitzkrieg" of aggression met stiff yet ill-prepared and hopelessly outgunned resistance. One after another the Indian positions fell like dominoes.

Four days into the war, Zhou again offered talks. Nehru's response combined pain with defiance. Nothing in his long political career had hurt him more than China's perfidy, he claimed, but India would talk only when the "Chinese invasion" had been reversed and the PLA was back behind the McMahon Line and beyond the Aksai Chin. Though gagging on a lifetime of rhetoric about nonalignment, he leaped at offers of arms from the United Kingdom and the United States. Within a week the Kennedy administration, despite its preoccupation with the Cuban missile crisis, was sending up to eight flights a day laden with ordnance and ammunition. Meanwhile, the Indian parliament approved a state of emergency, and for days its members vied with one another in talking up India's prospects. Patriotic gestures were all the rage. Recruitment offices were besieged and blood banks overwhelmed. Even the Communists rallied behind Congress. The nation was as one.

After a three-week lull, during which the Chinese built roads and the Indians juggled personnel (Menon was finally replaced, as were nearly all the field commanders), the Chinese offensive resumed. In NEFA the Indians opened a new front in the far east of the Agency; it was promptly rolled back with heavy losses. Meanwhile, from Tawang the main Chinese advance continued, as did the catalogue of Indian defeats. By November 20 "no organised Indian military force was left in NEFA or in the territory claimed by China in the western [Ladakh] sector." The advance in Ladakh had halted at the line claimed by the Chinese. But in NEFA the invaders were about 125 miles inside the McMahon Line, the last mountain passes had been taken, "the famous Fourth Division was cut to pieces, [and] the humiliation of the Indian army . . . complete."[9]

Ahead stretched the broad Brahmaputra plain of Assam. Tezpur, the nearest administrative center, was evacuated; further downstream, the Assamese capital of Gauhati looked doomed. A propos the Assamese, Nehru announced in a broadcast that "we feel very much for them and we shall help them to the utmost of our ability." It sounded more like a valediction than a pledge.

In a final throw of the dice, Nehru now appealed for direct US intervention. No US air strikes were forthcoming, but transport aircraft were supplied and the aircraft carrier USS *Enterprise* was diverted to the Bay of Bengal. Bombing raids on Calcutta were anticipated. "This Is Total War," declared a Bombay weekly.[10]

But even as these plans were being laid, they were becoming redundant. For on November 21, 1962, the Chinese again took New Delhi by surprise. Instead of pushing down into Assam, let alone bombing Calcutta, they announced a unilateral cease-fire, to be followed by an unconditional Chinese withdrawal to the positions occupied in 1959. In other words, they would pull back to the McMahon Line in the east while hanging on to the Aksai Chin in the west.

Though this was precisely what Beijing had been hinting at from the start, it was all so unexpected in India that Nehru scarcely knew how to respond. Instead he asked for clarification while he played for time and juggled platitudes. The United States and the Soviets urged acceptance. So, given the state of his forces, did India's chief of staff. The cease-fire was therefore tacitly observed, and the Chinese duly pulled back.

But public opinion, as represented in parliament and the press, detected just another humiliation. Indian-claimed territory, although regained in NEFA, was being surrendered in Ladakh, as was any chance of avenging the recent string of defeats and so redeeming the nation's honor. Nehru had promised that a peace-loving India, once aroused, would surprise its foes and that "the war with China will be a long-drawn-out-affair [and] may take years." But the balloon of war hysteria had no sooner been launched than it was being burst. With the enemy contemptuously turning its back, a deflated India was left to lick its wounds and rue its loss of reputation. What had been billed as a "Chinese invasion" had turned out to be merely a punitive exercise. Prisoners of war taken by the Chinese were swiftly repatriated, and captured vehicles were first cleaned and then left parked in line to await their Indian drivers. The war had impinged on no centers of population. It had, if anything, improved the local infrastructure. And it had lasted just thirty days.

To explain the Chinese retraction, it was suggested that with the onset of winter the Chinese high command had become mindful of the logistical problems posed by trans-Himalayan supply lines. Or perhaps it was the threat of US intervention that had done the trick. Perhaps too, Moscow had mended its crumbling fences with Beijing long enough to exert pressure on behalf of its Indian acolyte. Even more improbably, perhaps the strength of Indian resistance and the spectacle of national mobilization had prompted second thoughts in Beijing. Anything was better than the admission that around three thousand Indian lives (and possibly as many Chinese) had been lost, and the nation humbled, all because New Delhi had consistently misread Chinese intentions.

Nehru never fully recovered from the shock and "hurt" of the war. A year later he suffered a stroke, and in May 1964 he would die. "Wasted" or not, the Nehru years ended on a sour note. While in effect accepting the terms of the Chinese withdrawal—including a twenty-mile exclusion zone on either side of the 1959 lines of occupation—India had continued to decline any talks that might lead to recognition of the de facto frontier or to its demarcation. Subsequent governments would follow this example. Any agreement that implied the concession of Indian territory would remain anathema. Indian maps still showed the Aksai Chin as Indian territory, just as they showed Azad Kashmir and Pakistan's Northern Areas as Indian territory. But the Chinese retained control. In 2011 their Xinjiang-Tibet road was being upgraded, and in 2012 they announced plans for a space observatory in the Aksai Chin.

IRONICALLY, IN THE SAME WAY as a sharp reality check in the form of military defeat heralded the end of the Nehru era in India, so would a similar defeat signal the end of the Ayub Khan era in Pakistan. The wildly divergent trajectories of the two nations often obscure an underlying parallelism. But in Pakistan's case the consequences of a battlefield reverse, while dire for President Ayub Khan, would be even worse for Pakistan as a whole. India had rallied as one in the face of an external threat; as a result of another, Pakistan would be slowly sundered in two. A second partition loomed, and the very existence of Pakistan as a whole was about to be challenged.

In Pakistani eyes the culprit, inevitably, was India. Yet if any Pakistani leader appreciated the need for détente with India, it was Ayub Khan. Head of state in his role of chief martial law administrator and head of the armed forces in his assumed rank of field marshal, Ayub was virtually unchallenged during his first four years in power (1958–62). Without prejudice to Pakistan's stance on Kashmir, he could—and did—attempt to normalize relations with India. In 1959, as China's Aksai Chin road became common knowledge, he proposed a joint Indo-Pak defense pact against external aggression. "Of course I wanted the future of the people of Jammu and Kashmir to be decided according to their wishes," he would later recall, "but I was . . . also working for co-existence, for relaxation, and for understanding."[11] It came to nothing. Despite the Chinese threat, Nehru chose to interpret the offer of a joint defense arrangement as a bid to undermine his nonalignment and even insinuate Pakistani troops into India. Instead, New Delhi offered a no-war pact. But at the time this was unacceptable in Pakistan; it would preclude the freedom of action deemed essential by the more vulnerable of the two nations, and it might be interpreted as a weakening of Karachi's support for the Kashmiris.

Four years later, in 1962–64, a resolution of the Kashmir issue itself looked within reach. The initiative had come from the United States and the United Kingdom as a direct result of the Sino-Indian war. In return for supplying India with arms, and with a view to a united Indo-Pak front against the Chinese, the Western powers encouraged Nehru to enter into negotiations with Pakistan. This meant, above all, revisiting the question of Kashmir. Indeed, it was "one of the rare occasions when [the Indians] were obliged to depart from their established position over Kashmir," this being "that any discussions in some way implied that the status of Jammu and Kashmir was in doubt."[12] Six rounds of talks at ministerial level aired the options. They included some form of shared sovereignty over the whole state (which appealed to neither India nor Pakistan) and some form of partition (India would settle for the existing cease-fire line, Pakistan for nothing less than the whole of the valley). The gap was as wide as ever.

Meanwhile, Ayub Khan and the young Zulfikar Ali Bhutto, his foreign minister as of 1963, had followed Nepal's example by normalizing relations with China with regard to their own shared border. As inaccessible as any in the Himalayas, the border in question was of course that of the Northern Areas, a region that India still regarded as part of its Jammu and Kashmir state and that even Pakistan regarded as subject to whatever settlement might eventually be agreed upon for the state as a whole. According to India, the new Sino-Pak agreement involved bartering away 2,700 square miles of Indian territory in return for Chinese support of Pakistan's claim to Jammu and Kashmir. According to Pakistan, India's notions of the state's extent were as excessive in the north as in the Aksai Chin; no territory had been ceded and some had in fact been gained. The spat did nothing to improve the chances of agreement over Kashmir or to reassure the Western powers.

It did, though, confirm that the Karakorums were south of the border and that the world's second-highest mountain was therefore within the Northern Areas. But because the Northern Areas were themselves contentious, any attempt to give the mountain a name was rejected as premature. It remained just "K2," the designation given it by the surveyor who first plotted its position in the 1860s.

Within Kashmir nothing much changed until, in the winter of 1963–64, a treasured Muslim relic, a hair from the Prophet's beard, disappeared from the eponymous Hazratbal, a mosque just outside Srinagar. It was assumed it had been stolen, and Kashmiri Muslims readily accused Hindu zealots of being responsible. Angry crowds took to the streets throughout the Valley. Government forces responded with tear gas and bullets. Although the relic mysteriously reappeared, Kashmiri lives had been lost to Indian firepower, and for once Kashmiris had spoken out: Evidently they were no longer under any illusions about the shortcomings of Indian secularism. Nor were their Muslim co-religionists in Pakistan. Even in East Pakistan, a province so remote from Kashmir that it seldom shared in the national obsession with that state, Muslims were so incensed by the relic's theft and by India's heavy-handed treatment of the protesters that they turned on Hindus in Khulna and Jessore. Some hundreds of thousands duly fled toward the porous border into India as another wave of Bengali migration got under way. This was greeted by more outpourings of anti-Muslim communalism in India itself.

Partly to placate Kashmiri opinion, partly to right an old wrong, a Nehru chastened by the Chinese incursion had now agreed to the release of Sheikh Abdullah. During his six years behind bars, the "Lion of Kashmir" had been convicted of no crime; indeed, vindicated by his acquittal, he was now more respected than ever. He returned to the fray determined to convince his onetime friend Nehru to review what he called the "Kashmir problem." In Delhi he was Nehru's guest, and, according to the sheikh, the suggestion that he visit Pakistan to convince Ayub Khan to open negotiations came from Nehru. According to others, "it was Bhutto who stole a lead on the Indian leaders" by issuing the invitation.[13] Just back from New York, where in the course of the UN's 110th debate on the issue he had excoriated the West for its inaction in Kashmir, Bhutto was now setting the pace on Kashmir; but Ayub Khan approved. In May 1964 the sheikh flew to Rawalpindi and duly received a tumultuous welcome on what was his first and only visit to his Pakistani neighbor.

In amicable exchanges lasting a week, Sheikh Abdullah hinted at Nehru's more open-minded stance while registering his own opposition to any division of the state. Rather, he proposed demilitarizing Jammu and Kashmir and restoring its integrity within a tripartite confederal arrangement consisting of India, Pakistan, and Jammu and Kashmir. Ayub thought this both impractical and detrimental to Pakistan's sovereignty. But a proposal for the first-ever heads-of-government talks on Kashmir was agreed upon; Ayub in person would go to New Delhi to consult with Nehru. It was the most promising development in sixteen years of confrontation.

Tragically, it came too late. Before the month was out, Nehru suffered a second stroke and died within days. Bhutto and the sheikh did meet up in Delhi, but it was for the Indian prime minister's obsequies. The initiative then lapsed. Nehru's successor, Lal Bahadur Shastri, lacked the stature or the commitment to pursue it. Indeed, he approved further moves to integrate Jammu and Kashmir state into the Indian republic and in 1965 authorized the rearrest of the sheikh. Foreign Minister Bhutto responded by threatening "retaliatory steps." The year thus ended not with rapprochement but with the sheikh facing further detention, India and Pakistan more suspicious of each other than ever, and Bhutto promising "a thousand-year war" to "liberate" the Kashmiris.

Yet Ayub's Pakistan and Nehru's India were not incapable of mutual accommodation. A no less vital and contentious issue had already been partially settled. This concerned the flow of water to the irrigation-dependent farmlands on either side of Radcliffe's Partition line in the Punjab and Bengal. In essence the new frontier sliced through the Indus River and its tributaries in the west just as it did the Ganges and Brahmaputra Rivers in the east, so giving upriver India a stranglehold on the lifeblood of Pakistani agriculture. The problem had been recognized in 1947. Minor adjustments had been made by Radcliffe to ensure that the headworks of some of the affected canal schemes stayed within the territory of those dependent on them, and an arrangement based on previous usage plus an annual subvention from Pakistan had been accepted as a temporary expedient. Pakistan was happy to extend the principle of previous usage provided that the supply could be guaranteed. But India, anticipating heavier demand from the extension of irrigation to the dry regions of southeastern Punjab (Haryana) and Rajasthan, preferred a straight division of the waters: of the six main Indus basin feeders, the three more westerly rivers (Indus, Jhelum, and Chenab) might go to Pakistan, but the three more easterly (Ravi, Beas, and Sutlej) must go to India.

Discussions had opened in 1949, but, in countries where around 80 percent of the population depended on agriculture, the issue became heavily politicized. No government could afford to alienate rural voters by making concessions perceived as prejudicial to their crops.

On the other hand, Pakistan clearly needed some guarantee that it would not be held hostage by India, while India was understandably reluctant to surrender so obvious a bargaining counter. The talks dragged on until 1951 with much acrimony and minimal progress.

In 1952 they were revived on the initiative of the World Bank. Again agreement proved elusive until, in 1954, the bank came up with its own proposal. Pakistan, already the recipient of much US aid and weaponry, had just officially aligned itself with Washington by signing a treaty of friendship and joining SEATO; the bank's deeper involvement, not to mention its funding, could therefore be read as a quid pro quo. But India continued to insist on a division of the main feeder rivers and Pakistan on its prior right to water from all of them. After several more years of argument, it was the engineers who came up with a compromise and it was Ayub Khan's dictatorial rule that silenced the usual political opposition to it in Pakistan.

In signing the Indus Waters Treaty in 1960, Ayub and Nehru endorsed one of the very few international water agreements to be reckoned an abiding success. Neither two wars, later near-wars, the continued tension over Kashmir, nor sundry terrorist outrages would interrupt the operation of the treaty. To those who supposed India and Pakistan incapable of sharing anything, the slosh of the sluices was a salutary reminder that enmity need not inhibit development.

The treaty conceded India's argument for exclusive rights to the three eastern rivers. On the other hand, it also awarded to Pakistan a one-off payment for relinquishing them, plus an elaborate system of canals, dams, and reservoirs designed to offset the loss of the eastern rivers by diverting water from its western rivers to the areas affected. More important still, it set up a permanent commission to monitor the agreement and procedures for the settling of disputes. Both have been sorely tested over the years. Moreover, the treaty applied only to the Indus basin; in the east there was no such agreement on apportioning the waters of the Ganges and Brahmaputra between India and Pakistan. There India's construction of, for example, the Farakka barrage (to divert the main flow of the Ganges down the Hooghly River to Calcutta) would antagonize East Pakistanis and then Bangladeshis. In fact, Karachi's failure to defend the water rights of its eastern province with anything like the energy devoted to those of its Punjab province rated highly among the grievances being vehemently aired in Dhaka.

THE INDUS WATERS TREATY would serve its purpose well and have interesting side effects. Central to Pakistan's acceptance of it was the construction of the Mangla Dam across the Jhelum at a point where that river emerges from Azad Kashmir into Punjab province. The dam, more than 1.8 miles long and 125 feet high, with a hydroelectric capacity of 1,000 megawatts, was inaugurated in 1967 and at the time was one of the largest ever built. The World Bank and the international community shouldered the bulk of the financial cost, leaving Pakistan to bear the human cost, which was considerable. The Mangla reservoir flooded an area of almost a hundred square miles, most of it in Azad Kashmir. The important town of Mirpur was completely inundated, as were countless villages. In all, some one hundred thousand people were displaced, most of whom either moved to the cities of the Punjab or emigrated, their principal destination being Britain.

Under a work voucher scheme, admission to the United Kingdom of Commonwealth citizens was comparatively unrestricted in the early 1960s. Moreover, Mirpuris had already established some links with the country through prewar employment in shipping and wartime service in British India's armed forces. Partition and the 1947–49 war in Kashmir had led others to migrate, and the Pakistani government now endorsed further migration as a solution to the displacement caused by the dam. There ensued a rapidly growing exodus from the affected Mirpur area to Pakistan's Punjab and to the cities and mill towns of northern Britain. The scale of this migration could hardly compare with the upheavals occasioned by Partition, yet its narrow focus and international character highlighted certain specifics of the post-Partition diaspora and had a notable impact in parts of the United Kingdom.

With the addition of spouses and dependents, migrants of Pakistani origin would come to constitute Britain's largest South Asian community, and of these so-called British Pakistanis, "somewhere in the region of two-thirds [were] in fact of Azad Kashmir origin," mostly from Mirpur.[14] The majority of the United Kingdom's South Asian intake thus came to consist not, as commonly supposed, of Pakistani Punjabis but rather of Mirpuri Kashmiris, people who, though seldom Kashmiri-speakers, hailed from what was once part of the troubled Poonch region of Jammu and Kashmir state and was now Azad Kashmir.

Similar source-specific and destination-specific flows of migration would characterize the whole diaspora. In the United Kingdom, Sikh immigrants, many from Jalandhar, would make for west London, while East Bengalis would concentrate in parts of east London. Among the latter, whether known as East Bengalis, East Pakistanis, or Bangladeshis, more than 95 percent originated from Sylhet, which had been a district of Assam during British rule but had been detached in 1947 when its Muslim-majority areas voted to join Pakistan. Like Mirpur and like the Gurkha recruiting districts in Nepal, Sylhet was an agriculturally marginal region with a large percentage of owner-cultivators and a tradition of seeking work away from home. But while Mirpuris and Gurkhas had often enlisted in the British Indian army, Sylhetis had invariably opted for the navy and especially the merchant marine. Arriving in London's dockland, some had jumped ship and settled there. The skills learned at sea in engine rooms or galleys enabled them to find work in the engineering and catering industries.

Post-Partition Sylhetis followed in the footsteps of these pioneers. Often indebted to them for arranging work vouchers, they also relied on them as contacts and employment agents. Catering proved especially popular and led to Britain's proliferation of curry houses and "balti" takeout shops. By the 1970s almost every "Indian" restaurant in the United Kingdom was in fact Sylheti-operated, though the food was not obviously Indian, Bangladeshi, or Sylheti.

The migrants' objective was invariably to improve the social and financial status of their kin and community back home. Initially this meant they were overwhelmingly male and were intent on amassing savings to remit home for investment in land, housing, and marital alliances. By the 1970s more than half of Pakistan's foreign earnings, and nearly all of Azad Kashmir's, came in the form of migrants' remittances. Many migrants planned to return and often did so more than once. Emigration conferred status and influence back home. It also afforded a notable outlet for the expression of South Asian grievances through access to the press and parliamentarians in the United Kingdom. Mirpuris, for instance, took to airing their dissatisfaction with Pakistan's dismal record in restoring communications after the construction of the Mangla dam. Blaming Karachi for treating Azad Kashmir as a colony, they veered away from favoring Kashmir's integration with Pakistan and became "enthusiastic supporters of a Kashmiri entity which would be entirely independent of both India and Pakistan."[15] The 1977 formation of the Jammu and Kashmir Liberation Front, dedicated to achieving this independent Kashmir, would be announced in Birmingham and promoted largely by British Mirpuris.

In Pakistan, as in India, the construction of massive dams (another at Tarbela on the Indus would be begun in the late 1960s) served the crying needs for power generation, irrigation, and flood control while proclaiming the ambitious intent of Ayub's newly relaunched nation. In similar spirit, the field marshal in 1960 announced the relocation of Pakistan's capital. From its interim home in overcrowded Karachi it was to be removed to an airy Gotham purpose-built on scrubland near Rawalpindi in Punjab province. There was much to recommend the change. To be known as Islamabad, the site was more centrally located, albeit purely in terms of West Pakistan. Punjab was West Pakistan's most populous and assertive province, while Rawalpindi was the headquarters of the military; indeed, its firing ranges abutted the new city. Bureaucrats, politicians, and foreign diplomats would be more secure there—as well as more readily secured. Construction got under way immediately; occupation followed in stages throughout the early 1960s.

Ayub's model was Ankara and the Turkish national revival engineered by Mustafa Kemal Ataturk in the 1930s. Whether Pakistan could afford such extravagances was debatable, although the economy suggested it could. In a market less restricted than that of

India's "permit raj," manufacturing output grew by over 11 percent annually between 1960 and 1965, and the economy as a whole grew by around 5–6 percent. While India struggled to produce a trickle of outdated European vehicles indifferently made under license, nifty Japanese sedans began to replace Pakistan's worn-out Fiats and Morris Minors. Hilton, Marriott, and Pearl tendered for high-rise hotels to upstage the British-era watering holes of Faletti's in Lahore, Flashman's in Rawalpindi, and Dean's in Peshawar. Peeling posters and unsightly graffiti—a downside of democracy—were removed; everything that could be whitewashed was. Travelers braving the formalities of the only frontier crossing from India's Punjab to Pakistan's Punjab encountered smoother roads, more familiar billboards, fewer beerless bars, and almost no beggars. The country seemed to be touched by a recognizable modernity. There was no sign of a personality cult. Ayub's dictatorship looked to err on the side of leniency.

Yet, though per capita incomes were rising by around 3 percent per annum, "this was mostly because the rich got richer. The poor just got more."[16] Some 220,000 people a year dropped below the poverty line, the majority being in East Pakistan. Meanwhile, a mere twenty-two families, largely from the mercantile Muslim community once of Bombay but now of West Pakistan, were said to control an estimated 65–75 percent of the country's banking, insurance, and industrial assets. Such evidence of private enterprise reassured Pakistan's US backers, as did its excessive spending on defense. With the armed forces accounting for the lion's share of the budget, social services such as education and public health languished.

Ayub, the first soldier to exercise power in South Asia since Wavell had made way for Mountbatten, preferred the decencies of discipline and loyalty to the cerebral dictates of ideology. Beginning with a flurry of restrictions on everything from commodity hoarding to public urination, his corrective measures were directed especially at lax bureaucrats, corrupt businessmen, and venal politicians. Yet though named, shamed, and if necessary arraigned, few of them received heavy sentences, and anyway most of these were commuted. Supremely confident in his own notion of authority, Ayub was neither brutal nor vindictive. His land reforms, though relevant only in

West Pakistan and scarcely more effective than Nehru's, were a genuine attempt to reduce the larger holdings and endow the landless. Initiatives in favor of family planning and the reform of Muslim family law addressed discriminatory practices of gender and inheritance but were bitterly, and often successfully, opposed by conservative opinion. And with respect to education, though schooling was starved of funds, Ayub claimed that educating the nation was precisely what his "basic democracy" was all about.

The centerpiece of his innovations, "basic democracy" introduced electoral practices and some local accountability within a hierarchical framework that was probably modeled on the military's chain of command. The intent "was pure Ayub Khan": to induct the largely uneducated masses into the political process, so encouraging a sense of national responsibility while creating a popular base for the regime.[17] All adults were given the vote, but they might exercise it to choose only the 80,000–120,000 "basic democrats" in the lowest tier of the hierarchy. Each of these basic democrats represented about fifteen hundred voters and, political parties being banned, the first cohort consisted largely of newcomers. In 1960 they obliged their patron by overwhelmingly confirming him as president.

Ten to fifteen basic democrats constituted a "union council" (in rural areas) or a town council; each was responsible for local amenities and for electing one of its members to the next tier. This was the *tehsil* council, at which level unelected administrators might represent up to half the membership. *Tehsil* councils oversaw the work of their subordinate councils, distributed resources among them, and chose a representative for the next tier, that of district councils. These followed the same pattern, and so on up the chain of command. The higher the tier, the less the elected element and the greater the administrative presence, not to mention the more pronounced the directive input. It was basic, certainly, but it was not democracy. Though Hinduized as the panchayati raj by Nepal's King Mahendra, and later Bengalized by Bangladesh's leadership, it failed to win lasting acceptance anywhere.

In Pakistan it survived for nearly a decade mainly because Ayub's political opponents found easier targets. In 1962 Ayub, now president, gave Pakistan its second constitution. Based on his own ideas, drafted under the constraints of martial law, and rubber-stamped by a Legislative Assembly chosen by his basic democrats, it reserved sweeping powers to the president and was unmistakably the product of the military. Though it signaled the end of martial rule, it was welcomed only by bureaucrats and generals, the mainstay of the regime. The urban intelligentsia were embarrassed by it, East Pakistanis burned it, and politicians, whether feudalist, federalist, Islamist, or Marxist, contested it. It was hastily amended under pressure from both within the assembly and without. As a concession to the religious establishment, the country's name was changed back from the Republic of Pakistan to the Islamic Republic of Pakistan, and as a sop to the politicians the ban on political parties was lifted. Ayub knew when to give way and when not to. Because reinstating direct elections would have undermined the legitimacy of the regime, a proposal to that effect was shot down.

The reemergence of the old political parties and their combative leaders nevertheless obliged him to seek his own civilian constituency. "Basic democracy" having as yet failed to yield the desired base of support, he accepted the leadership of a faction of the revived Muslim League and, in 1965, mobilized it in support of his campaign for another five-year term as president. In a face-off with the combined opposition parties led by Jinnah's aged sister Fatima, Ayub triumphed. But it was a pyrrhic victory. As Ian Talbot writes, "He may have won the election but he lost the people."[18] Despite the advantage of having devised the electoral system, and despite all the resources of incumbency, only 62 percent of his basic democrats voted for him. Dictators expected better; to unite the nation behind him, an increasingly defensive Ayub needed a more emotive cause.

The contentious nature of the new constitution was not the only target of the regime's critics. Ayub's subservience to Washington and his failure to get India to relinquish Kashmir were also held against him. Even as the Constitution was being promulgated, New Delhi chose to flex its military muscle in Goa; then within a year India was reeling under the Chinese assault. To Pakistanis the invasion of Goa was bad enough, for it was all of a pattern with Nagaland and Kashmir and further evidence of India's irredentist ambitions with respect to the whole subcontinent.

Much worse, though, was the wave of Western sympathy that greeted the otherwise pleasing spectacle of India's Himalayan debacle. For at least a decade Pakistan had enjoyed preferential access to US weaponry and training, while India relied on purchases from the Soviet bloc and western Europe. Ayub had once told Congress that America had no greater friend in Asia than Pakistan. Hobnobbing with senior Americans, cultivating US aid donors, locking into SEATO and CENTO, and providing air bases for CIA spy planes (one of which, a U-2 flown by Gary Powers, was famously shot down over Sverdlovsk in 1960) were Ayub's ways of redressing Pakistan's physical and military vulnerability to India's supposed aggression. But Washington cared little about Indo-Pak relations and was wary of taking sides over Kashmir. Its prime concern was containing Communism. With its troops already engaged in Vietnam, it met the news of a Chinese breakout along the Himalayas with alarm, then alacrity. As C-30 transports began disgorging state-of-the-art ordnance at Indian airports, Pakistanis felt betrayed. They were no longer America's only arms-favored nation in South Asia. A decade of kowtowing to Washington had gotten them nowhere. Resentful mobs stormed through Karachi and sent foreigners scattering for cover at Flashman's in Rawalpindi.

By settling Pakistan's Himalayan frontier with China, Ayub too signaled his disquiet with Washington. But he was still seen as the architect and champion of the country's relationship with the United States and was thus tainted by what Pakistanis called the American "betrayal." Bhutto, his fiery foreign minister, had a better record in this respect. Berating India for its occupation of Kashmir, and the West for failing to condemn it, Bhutto welcomed Zhou Enlai to Pakistan and portrayed an India-hostile Beijing as a more sympathetic ally than Washington. Meanwhile, Kashmir was convulsed by the mysterious affair of the Prophet's hair; Sheikh Abdullah's olive-branch visit came and went; Nehru died; and Shastri provocatively pruned back Jammu and Kashmir's special status, then rearrested the sheikh. To Bhutto it was self-evident that neither diplomacy nor defeat had softened Indian intransigence over Kashmir. Moreover, there was no guarantee that India's newly supplied US arms would not be employed there. On the other hand, the untried Shastri was no Nehru, the Indian army had lately been exposed as incompetent, and nothing was better calculated to disarm criticism of the regime than a call to arms over Kashmir. Bhutto saw his moment.

Campaigning for Ayub during the 1965 presidential election, he savaged New Delhi's determination to "merge the occupied part of Kashmir with India" and vowed retaliation. "You will see better results in the very near future," he declared.[19] Then, the election out of the way, he delivered. In April 1965, while Ayub was in Washington, Pakistani armored vehicles advanced across the Rann of Kutch, the tidal expanse of salt flats where West Pakistan's long Indian border uncertainly dips its toe in the Indian Ocean. It was about as far from Kashmir as could be, but it was poorly defended and a good place for tanks.

More a skirmish over debatable frontier markers than a battle, the Rann of Kutch affair was hailed as a triumph in Pakistan. It might actually have become so had Ayub not intervened. Returning from Washington, the president restrained his gung-ho commanders, alerted his foreign minister to the danger of a counterstrike "at a time and place of India's choosing," as Shastri put it, and accepted a cease-fire pending negotiations. India agreed to international arbitration should the negotiations fail—something it had steadfastly rejected in the case of Kashmir. Ayub felt that a point had been made. His opponents felt that an opportunity had been wasted. In 1962 he had refrained from intervention in Kashmir when India was reeling under the Chinese assault; now he refused to move when Indian tanks were smoldering in the Rann of Kutch.

Undeterred, through the summer of 1965 Bhutto kept up the pressure. Lending credence to reports of widespread unrest in Kashmir itself, he informed the cabinet that, as in 1947, tribal volunteers were being recruited as "freedom fighters" to liberate Kashmir and that he had hatched a plan with the army to support them by infiltrating regular troops. He had no doubt both the troops and the irregulars would be welcomed by Kashmir's restless masses. He was also convinced that, after its mauling in the Himalayas and the Rann, India would not dare to escalate the conflict by deploying troops outside

Kashmir. On all counts he was wrong; but, recognizing the popular demand for action, Ayub gave the go-ahead. Thereupon the infiltrators were quickly captured, the Kashmiris proved indifferent, and in answer to a Pakistani incursion into Jammu, Indian motorized units cruised across the frontier in the Punjab and threatened Lahore. Far from scaring off the Indian tiger, tweaking its tail in Kashmir had merely led to its sinking its claws into Pakistan's vitals.

The 1965 war lasted only seventeen days, by the end of which India had lost slightly more men and Pakistan slightly more tanks. Aircraft losses were about equal, but the territorial advantage lay with India. Both sides were short of munitions, spare parts, and fuel, the United States having imposed an instant embargo, and both were under enormous international pressure to desist, Moscow being as adamant as Washington. Bhutto canvassed allies elsewhere, most notably in Indonesia, but it was Beijing's response that was crucial. Its offer of "unconditional support" had delighted Bhutto and had possibly deterred India from attacking Pakistan's almost undefended eastern wing. But the Chinese offer was in fact far from unconditional, for Pakistan must first commit itself to a Vietcong-type "people's war of resistance" in which "cities like Lahore might be lost."[20] Rightly concluding that the nation would split, if not fragment, in such a struggle, Ayub opted for the UN's cease-fire and an offer of talks with Shastri to be chaired by the Soviets. Held in Tashkent in early 1966, the talks restored the prewar status quo.

The difficulty now was persuading Pakistanis to accept the outcome. The relentlessly upbeat news coverage provided by the government had led the nation to believe the war was being won and that the cease-fire was India's way of signaling that it would back down, at least with regard to Kashmir's status. Hence, when nothing of the sort emerged in the final declaration—indeed, Kashmir was not even mentioned—riots broke out in Lahore and politicians united in decrying the "sell-out." The president brazened it out, but "the Tashkent Declaration dealt a mortal blow to Ayub's reputation."[21] Like Nehru after India's China war, Ayub lingered on, his health declining, until forced to resign in 1969.

Meanwhile, Bhutto completed his political somersault. Disclaiming responsibility not for the war but for its untimely conclusion, he dissociated himself from Ayub, blamed him for the Tashkent sell-out (though he had himself been party to the talks), and six months later resigned. By joining the agitation against Ayub's personal rule and forming his own Pakistan People's Party (PPP), he showed a nice awareness of the times. China was now convulsed by the Cultural Revolution, Paris was brought to a standstill by the événements de '68, and Washington was besieged by anti–Vietnam War demonstrations. Popular protest was all the rage. Bhutto, as much demagogue as democrat, endorsed even the strident demands for autonomy emanating from East Pakistan. Promising to outlaw dictatorship, reclaim Kashmir, and bring the economy into public ownership, he positioned himself for Pakistan's next flirtation with electoral democracy. But if the intent was to redeem the nation, the effect would be to rend it.

6

POWER TO
THE PEOPLE

ULFIKAR ALI BHUTTO IN PAKISTAN WAS NOT THE ONLY ONE advocating a populist agenda that would prove divisive. By the early 1970s a Nehru-less India was also confusing politics with personality, principle with slogans. Hunched on a wooden chest, Raj Narain leaned toward me and thumped the hut's floor of hard-packed mud with his stick.

"Madam is breaking the rules," he said as he surveyed the makeshift hustings outside. "These jeeps and *pandals* [electioneering platforms] are being paid for by the state. She has no right."

His stick jerked up and down in time with his words. Though he could barely walk without it, it was less a cane than a cudgel. Stout and steel-tipped, it was identical to the police *lathi* that had lamed him in the first place, he said. But that was long ago and in another cause; during a lifetime of obstreperous protest Raj Narain would claim to have been arrested more than eighty times. Now, in January 1971, he was standing for the Lok Sabha, the lower house of the Indian Parliament, as the Socialist Party's candidate for Rae Bareilly. A rural constituency in UP, Rae Bareilly conformed well to the description given by V. S. Naipaul of his own ancestral homeland elsewhere in the Gangetic plain: "wherever you looked there was a village, low, dust-blurred, part of the earth and barely rising out of it."[1]

But unlike the fastidious Naipaul, Raj Narain was quite at home here. He boasted of never having owned a suit, and he often covered his head with a bandana-like turban. Stubbled and stocky, in dirty white kurta and pajamas, the fifty-three-year-old was dressed for the campaign trail. To win the villagers' votes, he must remind them he was one of them. In an electoral battle with the incumbent prime minister, that should count.

Four weeks later, stick and stubble proved to have been of no avail. On polling day Raj Narain lost to Indira Gandhi by a crushing hundred thousand votes. Yet, never one to be easily cowed, he would contest the result. He took his grousing about his opponent's misuse of government facilities to the Electoral Commission and then the courts. Four and a half years later, the case would reach the highest court in the state, which decided in his favor. The Rae Bareilly result would be annulled, the prime minister disqualified from office, and India plunged into the Emergency, its greatest-ever constitutional crisis. Narain felt vindicated. Better still, when after the Emergency he again challenged his old adversary in Rae Bareilly, he would win.

The 1971 election thus had a sting in its tail. At the time it promised to be momentous, not least because it was unexpected. Given the standard five-year term, it was not actually due till 1972. That meant that for the first time India's parliamentary elections were not coinciding with elections to the state assemblies. As Raj Narain saw it, national issues were taking pride of place, principal among them being Mrs. Gandhi's claim to the legacy of Congress. Though already in her fifth year as prime minister, she had called the election a year early in a bid to confound her opponents and ratify her leadership. She herself put it even more bluntly. When a *Newsweek* reporter inquired what issues were at stake, "she answered without a pause: 'I am the issue.'"[2]

Nehru's immediate successor, Lal Bahadur Shastri, had never had to fight an election. As the world's most vertically challenged prime minister, he had enjoyed a suitably short tenure, just eighteen months. In 1966, within hours of signing the Tashkent agreement that ended the 1965 Indo-Pak war (also known as "Bhutto's war"), he had died of a massive heart attack. Once again the Congress Party's regional bosses, collectively known as the Syndicate, had put their heads together, and this time they had chosen Nehru's daughter. Born in 1917, the same year as Raj Narain, Indira Gandhi was not inexperienced. She had long acted as hostess for her father and had sometimes accompanied him on foreign trips. She had also involved herself in politics, serving as president of Congress under Nehru and as a minister under Shastri. More obviously, to an electorate primed on the heroics of the freedom struggle she sounded perfect. A Nehru by birth, she had become a Gandhi by marriage (that her now deceased husband was unrelated to the Mahatma was no secret, though neither was it a handicap). Yet she was a generation younger than most of the Syndicate bosses, added to which she suffered from the considerable handicap of being a woman. While recognizing her appeal to the electorate, the kingmakers felt reassured by this. Once in office she should pose no challenge to their authority over the party or the government.

In an age when women leaders were as much a novelty in Asia as anywhere else, only Sirimavo Bandaranaike, who became the prime minister of Ceylon in 1960, had preceded her. The Syndicate might usefully have studied this precedent, for "Mrs. B.," herself the widow of one premier and the mother of another, was proving a doughty operator in her own right. She had championed a program of nationalization and antagonized the Western powers, much as would Mrs. Gandhi. More ominously, she had curried favor with Ceylon's Sinhala-speaking Buddhist majority by promoting a nationalism that discriminated against the country's Tamil minority, most of them Hindus and originally wage migrants from south India. Naturally the DMK, the Tamil party in India's Tamil Nadu, had taken a dim view of this, and so, perforce, had the Indian government. Already under severe pressure from the DMK over the question of Hindi versus English as India's official language (in Ceylon Bandaranaike had outlawed the use of English despite Tamil protests), New Delhi had felt obliged to reach an agreement with Colombo: 375,000 Sri Lankan Tamils were to be given Ceylonese citizenship in return for India repatriating another 600,000. Thus began a staged migration of Ceylon's "estate Tamils" not only to India but beyond. For once it had nothing to do with Partition, although the Ceylonese Tamils and their diaspora would continue to set a dire precedent for the subcontinent as a whole.

In 1967, less than a year into her first prime ministership, Gandhi had had to fight her first election. She had won it comfortably if not convincingly. Congress's share of the vote had slumped from around 45 percent to 40 percent and its seat tally from around 360 to 280. A Communist-led coalition had recaptured Kerala, another edged out its rivals in West Bengal, and the DMK stormed to power in Tamil Nadu. Elsewhere, slender majorities won by patronage and bribes were soon eroded by patronage and bribes. Seemingly the broad church that once had been Congress could no longer take the strain of a myriad of assertive interest groups based on caste, religion, ethnicity, language, or ideological conviction. Politics was getting dirtier. Patriots with a social conscience, a decent education, and a law degree had once filled the ranks of Congress. Now few wanted any part in it.

Neville Maxwell, then of the London *Times,* reported the future for democracy in India as "dark" and "the crisis" as imminent.[3] Popular works such as Ronald Segal's *The Crisis of India* (1965) and Naipaul's *An Area of Darkness* (1967) faithfully echoed these sentiments amid a wrinkling of noses over "the dirt and the submission, the superstition and apathy, the greed and the corruption and the endless, astonishing and affronting poverty."[4] Over half of all Indians earned less than a living wage, and of these most habitually went hungry. A succession of poor harvests coupled with a hike in defense spending as a result of the China and Pakistan wars had just obliged Mrs. Gandhi to devalue the rupee by half and to negotiate another massive food aid package from the United States. Later assertions that famine in India had "disappeared abruptly with the establishment of a multi-party democracy" somehow overlooked the thousands starving in Bihar in 1966–67, just as they would overlook the estimated 1.5 million who would die for lack of food and adequate relief in a democratic Bangladesh seven years later. Arguably, if India was indeed experiencing fewer in the way of newsworthy famines, it had less to do with democracy and more with Partition having relieved New Delhi of responsibility for disaster-prone East Bengal.

With Congress heavily implicated in this catalogue of woe, Indira Gandhi needed to connect with the people by distancing herself from the party's "old guard" Syndicate and charting a new direction. Though usually diffident about her own beliefs, "she suddenly discovered a deep affinity for the poor and downtrodden, plus an unexpectedly dictatorial streak."[5] A program of radical reforms was announced. Banks and insurance companies were to be nationalized, a minimum wage introduced, and the ex-rulers of the princely states deprived of their "privy purses" (the privileges and annual state pensions awarded them in return for their accession). The plight of the nation's poorest demanded that India embrace more obviously socialist policies. Or as the prime minister's principal adviser put it, "The best way to vanquish the Syndicate would be to convert the struggle for personal power into an ideological one."[6] Nehru had embraced socialism as a matter of principle; his daughter seemed to be doing so as a matter of expediency.

Though agreeable to radical young Congress activists, the program met with stiff resistance from the Syndicate and especially from Morarji Desai, Mrs. Gandhi's deputy and finance minister. She simply relieved Desai of the finance portfolio and nationalized the banks anyway. Her confidence grew even as her "old guard" sponsors fumed. Matters had come to a head in early 1969 over the choice of the republic's next president. For an office that, though largely ceremonial, came with some constitutional powers as well as New Delhi's massive viceregal residence, the Syndicate nominated one of their own as Congress's official candidate. But Gandhi declined to endorse the Syndicate's man. Instead she finally broke ranks by lending her support to a more obliging rival. The predicted crisis had arrived.

In what amounted to a parliamentary vote of confidence in herself, the prime minister's candidate narrowly won the contest for the presidency. But the party retaliated by expelling her; she then formed her own breakaway Congress. Thus by 1970 there were two Congress parties. The prime minister's was known as Congress (R) (initially the R stood for "Requisitionist," an earlier attempt to requisition a special session of the party having failed, and then for "Reform"), but the name was later changed to Congress (I) (for "Indira"). The Syndicate's party was always Congress (O) (initially for "Organisation," but later interpreted as "Old" and ultimately "Obsolete"). Like the Muslim League in the early days of Pakistan, the mighty Congress, the juggernaut of the freedom struggle and the embodiment of the national consensus, had fractured.

Gandhi preferred to think of it as purged. She soldiered on, having cobbled together a parliamentary alliance with the less radical of the two Communist Parties. But with both bank nationalization and her assault on the princes stalled on constitutional grounds by the Supreme Court, and with other reforms opposed on principle by Congress (O), in late 1970 she took her opponents by surprise and announced the snap election of 1971. Both her future and the country's direction were in the balance. The upcoming election, and particularly the result in Rae Bareilly, could hardly have been more critical.

"*Indira hatao,* out with Indira," croaked Raj Narain. It was by way of a farewell as he hobbled away to find his lift into town. Coined by himself, the slogan had been adopted by the Congress (O) diehards with whom his Socialist Party was aligned.

"*Gharibi hatao,* out with poverty," countered the prime minister's supporters as their flag-waving motorcade trundled off into the dead-flat distance and the dust slowly settled.

Thanks to Gandhi's indefatigable campaigning, her catchier slogan, and her relentless assault on the "forces of reaction," even the pollsters were confounded. In 1971 the number of seats won by her Congress (R) was much the same as that chalked up by the undivided Congress under Nehru in 1962. It was an essentially personal triumph, and it heralded an increasingly personal rule.

Never much of a performer in the Lok Sabha, she could now afford to take her party's support for granted. Her mandate was from the people, not parliament, while her policies emanated from an inner circle of advisers, not the cabinet. In a spate of constitutional amendments, she reined in the Supreme Court's powers to interpret the constitution by arguing that the fundamental rights accorded to the individual must be subordinated to those of society as a whole if

India was to become more egalitarian. Nehru might have approved; a radical redistribution of wealth and influence to those who could only dream of such things looked possible. But it was for the state to determine what society needed, and since "Indira is India and India is Indira," as one of her supporters would put it, the state had gotten a lot more personal. It could be caring and responsive; it could also be detached and vindictive. A rush of power to the head was no guarantee against the misuse of all that power.

Thus armed, Gandhi pushed through the takeover of the banks, then the insurance and coal industries. Likewise, the ex-princes lost their stipends. The judiciary was encouraged to be more committed, which could mean less impartial, and the bureaucracy to be more engaged, which could mean less principled. Meanwhile, hostile or noncompliant state governments were being toppled like ninepins. At the national level, participatory democracy was being corralled into the twice-a-decade vote bazaars that heralded an election. "The drift was unmistakably toward a Jacobin conception of popular sovereignty," according to Sunil Khilnani.[7] In her new avatar as a many-armed deity, Gandhi bestrode the barricades, ballot box in one hand, progressive directives in all the others. Rae Bareilly was remembered only for her reincarnation. The skeleton in the cupboard that was Raj Narain's obsessive concern for the niceties of electoral practice looked destined to stay there, amid a whiff of sour grapes.

ACROSS THE BORDER IN PAKISTAN, Gandhi's triumph went largely unremarked. Islamabad's future bête noire was as yet rated no more highly than the geriatric leadership of the Syndicate she had toppled. At any rate, Pakistan faced a test of its own. In view of that country's erratic acquaintance with democracy, the chances of a Pakistani election coinciding with an Indian one were slim. But in 1970–71 they fell within a few weeks of each other. Both polls were reckoned fair and highly significant. And while in Indira Gandhi's India the election proved satisfactorily decisive, in bipartite Pakistan it merely highlighted the bipartite division. "People power," as yet so affirmative for New Delhi, was already proving calamitous for Islamabad.

After the fiasco of the 1965 war with India, President Ayub Khan had met the protests against his perceived sell-out in Tashkent with firmness. Colleges and universities had been closed and efforts to restore the army's morale got under way. A national conference staged by the leaders of the political parties became a pretext for their arrest and "revealed more about the divisions within the opposition than their capacity for unity."[8] Among those detained was Mujibur Rahman, the heavily bespectacled and mustachioed leader of the Awami League. An East Bengali party formed by H. S. Suhrawardy and others in 1949–50, the Awami League had just committed itself to a six-point program demanding for East Pakistan the fullest possible autonomy short of independence. As well as insisting on a parliamentary representation commensurate with its population, the province was to exercise its own fiscal powers, mint its own currency, manage its own trade and economy, and raise its own militia; only foreign affairs, defense, and certain coordinating responsibilities were to be delegated to the central government in Islamabad.

President Ayub Khan regarded Mujib's Six Points as tantamount to a demand for outright secession, and he was not alone: most of West Pakistan's politicians agreed. But they attributed the Awami League's demand to the repressive nature of military rule and accorded a higher priority to things such as the restoration of democratic rights, the revival of the provincial legislatures (i.e., an end to the "one-unit" amalgamation of West Pakistan), and the removal of Ayub himself. In effect, opinion in West Pakistan favored political participation as the prerequisite to addressing provincial grievances, while opinion in East Pakistan would not even consider participation until provincial autonomy was conceded. Faced with this conundrum, the now ailing Ayub responded with a mixture of overtures and threats: if the parties would work with him, he would lift the state of emergency imposed during the war, but, if not, he would reintroduce martial law.

Neither option held much appeal for Mujibur Rahman and the Awami League. Throughout East Pakistan, intermittent protest was turning into sustained violence. An observer in 1968 found Dhaka's students and teachers "readily admitting . . . that many student leaders carry knives and guns and use them frequently to settle political disputes." Alongside the campus rabble-rousers, "workers and street mobs" were now joining in the movement, attacking police stations, banks, and government buildings. Arms were being looted and "disagreements . . . increasingly settled by terrorist methods."[9]

The demonstrators demanded implementation of the Six Points as a guarantee against cultural disparagement and ethnic discrimination in the regime's allocation of government jobs, investment, and social programs. Lawrence Ziring writes in his history of Pakistan, "As the riots [in East Pakistan] spread and intensified, the years of martial law, political restrictions, press controls, educational neglect, static wages, escalating inflation, a self-serving entrepreneurial elite, and a callous bureaucracy spurred the anger."[10]

A further dimension was added by the so-called Agartala Conspiracy. In January 1968 Mujibur Rahman and thirty-five others were brought to trial for making treasonable contact with officers of India's army. A plan to do away with Ayub and declare East Pakistan independent had allegedly been hatched, and talks had certainly taken place, notably at Agartala, just across the East Pakistan border in the Indian state of Tripura. But they dated back to 1962, before the Indo-Pak war, and it was unclear to what extent senior figures on either side were involved. Ayub still felt that a state trial was essential. Well publicized, it would discredit the Awami League and bring home to his countrymen the seriousness of the situation in the eastern wing. In the event, though, it simply backfired. The prosecution faltered when it emerged that one of the accused had died in custody and that others had apparently been tortured; Mujib and his defense found the courtroom a congenial platform from which to proclaim their grievances; and East Pakistan celebrated its latest "martyrs to the cause" with additional massive demonstrations. Writes journalist Owen Bennett-Jones, "Before the trial few in Pakistan dared to discuss secession in public. But as the newspapers printed more and more details of the proceedings, debate about breaking away became a normal part of public discourse."[11] In Dhaka the trial itself came to be seen as the conspiracy, the prosecutor being Mujib, the accused Ayub, and his treachery that of blackening East Bengalis as India-loving traitors to Islam.

Recognizing that the whole exercise was becoming hopelessly counterproductive, Ayub called it off, released Mujib, and made a final attempt at conciliation. It took the form of roundtable talks held in March 1969. Ayub had already announced that on health grounds he would not contest the presidential election to be held under his "basic democracy" rules in 1970. He hoped that this news would concentrate minds. It did, but not the right minds. The top brass, including army chief of staff General Agha Muhammad Yahya Khan, began planning for the succession. Meanwhile, Mujib, having been denied his Six Points, walked out of the talks. More crucially, Zulfikar Ali Bhutto and his Pakistan People's Party boycotted them altogether.

Over the previous months Bhutto, once Ayub's most trusted adviser, had emerged as his most outspoken critic. Riding a wave of hostility directed partly at the Ayub regime he had once upheld, partly at the war he had promoted, and partly at the Tashkent talks he had attended, Bhutto now discovered his vocation as the voice of the people. Morarji Desai had once described Indira Gandhi as "a dumb slip of a girl," the implication being that supporters flocked to her because of who she was and what she stood for, not because of what she said. Bhutto was the opposite. He told his supporters what they wanted to hear. His histrionic oratory laced with cleverly marshaled arguments convinced even himself. Indira Gandhi's "Out with poverty" might be a well-intentioned slogan, but Zulfi Bhutto's cry of "Bread, cloth and housing" addressed the needs of the masses. Backed by his demands for social justice and the nationalization of all the most remunerative sectors of the economy, it carried conviction.

So did his heavily publicized meetings with China's leadership. While Ayub sucked his pipe and cast a fly like the Sandhurst product that he was, Bhutto sported a Chairman Mao forage cap and looked to Beijing for the arms shipments still denied to Pakistan by the US embargo imposed during the 1965 war. Of the great powers, China alone supported Pakistan's position over Kashmir, which was reason enough for a Sino-Pak alignment. Bhutto's own belligerent stance on Kashmir was not forgotten either. It played especially well in the Kashmir-adjacent Punjab and NWFP; it also served to deflect attention from the secessionist province in the east to the one in the north that had yet to accede. In an essay published in 1969 Bhutto argued that India's continued occupation of most of Kashmir lay at the core of all Pakistan's problems.

> Why does India want Jammu and Kashmir? She holds them because their valley is the handsome head of the body of Pakistan. Its possession enables [India] to cripple the economy of West Pakistan and, militarily, to dominate the country. . . . If a Muslim majority area can remain a part of India, then the *raison d'être* of Pakistan collapses. . . . Pakistan is incomplete without Jammu and Kashmir both territorially and ideologically. Recovering them, she would recover her head and be made whole, stronger, and more viable.[12]

To that end he revived the promise of a "thousand-year war" and taunted Ayub with having betrayed the Kashmiris in the Tashkent agreement. The people loved it. In mass rallies he lambasted the regime, castigated the United States, and savaged an economic system that enriched the few and did nothing for the many. Students, labor unions, and the intelligentsia responded with enthusiasm. Of all the parties, only Bhutto's PPP reached out across West Pakistan's ethnic, social, and linguistic divides. Even among the military his commitment to the country's defense and to the nation's integrity won respect and allies.

It was thus inevitable that, without Bhutto or Mujib, Ayub's last attempt at conciliation would collapse. At the instigation of General Yahya Khan, martial law was reimposed. Ayub's authority drained away, and on March 25, 1969, he resigned. In defiance of his own constitution, he nominated Yahya Khan as chief martial law administrator and his successor as president. Two years later, it would be Yahya Khan's regime that initiated the crackdown in East Pakistan that precipitated the province's rebirth as independent Bangladesh.

Like Ayub ten years earlier, Yahya immediately clamped down on various corrupt practices and promised a new constitution plus early elections at both the provincial and national levels, followed by a return to parliamentary government. But this time the elections were to be on the basis of "direct adult franchise," and, unlike Ayub, Yahya was as good as his word. New constituency boundaries were drawn, electoral rolls prepared, and a date for the poll set in late 1970. Meanwhile, a Legal Framework Order was promulgated to guide the soon-to-be-elected members of the National Assembly in developing what would be Pakistan's third constitution. The 1956 Ayub-Mirza constitution was therefore abrogated, Ayub's elaborate "basic democracy" was allowed to lapse, and his "one-unit" West Pakistan was rescinded in favor of West Pakistan's reinstated provinces.

The Legal Framework Order stipulated that the new constitution would be subject to presidential approval but was otherwise surprisingly inclusive. Islam was to be respected, elections were to be based on universal adult franchise, provincial autonomy was to be guaranteed save with regard to the central government's conduct of external and certain internal affairs, and the economic and employment disparities between the provinces were to be removed. Against considerable opposition from his supporters within the military, Yahya's advisers had come up with a formula that might just have worked.

Even Mujibur Rahman could live with it. Of the 326 seats in the new Assembly, 169 would be filled by members from East Bengal, finally reflecting that province's numerical superiority and giving it a majority over the combined membership from all the other provinces; the Awami League duly put up candidates for all of the East Bengal seats. But Mujib, under pressure from extremists among his supporters, kept his distance from the Yahya regime. He preferred to conduct the election as if it were a referendum on the Six Points and let it be known that secession was still a possibility. Bhutto, on the other hand, though a onetime supporter of Mujib's Six Points, now vehemently rejected them and, strengthening his links with the military, posed as the savior of the undivided nation.

Thus, twenty-three years after its creation, while India geared up for its fifth round of direct national elections, Pakistan launched into its first. Since "the activities and electioneering of the participants were nothing like anything yet experienced in the history of Pakistan," predictions about the outcome were understandably tentative.[13] In west Pakistan, against a kaleidoscope of parties representing purely provincial interests plus various shades of Islamic orthodoxy, ideological preference, and Muslim League tradition, Bhutto was expected to be a major contender; in Sind, feudal landowners were expected to secure the vote for Bhutto, who was one of their own; and in Punjab, whose eighty-one seats comfortably exceeded the combined total for the other provinces of West Pakistan, Bhutto could expect to carry the urban vote and, by dint of hard bargaining with landed interests and Sufi divines, make inroads into the rural vote.

Mujib's task in a heavily politicized East Bengal looked more daunting. In addition to the Islamic parties and the Muslim League factions, his Awami League was in danger of being upstaged by the quasi-Maoist and outright secessionist National Awami Party, led by the eighty-nine-year-old "Red Maulana," Abdul Hamid Khan Bhashani. Maulana Bhashani, however, was a man of inflexible principle. He would have nothing to do with Yahya's Legal Framework Order. Despite the boost to Mujib's prospects (or possibly to enhance them), he therefore instructed his supporters to boycott the elections. That cleared the way for Mujib's Awami League to make an exclusive claim to the votes of all those who increasingly called themselves "Bangla-desh" (Bengali-land) patriots.

As so often in ill-starred Bengal, it was a natural disaster that had the final say. First, monsoon flooding necessitated a postponement of the vote from October to December. Then in November a cyclone moved slowly up the Bay of Bengal. It struck the coastal districts of East Bengal on the evening of November 12. Coinciding with the high tide, a storm surge up to thirty-two feet high tore across the offshore islands and swept inland up the low-lying delta. Tens of thousands of villages were erased, and fields, fishing fleets, and livestock were carried away. Around half a million people are known to have lost their lives and more than three million to have been left homeless and destitute. In all probability, what is widely recognized as the deadliest cyclone ever recorded accounted for more fatalities than the combined toll for the massacres of Partition, the 1947–48 Kashmir war, the 1962 India-China war, and the 1965 Indo-Pak war.

The elections nevertheless went ahead, as it was thought that another postponement might attract accusations of bad faith. But such accusations could hardly have compared with those of complacency and incompetence leveled at Islamabad over the relief effort. The regime appeared not to take the disaster seriously, then to skimp on assistance when belatedly shamed into action by the international community. Eighteen helicopters were rushed to the scene by the United States and the United Kingdom; Islamabad managed just one. It blamed India for refusing transit rights, but India denied this and blamed Pakistan for not allowing it to fly its own considerable relief effort into East Bengal. Red tape and the misappropriation of resources further angered the survivors. Whatever their voting intentions might have been, East Bengalis now united in protest against a criminal indifference that seemed to epitomize West Pakistan's two decades of neglect in the province. Bhashani turned out before a crowd of fifty thousand to excoriate the regime's response. Mujib noted wryly that "we have a large army but it is left to the British marines to bury our dead."[14]

The cyclone effect, allied to Bhashani's boycott, carried the elections. Mujib's Awami League won an astonishing 160 of East Bengal's 162 seats (a further seven being reserved for women). Even Indira Gandhi would never achieve such a result. It was the most impressive performance ever recorded in a free election of comparable magnitude. Mujib was assured of an overall majority in Pakistan's National Assembly whatever the outcome in the provinces of West Pakistan. Yet there Bhutto too did better than expected, his PPP capturing 81 of a possible 138 seats. There were thus two clear winners. And just as Mujib had won not a single seat in the west, so Bhutto had won not a single seat in the east. Pakistan's first proper election had exposed the structural fault that decades of constitutional wallpaper and military whitewash had failed to obscure, let alone rectify.

The nightmare scenario foreseen by many, including Ayub and Yahya, had now materialized. Bengali supremacy was certainly no more acceptable to Punjabis—or, for that matter, to Pathans, Sindis, and so on—than Punjabi supremacy had been to Bengalis. While compromising on Mujib's Six Points would trigger a revolution in the east, denying Bhutto a share of power would spark a revolution in the west.[15]

Any chance of a political settlement now depended on negotiations between Mujib, Bhutto, and Yahya Khan. None of them was a free agent. Yahya had to contend with a military junta deeply suspicious of his intentions, Mujib with zealous supporters whose expectations no longer stopped at autonomy, and Bhutto with importunate power brokers in the provinces of west Pakistan. All three were guilty of inconsistent statements tailored to circumstance. Their motivations and strategies are thus hard to discern. Yahya strove for a peaceful accommodation while his junta busied itself with plans for military intervention, Mujib hinted at compromise on his Six Points while publicly ruling out anything of the sort, and Bhutto posed as a mediator while nursing designs as a principal.

Yahya's first response to the result was conciliatory. He accepted Mujib's claim to the prime ministership of all Pakistan and agreed that the National Assembly convene in Dhaka rather than Islamabad. Mujib took this as a commitment and expected to hold Yahya to it. Bhutto objected. Since Mujib insisted on making his Six Points the basis of the new constitution, Bhutto demanded that the constitution be settled before the Assembly met. Otherwise the PPP would not participate, which would be "like staging *Hamlet* without the Prince of Denmark," as Bhutto put it. Yahya thus had both a good reason (Mujib's recalcitrance) and a handy excuse (Bhutto's boycott) for postponing the Assembly.

But on March 1, 1971, an announcement to that effect just two days before the Assembly was due to convene was the last straw for Mujib and his supporters. "It struck the Bengalis with the force of an atomic bomb," according to one observer.[16] An indefinite general strike was called; millions took to the streets, and widespread fighting was reported. Pakistani flags were burned and replaced by ones displaying a golden outline of East Bengal within a blood-red disk against a lush green surround. The police were overwhelmed, and the army opened fire. West Pakistan in the persons of Yahya and Bhutto had betrayed the Bengalis once too often. "The struggle now is the struggle for our independence," Mujib told a mass rally on March 7. "Turn every house into a fort. Fight with whatever you have."

While in India Mrs. Gandhi was savoring her electoral triumph, in Pakistan Yahya was presiding over an electoral disaster. He named a new date for the opening of the Assembly, but it was only by way of playing for time. Echoing Bhutto, he now referred to Mujib as a "bastard" and "traitor," while his generals pressed ahead with plans for a military solution.

But this too proved to be far from straightforward, for mounting what they called "Operation Searchlight" had just gotten a whole lot harder, thanks to a seemingly unrelated incident. On January 30 an antiquated Fokker Friendship belonging to India's state airline had been hijacked to Pakistan's Lahore while on an internal hop from Srinagar to Jammu. There were no casualties, for the crew and passengers had been released, and the hijackers, being Kashmiris, had been fêted. But the plane itself had been deliberately burned, and, in protest, India hastily placed a ban on all Pakistani overflights of its territory. Though it would later be claimed that the whole affair was in fact the work of the Research and Analysis Wing (RAW) of Indian intelligence, the ban on overflights stood. For Pakistan, ferrying men, munitions, and supplies from west to east now involved an eight-hour flight with a refueling stop in what was still Ceylon.

By this roundabout route Yahya and Bhutto headed to Dhaka for last-minute negotiations in mid-March. The negotiations turned out to be little more than window dressing. In the East Bengal capital the visitors were made to feel like unwelcome foreigners, mobbed by black-flag-waving crowds and heavily guarded for their own security. Meanwhile, Mujib took the salute from student militias parading under the colorful new ensign of Bangladesh. An eleventh-hour compromise was rumored but was overtaken by events. Yahya flew home empty-handed on the twenty-fourth, Bhutto following within hours. When the PPP leader landed in Karachi, the Pakistani army's genocidal Operation Searchlight had already begun. Knowing this full well, Bhutto issued another of his rhetorical clangers. "By the grace of God, Pakistan has been saved," he announced.

THE WAR IN EAST BENGAL began on March 25, 1971, two years to the day after Ayub Khan had stepped down as president. Yet despite the election results and the frantic attempts at negotiation, it took the world by surprise. Foreign correspondents leisurely dissecting the outcome of the Indian election in Delhi were summoned to the telex and reassigned to Dhaka. A scramble for airline seats ensued, only to be aborted by the cancellation of all East Bengal–bound flights, as Dhaka's airport had been closed. The land the journalists were starting to call "Bangla Desh" was already under lockdown.

In what would prove to be a two-part war, the first phase, from March to June, pitched regular Pakistani forces against Bangladeshi irregulars and brought a quick but uneasy victory for the former. The Awami League's ill-prepared and uncoordinated militias were no match for the armor and superior firepower of the Pakistani army. By May all the main cities had fallen, the last being Chittagong, from where a weak signal from a radio station had carried a declaration of Bangladesh's independence. It was read by the then little-known Ziaur Rahman, a major in the Pakistani army's East Bengal regiment who had thrown in his lot with the resistance.

Mujib himself had been quickly arrested and taken to West Pakistan for trial. Other Awami League leaders had made their escape across the ever-permeable border into India, there to be joined by thousands, then millions, of fleeing Bangladeshis. The Pakistani army had locked down the cities but had done nothing to win over their teeming populations, nor did it control the countryside and the rural masses. Instead of pacifying the population, it seemed bent on decimating it. Hearts and minds were ignored; intimidation and vengeance prevailed. The despised Bengalis had challenged the two-nation theory and hence the very existence of Pakistan, so now they must pay the price.

The Pakistani army was not the only instigator of atrocities. Before the war, as law and order collapsed, Awami League activists had retaliated against the shooting of demonstrators by lynching west Pakistani officials and anyone seen as collaborating with them. The violence—killings, burnings, and rapes—echoed the horrors of Partition and targeted the most vulnerable groups, including East

Bengal's still-large community of Hindus (the whipping boys of both sides), along with its smaller community of "Bihari" Muslim migrants (the already twice-over victims of Partition) and the predominantly Buddhist "tribal" peoples of the Chittagong Hill Tracts.

With the launching of Operation Searchlight, the Pakistani army had responded in kind and on a much more ambitious scale. Disaffected units of locally recruited regiments that had not immediately deserted to the enemy were ruthlessly purged. So were suspect Bengali members of the administration. Students and intellectuals being in the forefront of the movement, Dhaka University was an early target. Its residence halls were shelled, hundreds were killed on the spot, and hundreds more, both students and academics, were bused away, their bodies to be later exhumed from mass graves. With official sanction, squads of killers prolonged the carnage in the cities; sweeps into the countryside left a swath of burned-out villages and a trail of raped and mutilated victims. Those on the run dodged between aerial bombings and overland raids.

> We spent a night in a village but next morning we heard that the [Pakistani] troops were headed for that village. Again we left along with the owner of the house. After a couple of days when we returned, we found the whole village burnt to ashes. Many of the people who could not escape were killed. The carcasses of livestock were strewn all over. The stench was unbearable. It was hell![17]

Once again Hindus, seen by the Pakistani army as India's fifth columnists, suffered disproportionately. Muslim Biharis, whose pre-Partition roots in India were no different from those of *muhajir* elements in the Pakistani army, fared better. A few were transported to West Pakistan for their own safety; others were recruited as informants and auxiliaries, for which services they would pay dearly when the tide of war turned.

As usual, the actual figures are disputed. Pakistan admitted to substantial military losses; Bangladesh claimed civilian losses of up to three million. It was the same with the refugee exodus across the border into the neighboring states of India. Islamabad sanctioned a final figure of two to three million refugees, New Delhi one of eight to ten million. Either way, observers again noted similarities with Partition, this time with the mass migrations witnessed in the Punjab in 1947–48. Less remarked, though, was the similarity in the confessional allegiance of the refugees. Whatever the total, as many as 90 percent of the migrating refugees were not in fact Awami League sympathizers from East Bengal's Muslim majority but members of East Bengal's embattled Hindu community, many of them low-caste cultivators and menials. To West Pakistanis, the ten-million-strong Hindu community was the canker at the heart of the problem. Regarded as a subversive element whose real loyalties lay with India, East Bengal's Hindus stood accused of undermining Muslim solidarity and instigating secession. Targeted accordingly, their flight replicated that of other East Bengalis in the 1950s and 1960s and was seen by many of the migrants as a prelude to permanent settlement in India.

In this they were disappointed, for New Delhi was adamant that all must eventually return. While shouldering the burden of relief, it therefore detained the refugees in temporary encampments, most of which were dotted along the border and soon fell prone to cholera. The sheer scale of the exodus was said to preclude the possibility of rehabilitation elsewhere in India. Additionally, the plight of the massed refugees was a powerful weapon in India's management of international opinion.

In a major diplomatic offensive of April 1971 Indian officials set out to alert world leaders to the humanitarian crisis and to press them into prevailing on Islamabad for a settlement with the Awami League that would enable the displaced to return. Sympathy and pledges of aid were forthcoming, but no government relished the consequences of intervening in what was regarded as a purely Indo-Pakistani affair. In Washington, President Richard Nixon thought too well of Yahya Khan, whose good offices were essential to Henry Kissinger in arranging his groundbreaking visit to Beijing that summer.

The one exception was Moscow. There India's foreign minister reaped the benefit of earlier overtures and returned with a draft agreement. Under the new Indo-Soviet Treaty of Peace, Friendship and Cooperation, signed in August 1971, the pretense of Indian non-alignment was finally laid to rest. To offset China's budding relationship with Pakistan and to cut off a trickle of Soviet aid and arms to Pakistan, India subscribed to a version of the Brezhnev Doctrine. Under it, each country undertook to consult and assist the other in the event that either of them was attacked or came under threat of attack. In effect, should India feel so menaced by the situation in East Bengal as to contemplate intervention, it could count on the support of an ally powerful enough to discourage China or the United States from intervening on behalf of Islamabad.

That India was indeed an interested party in the possible breakup of Pakistan was taken for granted. But, aside from the question of who had been responsible for the timely hijacking that had closed Indian airspace to Pakistani flights, it seemed as if Pakistan was imploding of its own accord. Restraint rather than intervention looked to be New Delhi's best option. When, therefore, the director of India's Institute of Defence Studies and Analyses saw in the breakdown of negotiations in Dhaka "an opportunity the like of which will never come again," he was silenced. Yet six weeks later Indira Gandhi was coming around to the same opinion. Events in East Bengal were running contrary to all that India stood for. A democratic mandate was being flouted, Hindus were being massacred, and the Pakistani army was now massed in force along India's porous and hitherto unmilitarized eastern border. Moreover, according to Mrs. Gandhi, the growing number of refugees served as evidence that Islamabad was pursuing a solution "at the expense of India and on Indian soil." This, according to her advisers, constituted "indirect aggression."[18]

Further evidence of active Indian interest came with New Delhi's decision to host the activities of a Bangladesh government-in-exile. Formed by Awami League officials loyal to Mujib who had escaped to India, the interim government was installed at "Mujibnagar," or "Mujib Town." This was a movable venue—initially it was located on a property in Calcutta but was later shifted to a disputed sector of the nearby border so that it could claim to be operating from Bangladeshi soil. In the same mischievous spirit, the Indian army was instructed to equip and train Bangladeshi guerrilla units, known collectively as the Mukti Bahini, that were conducting sabotage raids into East Bengal from Indian territory. Both initiatives were in marked contrast to Delhi's hands-off attitude toward the Tibetan refugees a decade earlier. Then, in deference to Beijing, Nehru had refused to countenance a Tibetan government-in-exile and had denied support to those Khampas and others who were actively engaged in opposing the Chinese. Now, in deference to no one, Indira Gandhi took it upon herself to arm and actively support East Bengal's "freedom fighters," sponsor their self-declared government, and protest to Colombo over Ceylon's airports being used to refuel Pakistan's Dhaka-bound airlift of munitions and troops (the troops slipped into civilian clothes for the Colombo stopover). India's earlier restraint with regard to what was still part of Pakistan was giving way to hostile engagement. Critics saw parallels with the last days of Goa, Hyderabad, and Kashmir. Evidently neighborly noninterference was on a short fuse within the confines of what had been pre-Partition India.

Within East Bengal/Bangladesh, Pakistan's military lockdown was followed by the monsoon shutdown. From June till August the rivers flooded and the countryside became impassable; supplies for the Pakistani forces ran short and for the general population even shorter. Across the border in India the refugee camps turned into quagmires. The number of cholera cases there rose to forty-six thousand. Both sides became dependent on international food aid. Meanwhile, another source of Indian concern brought the prospect of intervention still closer.

Quite apart from the strain of the refugees, Gandhi and her advisers were increasingly alert to the impact East Bengal's defiance of Islamabad was having on disaffected peoples within India itself. In Tamil Nadu the DMK chief minister had pointedly warned that, in India too, excessively centralized rule would only encourage autonomous tendencies. These tendencies were already evident in Jammu and Kashmir and especially in the northeastern states that actually fringed East Bengal: namely, a Communist-inclined West Bengal, an exploited and ethnically divided Assam, and a Nagaland that was practically a no-go area. From across the unpoliceable border, the unrest and lawlessness in East Bengal threatened to spread to these states and further destabilize them. There was much to be said, then, for a show of force on foreign territory to forestall trouble on the home front.

On the understanding that it was still the refugee burden that was exercising Delhi, in July the secretary-general of the UN suggested that the office of its High Commissioner for Refugees (UNHCR) should step in. UNHCR representatives could be stationed on either side of the border to facilitate the return of the displaced and as a guarantee of their security once returned. But Gandhi, notwithstanding her complaints about the migrants' presence being "indirect aggression," would have none of it. As over Kashmir, India objected on principle to any international presence, which might circumscribe its freedom of action or, worse still, expose its existing involvement with the Mukti Bahini. Even international aid workers in the camps were being expelled. Gandhi therefore declared herself to be "totally opposed" to UN observers being posted on Indian territory and opined that they could serve no useful purpose in East Bengal either, at least until such time as Islamabad backed down and accepted the Awami League's mandate. As Richard Sisson and L. E. Rose point out, "New Delhi opposed almost everything the U.N. secretary-general sought to do on this matter," right up to the last minute.[19] In October, by which time the military buildup on both sides of the border was well under way, Yahya Khan expressed his willingness to accept a UN plan for withdrawing his troops from border areas, but again Gandhi declined to reciprocate with respect to India's forces.

This last proposal about troop withdrawals resurfaced in November during a famously frosty encounter in Washington between the Indian prime minister and President Nixon. Kissinger would call it "a classic dialogue of the deaf," with the perspiring Nixon and the bristling Gandhi "not intended by fate to be personally congenial to one another."[20] By now Yahya was willing to withdraw his forces from the border unilaterally. Nixon called it a "capitulation" and looked to Gandhi for a reciprocal gesture. None came until, back in Delhi, she made the call for Pakistan's unilateral withdrawal her own and simultaneously "authorized the Indian military to cross the border as far as necessary to counter Pakistani shelling." According to Sisson and Rose, it was the resultant digging in of Indian forces within East Bengali territory on November 21 that turned Pakistan's civil war into the third Indo-Pak war.[21]

Indian apologists dispute this. They point out that cross-border shelling in both directions had started in October, and, that for months before that, the Mukti Bahini had been operating inside the country with Indian support. Therefore, nothing much changed on November 21. It was not until December 3 that the war actually began, according to New Delhi. On that day, without further provocation or warning, and more than 900 miles from East Bengal, the Pakistani air force launched bombing raids on nine local airports in western India, while the Pakistani army probed western India's land frontier in Sind and Kashmir.

Less debatably, two weeks later the war would be over. On the western front, Indian forces rolled back Pakistan's advance and over-ran a few Pakistani positions in Kashmir. In the east an already well-planned Indian offensive was simply brought forward. An immediate bombing raid on the Dhaka airport prevented Pakistan from deploying its US-supplied fighter jets. It also ended the shuttle of supplies via Colombo and gave India complete air superiority. The Indian navy cut off Chittagong and, by also threatening Karachi, ended any chance of maritime reinforcements. On the ground, India's half a million troops, aided by a hundred thousand Mukti Bahini, outnumbered the Pakistani forces by perhaps eight to one.

In desperation, Yahya Khan turned to China and the United States. Nixon, busy with his own China initiative, offered only diplomatic support. Beijing followed suit; at any rate, the Himalayan passes were becoming snowbound. With East Bengal's civilian population overwhelmingly hostile, the Pakistani forces could neither maneuver nor withdraw. "Military situation desperate," wired the province's governor on December 9. "The front in Eastern and Western sectors has collapsed. . . . Food and other supplies running short. . . . Millions of non-Bengalis and loyal elements are awaiting death. . . . If no help is expected I beseech you to negotiate. . . . Is it worth sacrificing so much when the end seems inevitable?"[22] The appeal brought authorization for a surrender, and a week later India announced a unilateral cease-fire.

From Delhi's perspective, it was perhaps the perfect war—short, morally defensible, not excessively bloody, largely fought on foreign soil, domestically popular, and above all devastatingly conclusive. Previous Indo-Pak wars had invariably been aborted under international pressure. Thirteen days long, this one was over before the olive-branch emissaries could get airborne. As the many-pronged Indian offensive homed in on Dhaka, all the niceties of victory were observed. The Mujibnagar government-in-exile was officially recognized as "the Provisional Government of the People's Republic of Bangladesh." On December 16 the surrender of Pakistan's ninety-three thousand troops in Bangladesh was formally staged at the stadium in Dhaka's Ramna Race Course. The stadium was where Mujib had been wont to address his supporters, but this time the victory was essentially India's. The surrender was taken by the Indian top brass along with a single Bangladeshi representative in doubtful attendance.

Yahya had responded with his own cease-fire. Having presided over the catastrophic loss of half the nation, his position was now untenable. On December 20, amid widespread unrest throughout West Pakistan, Yahya was persuaded to hand over the presidency and the martial law administration to Zulfikar Ali Bhutto.

Bhutto's first act was to release the imprisoned Mujibur Rahman, who immediately departed for Dhaka. Flying via London, where he arranged for himself to be sworn in as Bangladesh's first president, and then Delhi, where amid mutual congratulations Gandhi updated him on conditions in Bangladesh, Mujib arrived in Dhaka to a tumultuous reception in January 1972. Within the year most of the refugees had returned, an interim government was in operation, and Mujib had relinquished the presidency to become the first prime minister of a newly independent Bangladesh.

Another partition had resolved the absurdity of a bipartite Pakistan. Instead of two successor states, there were now three. Many South Asians supposed that that was it. The unfinished business of the Great Partition had finally been concluded. India had assumed the role of the region's policeman. Bangladesh and the residual Pakistan had emerged as manageable entities. Expectations ran high.

7

AN ILL-STARRED CONJUNCTION

THE INSTALLATION OF ZULFIKAR ALI BHUTTO IN PAKISTAN and of Mujibur Rahman in Bangladesh signaled another sea change in South Asia: for the first time ever, all of the subcontinent's now three principal states were under directly elected civilian governments. All three were committed to socialist policies aimed at removing inequalities and boosting living standards. All three were led by outstanding figures. And of this revered triumvirate, all three commanded unassailable majorities and were committed to the democratic process.

The wounds of war were quickly stanched. When in March 1972 Indira Gandhi paid her first visit to Bangladesh, crowds of a hundred thousand fêted her and Mujib and applauded the inevitable treaty of Indo-Bangladeshi friendship. A year later, the last Indian troops left Bangladesh. A year after that—so just two years after being released from detention—Mujibur Rahman revisited Pakistan at Bhutto's invitation. He came to attend the Lahore summit of the Organization of the Islamic Conference, following which the ninety thousand Pakistani prisoners of war taken in Bangladesh were repatriated.

Though most Pakistanis would always hold New Delhi responsible for the loss of Bangladesh, even Bhutto was now talking of "an entirely new relationship with India." Meeting with Indira Gandhi at Simla in June 1972, he signed an agreement whereby both parties renounced the use of force and agreed to settle their outstanding differences "by peaceful means." Territory taken by India on the western front was evacuated and, with minor adjustments and a name change, the old Kashmir cease-fire line was reinstated as the "Line of Control." Notable too was the fact that the more contentious question of Kashmir's status and the promised plebiscite, though discussed at Simla, did not figure in the final agreement. Instead, the now sixty-six-year-old Sheikh Abdullah was released from his latest detention and allowed to make a triumphant return to Kashmir. Following talks with Indira Gandhi, it was understood that although the sheikh would again seek—and in 1975 secure—the chief ministership of Jammu and Kashmir, he would do so without challenging the state's incorporation into India. Everywhere, peace was being given a chance. The fortuity of three popularly elected governments happening to coincide was paying a dividend.

But this favorable conjuncture would last barely three years, and after that it would not come around again for a couple of decades. As if "predestined to commit the same follies," the populist trio of Indira, Bhutto, and Mujib followed parallel paths to a common nemesis.[1] All would succumb to the delusions of power, all would fall from grace, and all would be brutally eliminated. Additionally, all would leave offspring to reclaim their prime ministerial mantles, perpetuate the "same follies," and court a similar fate. The legacy of the people-powered 1970s would linger on. Pakistan and Bangladesh would continue to be convulsed by the fallout from the Bhutto and Mujib governments well into the twenty-first century. India too was scarred. The war had fostered a hegemonic mind-set that would dog future relations with its neighbors. And in Indira Gandhi it had bred the authoritarian tendencies that led to her imminent Emergency and the severest test yet of India's commitment to democracy and secularism.

Mujib was the first to go. Apparently the least vulnerable of the three, he faced by far the most formidable task and brought to it the least experience of government. Bangladesh in 1972 was more desperately disadvantaged even than Pakistan in 1947. To the challenges of turning a nation into a state, improvising a government, reconstructing an economy, restoring law and order, and resettling several million refugees, there had been added the physical and psychological devastation caused by the war and the 1970 cyclone. Reconstruction required time and purpose along with inclusive policies, massive investment, and inspired leadership, none of which was forthcoming.

Like the Muslim League of 1947, the Awami League of 1972, once it had achieved its primary goal of independence, had no ready-made program to deal with the situation. Members of the government-in-exile, themselves representing different interests and shades of opinion, clashed with those who had opposed the Islamabad regime from within the country, those who had fought against it from India, and those who had been stranded in (west) Pakistan. Radical parties, some of which had boycotted the 1970 election, lobbied for the formation of a national coalition. Mujib rejected the idea. His mandate still stood and his status as Banglabandhu—"Bengal's Big Brother"—and founder of the nation was universally acknowledged. Years in opposition and detention had equipped him more for confrontation than for consensus. As Lawrence Ziring puts it, "Conciliation was not part of his repertoire."[2]

There was a wider human deficit too. With the departure of west Pakistan's detested business elite, the expectations of Bangladesh's indigenous entrepreneurs, labor leaders, and surplus farmers soared. Willem van Schendel notes that "each expected that their support for the Awami League would translate into greatly expanded economic opportunities"— and some were not disappointed.[3] The government acquired the assets of all Pakistani firms, nationalized even Bengali-owned banks and businesses, and was, in addition, in receipt of substantial aid. It had the wherewithal to reward supporters and did not hesitate to use it. In a display of what has been called the "politics of patronage," important enterprises were placed under the direction of favored clients who lacked competence, experience, and often probity. A five-year plan was trotted out but indifferently implemented. The money supply was increased substantially. Inflation raged and GDP nosedived. In 1973, agricultural production was 84 percent below what it had been prior to the war, and in industry production had dropped as well, by 66 percent.[4]

Worse followed. After the 1973 Arab-Israeli War, world oil prices began rising and with them the cost of manufactured goods and most other commodities. Bangladesh's undermechanized economy was less affected than some, but the price of imported goods shot up and the cross-border smuggling of everything from pharmaceuticals to rice, cattle, and consumer durables became a national pastime. Elsewhere floods, poor harvests, and the misappropriation and erratic distribution of aid led to scarcity, then famine. While the situation was most acute in the still lawless northern provinces of Rangpur and Mymensingh, the effects spread to Dhaka, where by the middle of 1974 thousands of famine victims were invading the city. Others drifted over the border in another wave of migration into India.

Mujib would concede a death toll of thirty thousand from the famine; international agencies put it at fifty times that. With India and the Soviet Union unable to help, Mujib suddenly reversed his previous insistence on accepting only bilateral aid from friendly nations and went, cap in hand, to the United Nations and Washington. A World Bank–led consortium duly came to the country's rescue, though not before Mujib had been persuaded to ditch his command economy. Tajuddin Ahmed, his socialist finance minister and previously prime minister of the Mujibnagar government-in-exile, was sacked, the currency was devalued, state industries were denationalized, and reforms favorable to the private sector and foreign investment were introduced. "Critics of the new aid consortium argue that Bangladesh has had to barter away the last vestiges of its original commitment to the ideals of 'socialist planning' in return for short-term relief," noted the *Far Eastern Economic Review*.[5]

Other critics vented their disillusionment in less measured terms. Never an organized force, the Mukti Bahini had been only partially absorbed into the army. Bands of armed fighters still infested the countryside and, losing all confidence in Mujib, increasingly turned on members of his government and party. Mujib responded by raising his own vigilantes, the Lal Bahini and then the Rakhi Bahini. But these too rapidly got out of hand and began selecting their own targets. A reign of ill-directed terror began, and by the end of 1974 the death toll among members of the Awami League had reached four thousand, with five of those being members of parliament.

Distancing himself from all these paramilitaries, Mujib now performed another about-face. He called in the army, ostensibly to suppress the smuggling that financed the insurgents; then in December 1974 he effectively abrogated his own two-year-old constitution by declaring a state of emergency. His well-drilled National Assembly endorsed it, so ending all further pretense of parliamentary government. Mujib declared himself president indefinitely, the press was muzzled, political parties were banned, and the rights of protest and assembly were suspended. After just three years, Bangladesh was not only in deep trouble but also back under one-man rule.

Bhutto, when he took up the reins of power from Yahya Khan in January 1972, was described as the first-ever civilian to be a chief martial law administrator; Mujib now had a good claim to being the second. In imposing a state of emergency he had also reversed his pupil-mentor relationship with Indira Gandhi in that his own "emergency" anticipated by six months Gandhi's identical response to disruption and collapse in India.

But it was in Bangladesh itself that the betrayal was most sorely felt. For a politician whose entire career had been built on electoral arithmetic, and, for a nation that owed its statehood to democratic consensus, the lurch toward authoritarian rule was unforgivable. In a vain attempt to revive his moribund reputation, Mujib formed a new national party, which rejoiced in the acronym of BAKSAL (Bangladesh Peasants and Workers Awami League). This heralded another about-face, this time back to the left in an attempt to enlist the support of those worst affected by the failure of his earlier economic policies. But by now Mujib had taken a turn too many. He had lost touch with reality. "In a country overrun by self-styled enforcers, gouged by profiteers, and raped by government officials . . . [he] presided over a court corrupted by power," writes Ziring.[6] Once the symbol of the nation's hopes, Mujib was now the butt of its failure, a Groucho Marx look-alike floundering amid his own delusions.

With all other opposition stifled or divided, only the army saw itself as capable of challenging his all-powerful BAKSAL. By mid-1975 it was not so much a case of whether the military would intervene but of how, when, and in whose name. The last question has yet to be conclusively answered, but of the how and when there is a grim certainty. On the night of August 15, tanks rolled up before the Rahman residence in Dhaka. Troops then stormed the building. Mujib was gunned down on the stairs; his family—some twenty people, mostly women and children—died along with him. Only two daughters, both of whom were in Europe at the time, survived, one being Hasina, a future Awami League prime minister and redoubtable champion of her father's reputation.

That the bloodbath had the backing of senior military figures was self-evident. The trigger-happy majors responsible for it were promoted, granted immunity from prosecution, and given safe passage into exile. But so convoluted was the 1975 power struggle, and so partisan the testimony of the participants, that the spate of attempted coups and countercoups that followed has yet to be satisfactorily untangled. Suffice it to say that by the end of 1975, army chief of staff General Ziaur Rahman—he who had first broadcast the news of Bangladesh's independence in 1971—had commandeered a rank-and-file army mutiny and, tearing a leaf out of Ayub Khan's book, declared himself Bangladesh's first official chief martial law administrator.

THUS WITHIN FOUR YEARS Bangladesh had succumbed to military rule under a general called Zia. If the Awami League could so traduce its mandate as to endorse autocratic government and invite military intervention, then the PPP could do the same in what remained of Pakistan. Bhutto should have been warned. Yet eighteen months later he too stood accused of so prostituting the apparatus of power as to trigger a coup, which was conducted under the glassy-eyed stare of another General Zia.

As with Mujib in Bangladesh, much had been expected of Bhutto in his truncated Pakistan. "If ever a Pakistani ruler wielded absolute power, it was Zulfikar Ali Bhutto following the 1971 war with India," writes Lawrence Ziring.[7] Unlike Pakistan's later prime ministers, he was not beholden to the army, which anyway had been discredited and maimed by the defeat in Bangladesh. More experienced and more intellectually formidable than Mujib, the urbane

Bhutto looked equal to any occasion. He delighted the international community with his literary quips, commanded the adulation of his followers with earthy jibes, and silenced rivals with biting sarcasm. Appreciating the need for a reappraisal of Pakistan's purpose and convinced that he personally embodied that purpose, he articulated it much more confidently than Mujib.

In a Pakistan minus its eastern wing, the doubtful parity implicit in the original idea of the subcontinent's "two nations" was no longer sustainable. There were as many Muslims in India as in what now constituted Pakistan (or indeed Bangladesh). While mindful of its origins as a homeland and haven for the subcontinent's Muslims, post-1971 Pakistan's destiny now lay as a compact nation-state astride the crossroads between an Islamic West Asia, a still Soviet Central Asia, and the Indian subcontinent.

Such repositioning called for some historical revisionism. Aitzaz Ahsan, a stylish lawyer and leading light in the PPP, would argue that, contrary to received opinion, the new Pakistan, however fortuitous, was anything but artificial. As a distinct sociopolitical entity cradled by the Indus River rather than the Ganges, "Pakistan had existed for five and a half of the last six thousand years."[8] According to Ahsan, only in the last half millennium had its identity been obscured by a succession of outside rulers and the constant passage of arms. Islam had provided solace and a wider sense of community, but it was not the Indus people's only distinguishing trait. A predilection for clannish fraternities based on kinship and convenience, a preference for ostentatious consumption over thrift and capital accumulation, a high tolerance of exploitative rulers, a readiness to switch allegiances, and a tendency to blame any but himself represented "Indus man's" characteristic response to constant pillaging and subjection. Fashioned by adversity, he was a tough nut, parochial, resilient, intemperate, and largely impervious.

Ahsan would write *The Indus Saga and the Making of Pakistan* during several long spells of post-Bhutto detention. He lacked the resources of the historian, but, as a persuasive advocate, he made a noteworthy case for not judging Pakistan by the standards applicable to less troubled regions. An elite long inured to authority, indeed "conditioned to brutality," could take in its stride the brickbats of repressive fortune and the comings and goings of regimes. "The Bengalis did not have the same tolerance threshold as [the] Indus [peoples]. And so they separated."[9] Without them, Pakistan could again become its robust old self.

Whether Bhutto was aware of Ahsan's thinking is uncertain. But he acted as if he was, pushing the Indus persona to its limits. While touting his democratic credentials and endearing himself to the masses with a flurry of nationalizations (heavy industries, insurance, cooking oil, rice husking, banking, etc.), he tightened his iron grip on party, patronage, and power. Martial law was terminated, and in 1973 Pakistan's third and most enduring constitution ushered in a genuinely parliamentary form of government. This transferred all executive authority from the president to the prime minister, in which office Bhutto, as chairman of the PPP, was duly confirmed by a National Assembly composed of the victors of the 1970 poll.

On paper the new constitution was unexceptionable. Orthodox opinion was assuaged by the designation of Pakistan as an Islamic state, by the promotion of Quranic teaching, and by the creation of an advisory council to ensure that legislation conformed with Islamic precept. Yet initially Bhutto, a Shi'ite by birth and a libertine by inclination, shunned the Sunni Islamic parties and made no adjustments to his decidedly secular lifestyle. In a similar vein, the constitution awarded more autonomy to the provinces by specifying the responsibilities reserved to their governments. But as in India, the list of "concurrent subjects" (i.e., those for which the federal center and the provinces shared responsibility) was long and contentious. In effect, writes Ian Talbot, "Bhutto, despite his often expressed sentiments in favor of federalism, was no more willing to shift power from the centre to the provinces than any of his predecessors."[10] Constitutional concessions extracted by the opposition parties were swiftly negated by prime ministerial ordinances that, though couched in terms of the national interest, were deployed in the interests of the PPP.

The party itself was regularly purged and just as often diluted by the induction of sycophantic allies. Instead of shoring up its grassroots support by establishing a structure of representative local committees, Bhutto took it upon himself to select the party's functionaries and dictate its policies. Intolerant of even the mildest criticism, he relied on his own undoubted charisma, plus the services of the newly raised FSF. The initials stood for "Federal Security Force"—or, to those singled out for its thuggish attention, "Fascist Security Force." Recruited from unsavory elements, the FSF was outside the purview of the armed forces, more amenable than Mujib's Rakhi Bahini, and answerable only to Chairman Bhutto.

History might have forgiven Bhutto his authoritarianism had he lived up to his egalitarian principles. In a society with more bastions of privilege than even caste-ridden India, targets were plentiful. The twenty-two familial conglomerates that supposedly controlled most of the economy were scattered by his nationalization program, many preferring to take themselves and their capital overseas. As in Bangladesh, the economy then contracted and the growth rate slowed. Private investors took fright, while the public sector was hamstrung by the "politics of patronage." It was the same with the bureaucracy. The elite Civil Service of Pakistan was dissolved in favor of a graded and more accessible administrative structure. But in practice many former bureaucrats simply resurfaced as born-again "Bhuttocrats," and it was not talent that enjoyed easier access but influence. Likewise, the great landowning baronies of Punjab, though subject to two attempts at radical land redistribution, remained substantially intact thanks to favors rendered to the PPP and the usual cut-and-paste ploy of dividing holdings among relatives and dependents.

Most important of all, the army's presumed role as the savior of the nation cried out for curtailment. As well as awarding some peace-keeping responsibilities to the FSF, Bhutto worked to dilute the armed forces' monopoly of national defense and to influence the selection of their most senior personnel. But again all three moves backfired. The FSF became more detested than the miscreants it was supposed to control. Moreover, it proved no match for the army when it came to containing mass insurgency. From 1973 to 1976 some eighty thousand regular troops were engaged in ruthlessly suppressing a secessionist movement in Balochistan; it was nearly as many as had been deployed in Bangladesh in 1971. And as early as 1972 the military had been called to Sind province when the Urdu-speaking *muhajir* community rioted against Bhutto's privileging of the native Sindi-speakers. Both interventions "carried echoes of Yahya's ill-conceived actions in East Pakistan and depressingly repeated the pattern of the state hampering national integration by provoking regional opposition through its violent suppression of legitimate demands."[11]

Another way to reduce the army's influence was to upstage its monopoly of firepower. At the time of the 1965 Indo-Pak war, Bhutto had famously vowed that, were India ever to develop a nuclear bomb, "then we should have to eat grass and get one, or buy one of our own."[12] The prospect of buying the technology and eating grass to pay for it came a lot nearer when in May 1974 Indira Gandhi opted to test India's first "nuclear device." Allegedly developed to deter further aggression from China, and then tested for domestic reasons, it lacked the warhead of a nuclear bomb, and there was as yet no means of delivering it. But the explosion beneath the Rajasthan desert clearly advertised both intent and capability.

Pakistan too had a small nuclear program. A plutonium power station had been supplied by Canada, and France had signed an agreement for a reprocessing plant. Reprocessed plutonium could be used for weapons. But under pressure from the nonproliferation lobby and the United States, in the mid-1970s Canada halted fuel supplies and the French contract was put on hold. Bhutto, who had already urged Pakistan's Atomic Energy Commission to achieve "fission in three years," would persevere with plutonium, but he also let it be known he was open to alternatives.

This news reached the ears of Dr. Abdul Qadeer Khan, a senior nuclear physicist then working at a uranium processing facility in the Netherlands. Born in Bhopal, India, from where his family had removed to Pakistan at the time of Partition, Khan was a leading expert in the design and engineering of centrifuges suitable for uranium enrichment. He had a wide understanding of the whole process and access to international suppliers and scientists. With Bhutto's backing, in 1976 Khan and his assets were transferred to a new research center at Kahuta, near Rawalpindi. He would remain there for a quarter of a century, being credited with making possible Pakistan's first nuclear tests in 1998, and would become a national hero, the country's most decorated scientist, and the world's most notorious purveyor of nuclear know-how and materials.

Bhutto would rate his own role in the development of what he called the "Islamic bomb" a greater achievement than his master-minding of the strategic alliance with Communist China. "I put my entire vitality behind the task," he would write, and "due to my sin-gular efforts Pakistan acquired the in[f]ra-structure and the potential of nuclear capability."[13] Thanks to Bhutto, the nation would finally possess a credible deterrent against Indian aggression. It would also have a useful bargaining counter in negotiations with Washington; discontinuing nuclear development—or pretending to—could be traded for aid packages and conventional weapons. Better still, with the program and its control under civilian direction, the government could boast a defense capability that upstaged the heavy armor on offer from the armed forces.

Having rescued the nation after the Bangladesh debacle, Bhutto would now claim to have underwritten its security for generations to come. But the bomb would take time to develop, and there was no guarantee that the nuclear program would remain under civilian control. Fatally, in May 1976 he took another swipe at the military by picking as the army chief of staff an unknown, unregarded, and supposedly amenable general called Zia ul-Haq. Then eight months later he called for elections. Although they were due within five years of the new constitution having been approved, Bhutto gave minimal notice of the poll and was confident of sweeping the board.

"Perhaps I have embedded myself too deep in the poor of this land," he wrote. "I am a household word in every home and under every roof that leaks in rain . . . I have an eternal bond with the people which armies cannot break."[14] Anything other than a vote for Bhutto would therefore be treachery, and anything less than a clean sweep unthinkable. The opposition parties nevertheless cob-bled together a grand Pakistan National Alliance and went down fighting. The PPP won the 1977 election handsomely, but it was amid such widespread accusations of having disqualified potential opponents, rigged the vote, and tampered with the ballot boxes that the real cut-and-thrust only got under way after the results were declared.

As in East Bengal when Yahya Khan had postponed the 1971 National Assembly, protesters took to the streets while a succession of general strikes paralyzed the economy. In Lahore and Karachi martial law was imposed. In Sind, *muhajir* students, among them Altaf Hussein, the future leader of the formidable MQM party, were still agitating against the reservation of educational places and jobs for Sindi-speakers. At least in Sind, Bhutto was on home territory. In the NWFP he barely dared show his face. There Khan Abdul Wali Khan, the six-foot-something Pathan patriarch who led the main opposition party and should have been heading the Pakistan National Alliance, had been arrested on a trumped-up charge and consigned to jail. Nationwide, in a matter of weeks in the early summer of 1977, more than two hundred protesters died in armed clashes involving either the FSF, the police, or the army. Students and small traders, once the backbone of the PPP's support but now alienated by rising prices, rampant corruption, and lack of jobs, rallied to the opposition's Pakistan's National Alliance and backed its demand for a rerun of the elections.

Bhutto, with his mandate sullied and the army increasingly reluctant to gun down his opponents, had no choice but to backtrack. "Too clever by half" (and more questionably the man who "gave political opportunism a bad name in Pakistan"), he indicated that there might indeed have been improprieties in the recent election and offered the National Alliance a dubious compromise.[15] Simultaneously, he tried to detach the Islamic parties from the Alliance by volunteering to ban gambling, close nightclubs, and restrict the sale of alcohol. Coming from the clean-shaven, cigar-smoking Bhutto, it was a blatantly cynical attempt to cling to power. By pandering to the intolerant sentiments of religious radicals, it also set a dangerous precedent.

But none of these concessions brought an agreement on rerunning the elections. Nor did they reassure those several brigadiers whose troops were trying to reimpose order in the streets. It was seemingly on the insistence of the latter that General Zia ul-Haq, fearful of the army itself being divided by the ferment, staged his coup of July 5, 1977.

At the time the coup seemed even more benign than Ayub Khan's in 1956. There was no bloodshed, no overt protest. The 1973 constitution was not abrogated, merely suspended pending arrangements for new elections; Zia promised they would be held within ninety days, after which he would stand down. Meanwhile, martial law was reimposed, political life ceased, and the nation went back to work—all, that is, except the FSF, which was disbanded and its leaders arrested. Under interrogation they confessed to numerous crimes and evinced a willingness, as suspicious as it was plausible, to implicate Bhutto. But Bhutto himself was treated with caution. Whisked off to the cool comforts of a hill station, he and his party henchmen enjoyed a spell under vacation-cottage arrest; the arrangement was temporary and supposedly for their own safety.

A month later they were duly released, since elections held while the principal contender was still under restraint would have been a farce. But if Zia was counting on Bhutto's followers having by now despaired of him, he was mistaken. Massive crowds welcomed back the self-proclaimed "Leader of the People" in Karachi, Lahore, and his native Sind. As so often is the case, disgrace and detention had done his reputation no harm whatsoever. Though unforgiven by many, he was forgotten by none.

It was this outpouring of support that seems to have decided his fate. In early September, little more than a month after his release, he was rearrested, charged with murder, bailed out, and then re-rearrested, this time for good. It is not clear whether Zia had been nudged into action by the officers who had urged the July coup or whether he was now more mindful of his own vulnerability, for if the PPP were to win the promised election, it would be the general who would have to stand trial. To scotch any such possibility, on October 1 Zia announced that the elections would have to be postponed for another ninety days. More postponements would follow as the ninety days stretched to ninety months and beyond. Bhutto lived to witness only eighteen of them.

For high-profile prisoners in South Asia, detention was not necessarily a hardship. Often it was served under house arrest; even in jail the prisoner might enjoy access to creature comforts plus the services of a retainer or two. Sentences might be commuted for those willing to embrace exile; judicial executions were comparatively rare (and still are), even in the case of convicted terrorists. Mustafa Khar, governor of Punjab province as Bhutto's strongman and then Punjabi jailbird as his deadly rival, would set up his own poultry farm while in prison and, having taken his jailers onto his payroll, would want for nothing. "He had been allocated seven rooms . . . his cell was air-conditioned. He had a fridge and a deep freezer . . . ," noted Tehmina, the latest of Khar's glamorous wives.[16] On prison visits, she was hard-pressed to think of any little luxury to take him.

But Bhutto's incarceration was different. For more than a year, while his case was being decided and an appeal rejected, he languished in the solitary confinement of a cramped death-row cell, "hemmed in by its sordidness and stink throughout the heat and rain of the long hot summer."[17] Few visitors were allowed; his eyesight deteriorated and his gums rotted. Although the most political of prisoners, he was not being treated as a political prisoner.

Accused, tried, and convicted of instigating the FSF's elimination of an opponent, he was sentenced to death as a common criminal. The appeal against the sentence was rejected by a four-to-three majority of the doubtfully constituted Supreme Court. International pleas for clemency from the Western powers and the Arab world also fell on deaf ears. After a farewell visit from his wife, Nusrat, and his daughter, Benazir, both of whom would succeed him as leader of the PPP, he was led from his cell in the early hours of April 4, 1979, and hanged.

Mujib had been assassinated, and Indira Gandhi too would die in a hail of bullets; only Bhutto was judicially executed. Throughout his prison ordeal he had remained defiant. He allegedly refused the options of exile or retiring from politics ("It was like asking a human being to live, but without oxygen," wrote his wife).[18] He refused even to lodge his own appeal lest it lend legitimacy to the proceedings. The Bhutto legend would owe much to the manner of his death and the courage with which he met it, more perhaps than to his rhetoric or his tarnished record in government.

Zia's refusal to commute the death sentence was nevertheless curious. There were ample grounds for clemency: The conviction was shaky, the appeal had been rejected by just a single vote, and world opinion was unanimously in favor of a reprieve. Bhutto himself, and later Benazir, sensed a conspiracy. Zia, they argued, stood firm on the instructions of Washington. Often the target of Bhutto's jibes, the United States had come to regard him as a dangerous demagogue and the last person to be trusted with a nuclear capability. In other words, Bhutto died because of the bomb; cherishing martyrdom, he had sacrificed his own future for that of his country. But although Zia would indeed enjoy close relations with Washington, they dated from later in 1979, by which time the shah of Iran had been overthrown and Russian troops had begun rolling into Afghanistan. At the time, Zia was more concerned with strengthening his hold on power and ridding himself of the turbulent premier who was sworn to contest it.

In line with titles such as Quaid-i-Azam (Leader of the People) for Bhutto and Mujib's Banglabandhu (Bengal's Big Brother), the *Economist* had capped its coverage of the Bangladesh war by declaring Indira Gandhi "Empress of India." Villagers joined the national press in hailing her as a reincarnation of the goddess Durga, the all-conquering manifestation of the wife of Lord Shiva. The victory in Bangladesh had been her apotheosis.

Apart from Pakistan's poorly executed bombing of some small airports in Punjab and in Jammu and Kashmir, Indian territory had scarcely been affected by the war. The population, though, had been affected. In anticipation of further air raids, security had everywhere been tightened and the major cities put on high alert. Civil defense drills disrupted the workday; sirens were tested at night. Even distant Bombay was subject to a citywide blackout. This made after-dark excursions along pavements that habitually doubled as dormitories so perilous that Christmas shopping had to be curtailed. Out at the airport, fighter pilots had rigged canvas awnings from the wings of their jets, beneath which they ate and dozed while waiting for the order to scramble.

It was, of course, a false alarm and lasted less than a fortnight. But such precautions ensured maximum awareness of the war and then universal delight at its outcome. The delirious crowds could hardly believe it. Pakistan had finally gotten its comeuppance. After centuries of humiliation at the hands of Muslim and British invaders, India had a battlefield triumph to celebrate. The nationalist greeting "Jai Hind"—as much "Victory to India" as "Hail India"—was no longer a pious hope; it was a joyous statement of fact. The army had redeemed its failures of 1962 and 1965, and the prime minister, who had assumed personal responsibility for the conduct of the war, had emerged as a master strategist. Outwitting Pakistan's mustachioed generals while deftly deflecting Washington's disapproval, the leader once dismissed by Morarji Desai as a "dumb slip of a girl" now deserved every encomium going. Indira Gandhi could do no wrong, and had she chosen the moment to call another snap election, she might well have whitewashed the opposition as comprehensively as Mujib had in 1970. As it was, in March 1972 Congress won 70 percent of the seats contested in the state elections.

But the trouble with such a soaring approval rating lay in the near impossibility of sustaining it. Though gratified by all the plaudits, Gandhi urged the nation to put the Bangladesh war behind it and concentrate on the war against poverty. It was a timely reminder. With more than 40 percent of the rapidly growing population still below the poverty line, there were far more poor Indians than in 1960. As in Pakistan, the "Green Revolution" (affording higher crop yields through the use of hybrid seed, better irrigation, and more fertilizer) had substantially increased wheat production in the northern states. Self-sufficiency in cereals was at last within reach. But when the monsoons of 1972 and 1973 both failed in large parts of the country, grain prices shot up and food riots followed.

In the economy as a whole the growth rate remained stuck at 3–4 percent per annum. The earlier investment in infrastructure and heavy industries had stalled. Inflation was in double figures even before the 1973 oil price hikes sent it up to over 20 percent. Like her father, Indira Gandhi claimed to be running an economy that combined socialist uplift with capitalist incentive. But according to one economist, it had failed on both counts: "It had grown too slowly to qualify as a capitalist economy, and by its failure to eradicate illiteracy or reduce inequalities had forfeited any claims to be 'socialist.'"[19]

Throughout South Asia, nationalization was seen as the touch-stone of a socialist economy. Taking ever more industries into the state sector (Gandhi added first coal and then oil and gas to her government's portfolio) was supposed to ensure that they were run for the national benefit, that prices were not inflated by profit taking, and that workers enjoyed some security of employment. But in practice what endeared nationalization to the populist governments of the day was the inviting reservoir of desirable posts and perquisites that it made available. In return for awarding to an applicant a direc-torship in a state-owned bank, for instance, the government could expect cheaper loans for its favored projects plus a substantial do-nation to party funds. The operation of the permit raj in the private sector had much the same effect. Well-meant policies aimed at social betterment were being commandeered by the politics of patronage.

Cronyism and nepotism thrived as a result. The highest-profile case was provided by Sanjay Gandhi, the younger of the prime min-ister's two sons. Despite a doltish reputation and a dismal school record, on the strength of an apprenticeship with Rolls-Royce in En-gland the twenty-five-year-old Sanjay tendered for a coveted license to set up India's first indigenous automotive plant. Government-backed, it was to mass-produce an affordable "people's car" at the rate of fifty thousand units per year to challenge the Fiats, Morrises, and Tri-umphs built to outdated designs from Europe. The newspapers were full of buzz, dealerships were sought, orders were placed. With little discussion and despite a total lack of managerial experience, Sanjay's company, Maruti, was awarded the contract ahead of eighteen other applicants. He was then practically gifted the site for his factory by a chief minister keen to ingratiate himself. Eyebrows were raised and the misgivings of Mrs. Gandhi's principal adviser were noted. But such was her national stature and her command of both party and parliament that few dared openly object.

Maruti's promise of "horsepower to the people" became a bad joke. During its ten years under Sanjay's stewardship the company produced not a single production-line vehicle and only a handful of barely drivable prototypes. It did, though, alert Sanjay to the ways of patronage and the political possibilities afforded by his birth and his mother's confidence in him. Though without either a seat in parliament or an office within the party, he increasingly acted as a political troubleshooter and a gateway to the prime minister's office.

Egged on by Sanjay and her all-powerful secretariat, in 1973 Indira resumed her vendetta against the Supreme Court and its reluctance to sanction constitutional amendments. She did so by setting aside both seniority and tradition to appoint a little-known but pliable figure to the post of chief justice. "The choice was politically motivated," notes the historian Ramachandra Guha, "a manifestation of the government's increasing desire to control the judiciary."[20] Many senior figures remonstrated, though to little immediate effect, prominent among them being the revered Gandhian and socialist J. P. Narayan. In the same year a petition citing serious irregularities in the 1971 Rae Bareilly election was lodged with the UP High Court in Allahabad; the stick-waving Raj Narain was still on the warpath. With the parliamentary opposition ineffective, resentment over corruption and the high-handedness of the prime minister's secretariat was finding extraparliamentary expression. In a two-pronged assault, Narayan publicly championed growing disgust over the venality and exploitation at every level of government, while Narain doggedly pursued the prime minister herself through the courts.

Early in 1974 remonstrations gave way to demonstrations. In the state of Gujarat students took to the streets to protest against rising commodity prices and the blatant corruption of the Congress-run state government. Bihar, J. P. Narayan's home ground, followed suit; similar demonstrations involving organized labor as well as students brought the entire state to a standstill. And to cap it all, in May the socialist-led railway workers' union called a national rail strike.

The government responded with force rather than concessions. In Gujarat more than a hundred protesters died in confrontations with the police before Indira Gandhi suspended the state government. The train strike was also ruthlessly suppressed, some twenty thousand railway workers being imprisoned without trial under the draconian new Maintenance of Internal Security Act (MISA—otherwise known as the "Maintenance of Indira and Sanjay Act"). Only in Bihar were the protests left to run their course. This was largely due to J. P. Narayan's unassailable reputation. The seventy-two-year-old

"conscience of the nation," who rather than seeking office had devoted his life to a variety of noble causes, now lent his name and his
leadership to the whole protest movement (which came to be known
as the "JP Movement"). Calling for a nonviolent "total revolution"
that would be "political, economic, social, educational, moral, and
cultural," he toured Bihar addressing massive crowds and promising
"a real people's government" within one year.

Suddenly Indira Gandhi seemed to have lost her touch. The bounce
from Bangladesh had subsided. A new distraction was needed, and,
like a conjuror pulling rabbits from under her sari, she came up
with two, one explosive, the other acquisitive. In May, in the midst
of the rail strike, she gave the go-ahead for that test of India's first
nuclear device. Though the test had been in the cards for months, the
timing was entirely of her own choosing. Euphemistically billed as a
"peaceful nuclear experiment," it was portrayed as an important step
in "building up a better future of the people." It was also hailed as a
triumph for the nation's scientists and was accompanied by fulsome
disclaimers of any intent to weaponize the technology. Nevertheless,
a national outburst of unseemly chauvinism followed, then an international outburst of hypocritical condemnation. The existing nuclear
powers deplored proliferation, as did India's South Asian neighbors,
none more so than the incensed Zulfikar Ali Bhutto in Pakistan.

Four months later, with the JP Movement spreading beyond Bihar and a mass march on Delhi in the offing, the second rabbit was
revealed. It took the form of a carefully engineered and decidedly
brazen assault on Sikkim, the smallest of the sovereign states along
the Himalayan glacis. Nehru would have been appalled. While keen
to claim Kashmir and gobble up the colonial enclaves of Pondicherry
and Goa, he had always acknowledged Sikkim as a sovereign kingdom, just like Nepal and Bhutan. Its historical and religious ties were
with Tibet. It had long commanded the main trade route with Tibet
and had once been on a territorial par with Bhutan. It was not, and
never had been, part of political India.

True, like Bhutan, it was otherwise wholly dependent on India
and had long since assigned to Delhi its defense and the conduct of
its external affairs. Yet the sovereignty of the kingdom as enshrined

in its *chogyal* or "righteous king" was uncontested. It flew its own flag, minted its own currency, communicated directly with its Himalayan neighbors, and maintained its own small corps of national guards. Though for convenience the British had sometimes grouped it with the princely states of India proper, it had not been considered one of them. Hence in 1947 the *chogyal* had not been among those princes from whom Mountbatten extracted Instruments of Accession. Instead, in 1950 there was a new "treaty"—the term itself being indicative of the equal status of the signatories—whereby Sikkim now accorded to India responsibility for its defense, foreign affairs, and communications.

There matters might have stood but for three countervailing factors. One was the strategic location of Sikkim, squeezed between Nepal and Bhutan. Its southern border abutted the narrow corridor that linked Assam to the rest of India, while its northern border marched with Chinese Tibet. As India's relations with China soured in the late 1950s, the latter border had looked as vulnerable as Ladakh's or that of the North-East Frontier Agency. Beijing not only disputed its precise alignment but, courtesy of its position in Tibet, could claim an ill-defined suzerainty over the *chogyal* and his kingdom. By way of a reminder, in 1963 Chinese Communist Party chairman Liu Shaoqi had sent directly to Gangtok, the Sikkimese capital, a telegram of condolence on the death of one *chogyal* and in 1965 another of felicitations to his successor. New Delhi immediately protested over these infringements of its monopoly of Sikkim's external relations and suspected some Sino-Sikkimese intrigue. If for no other reason than to preempt Chinese influence in the state, any assertion of Sikkimese independence had to be resisted and any opportunity for closer Sikkimese association with India welcomed. Meanwhile, in the wake of the Sino-Indian war, the Indian military presence along the Sino-Sikkim border was so increased that Sikkim began to feel like an occupied land.

The second factor was the steady influx of settlers from neighboring Nepal. By the 1970s, of Sikkim's population of two hundred thousand, its native component of Buddhist Lepchas and Bhutiyas-was outnumbered three to one by Hindu Nepalis. Hungry for employment and land, and unconstrained by border controls, the Nepali diaspora also poured into Bhutan and the neighboring districts of West Bengal. In time the Bhutanese would try forced repatriation and the Indian authorities would be obliged to offer incentives to assimilation. Sikkim, and especially its fragile Buddhist monarchy, was more vulnerable to the Nepali influx, for the *chogyal,* however anxious to conform to India's democratic principles, was constrained by the near-certainty that Nepalis would dominate any representative bodies. They could then be expected to use them to dismantle the traditional patterns of land ownership and hereditary authority, and even the monarchy that upheld them. It was by exploiting this politico-ethnic imbalance that successive Indian representatives in Gangtok, whether as political officers, dewans, chief executives, or chief ministers, were able to manipulate the situation and steadily extend their influence at the expense of the *chogyal*'s prerogatives.

Finally, and much to New Delhi's annoyance, Sikkim's endangered existence was suddenly exposed to international scrutiny by the new *chogyal's* infatuation with a long-haired American girl, seventeen years his junior, called Hope Cooke. Sensationalized by the world's press, their royal wedding in 1963 became "the catalyst that completely changed the situation."[21] Sunanda Datta-Ray, the Bengali responsible for the most authoritative, if highly critical, account of Sikkim's last days, knew Cooke well. She was "a strange unhappy woman, unable to reciprocate her husband's doting love [and] neurotically conscious of her loneliness in a court that found her faintly ridiculous," yet she gamely championed all things Sikkimese, insisted on the titles and trappings of monarchy, and unwittingly isolated her husband from many of his traditional supporters.[22] With Queen Hope as hostess, ambassadors and other distinguished visitors to Gangtok flocked to the palace, leaving New Delhi's political officer glaring in disgust from the trellised verandah of his India House. It was unfortunate that the designation of the state as a protectorate left the Republic of India looking like an imperialist suzerain and worse still that the protocol of this relationship was being casually ignored.

When in the late 1960s the *chogyal* had requested a revision of the 1950 treaty, New Delhi had been almost accommodating. In return for closer control of the state, various inducements had been offered, including a "permanent association" instead of a protectorate plus qualified "autonomy in regard to internal affairs." But this conciliatory approach found no favor in the following decade. Mrs. Gandhi's electoral triumph in 1971, followed by victory in Bangladesh and then the "peaceful nuclear experiment," heralded a more assertive role for India in South Asia. With respect to Sikkim, "there was no longer any question of accommodation."[23]

The *chogyal* would later describe the annexation of his kingdom as a case of "smash and grab." This suggests more haste and less premeditated guile than was the case. But he was right in that first his own authority was smashed, then the state grabbed. The smashing involved discrediting the ruler by masterminding the antimonarchist challenge of a scruple-free opponent, then flooding Gangtok with this pretender's unruly supporters. "Police stations were burned down, loyal officials beaten up, the country's few armouries were looted and wireless equipment and petrol were seized."[24] With the *chogyal* a prisoner in his own palace, an Indian army division was given the responsibility of restoring order. Thus isolated and powerless, in April 1973 the *chogyal* was prevailed on to hand over administrative control to India's political officer. The latter then became chief executive and speaker following elections and the formation of a national assembly. With the ruler sidelined, it remained only to annex, or "grab," his kingdom.

In 1974, amid further attempts to bully the *chogyal* into cooperating in the liquidation of his kingdom, Queen Hope took off back to America. It was said to be for a vacation, but she never returned and the royal couple were later divorced. A bill, drafted for the new Sikkim Assembly by the Indian chief executive, was supposed to define Sikkim's constitution, but that too ran into trouble when both the *chogyal* and the Assembly tried to introduce amendments. The impasse brought the *chogyal* to Delhi for his last encounter with Mrs. Gandhi. It was time for what he called a "final and frank talk." But "it was never Mrs Gandhi's style to face unpleasant truths or attempt an honest answer," says Datta-Ray.[25] On the contrary, her long silences and "drawing-room duplicity" suggest that the die was already cast. The *chogyal* returned to Gangtok empty-handed, while Gandhi bided her time and awaited the moment to strike.

In India the year 1974 ended with the JP Movement apparently running out of steam. New elections were promised in Bihar; the universities reopened and students returned to class. Narayan was still bent on toppling Gandhi as part of his "total revolution." Moreover, his movement could now count on the support and crowd management skills of most of the opposition parties. But it lacked any clear ideological focus and had made little headway in Bombay and the south. With national elections due within eighteen months, it looked possible that the inevitable trial of strength would be left for the voters to decide.

All this changed when in March 1975 both Narayan and Narain upped the stakes. Calling on all government servants, including the army and the police, to defy orders that ran contrary to the spirit of the Constitution, Narayan staged a march to Parliament in Delhi and then addressed a crowd estimated at three-quarters of a million. It was probably the largest gathering since the Independence Day celebrations in 1947. Simultaneously Gandhi received a summons to appear before the Allahabad High Court in connection with Raj Narain's interminable petition about the Rae Bareilly election of 1971. This was the first time an Indian prime minister had been called on to testify in court, and it was not a good sign. Judge Jagmohanlal Sinha was evidently as much a stickler for electoral niceties as the stick-waving plaintiff was. Meanwhile, Morarji Desai, Indira's onetime challenger for the leadership of Congress, was poised to undertake a hunger strike in protest over the delay in calling elections in his home state of Gujarat. The public was getting restive again; it was time to release the remaining rabbit.

Up in Sikkim there had been no shortage of pretexts for leveling accusations of treason at the wretched *chogyal*. In February 1975 he had accepted an invitation to attend the coronation of King Birendra of Nepal in Kathmandu. There his brief encounters with a US senator, a Chinese vice premier, and an aging Mountbatten sparked wild charges of conspiracy and some avid speculation in the Indian press. Rumors that the *chogyal* was seeking sanctuary overseas proved wrong; he headed back to Sikkim "to live and die there," as he put it. But approaching Gangtok, his motorcade was halted by Nepali protestors, one of whom was wounded in the ensuing fracas by a member of the royal escort. To the possible accusation of treason was now added that of attempted murder.

A similar string of trumped-up charges was laid against Sikkim's heir apparent. But Prince Tenzing, more spirited than his father, struck back by circulating a written demand aimed at reining in Indian interference and clawing back powers already ceded. More controversially still, the demand appeared to have the backing of those Sikkimese and Nepalis who had hitherto been foremost in obliging India by opposing the *chogyal* and who now constituted Sikkim's puppet Assembly. For New Delhi, this was the final straw; and for an embattled Indira Gandhi it was perfect timing. While the Assembly's turncoats were being made to recant, plans were laid for an outright takeover of the state.

On April 9, in a scenario that could have been borrowed from Rawalpindi's military handbook, Indian troops took up positions throughout Gangtok. Phones went dead, roadblocks went up, and Assembly members were plucked from their homes for an extraordinary session. On the agenda were two motions. One abolished the institution of the *chogyal* and declared Sikkim a constituent of India; the other announced a referendum authorizing India to implement these changes. Both motions were passed unanimously.

The referendum was conducted just three days later and under Indian supervision. Regardless of the absurd schedule, despite widespread disorder, and in defiance of legal opinion to the effect that the whole procedure was unconstitutional, 63 percent of the electorate was said to have voted, and, of this improbable turnout, an even more improbable 97 percent supposedly supported the motion. Delhi's *Hindustan Times* was one of several papers to express acute embarrassment. It called Sikkim's vote for constitutional suicide a "mockery," adding, "And this in the India of [Mahatma] Gandhi and Nehru."[26]

With more unseemly haste a constitutional bill for a thirty-fifth amendment calling for the "association" of Sikkim with the Union of India was rushed through the Indian parliament and ratified on

April 26. "Not a voice was raised in the Parliament, no political party questioned the legality of the measure," writes historian Amar Kaur Jasbir Singh. "The curtain had finally come down on the once sovereign kingdom of Sikkim."[27]

THE FINAL ACT IN THE SIKKIM DRAMA had lasted little longer than the Bangladesh war; from armed intervention to constitutional extinction had taken just seventeen days. Another high-speed triumph brought another burst of applause, most of it from irredentist nationalists on the right wing of Congress. But the sheer speed of Indira Gandhi's legerdemain left others bewildered. If Sikkim was so keen on union, why had the exercise not been conducted with greater transparency and decorum? Likewise, if the *chogyal* was such a villain, why was he still in his palace? The *Hindustan Times* was not alone in its skepticism. A later chief justice of the Supreme Court found the whole legal process to have been riddled with constitutional anomalies.

Outside India it attracted mixed attention. A Bangladesh convulsed by the last days of Mujib paid little heed, but in Pakistan protesters took to the streets and Bhutto characterized the annexation as further evidence of India's expansionist intent. The same fears were expressed in Nepal. Mobs there set fire to Indian buildings and vehicles. Even B. P. Koirala, the former prime minister and leader of the Nepal Congress who was now in exile in India, noted that the Sikkim referendum had been a sham.

In India it was perhaps fortunate that more momentous events quickly swept the whole affair under the carpet. On June 12 Gandhi learned that she had lost the state election in Gujarat. In what had been a direct challenge to her leadership, the Janata Front, a combination of opposition parties led by Morarji Desai and J. P. Narayan, had edged Congress out of one of its traditional strongholds. Then, later the same day, there came news from Allahabad: Chief Justice Sinha of the UP High Court had upheld two of Raj Narain's complaints about the 1971 Rae Bareilly election. Though mere "technicalities," according to the prime minister's supporters, the two infringements sufficed to overturn the result and disqualify her from holding office for six years; she was given twenty days to appeal to the Supreme

Court. She in turn appealed against the twenty days. The term was extended, but only on condition that she refrain from voting in parliament. Given her majority, this in itself scarcely mattered. But it left her in a legal limbo, at the mercy of the court and her opponents.

There ensued an exercise in mobilizing mass support on the streets of New Delhi. As J. P. Narayan's followers besieged Rashtrapati Bhawan in an attempt to force the president to dismiss Mrs. Gandhi, Sanjay and her other lieutenants bused in hundreds of thousands of her own supporters to protest on her behalf. It was the middle of June, the hottest of months; tempers frayed, reason wilted, and the political mercury soared. Sanjay and his associates drew up lists of those they hoped to see arrested; Indira explored the constitution for legal options. In the end it was the threat of Narayan renewing his call for noncooperation that carried the day; such a call, when directed at the police and the security forces, amounted to incitement to mutiny. Citing all the usual culprits—"communal passions," "forces of disintegration," "a widespread conspiracy," and "a foreign hand"—the prime minister saw it as her duty to take control. Hence the declaration of a state of emergency. "What else could I have done except stay?" she later claimed. "I was the only person who could [lead the country]."[28]

In the early hours of June 26, in what anywhere else in South Asia would have been accounted a civil coup, all the main opposition leaders—J. P. Narayan, Morarji Desai, and Raj Narain among them—were arrested. First hundreds and then thousands of others, including members of parliament and of the state legislatures, student leaders, journalists, academics, and union bosses, followed them into jail under the MISA's provisions for detention without trial. The newspaper presses were halted by turning off the power; a rigorous censorship was imposed. The cut and thrust of political life ceased, the elections due in 1976 were postponed. "And this," as the papers might have put it if they could, "in the India of Mahatma Gandhi and Nehru."

The wider world was aghast. Obituaries for Indian democracy, both tearful and patronizing, featured prominently in the Western press. Bhutto, on the other hand, was unusually reticent. He noted only that "gloating" was inappropriate and warned Gandhi not to "seek to extricate herself from this mess by embarking on an adventurist course against Pakistan."[29] Elsewhere, while India's friends wrung their hands and volunteered their services, India's critics preferred to say "I told you so." V. S. Naipaul characterized the JP Movement as retrogressive, a throwback to Mahatma Gandhi's vision of an apolitical India consisting of village republics. The Emergency was a requiem for Western-style democracy and also a long-overdue wake-up call. By "dramatiz[ing] India's creative incapacity, its intellectual depletion, its defencelessness, the inadequacy of every Indian's idea of India," it would finally dispel Gandhian complacency.[30] He expected the crackdown to last and noted that by 1976 the JP Movement was already "evaporating."

"Condensing" would have been a better choice than "evaporating." In late 1975 Narayan's precarious health had taken a turn for the worse. To forestall the explosive potential of his dying in detention, he was rushed to a hospital in Bombay and there "chained to a dialysis machine." According to Ramachandra Guha, there were now "an estimated 36,000 . . . in jail under MISA." A constitutional amendment deprived them of any legal redress; other amendments, all rubber-stamped by the Supreme Court, prevented any judicial review of the Emergency, quashed Raj Narain's action, allowed Parliament to extend its own life and make its own changes to the constitution, and gave the central government new powers to suspend or dismiss state governments. The murder of Mujibur Rahman in Dhaka in August only made matters worse. Mrs. Gandhi interpreted the assassination of her friend and ally "as an omen of what could happen to her and her own family."[31] Surveillance was increased and more suspects were hauled in. As ever, paranoia stalked autocracy.

There was, though, an upside to the Emergency. Even critics recognized it. Like dictators elsewhere, Indira Gandhi made much of the need for discipline. Among those rounded up, the tax evaders, black-marketeers, smugglers, and bribe takers greatly outnumbered the political detainees. As demonstrators trooped back to work aboard buses customized with slogans such as "Talk less, work more" and "Efficiency is our watchword," industrial strife subsided. The crime rate plummeted, as did the rate of inflation, and the trains ran closer to schedule. Denied the usual scandals, those journalists who were at liberty to file reports found that there was disappointingly little to write about. Beggars betook themselves elsewhere, taxi meters sometimes worked, and big business generally approved.

While Mrs. Gandhi adopted a twenty-point program full of rehashed socialist pieties, Sanjay hobnobbed with multinational corporations and diverted funds from his Maruti car company into a variety of dubious enterprises. Instead of land reform and debt relief, he spoke out in favor of enterprise and efficiency. Decrying nationalization, in one interview he looked forward to a liberal economic regime in which the public sector would die "a natural death." In this he was, of course, well ahead of his time. Not for another fifteen years would such radical rethinking about the economy be officially contemplated; indeed, so objectionable were Sanjay's methods that his advocacy probably hampered liberalization rather than hastened it.

His mother, though disapproving, seemed incapable of censuring him. Instead she encouraged him to concentrate on his political future. By shoehorning him onto the executive committee of the Congress Party's Youth Wing, she effectively anointed him as her preferred successor. Packed with his minions, the Youth Wing would become Sanjay's power base and a rival to the party itself. He was already ensconced in the prime minister's residence at the head of a "kitchen cabinet" that short-circuited both the official cabinet and the prime minister's secretariat. In what the wags called the "Land of the Rising Son," it was Sanjay who called the shots. The Emergency seemed as much his creation as his mother's.

To kick-start the modernization of the country, he came up with a five-point program of his own. A mixture of the worthy and the quixotic, it prioritized family planning, slum clearance, mass literacy, afforestation, and the abolition of dowries. The last three being the least susceptible to speedy implementation, they had to wait. That left the slums and the birth rate; it was for bulldozers and vasectomies that Sanjay would be remembered.

The slums he targeted were principally the shanty townships in Delhi. Sanjay had already adopted the city as a trial ground for his rough-and-ready brand of enforcement and had there found an able collaborator in the person of Jagmohan Malhotra, vice chairman of the Delhi Development Authority and later a controversial governor of Kashmir. While Sanjay provided political cover plus police backup, and with the Emergency regulations ensuring a publicity blackout, Jagmohan ordered in the bulldozers. Sometimes the residents received ample warning; sometimes they were directed to remote alternative sites; sometimes neither. In the space of eighteen months around 150,000 families had their homes demolished, and since most of these were rented and had been illegally constructed in the first place, there was little prospect of compensation. Resistance was met by baton charges, tear gas, and occasionally live rounds. The numbers wounded or killed went largely unreported, like the action itself. No doubt the slum settlements were an eyesore and a health risk. But this most undemocratic method of dealing with them belied Mrs. Gandhi's claim that her Emergency was in defense of democracy.

Much the same could be said of Sanjay's efforts at population control. These had a far wider effect and just as much to recommend them. The population had doubled in the last half century. Reducing the birth rate had long been government policy; planners regarded it as essential, and, with life expectancy increasing and infant mortality falling, it was the obvious way to reduce the poverty statistics. But this was less obvious to laboring families, who regarded every infant as a potential source of earnings. Moreover, condoms were unpopular and contraceptive pills in short supply. Easier to quantify and much more effective was the "snip." Mass vasectomizing could be conducted in roadside tents and mobile clinics. Like immunization, it could also be incentivized.

This was Sanjay's brainchild. From attracting individual volunteers with promises of cash or a radio, he began setting targets for the number of vasectomies to be performed by each state. Passed on down to the districts and subdistricts, the targets introduced a competitive element. To meet or exceed them, and so impress the Rising Son, officials vied with one another and resorted to methods that might be both discriminatory and coercive. In some areas the clinics directed their attentions disproportionately to the homeless, Muslims, tribal peoples, and *harijans*. Elsewhere, the entitlement to benefits, jobs, and licenses might be made contingent on the production of certificates of vasectomization. The results were impressive. "In the six months between April and September 1976, two million Indians were sterilized," with as many as six thousand per day in Delhi alone.[32] But resistance was widespread and visceral. Nothing in the entire Emergency was as much resented as Sanjay's clumsy assault on the masculinity of the nation.

Isolated among the obsequious members of her kitchen cabinet and lulled by her compliant press, Mrs. Gandhi was apparently unaware of the worst excesses. When they were finally brought to her attention, she called a halt to them, though without censuring Sanjay or appreciating the scale of the damage. Just how out of touch she had grown became clearer in January 1977. Taking both friend and foe by surprise, she blithely announced that elections were to be held. They were to take place in March, allowing just eight weeks for the campaign. Most of the political detainees were released, censorship was lifted, and campaigning began immediately. Like Bhutto in Pakistan—indeed, possibly prompted by his announcement of elections there a few days earlier—she supposed her opponents were in disarray, and she was confident of victory,

Bhutto's reading of his own electoral prospects would prove right; his mistake lay in trying too hard to ensure his victory. Mrs. Gandhi's reading was hopelessly wrong; her mistake lay in trusting her own propaganda machine. Both had become dangerously isolated from the realities of life—and not just in South Asia. For as of 1973 an economic tsunami had been racing out of the Arabian Gulf and across the world's oceans. No place was spared. Currency markets shook and stock markets crumbled. In what might well qualify as the late twentieth century's first wave of globalization, the price of oil had gone through the roof. Buffeted by the shock, Mujib in Bangladesh, Bhutto in Pakistan, and Gandhi in India might console themselves with the thought that their woes were not entirely of their own making. Yet the long-term effects for South Asia would prove far more complex, indeed a blessing, albeit a mixed one and in disguise.

8

TWO-WAY TICKETS, DOUBLE STANDARDS

T HE HIKE IN OIL PRICES HIT HARDEST IN 1973–74, WHEN IN A matter of weeks the price of crude shot up from $3 a barrel to $12. Though this was in part a response to the devaluation of oil assets occasioned by Nixon's detaching the dollar from the gold standard, Arab producers insisted they were raising prices and cutting back on production in retaliation for Washington's rearmament of Israel after the 1973 October War. In other words, the dreaded "oil weapon" had finally been unsheathed. Since practically everything depended on oil, practically everything was affected, from steel output to textile and fertilizer production. In Japan the panic extended even to toilet paper.

Then in 1979–80 the same thing happened all over again when the price of crude soared to $40 a barrel. This time it was supposedly because of uncertainties over supply following the fall of the shah of Iran, the Soviet invasion of Afghanistan, and the beginning of the Iran-Iraq War. But an element of panic was noted and some corporate manipulation was suspected. Throughout a rapidly industrializing world, the dangers of depending on any globally traded commodity that was in limited supply were becoming painfully manifest.

Higher oil prices were not always bad news, though. As well as bringing untold spending power and an almighty construction boom to the otherwise impoverished Gulf region, price hikes quite suited the industrialized countries. Those with their own reserves could charge more for them, while to those without reserves, higher prices provided an incentive for developing alternative sources of energy. South Asia was badly placed in both respects: its known oil reserves were limited to a few wells in Assam, and, in regard to alternatives such as gas and nuclear energy, its technical expertise was limited.

Here too, though, ill winds worked their proverbial magic, for on balance the bonanza in the Gulf opened up other reserves—of employment, foreign exchange, and cross-border investment—that would offset the region's exposure to the rising cost of imports and substantially boost GNPs. Though unforeseen at the time, and indeed a mild source of embarrassment, such spin-off opportunities would buoy all the economies of South Asia well into the twenty-first century.

V. S. Naipaul had noted the relevance of the Gulf as early as 1976. Rattling around Delhi during Indira Gandhi's Emergency, he had been surprised to learn that his Sikh taxi driver was planning to emigrate: "He wanted to go to one of the Arab Gulf states. He had paid a large sum of money to a middleman, a 'contractor.' His papers were almost in order now, he said; all he was waiting for, from the contractor, was his 'no objection' certificate."[1]

"No objection" pretty much characterized the official attitude toward emigration at the time. It was neither promoted nor prevented; as yet irrelevant to the general mass of South Asians, its appeal was limited. Naipaul reckoned his Sikh driver to be someone who was "better off than most people in India." He spoke excellent English, his taxi was his own, and it occupied a sought-after station in the rank outside Naipaul's no doubt comfortable hotel. Postcolonial emigration, whether to the West or to the Gulf, seldom benefited the poorest classes or the lowest castes. Far from being an option of last resort, it was seen as a promising investment, the capital outlay required having the potential to transform not just the life of the migrant but the prospects of those he left behind.

Sikhs had been wise to the advantages of foreign earnings since long before Partition uprooted many from their homelands in what was now Pakistan. Untroubled by the caste-conscious Hindu's need to undergo expensive post-travel purification ceremonies, they had acted as diasporic pioneers, establishing communities in parts of California, British Columbia, East Africa, and the United Kingdom even before World War I. The beturbaned journeymen who in the 1970s were still selling dusters and detergents out of battered suitcases in places as remote as Orkney and New Zealand were often second- or third-generation migrants.

The new wave of migration differed in that the Gulf offered fewer incentives for permanent settlement. On the other hand, it was nearer and cheaper with respect to visits home. Most migrant workers were destined for the construction or service industries and went on fixed contracts, typically of two years. Although these might be extended or repeated, the conditions, both contractual and physical, were seldom such as to encourage workers to summon their families and so make the transition from sojourners to settlers. Instead, like the earlier wave of South Asian migrants to the United Kingdom and North America, they saved up to 50 percent of their earnings and remitted these sums by various means to kin and sponsors back home.

The economic impact of such transactions would be enormous, but so too would the social consequences. According to one study, albeit based on the expectations not of sojourners in the Gulf but of settlers in California, remittances were employed "to enhance status; gain philanthropic prestige; maintain *izzat* or honor; improve marriage potentials familywide; acquire political power or influence; demonstrate religious devotion; increase the potential for the education of siblings or more distant kinsmen; and, of course, finance additional migration."[2] Very few first-generation migrants, and not many of the second or third generation, severed their links with their kinsmen back home. If anything, South Asians abroad clung to family and community even more tenaciously than they did at home. Empowering his brethren back in South Asia validated the migrant's experience and enhanced his standing among them. They in turn might defer to his suggestions on the use of his remittances and heed his advice in other matters of community interest, including those of doctrinal and political allegiance.

Initially it was not India but Pakistan that benefited most from the Gulf's appetite for labor. Being for the most part Muslims, Pakistanis were already welcome in the Arabian peninsula. There were ancient commercial and trading links between Sind and the Gulf ports, and many thousands of Pakistanis headed to Mecca on the annual pilgrimage. Hajj organizers were trusted figures and were acceptable to all parties as labor contractors. Though in India migration to the Gulf was principally from Kerala—and though in Pakistan migration streams to countries other than those of the Gulf were also origin-specific (e.g., Azad Kashmiris to the United Kingdom)—the Gulf appealed across the board, attracting unskilled and semiskilled manual workers from all over Pakistan. Pathans and Punjabis flocked through emigration control at the Islamabad airport as readily as did Sindis and *muhajirs* at the Karachi airport. Unusually for Pakistan, here was an enterprise in which all the nation's fretful ethnic groups might jointly participate and profit.

It was therefore somewhat ironic that the PPP, the main political party with an all-Pakistan appeal, was unable to reap the rewards of Gulf migration. Bhutto had been in dire need of good economic news, but, when his government had been ousted by the military, the exodus to the Gulf was still a trickle. Only thereafter did it become a flood. From perhaps 300,000 Pakistanis working in Saudi Arabia and the Gulf states when Bhutto was arrested in 1977, the figure quickly increased sixfold, so that by the time he was executed in 1979 it stood at around 1.8 million. It would remain at this level until 1983, then fall away, only to surge again as oil prices soared further in the late 1980s. The principal beneficiary was thus the eleven-year regime of General Zia ul-Haq.

The same poor timing did Bangladesh's Mujibur Rahman and his Awami League no favors either. Augmented by remittances from the Sylheti community in the United Kingdom, the earnings of Bangladeshis in the Gulf would come to constitute the country's main source of foreign exchange. But the outflow of migrant labor to the Gulf only reached appreciable dimensions three to four years after Mujib's death. Once again it was the military regimes, first that of General Ziaur Rahman and then of General Mohamed Ershad, that benefited.

Although available statistics on the scale of remittances are reckoned inadequate (because they generally fail to distinguish between different streams of migration) and unreliable (because they mostly ignore informal money transfers), it seems that the value of foreign exchange reaching Pakistan in the form of recorded remittances from the Middle East rose from $434 million in 1976–77 to a peak of $2.4 billion in 1982–83.[3] By then Gulf earnings covered nearly 75 percent of Pakistan's trade deficit and were bringing in more foreign exchange than either exports or American aid. The World Bank calculated this to mean that in the decade 1977–86 Pakistan profited from Gulf migration to the tune of nearly $16 billion.

In reality it was probably more. Cash transferred not through banks but through the informal *hundi* system of brokers—or indeed stashed about the returning migrant's luggage and person—is thought to have added another 50 percent. Moreover, the Pakistani economy profited indirectly too. Lower deficits meant lower borrowing costs, and siphoning off excess labor to the Gulf may have reduced domestic tensions; plus the demand for Pakistani products from the roughly 10 percent of the country's male labor force who were now working in the Gulf saw exports to that region double.

Nor was this a flash in the pan. As of 1983 Pakistan's participation in the Gulf bonanza showed a slight decline. Oil prices were slipping, and the resultant belt tightening in the Gulf reduced the demand for labor. Meanwhile, migrants from India, Bangladesh, Nepal, and Sri Lanka who were either more amenable to lower pay rates or better equipped in terms of skills provided stiff competition. Yet the reduction in remittances to Pakistan was nicely offset by the lower cost of oil imports, and, when oil prices again surged, so did the flow of migrants and the value of their remittances. After several more such seesaws, by 2012 the value of all foreign remittances reaching Pakistan (so from Europe and North America as well as the Gulf) was estimated at a mighty $13.5 billion a year.

How much of this was being put to productive use—indeed, what constitutes productive use—has been much debated. A survey published in 1987 by the Asian Employment Programme of the International Labour Organization indicated that in Pakistan around 50 percent of remittance funds were spent on "recurring consumption plus [consumer] durables," with another 10 percent going to marriage and hajj costs and 17 percent to acquiring land and property. That left around 20 percent for "other investment." Some of this 20 percent "was directed towards commercial avenues such as trade and [the] restaurants business," but only 7 percent went to "agricultural and industrial machinery and commercial vehicles."[4] Greater spending power obviously benefited the wider economy and boosted GDP, but the government-sponsored savings schemes and investment incentives that might have generated long-term productivity were scorned. The abiding preference of "Indus man" for ostentatious consumption over thrift and capital accumulation was still in evidence.

Something similar was true of Kerala. Though one of India's smaller states, Kerala—densely populated, well educated, and with a substantial Muslim minority—accounted for half of the nation's annual migrant outflow to the Gulf. The stream of remittances into the state was thus considerable, yet it did not seem to make much of an impact on the state's economic growth rate nor to have any substantial effect on the employment rate, agricultural development, or industrialization.[5] Instead Keralans plowed their earnings into day-to-day necessities, consumer goods, and construction materials for new housing.

But just across the border from Pakistan in the Indian state of Punjab the situation was rather different. In Jandiali, a Sikh village with a long tradition of migration, Arthur Helweg's research in the 1980s found that investment from remittances had overtaken the needs of production: "Emigrants sent back much money which enabled farmers to mechanize and invest heavily in machinery and technology. . . . To illustrate, Jandiali had 22 tractors to till her 646 acres. Tractors in Jandiali did hire out, but the figure is indicative of an investment above that warranted by the output, possibly 20 times the amount. Part of the reason for excessive tractors is that they are a prestige item."[6] Jandiali was an extreme example. Located in Jalandhar district, long an area of high emigration, by the 1980s more than half of the village's natural population was living abroad. And since earlier patterns of migration had established Jalandhar's

Sikhs in the United Kingdom, Canada, and the United States, it was from these places rather than the Gulf that the bulk of the remittances were coming.

Punjab itself was not exactly typical either. The tractor-cluttered roads and the thump of newly sunk tube wells advertised its preeminence as the most agriculturally productive state in India. In fact, by 1985 India's Punjab seemed no longer to belong to the Third World and to have left the rest of India behind. Bullock carts were being forced off the roads by combine harvesters. The shops had plate-glass windows and the Yamaha had ousted the bicycle. "There were no mud huts in the villages; it was all brick and stone. . . . If any one part of the country could be called a success story, this was it."[7]

But the good news had a downside: Punjab was in danger of becoming the victim of its own success. Mechanization had reduced the demand for labor, while inflation plus greater productivity had pushed up the price of land. Those not in receipt of foreign earnings were having to sell out and join the ranks of the landless. In what was acclaimed as India's breadbasket, some 40 percent did not make enough to pay for their own bread. Meanwhile, the prosperity generated by the combination of green-revolution technology and greenback remittances had so roused the envy of other states that Indira Gandhi felt justified in discouraging industrial development in Punjab and directing it elsewhere. Thus the easiest means of taking up the slack in the labor market was ruled out. According to Helweg, disparity between rich and poor was becoming ingrained. Only those with emigrant connections could purchase land, make investments, and maintain an acceptable standard of living.[8]

From competition for land and jobs, the growing tension between the remittance haves and the remittance have-nots spread to issues of local leadership. In affairs of common interest the haves expected a say commensurate with their newfound status; the have-nots resented this and were inclined to see emigrants as scapegoats for all of India's problems. Such factionalism was not unusual and anywhere else might have been ignored. But Punjab in the 1980s was a special case in more respects than one. The most progressive state, it was also one of the most assertive and distinctive. Claims that it was Punjabi farmers who fed the nation and Punjabi soldiers who defended it were not without foundation, although no doubt exaggerated. Punjabis were as preeminent and overrepresented in the armed forces as they were in cereal production. But above all, and as a result of some opportunistic redrawing of federal boundaries, Punjabis were now deemed synonymous with Sikhs.

Ostensibly this was the outcome of the belated reorganization into language-based states of India's post-Partition half of the British Punjab province. Back in the 1950s Jawaharlal Nehru, though accepting the principle of linguistic states in the south, had resisted it in the case of Punjab. He reasoned that since all Sikhs spoke Punjabi, partitioning what remained of the already partitioned province into Hindi-speaking and Punjabi-speaking units would make the latter in effect a Sikh state. This would undermine the nation's secularism and encourage divisive sentiments elsewhere. But in 1966, shortly after her selection as prime minister, Indira Gandhi had decided otherwise. Anxious to win support wherever she could in her battle with the Congress Party's Syndicate, she had acceded to demands for Punjab's trifurcation. Its hill districts, many of them once princely states, were grouped together as Himachal Pradesh (the state capital being Simla), while its mainly Hindi-speaking southern and eastern districts around Delhi were detached to form the new state of Haryana and its now mainly Punjabi-speaking heartland continued as Punjab.

Strategically crucial because it bordered both Pakistan and Kashmir, it was this last creation that had become such a success story. The agreement with Pakistan over the sharing of the Indus waters, the higher productivity associated with the green revolution, and the boom in migration and remittances were all working in favor of the mini-Punjab. Additionally, apart from the trouble spots of Kashmir and Nagaland, Punjab was as yet the only state in India with a non-Hindu majority, for as Nehru had foreseen, those who claimed Punjabi as their first language (and the Gurmukhi script as its written expression) were overwhelmingly Sikhs. More important still, the state embraced the Sikh holy city of Amritsar along with its Golden Temple complex, the revered Mecca-cum-Vatican of the Sikh religion.

Not surprisingly, Sikhs, both in India and abroad, came to regard their new Punjab more as a hallowed homeland than an administrative division of the Indian republic. Though far from united, all Sikhs subscribed to a tradition that, like Islam's, stressed the relevance of doctrine to every aspect of life, politics included. At the time of Partition they had been promised the freedom to exercise their faith plus such autonomy as this required. The main Sikh political party, the Akali Dal, was pledged to realizing this autonomy, and, in 1973, at a place sacred to the memory of the last guru, it had adopted a radical resolution to that effect.

Known as the Anandpur Sahib Resolution, it advanced forty-five demands, some essentially parochial or economic, others distinctly incendiary. One revived the British Cabinet Mission's proposal that what the Akali Dal called "interference" by New Delhi in the governance of the states should be limited to defense, foreign affairs, currency, and "general administration." In this it also echoed the six-point program of Mujibur Rahman's Awami League. And just as the latter had led to the breakup of Pakistan, so the Akali demand could be seen as threatening the integrity of India.

Other demands in the Anandpur Sahib Resolution referred to the Sikhs as a *qaum,* an Urdu word that could be understood as meaning "community" (which was acceptable) or "nation" (which echoed the two-nation theory of Pakistan's founders and was quite unacceptable). Additionally, the Akali Dal insisted that Chandigarh, the bleakly futuristic city designed by Le Corbusier as the capital of India's pre-1966 Punjab, should be awarded to their own truncated Punjab. This was anathema to Hindi-speaking Haryana and had already provoked riots and rival fasts unto death. Solomon-like, Indira Gandhi decreed that both states should share Chandigarh's capacious facilities. Under further pressure, she then changed her mind and awarded the city to Punjab. But there was a quid pro quo. Punjab would have to relinquish two districts to Haryana by way of compensation. This suited neither state and provoked trouble in both. It remained unimplemented until, in 1984, renewed Punjabi demands for Chandigarh would goad Gandhi into waging her "Last Battle." Otherwise known as "Operation Blue Star," this Indian Army assault on Amritsar's Golden Temple would be regarded by many as the century's greatest sacrilege.

IF A RAMPANT POPULISM had typified the whole South Asian political scene in the 1970s, a rabid communalism was more in evidence in the following two decades. Earlier the importance attached to nation building had encouraged Nehru, and to a lesser extent Jinnah and Mujib, to play down confessional identities and promote a supposedly inclusive secularism. But such neutrality in matters of religion antagonized those who favored a more public role for their preferred belief system and was often belied in electoral practice by confessional communities voting en bloc for parties pledged to defend their interests. Protestations of secularism notwithstanding, religious identities were far from dormant and were eminently susceptible to new stimuli.

One such stimulus was another by-product of emigration. With regard to Islam, migrants coming and going to the Arabian peninsula often brought home a sounder notion of their faith's supranational profile and a new regard for the fundamentalist tenets and uncompromising attitudes of Saudi Arabia's Wahhabi elite. Likewise, remittances, whether they originated from sojourners in the Gulf or settlers in the West, often came with doctrinal strings attached. So of course did the devotional and educational endowments that were increasingly directed at South Asia by charitable foundations in the Middle East and the West. Moreover, such patronage could prove provocative. Being funded to speak out on matters of faith and promote a particular doctrine could amount to proselytization. When in 1981 several thousand Dalits (*harijans* or untouchables) in Tamil Nadu opted to mass-convert to Islam, it was widely reported that Muslim inducements, including Gulf cash, had played a greater part in their decision than the discriminatory practices to which they had previously been exposed as Dalits. By the adherents of other cults and creeds, among them India's vast Hindu majority, such conversions were seen both as a threat and as a challenge. To meet it they would mobilize their own resources—financial, organizational, and agitational.

Affirming a national religious identity could also pay political dividends. In both Pakistan and Bangladesh the Generals Zia cultivated support for their military regimes at home and abroad by stressing their Muslim credentials and appeasing their countries' Islamic leaderships. Thus in the late 1970s Ziaur Rahman scrapped all reference to secularism in the Bangladesh constitution, and in the late 1980s General Ershad finally decreed that Bangladesh should call itself an "Islamic state." Meanwhile, Zia ul-Haq in Pakistan had given statutory expression to what this vexed concept might mean in practice. All were no doubt sincere believers, yet they were also aware that to generals who badly needed legitimacy, securing the approval of Muslim ideologues was the next best thing to a democratic endorsement.[9]

India remained avowedly secular. Indeed, Mrs. Gandhi wrote a new clause to this effect into the constitution during her Emergency. But secularism meant different things to different people. For the agnostic Nehru it had been an intellectually persuasive proposition; for his daughter it was a shibboleth to be trotted out when required; and for J. P. Narayan it was something of a religion in itself. As a onetime colleague and disciple of the Mahatma, Narayan was convinced not that religious belief should be denied a role in public life but that public life, once it had been cleansed and devolved to the village level, would no longer provide a congenial arena for the universalist claims of competing belief systems.

As someone who had once acted as a government go-between with both Kashmir's Sheikh Abdullah and the Naga leader Angami Zapu Phizo, Narayan brought a similarly eclectic vision to matters of political allegiance. In fact, his "total revolution," after restoring power to the people, was supposed to usher in a homespun utopia that would be as devoid of politics as it was of religious bigotry. This conviction, plus his untainted reputation, enabled him to command the loyalties of a decidedly kaleidoscopic coalition. To Indira Gandhi, the sight of diametrically opposed ideologues marching shoulder to shoulder under the JP Movement's umbrella seemed a travesty of electoral democracy—indeed evidence of some kind of conspiracy. But Narayan's unlikely coalition held together, and come the Emergency detentions, it was actually strengthened. Scions of the former princely families found themselves sharing cell space with revolutionaries of Marxist-Leninist persuasion; one-nation Hindu fanatics bedded down beside bearded Jamaati mullahs, and social-ist mavericks such as Raj Narain bandied anti-Indira slogans with business-friendly Congress stalwarts such as Morarji Desai.

Weirdest of all, and yet crucial to the success of the JP Movement, was the coming together of nonviolent disciples of the Mahatma, like JP himself, with the successors of Nathuram Godse, the man who had assassinated the Mahatma. After Gandhi's 1948 shooting, Godse had quickly been disowned by the ultra-Hindu RSS (the extra-parliamentary organization that Nehru believed to be "in the nature of a private army . . . proceeding on the strictest Nazi lines"). Yet there was no denying that Godse had once belonged to the RSS and that he had been swayed by its outspoken attacks on the Mahatma's even-handed stance toward Muslims. Following Godse's conviction, the RSS had been banned and thousands of its activists arrested. Although the ban was soon lifted, the Jana Sangh, the political wing of the RSS, had since been treated as a pariah by the more secular political parties and had struggled to make an electoral impression. Its decision to join the JP Movement, and even "assimilate" with it, represented an important change of tactics. Still the voice of a pa-triotic and determinedly one-nation Hinduism, the Jana Sangh was bidding to enter the mainstream of Indian politics.[10]

In return, the Sangh made available to the JP Movement a nation-wide structure and organizing capacity that the movement otherwise lacked. Derived from the party's association with the well-drilled cadres of the RSS, these assets had proved crucial to mounting the movement's massive pre-Emergency demonstrations in Delhi and had become even more germane in the politicking that went on inside prison. In fact, by January 1977, when Mrs. Gandhi lifted the Emer-gency, announced elections, and released those still in detention, the JP Movement had metamorphosed into a formidable electoral con-testant. Comprising the Jana Sangh, the Socialists, Congress (O), and a powerful farming caucus, it emerged into the light of day as the newly fledged Janata Party.

By giving just a few weeks' notice of the 1977 election, Gandhi had again counted on taking her opponents by surprise. But this time she had miscalculated. Whatever credit she claimed for her Emergency was more than offset by popular outrage over its excesses. Janata was ready to take up the cudgels and had merely to stress the obvious. Savaging Sanjay's slum clearances and forced sterilization programs, and decrying the arrests and the press censorship, it promised an immediate return to constitutional integrity, democratic normality, and Gandhian values. Important figures in Indira's Congress sympathized and defected to it; meanwhile, seat-sharing arrangements with regional parties such as the Tamil AIADMK (like other parties, the original DMK had split) and the Sikh Akali Dal ensured that the anti-Indira vote was not fragmented.

The result was a sweeping Janata victory. In the national parliament the new party won 295 of the 542 seats and performed equally well in most of the states. Indira's Congress slumped to 154 seats, at the time its lowest-ever representation. In Rae Bareilly the prime minister herself was roundly defeated by Raj Narain; in a neighboring constituency Sanjay's attempt to win a seat bombed. For the first time ever India had a non-Congress government. The Emergency had been discredited and with it the lurch toward authoritarian rule. Portraying the result as less a critique of Gandhi's constitutional tinkering and more a test of the nation's commitment to democracy, a standard history of the period reassures its readers that there was "no doubt that the Indian people passed the test with distinction if not full marks."[11]

But while the Janata Party had triumphed in the polls, it was former Jana Sangh members who had triumphed in the party. Their tally of ninety-three seats was twice that achieved by ex-members of any of the other Janata components. There followed much jockeying for position, and eventually J. P. Narayan was asked to arbitrate over the choice of a leader; he installed the octogenarian Morarji Desai as prime minister. But Jana Sanghis also got portfolios, among them the party's president, Atal Bihari Vajpayee, as minister for external affairs. In this role Vajpayee belied his party's reputation for intransigent Hindu triumphalism by visiting Beijing and Islamabad. Fences were mended with both, and, while good terms with Moscow were maintained, a new relationship with Washington was signaled when in 1978 President Jimmy Carter paid an official visit to India. Carter gratified his hosts by likening the shock of Delhi's recent Emergency to that of Washington's recent Watergate crisis. Clearly Hindu nationalists, once in power, were not necessarily a liability and could act as responsibly as any Congress minister.

The same could hardly be said of the Janata party's non–Jana Sangh membership, nor of its domestic policies. *Jana* means "people," with *janata* being its adjectival form, "people's." Under the influence of Nehru's social leveling policies, so-called *janata* amenities had been popping up everywhere. There were *janata* banks and *janata* housing schemes, and in the railway timetables a number of trains were billed as "*janata* expresses." These connected the country's main cities and were to be avoided if at all possible, for a "people's express," though certainly popular, was not expresslike in terms of luxury or speed. Consisting entirely of non-air-conditioned third-class carriages, it stopped at every station (plus points in between), was jam-packed even by Indian standards, lacked adequate toilet facilities, and invariably arrived late. On the railways as elsewhere, *janata* represented the lowest common denominator, with its combination of universal access and rock-bottom standards. As a brand, it was one to avoid; it was not a promising name for a political party.

Insofar as the excesses of the Emergency were quickly addressed, the Janata government may be said to have gotten off to a good start. Mrs. Gandhi's constitutional amendments were reversed, and a legal minefield was laid down to prevent any repeat of the Emergency. The former prime minister herself was humbled with a flurry of judicial inquiries into her conduct in office. Additionally, in deference to Narayan's Gandhianism and Janata's farming lobby, the government nudged economic policy away from centrally planned industrialization and toward rural development and small-scale manufacturing. Ironically, it also improved conditions on the railways, including the dreaded *janata* expresses. A quasi-computerized system of seat reservations was introduced along with what Guha calls a "far-reaching measure" to pad the hard wooden berths of second-class sleepers with a little over an inch of foam rubber.[12] But more village crafts, less central planning, and a marginally more comfortable berth were not a lot to show for a government with such an overwhelming majority.

In fact, the majority was proving to be the problem; for the solidarity that had carried the Janata Party to power instantly deserted it in office. Its ex–Jana Sangh members refused to forswear their allegiance to the RSS and insisted on a nationalist agenda with respect to such things as the rewriting of school textbooks. Neither of these reassured their associates in office, who favored preferential treatment for farmers, money-for-work schemes, and extending the educational and job opportunities reserved for the "scheduled" tribes and lowest castes to other backward castes. However well-intentioned, all this merely stirred up caste conflict, leading to violent clashes and some notable atrocities. Thus it took only nine months for the regime to lose its political momentum and for the Janata Party's uneasy coalition to begin to fall apart.[13] A Janata government lingered on until 1979, but it was amid bitter internal struggles plus growing unrest in the country as the second round of oil price hikes sent inflation back up to 20 percent.

Indira Gandhi had only to bide her time. The Jana Sangh's obsession with "Mother India" (Bharat Mata, a supposedly indivisible and primordially Hindu personification of the nation) was countered by the nation's rediscovered affection for "Mother Indira" (Indira Amma). Her star rose with every move to impeach her or impede her rehabilitation. Janata's pursuit of justice began to look like a vendetta; Sanjay's strong-arm tactics were forgotten. Reelected to parliament in a 1978 by-election in Karnataka, Mrs. Gandhi once again purged her party, then mobilized it to support a breakaway Janata coalition. This arrangement lasted but a matter of weeks. J. P. Narayan was now a dying man, and with him was expiring all hope of his Janata being reconstituted. When in August 1979 Gandhi's Congress withdrew its support of the breakaway coalition, the government lost its fragile majority. New elections were called for in early 1980. India's first ever non-Congress government had lasted less than three years.

Considering how effectively she and Sanjay had masterminded her return to power, and how she then swept the polls to win a majority comparable to that of 1971, the reinstated Gandhi appeared as formidable as ever. She was isolated, certainly. She trusted no one save Sanjay, surrounded herself with sycophants, supposed herself the embodiment of the nation, and took all expressions of dissent as personal affronts. "'Paranoia' may be the most appropriate word here," says Guha.[14] But a rival suggestion that "she no longer had a firm grasp over politics and administration . . . [and] showed signs of being a tired person" was not borne out by events.[15] Still in her early sixties, she enjoyed reasonable health, the close support of her family, and the conviction that only she could hold the nation together.

Arguably, the initiatives of her last four years in power were no more ill-conceived than those of her first four. But whereas in the late 1960s she had embraced leftist policies to discomfit her opponents, in the early 1980s she wheeled to the right for the same reason. Reasoning that Janata had owed its short-lived success entirely to the Jana Sangh and its emphasis on Hindu nationalism, she tailored her public conduct to the new communalism. A Hindu holy man took up residence in the prime ministerial home, and in the weeks immediately after her return to power she made a point of being photographed at temples all over India.

A more communalist approach was also evident in her ritual toppling of non-Congress governments in the states. Though formerly a supporter of Sheikh Abdullah's National Conference in Jammu and Kashmir, she now championed the sense of alienation felt by Hindus in that state's Jammu region and accused the National Conference of "anti-nationalism." Apparently Farooq Abdullah, the Conference's leader since the death of his father, the sheikh, in 1982, had sought Gulf money to develop the state, hoping to place Kashmir on the international map. This was neither particularly sinister nor well substantiated, but it gave Gandhi a pretext for changing tack. Moreover, her attempt to outbid rightist opponents paid off. In the 1983 state elections her Congress comfortably upstaged the challenge of the Hindu right in Jammu as now represented by the Bharatiya Janata Party (BJP), a reincarnation of the Jana Sangh in the wake of the Janata Party's collapse. Mrs. Gandhi's move was nevertheless questionable in that it ran contrary to Nehru's insistence on secular neutrality. Indeed, though most of the BJP's candidates had lost, Gandhi's showing in Jammu could be construed as an endorsement of their platform. As a contributor to the BJP's official organ consoled its readership, "ideas are more important than seats."[16] The ploy also failed in its primary objective of toppling the Abdullahs' National Conference. In what was widely regarded as the state's fairest poll to date, Farooq Abdullah brushed off his rejection in Jammu and was returned to power thanks to the overwhelming support of the Muslim vote in the Kashmir Valley.

No less mischievous interventions in Assam and Punjab were equally counterproductive and would ultimately prove much more disastrous. But it was not just in the center's relationship with the states that Gandhi's cavalier attitude to her father's principles was evident. Regional relations also suffered, most notably with respect to Sri Lanka.

On that troubled island, as in Bangladesh, an upsurge of violence in the 1970s was already concerning New Delhi. A combination of India's ethnic links to the island's Tamil-speaking minority, growing anxiety over possible superpower involvement in resolving the violence, and resentment over the transit facilities afforded to Pakistan in the Bangladesh crisis argued strongly for another assertion of India's regional responsibilities. Additionally, a prime ministerial reputation already built on popular success beyond India's northern borders in Bangladesh and Sikkim might well be reinvigorated by timely engagement with an unhappy island just off the country's southern seaboard.

In a city notably short of landmark buildings, Colombo's Galle Face Hotel stands out as much by reason of its prime location as because of its teak and stone colonnades. To the west the Arabian Sea pounds the hotel's open terraces, to the east runs the city's main traffic axis, to the south lie the Indian High Commission and the US embassy, and to the north, facing the hotel's palm-fringed entrance, stretches a broad grassy esplanade from which strolling couples can watch the sun set. On this breezy sward on the morning of June 5, 1956, some two hundred Sri Lankan Tamil parliamentarians and supporters had assembled in silence. Primed on Gandhian tactics, they sat down and they stayed there, saying nothing, offering no resistance, while organized mobs converged on the park and set about them with sticks and stones. The police were under orders not to intervene. In the nearby Parliament Building the debate on the Official Language Act went on regardless.

"Miraculously," according to later reports, no one was killed. One protester had an ear bitten off, another was thrown into a lake, and dozens were so badly beaten as to need hospitalization. But it was not a massacre and it was all over by 1:00 P.M. That evening guests at the Galle Face Hotel might sally forth to take the ocean breeze as usual. Yet Sri Lanka would never be quite the same again, as historian K. M. De Silva notes: "The riots that erupted on this occasion and spread to many parts of the country brought an end to . . . 40 years of communal peace. . . . The rancour and the bitterness they left behind did not augur well for the governance of the country."[17] The island's fifty-year agony had begun.

A vast nation ringed by lesser entities is bound to regard them as its legitimate concern; no less certainly it is bound to be regarded by them with deep suspicion. This is the case with India and Sri Lanka. In 1956 Sri Lanka's population stood at around ten million. This was under a fifth of Pakistan's or Bangladesh's and around a thirty-third of India's. Most of India's constituent states are in fact larger and more populous than Sri Lanka. The equality implicit in Sri Lanka's sovereign status and UN membership could thus be deceptive. Likewise, the bullying hegemonism of which New Delhi is habitually accused should occasion no surprise. Both are par for the course. In Sri Lanka, as in Nepal, physical proximity to India, historical links, population exchange, a shared cultural matrix, and a considerable degree of economic dependency have long limited the exercise of sovereign prerogatives.

Colonial rule had done nothing to change this. Acquiring Sri Lanka in 1796 on the whim of an enterprising academic called Cleghorn, the British government had not regarded "the island of Ceylon" as pertaining to India or to the East India Company. In time it was run by Britain's Colonial Office rather than the India Office, and it took no part in either the Great Indian Rebellion of 1856–57 or

India's protracted freedom struggle. On the other hand, links with India were if anything strengthened. Under British rule, business houses and the administration relied less on the island's Sinhala-speaking Buddhist majority than on its long-established Tamil-speaking and mainly Hindu minority. Meanwhile, more Tamils were recruited from the Indian mainland as bonded labor to work the island's new tea and rubber plantations.

Of these two Tamil-speaking communities, the semi-indigenous Sri Lankan Tamils were concentrated in the north and east of the island and the less favored and more transient estate (or Indian) Tamils were found throughout the interior. When Sri Lanka attained its independence in 1948, each group represented around 12 percent of the island's total population.

In the 1950s and 1960s Indian concern focused mainly on the fate of the estate Tamils. Nearly two decades ahead of India, Sri Lanka had adopted a system of universal franchise that effectively defined who was a Sri Lankan citizen. Estate Tamils qualified only if they could prove five years' residence. This excluded many, some of whom had migrated back to India during the Depression years of the 1930s or moved overseas. More followed when in 1948 independent Sri Lanka's first government redefined citizenship in such a way as to disenfranchise most of the remaining estate Tamils. The move also incensed the much larger Tamil community in mainland India, prompting Nehru, Shastri, and then Mrs. Gandhi to intervene on behalf of these now stateless (and often estateless) Tamils. In 1964 and again in 1974 pacts were signed to resolve the problem. India would ultimately repatriate about half of the one million remaining estate Tamils, while Sri Lanka extended citizenship to slightly fewer; others swelled the ranks of the Tamil diaspora, mostly in Canada and the United Kingdom.

By contrast, the long-resident Tamil community in the north and east of the island was at first little affected by these arrangements. Better educated but much divided by caste and profession, these Sri Lankan Tamils did qualify as Sri Lankan citizens. They participated in the political process, and in the Jaffna Peninsula (just across the Palk Strait from India) they actually constituted a majority. They were also well represented in the offices and bazaars of Colombo and other cities. But after independence, such prominence came to be resented by the island's non-Tamil majority. Though riven by divisions of its own, this Sinhalese majority began asserting a national identity based on its shared allegiance to Buddhism and the Sinhala language. As a result, constitutional provisions originally conceived as necessary for the protection of minorities such as the Sri Lankan Tamils were increasingly portrayed as discriminating against the Sinhalese majority. To redress the situation, successive governments embarked on a program of affirmative action, albeit with the unusual object of empowering not a minority but the vast majority.

Access to the country's sole university and schemes for the development of new lands proved especially contentious. Tamils objected to the Sinhalese being settled on reclaimed tracts in the north and east, diluting the Tamils' numerical strength in the provinces they considered their homeland. They, and especially their youth, also took strong exception to a weighted system of admission requirements for the Colombo Schools of Medicine and Engineering, for to reduce the disproportionate imbalance between Tamil-speakers and Sinhala-speakers in these cherished professions, Sinhala-speakers were to be admitted with lower scores than those required of their Tamil-speaking peers.

But it was the issue of language itself that, in Sri Lanka as in Indian Tamil Nadu, provoked the greatest outcry. At the time of independence, Sinhala, Tamil, and English served as the official languages. English was soon to be phased out, and so, it seemed, was Tamil when in 1956 the Official Language Act was passed, for under it Sinhala was to become the sole national language within five years.

The main Tamil political party countered with demands for Tamil's reinstatement and for greater autonomy for the northern and eastern provinces. The first demonstration in support of these demands was the nonviolent protest mounted on the breezy sward outside Colombo's Galle Face Hotel on June 5. Following the rout of the protesters, the attackers turned their attention to Tamils in other areas of the city. Elsewhere in the country 150 people were reported to have died in related incidents before the situation was brought under control.[18]

Worse followed when in 1958 the government of S. W. R. D. Bandaranaike (who would be assassinated a year later and whose wife, Sirimavo, would eventually become prime minister), under pressure from members of the Buddhist monastic community, reneged on a later compromise permitting the official use of Tamil in the northern and eastern provinces. Tamils again protested, and this time the attacks spread to the north, where Tamils responded in kind.

All this coincided with the rise to power in India's Madras province of the Tamil DMK, followed by the creation of the Tamil-speaking state of Tamil Nadu and the eventually successful protests there against the adoption of Hindi as India's official language nationwide. Delhi seemed a lot more responsive to Tamil concerns than Colombo did, and this would remain the case when the ruling Congress in New Delhi habitually sought the support of the ruling DMK (or its breakaway AIADMK) in Tamil Nadu. Sri Lankan Tamils took heart from this example. Their main political mouthpiece called itself the Federal Party and increasingly presented its linguistic grievances in terms of a demand for the island's northern and eastern provinces to be granted the autonomous powers enjoyed by the Indian states.

The act making Sinhala the only official language duly came into effect in 1961. But with the Tamils' Federal Party holding the balance of power in parliament, the implementation of the act was again diluted by concessions to the Tamils—concessions that were once more withdrawn under pressure from Sinhala nationalists. In 1970 the electoral triumph of Sirimavo Bandaranaike at the head of a left-supported United Front government ended this stop-start shuffle. A new constitution awarded the prime minister and parliament additional powers, enshrined Sinhala as the official language, favored Buddhism as the majority faith, and effectively ruled out any further concessions. The die was cast. Feeling excluded from power, constitutionally hobbled, and educationally disadvantaged, Sri Lankan Tamils of different castes, age groups, and ideological persuasions drew closer together. The leader of the Federal Party, a mild-mannered Christian called S. J. V. Chelvanayakam, resigned his parliamentary seat, and in 1973 the party moved toward an uncompromising separatism.[19]

In the north and east of the island many Tamils now regarded the army and the police as hostile forces of occupation, to be resisted and targeted as the agents of Sinhala supremacism. Throughout the 1970s murders and other acts of violence increased. They included the assassination of an MP by radical Tamil youths answering to the twenty-three-year-old Velupillai Prabhakaran. As of 1975 Prabhakaran's militant Tamil Students' Federation adopted the name Liberation Tigers of Tamil Eelam (LTTE). Other militant groups proliferated, among them the ill-named EROS (Eelam Revolutionary Organisation of Students), founded in London in the same year. Soon after, in 1976, a national convention of the Tamil United Liberation Front (TULF), a constitutionally minded grouping rather than a militant one, resolved on a "sacred fight for freedom . . . [for] the goal of a sovereign socialist state of Tamil Eelam."[20] The rhetoric, no less than the reality, was threatening war. Another South Asian partition looked to be on the cards.

With the example of Bangladesh fresh in Tamil minds, "the hope and assumption was that what India had done for the people of East Pakistan it could be persuaded to do for the Tamils of Sri Lanka," writes K. M. De Silva. Nor would the Tamil secessionists be disappointed. The expansion and progress of their struggle "would have been impossible without the support and encouragement of the political parties of Tamil Nadu and . . . the more calculating, self-serving, and yet vital assistance of the Indian government to Tamil separatism in the 1980s."[21]

In 1977, the year in which Gandhi was defeated in the polls by the Janata Party, Bandaranaike shared a similar fate. With the election of J. R. Jayawardene as Sri Lanka's premier, another constitution ushered in a presidential form of government and proportional representation. TULF, campaigning on the platform of a separate Tamil state, won the second-largest number of seats and headed the parliamentary opposition. But these developments, while insufficient to reassure the separatists, more than sufficed to alarm Sinhala opinion. Riots and reprisals followed in 1978. The LTTE was banned, a state of emergency was declared in Jaffna, and vigorous counterinsurgency operations by the security forces triggered another Tamil exodus. Militant Tamil groups began to withdraw across the Palk Strait to Tamil Nadu; sympathizers—plus many Tamils who simply despaired of their future in Sri Lanka—either followed them or joined the wider diaspora.

In Indian Tamil Nadu an AIADMK government headed by M. G. Ramachandran, the corpulent but quasi-divine hero of innumerable Tamil films, was decidedly sympathetic to the plight of the Sri Lankan Tamils. Accommodation and funds were found for the newcomers. But no clear distinction was made between refugees and those whom the Sri Lankan government regarded as terrorists. Nor was it easy to distinguish the role played by the government in New Delhi from that of its AIADMK ally in Madras. From later reports it appears that "India's covert training of Tamil militant groups in Tamil Nadu may have started as early as May 1982."[22]

India's diplomatic involvement in attempts to mediate a settlement between the militants and the Jayawardene government also dates from this period. But it assumed much greater urgency as of July 1983. In that month an LTTE ambush in which thirteen Sinhalese soldiers were killed sparked islandwide attacks on Tamils. The violence was communal but otherwise indiscriminate. Sinhalese mobs turned on Tamil neighbors regardless of whether they were in sympathy with the separatist movement; the same innocent parties might be targeted by Tamil militants as suspected traitors to the separatist cause. Though officially classed as "riots," the killings and burnings reminded observers of the madness that had overtaken Calcutta in 1946 and the Punjab in 1947. Again the government was slow to intervene, leading to suspicions of complicity. Here too the death toll is disputed: estimates range from three hundred to three thousand. And again there was a massive movement of population. Up to two hundred thousand Sri Lankan Tamils were displaced, many of them preferring exile in India or the West. The only big difference was that whereas in India and Pakistan the killing had been stopped in a matter of weeks, in Sri Lanka it marked the beginning of the twenty-six-year war.

The Jayawardene government's barely disguised sympathy for the Sinhala nationalists continued to make matters worse. By rushing through a constitutional amendment that obliged all parliamentarians to forswear separatism, it gave TULF MPs little option but to resign. The consequences proved fatal, as their departure from politics resulted in a vacuum that was filled by Velupillai Prabhakaran and the LTTE. In the north and east, LTTE attacks kept pace with the increased deployment of Sri Lankan police and troops. Soon the Jaffna Peninsula was effectively under guerrilla control. Funds raised by the diaspora were now channeled principally to the militant groups, and it was their recruits who were dispatched to training camps in Tamil Nadu and elsewhere in India. Writes the historian Nira Wickramasinghe, "The events of 1983 [had] made them 'terrorists.'"[23]

While the LTTE waged a war of attrition against the Sri Lankan forces plus a no less bloody vendetta against its own guerrilla rivals, Indian concern mounted. The Tamil Nadu factor was probably uppermost. "Seldom has a constituent unit of one country influenced the relationship between it and a neighbouring country with the same intensity, persistence, and to the same extent that Tamil Nadu does in the case of India's relation with Sri Lanka," writes De Silva.[24] The prospects no less than the instincts of Tamil Nadu's AIADMK government demanded that it act as the protector of Sri Lanka's Tamils. As well as providing the guerrillas with support and sanctuary, it facilitated their acquisition of arms and urged New Delhi to deploy its international clout on their behalf.

In New Delhi, Gandhi obliged because she had an agenda of her own. The Jayawardene government in Colombo, which had toppled the United Front of her friend Sirimavo Bandaranaike, was already looking beyond India for assistance. For help in containing the Tamil challenge and mediating a settlement, Colombo openly approached neighbors other than India, including Pakistan and, further afield, the United Kingdom and the United States. Much to Gandhi's fury, Washington was already arming and bankrolling Zia's Pakistan in response to events in Afghanistan. Indian policy makers were alarmed by the prospect of their least favorite superpower acquiring yet another role in the region. To safeguard its own regional superiority, New Delhi badly needed to assert an exclusive interest in Sri Lanka.

The Tamil Nadu dimension lent further cogency to this analysis, as did reports that some Indian citizens had already fallen victim to the strife. India could not therefore remain indifferent. Yet critics noted only the parallels with the run-up to the Bangladesh intervention. Now as then, the Indian government emphasized its humanitarian concern for the refugees, denied any involvement in the training and funding of the guerrillas, and eagerly embraced the chance to act as arbitrator. This has led one scholar to note "a new Monroe Doctrine in Indian foreign policy after 1983." Another explains the reference by insisting "that India had to manage the ethnic conflict in Sri Lanka itself, in order to both maintain its hegemonic role and keep external powers out of its "backyard.'"[25]

In mid- to late 1983 senior Indian emissaries were twice dispatched to Colombo, and Jayawardene visited India. It was believed that plans for an armed Indian intervention had already been drawn up, and, to forestall this, Jayawardene welcomed the diplomatic initiative. TULF, LTTE, and other militant Tamil groups also endorsed the talks in the hopes of winning some recognition for their separatist agendas. But at the time Gandhi was preoccupied with more pressing separatist challenges closer to home. When in late 1984 one of these claimed her life, it fell to her son Rajiv (Sanjay had been killed in a plane crash four years earlier), as her successor, to resume the search for a role in Sri Lanka. This he would do, bringing the Sri Lankan parties together, then edging them toward the ill-fated 1987 accord under which Indian troops were finally ordered to the island. Proudly deployed as a guarantor of the peace, the Indian peacekeeping force would quickly become fair game when the accord unraveled.

Indian involvement in the Sri Lankan war officially internationalized the conflict, which had in fact long been so. The Tamil diaspora in the United Kingdom, the United States, the Gulf states, and especially Canada (where Toronto soon hosted 150,000 Sri Lankan "asylum seekers") had been funding the militant groups for years and now managed procurement agencies for weaponry, communications equipment, and bomb-making materials plus the shipping to deliver them. The diaspora also lobbied foreign governments on behalf of these groups, with New Delhi's diplomatic representatives reportedly offering their support. In a decade when India's own integrity was coming under greater threat than at any other time since Partition, some saw this as hypocritical.

The irony was not lost on President Jayawardene. When the weekly *India Today* had published the first hard evidence of direct Indian government involvement in supplying and training Tamil guerrillas, the Sri Lankan premier was incensed. "This is not a friendly act at all," he had declared. Nor was it one that he had brought on himself; for as he pointedly added, "I am not harbouring the people who want to separate Punjab and Assam from India."[26]

9

THINGS
FALL APART

Come, come,
Come out of your homes.
Chase, chase,
Chase the foreigner away.

THIS 1980S CHANT—"THE RALLYING POINT OF EVERY MEETING, the call to arms of every procession and protest"—could well have been that of Sri Lanka's Sinhalese majority baying for the suppression of the Tamil guerrillas.[1] It too was inspired by what has been called the "politics of citizenship," and it was providing Indira Gandhi with another stern test of her commitment to the secular and noninterventionist principles bequeathed by her father. But the chant in its pithier original was in fact in the Assamese language, and the "foreigners" whom Assam's activists wished to expel were largely Muslim Bengalis from across India's soft and ever-problematic border with Bangladesh.

Assam, in India's far northeast, had long been noted for an exceptional rate of population increase: Through the first half of the twentieth century it was the world's second-highest, at 137.80 percent, exceeded only by Brazil's.[2] In the census period 1961–71 Assam's population had continued to grow by around 35 percent; hence the 1961 population figure was expected to have doubled by 1991. This was not because the indigenous people—a mixture of Assamese and numerous smaller groupings—were exceptionally fertile. Rather, it was mostly a result of massive in-migration.

Like the Lepchas and Bhutiyas in Sikkim, though on a much larger scale, those who considered themselves natives of Assam were in imminent danger of being outnumbered in their own state. The same phenomenon was notable in neighboring states such as Tripura and Nagaland. And everywhere the ill-regulated immigration brought increased pressure on resources, especially land and jobs, leading to fierce competition over the conventional means of redress, the ballot box.

The Assamese, like the Sinhalese majority in Sri Lanka, had begun protesting against this "foreign" presence soon after independence. Riots followed in the 1950s and 1960s. The immigrants demanded that their own language, Bengali, be given parity with Assamese; the Assamese retorted with demands for the immigrants to be sent home to what was then East Bengal (East Pakistan). But it seems to have been the mass movement of refugees from East Bengal during the 1971 war that elevated the sporadic native protests into a sustained assertion of Assamese subnationalism.

Spearheaded by the All-Assam Students Union (AASU), a campaign of civil disobedience had by 1979 brought the local economy to a standstill and was holding the state government in Gauhati hostage. Targeted were tea plantations and oil installations, both of them vital to India as a whole and neither of them controlled by the Assamese themselves; additionally, government offices were picketed, roads and railways blocked, and schools and colleges closed. In a bid to reclaim the state for its indigenous people, the AASU insisted on its "three D's": detection of the immigrants, deletion of their names from the electoral registers, and their deportation back to Bangladesh.

Of these, deletion was the most controversial. The state had been something of a Congress stronghold, yet on good evidence many

Assamese attributed this to immigrants being permitted to cross the border and register as citizens in return for their voting for Congress. Partition's least convincing border, ill-defined, traversed by countless rivers, straddled by the potentially shifting mud banks known as *chars,* and pocked by enclaves, was a valuable asset. It kept the smugglers in business, the border guards in pocket money, and the Congress in power.

Since most Assamese are Hindus and most of the immigrants were Muslims, the conflict inevitably took on a communal character. Those indigenous Muslims who for generations had supplied Assam with clerks and professionals found themselves classed with the later waves of wretchedly poor and landless Bangladeshis. Conversely, many of the state's native but barely Hinduized tribal peoples aligned themselves with the disgruntled Assamese. The BJP and its RSS allies, the champions of *hindutwa* or Hinduness, also sided with the Assamese, while Mrs. Gandhi's Congress here preferred to stress its secular traditions; anxious about its electoral prospects, it upheld the rights of the immigrants and called the AASU's leaders communalist agitators.

Negotiations in 1980–82 got nowhere. The government offered to examine the electoral rolls and weed out the names of those who had entered the state illegally since 1971. The AASU preferred a cutoff date of 1951. There was talk of a compromise on 1961, but this too was unacceptable to the government, although nearly a million of the 1961–71 immigrants had in fact been Hindus. Fleeing what was then East Pakistan in the wake of the anti-Hindu riots triggered by the 1965 war and events in Kashmir, these Bengali Hindus might have been expected to vote against the Muslim-inclined Congress and for the AASU's agenda. Yet, fearing the opposite, the government resisted the chance to disenfranchise them.

With the state unable either to quell the troubles or to reach a settlement with the AASU, its ruling ministry was dismissed in 1982. Delhi in the person of Indira Gandhi now called the shots. Ably assisted by local Congress boss Hiteswar Saikia, "a stocky politician with the guile of a fox and the organising skills of an army general," she plumped for fresh elections as the only way forward.[3] Arguing that she had no choice in the matter since it was a constitutional obligation, she dismissed objections from many senior figures that the state was too disturbed for a meaningful contest and that the vote was sure to provoke violence. She nevertheless poured in more security units.

In the run-up to the poll in February 1983, the communal situation rapidly deteriorated. The AASU declared a boycott of the election and did its best to interrupt preparations and discourage intending voters. Shootings and bombings became a daily occurrence, with some five hundred related deaths, many at the hands of law enforcement personnel. Strikes were met with curfews; the formalities of electioneering were being conducted amid the security trappings of a military crackdown. In the end, though few voted, they were deemed enough for Congress to declare victory.

On the morning of February 18, four days after the main poll, the residents of a cluster of fourteen villages near the town of Nellie, a little over thirty miles northeast of Gauhati, received some welcome reassurance. Mostly non-Assamese and all Muslims, the villagers had, as "rightful citizens of a democratic country" (in the words of one of them), cast their votes. Now all they wanted was to get back to their rice fields. News that it was at last safe to do so was confirmed by a local official apparently ignorant of a military dispatch warning of trouble.

The villagers sallied forth soon after sunrise, men, women, and children straggling companionably from their homes in the slanting light. As they reached their fields, smoke was seen coming from their villages. Then the surrounding scrub erupted. Dressed in white kurtas and dhotis, an estimated one thousand ambushers fell upon them. The attack had been well prepared, and the attackers set about their work with whatever implements they had been able to lay their hands on—machetes, spears, pitchforks, bows and arrows, and the odd gun. According to one survivor, the massacre lasted six hours. But by the time the police appeared, it was over. The attackers had fled, the villages were smoldering, and the gruesome evidence of the worst single atrocity in post-Partition South Asia lay strewn across the glistening paddy fields.

Photos showed the mutilated bodies of toddlers and children laid out in rows on the bare earth like something from the killing fields of Cambodia. Even the government put the fatalities in this one "incident" at well over eighteen hundred; most independent sources say the number was over three thousand. The living wounded numbered less, the escapees less still. Of their assailants it was said that many were from the local Liwa tribe, that AASU activists accompanied them, and that the RSS had approved the attack. But apart from the appalling death toll, little is known for sure. Though criminal actions were subsequently brought, none was ever heard. A six-hundred-page government report was compiled but never made public.

Twenty-three years later Teresa Rehman, a reporter from the crusading weekly *Tehelka,* visited Nellie. She found the survivors still resentful and their villages little changed. Most had accepted the compensation on offer—"Rs 2000 [about $160] and three bundles of tin to build a new house . . . [and] for every person who died Rs 5000 and every wounded person Rs 1500." But they had had to wait many months in resettlement camps. Even then the payouts had been subject to peculation and their new homes were no better than the ones they had lost. Mrs. Gandhi, visibly moved during a whistle-stop visit soon after the massacre, had "promised us everything, right from a lamp to light our houses," said a survivor, "but we have been waiting and waiting." In 2006 there was still no electricity. Many of the fourteen villages had no road, and only four of them had primary schools, often without teachers. Wrote Rehman, "The Nellie survivors wage a daily fight to numb their senses and their pain. . . . The grim reality that is their present does not offer much succour as they grapple with the demons of the past."[4]

Throughout the state thousands more had died as a consequence of Gandhi's insistence on holding the elections. Nor did her victory do anything to stem the violence or to reassure the Assamese. The AASU grew into a political party, the Ahom Gana Parishad (AGP), and, following an accord with the government, in 1985 the AGP did contest new elections, which it won handsomely. But just as the TULF in Sri Lanka was overshadowed by the militant LTTE, the AGP would soon be upstaged by the United Liberation Front of Assam

(ULFA). Composed of radical separatists, ULFA drew its inspiration from "that mother of all revolutions," the national struggle still being waged in nearby Nagaland.

And all the while the immigrants kept coming. Some observers would see the border's double-wired fence, if and when completed, as more a sop to Assamese sensibilities than as an effective means of ending illegal transit. As in the case of Nagaland, Assam and its myriad grievances would remain a running sore well into the twenty-first century.

INDIA HAS ONE OF THE FREEST and liveliest presses in the world. The newspapers and news magazines invariably reported on Gandhi's ill-fated interventions and often commented on them unfavorably. But to Indians who were neither Tamils nor Kashmiris nor living in Assam, these obscure affairs seemed exceptional and peripheral. Sri Lanka was another land, Kashmir a matter of national security. As for Assam, it was a victim of the northeast's unfathomable ethnic complexity. The casualties there were often tribal people or poor immigrants from Bangladesh, legal or otherwise. They scarcely counted in the great scheme of things. Painful memories such as those of Nellie were best forgotten.

And there was a more obvious reason for downplaying them. Much nearer to Delhi, closer to the corridors of power and more subversive of the Indian consensus, another separatist gauntlet was being thrown down almost simultaneously. In tractor-rich, remittance-fed Punjab, fanatical Sikhs were on the warpath.

Except that it was anything but peripheral, the Sikh challenge had much in common with the others. As with the Sri Lankan Tamils and the Assamese activists, many Sikhs had long felt that their identity was under threat and their particularist interests were being ignored in a majoritarian nation-state. Grievances were voiced; demands for greater recognition and more autonomy followed. When these too were shunned, groups with more radical agendas vied with one another to raise the stakes: More autonomy became outright secession, and civil disobedience gave way to acts of violence. Meanwhile, cynical interventions by the central government only compounded the activists' sense of injustice and brought conflict nearer. Gandhi never doubted that she was serving the wider national cause, but, whereas in Assam and Sri Lanka a case could be made for her having acted in the best interests of party and country, this would be harder to sustain with respect to Punjab.

Following the 1977 elections—those that, in the aftermath of the Emergency, had brought the ill-fated Janata Party to power in Delhi—the preeminent Sikh "nationalist" party, the Akali Dal, had formed a government in Punjab. But once in power the Akalis had made little progress with implementing the devolutionary demands of their Anandpur Sahib Resolution. Like other non-Congress state governments, theirs was then dismissed on doubtful grounds by Gandhi following her return to power; and in 1980 Congress duly won back Punjab in a state election.

In the same year, and by way of response, a Sikh student body, disillusioned by the gradualist approach of the Akali Dal, revived the pre-Partition demand for an independent Sikh state. It was to be known as Khalistan (like "Pakistan," the name means "land of the pure"), and it was being heavily promoted by Dr. Jagjit Singh Chauhan, once an Akali Dal minister and now a medical practitioner in the United Kingdom. A Bangladesh-like breakaway was being urged as part of yet another partition.

The Khalistan movement has been described as "primarily an emigrant endeavour."[5] Chauhan, like Velupillai Prabhakaran of the Tamil Tigers, drew most of his support from extremist elements of the diaspora in the United Kingdom, the United States, and Canada. In Canada the large Sikh community in British Columbia nursed a tradition of militancy reaching back to World War I, when Canadian Sikhs had organized a return to India to foment an anti-British "revolution" (or *ghadr,* which was also the title of their weekly newsletter). On that occasion the revolutionaries had been rounded up as soon as their ship docked in Calcutta, but their sacrifice as early martyrs in the freedom struggle was respected both in India and among the diaspora. Drawing on such traditions, in the 1970s Chauhan and a National Council of Khalistan drafted territorial claims, planned diplomatic representation, lobbied the UN for counselor status, and printed passports, banknotes, and postage stamps. But the revoking of Chauhan's Indian passport curtailed his direct involvement in Punjab. There, although his Khalistan excited Sikh youths who were worried about their career prospects or who had diasporic connections, the impact of his movement remained marginal.

This changed somewhat in the early 1980s. With the Akali Dal now out of office, some of its leaders rediscovered an appetite for inflammatory rhetoric and extraparliamentary tactics. The Anandpur Sahib demands were redrafted, with greater emphasis being given to the demand for Chandigarh plus another in favor of canceling plans to divert excess water from Punjabi agriculture to other, drier states. An agitational front was formed; mass demonstrations and religious stunts mobilized support. The Congress leadership, fearing defeat in Punjab in the next nationwide election, cast about for a response that would undermine the Akali threat.

Since discrediting the Akali Dal had been a Congress priority ever since 1977, Sanjay Gandhi had already hit on an answer. Fresh from his vasectomy crusade and even less wary of betraying his party's secularist credentials than his mother, he had opted for the tactics that had succeeded against the BJP in Jammu, namely, stealing the agitators' thunder. Thus, to expose the Akalis as tepid opportunists, he gave free rein to a formidable stalking horse in the shape of the ferociously doctrinaire Sant Jarnail Singh Bhindranwale.

How much actual contact Sanjay and his mother had with Jarnail Singh Bhindranwale is unclear. Sanjay seems to have been the prime mover in the original idea, but his death in October 1980 did not halt progress of the plan, which had acquired a life of its own. Mark Tully, doyen of the Delhi press corps and voice of the BBC in India for as long as anyone can remember, identifies none other than the home minister and soon-to-be president of India, Zail Singh, himself a Sikh, as Bhindranwale's co-handler. Together, says Tully, Zail Singh and Sanjay chose Bhindranwale and then "found for him a cause which was both political and religious."[6]

At the time the youthful and generously bearded Bhindranwale enjoyed only a modest reputation as an effective rural preacher and a stern champion of Sikh orthodoxy. Posthumous portrayals of him as "bin Dranwale," a prototype for Osama bin Laden, owe much to a physical resemblance but belie his modest origins. His new role required him to adopt a much higher profile: he was to take on the Akali Dal in their religious citadel of Amritsar.

It so happened that the Akali Dal leadership had authorized members of the Nirankari sect to hold a convention in Amritsar. Though claiming to be good Sikhs, the Nirankaris controversially revered a twentieth-century guru much as the persecuted Ahmadis in Pakistan revered a nineteenth-century prophet. Bhindranwale's not uncongenial job was to protest against such heresy in the name of Sikh orthodoxy. He duly did so, but in such inflammatory terms that a fracas broke out in which three Nirankaris and twelve of his own supporters died. Bhindranwale thus acquired the first martyrs to his cause, and the Akalis had been exposed as less than zealous in their commitment to the doctrines of purist Sikhism.

This was in 1978. In the 1980 elections Bhindranwale campaigned actively for the Congress while stirring up more hatred of the Nirankaris. But when the Nirankaris' leader was murdered, there began a catalogue of unexplained shootings in which the targets were all too frequently Bhindranwale's opponents and critics. In 1981 the gunning down of a respected newspaper owner in his own home finally produced a warrant for Bhindranwale's arrest. Yet he still somehow evaded capture, then coolly negotiated for his voluntary surrender in front of massed supporters at a time and place of his choosing. A firefight ensued at this custodial rally, quickly followed by a string of terror attacks including train derailments, a skyjacking, and numerous shootings by motorcycle-mounted gunmen. Innocent parties, Hindus as much as Nirankaris, were now being killed, and the perpetrators were rarely captured. Evidently some of Punjab's largely Sikh police sympathized with Bhindranwale; other policemen seemed either intimidated by him or under highly ambivalent direction.

Arrested at his own convenience, Bhindranwale was detained on his own terms, then released without trial in less than a month. The release order reportedly came from either Home Minister Zail Singh or the prime minister herself. Bhindranwale celebrated his charmed existence with a victory parade of heavily armed followers through the heart of Delhi. Sikhs sympathetic to his call for a rejuvenated Punjab now hailed him as "a hero who had challenged and defeated the Indian government." The stalking horse, in other words, was breaking its traces and running amok, its handlers floundering in its wake, carrots outstretched, sticks out of sight. "By surrendering justice to petty political gains the government itself created the ogre who was to dominate the last years of Mrs. Gandhi and to shadow her until her death," says Tully.[7]

As in Assam, on-and-off negotiations throughout 1982–83 went nowhere. The Akali leadership was both divided as to its objectives and apprehensive about Bhindranwale; at one moment they welcomed him into their front, the next they disclaimed him. As was his way, he favored invective over discussion; though his student affiliates continued to promote the idea of an independent Khalistan, he merely taunted the government and incited Sikhs to fight for an undefined "liberation from Hindu enslavement."

Meanwhile, Indira Gandhi and her go-betweens waxed hot and cold. Aided by her elder son Rajiv, formerly an Indian Airlines pilot but now reluctantly shoehorned into Sanjay's seat as co-pilot of the Congress Party, they offered concessions that were promptly withdrawn plus threats that were not carried out.

The 1982 Asian Games in Delhi came and went without incident. Rajiv surprised everyone by getting the venues built on time; Bhindranwale's call for Sikhs to disrupt the games was frustrated by highly intrusive security checks on all transport links between Punjab and the capital. He nevertheless contended that Sikhs had been humiliatingly excluded from the games, a claim that joined the string of others in his long cartridge belt of grievances.

For greater security he was now occupying part of a large hostel complex immediately adjacent to the Golden Temple in Amritsar. When Tully interviewed him there in early 1983, "he was sitting on a string bed . . . surrounded by young men, some armed with automatic weapons, some with old fashioned Lee-Enfield rifles . . . and some with traditional spears. His answers to my questions could best be described as enigmatic."[8] Although the hostel did not partake of the Golden Temple's status as a recognized place of sanctuary, the authorities found it convenient to pretend that it did. Here, safe from arrest, Bhindranwale held court, directed operations, amassed a formidable armory, and afforded safe haven to various wanted individuals, among them bank robbers, Marxist revolutionaries (Naxalites), people traffickers, and even some smuggled Bihari Muslims trying to make their way across India from the refugee camps of Bangladesh to a new life in Pakistan.

In April 1983 they were all joined by a man who, in the main entrance to the temple, had just shot dead the state's deputy inspector-general of police. Despite a national outcry—one in which most Sikhs joined—no one came to arrest the murderer. Bhindranwale and his people appeared immune, their reign of terror unstoppable. Besides working their way through a hit list of enemies, his killing squads began waylaying interstate buses, segregating the Hindus on board, and massacring them by the roadside. Separatism seemed to be about not just seceding from India but separating Sikhs from non-Sikhs in a communal bloodbath. Hindus in neighboring Haryana duly retaliated.

Under growing pressure to act, Gandhi at last did so. She dismissed her own Congress government in Punjab and imposed president's rule. The president in question was now Zail Singh, who with Sanjay Gandhi had sponsored Bhindranwale in the first place.

Meantime, the Akali Dal, still trying to recapture the radical agenda, raised its own game. With Harcharan Singh Longowal, the most consistent of the Akali leaders, already holed up in a nearby hostel, fights broke out between the two factions, and Bhindranwale's men faced the threat of expulsion. Their leader responded by shifting his headquarters from the hostel to the sacred precincts of the Golden Temple itself, across the road. Neither the Akalis nor the police saw fit to prevent this move, although its enormous religious and tactical significance was known to all.

Bhindranwale had chosen as his new quarters the Akhal Takht, a large and ornate four-story building with a golden dome that overlooked the rectangular Holy Pool, in the midst of which stood the Harmandir Sahib, the gilded sanctum sanctorum of the whole Temple complex. The Akhal Takht also commanded the *parikrama*, the marble-paved walkway that surrounded the pool, along with most of the Temple's other buildings. Second in sanctity only to the Harmandir Sahib itself, it was from the Akhal Takht that directives were issued to the Sikh faithful and that war parties had been dispatched in ancient times. Its symbolism was as unassailable as its position; desecrating it was unthinkable.

Regardless, Bhindranwale turned the Akhal Takht into his command-and-control center. The Akali Dal responded by calling a Temple rally of Sikh ex-servicemen. This backfired when several of the veterans offered their services to Bhindranwale. Among them was Major-General Shahbeg (Shubeg) Singh, a hero of the Bangladesh war who had trained the Mukti Bahini. This remedied the deficit of military experience in the Akhal Takht. The command center had acquired a commander.

During April and May 1984 the death squads issuing from the temple upped their strike rate. Terror atrocities multiplied; some eighty killings claimed increasingly high-profile figures. The ineffectual state police had to be augmented by units from the more disciplined Central Police Reserve Force; and it was this force's efforts to waylay the terrorists that led to the first rooftop exchanges of fire. Bhindranwale and General Shahbeg Singh had by now seen fit to fortify the Akhal Takht with sandbags and slit apertures. They had also established sniper positions at vantage points in and beyond the temple. Resistance was becoming open defiance. As well as introducing more police, Gandhi alerted the army.

Last-minute talks might yet have averted catastrophe. Despite the flying of the odd Khalistan flag, Bhindranwale continued to deny he had any political ambitions and to skirt the issue of secession. The government was now offering concessions on Chandigarh and most of the other Anandpur Sahib demands. It insisted only that the awards be made by a specially appointed commission. Bhindranwale seemed tempted yet balked at the fig leaf of a commission. He wanted a public backing down by the *pandit*'s daughter herself. Failing that, he welcomed the prospect of a long siege in the expectation that it would bring the Sikh faithful rushing from all over Punjab to the defense of their spiritual capital.

In response, the Akali Dal also sought to widen the struggle. With exquisitely bad timing, in May 1984 its leaders announced that all grain shipments from the Punjab would be halted as of June 3. This was the final straw for the government. While Bhindranwale's defiance affected only Punjab, a stoppage of cereals threatened the entire nation. The next day police marksmen took up positions around the Temple. Then on June 2, the day before the grain stoppage was due to come into effect, Operation Blue Star got the go-ahead. Gandhi went on the radio; the army advanced on the temple.

The next day was for Sikhs the anniversary of the martyrdom of their fifth guru. Pilgrims piled into the Golden Temple to commemorate the event even as the military opened up with machine gun, mortar, and rifle fire. The significance of the day was not lost on the would-be martyrs either. Bhindranwale's arsenal responded with deadly effect, and the disposition of Shahbeg Singh's sharpshooters convinced India's General Brar that a surrender was unlikely. The temple would have to be cleared by force. Storming it under cover of darkness was the only solution, and this might mean bringing in heavy artillery.

Operation Blue Star was supposed to avoid damage to the temple and to be all over within forty-eight hours. It failed on both counts. Not until the stiflingly hot night of June 5 did the big guns open fire and the tanks begin forcing a way in. And not until June 7 were the defenders silenced and the bodies of Bhindranwale and Shahbeg Singh found among the dead in the ruins of the Akhal Takht.

By then the Temple looked as if it had been struck by an earthquake. Tank tracks had chewed up the marble *parikrama,* shells had demolished a whole frontage of the Akhal Takht, and bullets had pocked even the island jewel that was the Harmandir Sahib. The military claimed to have killed around five hundred "terrorists" and suffered the loss of eighty-three men. As usual, unofficial calculations suggest otherwise. The troop losses were almost certainly higher, as were those of the "terrorists," including an unspecified number of non-combatant pilgrims.

OPERATION BLUE STAR had done its job: The Golden Temple had been cleared of "terrorists," Bhindranwale killed, and the Akali leaders taken into custody. The army had shown, in the words of one account, "that the Indian state was strong enough to deal with secession and terrorism."[9] But in many eyes the appalling destruction and desecration within the Temple bore greater testimony to the courage of the defenders. Many Sikhs who had been horrified by Bhindranwale's previous antics now applauded his resistance and "martyrdom." His defense of their holiest shrine atoned for his past; the army's sacrilegious assault ranked as a greater outrage. Bhindranwale, who in life had become a liability, in death became a legend.

It was said he had somehow survived and would rise again. Journalists in Punjab found Khalistani flags much in evidence and the people sullen and alienated. Heavy-handed mopping-up operations by the military didn't help. Of the five thousand arrested over the following weeks, many had just been in the wrong place at the wrong time. In Delhi, President Zail Singh, who had been kept in ignorance of the attack on the temple till the last minute, threatened to resign.

The tension was augmented by rumors, soon confirmed, that some Sikh units within the Indian army had mutinied in sympathy with their brethren in the temple. This was the nightmare feared by every South Asian ruler to this day—that of intercommunal conflict infecting the nation's defense agencies. Sikhs constituted some 10 percent of the Indian army and formed the entire complement of two regiments. Worst affected was the Sikh Regiment itself. On the day after the Golden Temple fell, men of the regiment's 10th Battalion, stationed on the Pakistan border, rose up. Following the example of the Indian mutineers of 1857, they first raided the regimental armory, then "drove through the streets of Ganganagar shouting 'Long Live Sant Jarnail Singh Bhindranwale' and firing indiscriminately. A policeman was killed and another injured."[10] The mutineers then split up, half heading for Delhi, the others for Pakistan.

Mark Tully filed a report on this incident for the BBC. It was heard in India and four days later sparked a copycat insurrection at the regimental depot in distant Bihar. Again the mutineers, this time fifteen hundred strong, helped themselves to arms and ammunition, killing their brigadier in the process. They then set off in convoy for Amritsar, more than 750 miles away. Helicopters scoured the highway, but it was the roadblocks that halted them. In the final shootout near Varanasi some thirty-five were killed. The rest were rounded up, as were the earlier mutineers, and later outbreaks in Jammu and Pune (Poona) came to nothing. The most serious crisis of discipline the Indian army had faced since independence fizzled out in dissension over whether or not it would be wise to court-martial the offenders. But at least the nightmare scenario had been preempted, and India was not about to experience the military infighting that racked Bangladesh.

Further afield, the Sikh diaspora responded to events in Amritsar with less fear of the consequences. In Vancouver the "We Love Bhindranwale" bumper stickers were replaced by "Death to Indira" ones. Five thousand Sikhs demonstrated in Toronto, three thousand in New York's Madison Square Garden, and thirty thousand in Birmingham. From London Dr. Jagjit Singh Chauhan renewed the diaspora's financial support for Bhindranwale's pro-Khalistan students and announced the formation of a Khalistan government-in-exile. He also informed one of the BBC's domestic channels that Indira Gandhi's life would be forfeit. She and her family might expect to "be beheaded . . . in a few days," he said, adding, "that is what the Sikhs will do." The Thatcher government reprimanded him for incitement.

Similar threats reverberated in certain Sikh circles in India. Privately Gandhi heeded them; in a handwritten testament she mused about dying the "violent death . . . some fear and a few are plotting." But publicly she dismissed such thoughts. "I do not care if I live or die," she told a rally in Orissa.[11] When advised to replace Sikh members of her personal bodyguard with non-Sikhs, she retorted, "Aren't we secular?"[12] The put-down was delivered without a hint of sarcasm.

A political animal to the last, she promptly picked another fight with the Sikh orthodox over the repairs to the damage in the Golden Temple. The temple's management insisted that on religious grounds the work must be done by Sikh volunteers; she insisted it be performed by the government, which might then claim the credit for it. In other words, it was business as usual. Within a month of Operation Blue Star she was engineering the downfall of another state government.

The victim this time was the administration of Dr. Farooq Abdullah in Jammu and Kashmir. Relations between the Abdullah family and the Nehrus merit a book of their own. Both were proud to call themselves Kashmiris, yet neither did much to resolve the ambiguities of Kashmir's status. Just as Pandit Nehru had valued Sheikh Sahib's friendship yet kept him in detention, so Indira had engineered his National Conference's return to power only to turn against it.

The reason given for this last twist was that Farooq Abdullah, though the state's chief minister, was flirting with dissident Kashmiris whom the Indian government believed to be backed by Pakistan. Similar accusations of accepting Pakistani support had been leveled at Bhindranwale but were never substantiated. In reality, the prime minister's hostility to Farooq seems to have been more personal. Primed by a lifetime of electoral triumphs, she took defeat as an affront to her authority. The affront had to be repaid, her authority reasserted. Like the 1980 electoral victory of the Akali Dal in Punjab, that in 1983 of Farooq's National Conference in Kashmir could not be allowed to stand. Farooq was also throwing his weight behind a group of opposition parties elsewhere in India who were of a mind to fight the imminent national elections as a coalition. This recalled the Janata Party's ganging up on her. He had to go.

Advised by a crisis management team that now included her son Rajiv instead of Sanjay, Indira picked the amenable Ghulam Mohamed Shah, Farooq's brother-in-law, as her candidate to replace Farooq. Since the governor of Kashmir—the man who would have to handle the switch—was her own cousin, B. K. Nehru, it looked straightforward. The battle lines were drawn for another round in the interfamily feud. But when instructed to dismiss Farooq, B. K. Nehru put his foot down. A distinguished and impartial diplomat who had once dared to criticize Sanjay Gandhi's program of forced sterilizations, Nehru declared any such move purely vindictive and wholly unconstitutional. Thus it was he who had to be removed first. He was replaced as governor by Jagmohan Malhotra, once Sanjay's right-hand man in clearing Delhi's mostly Muslim slum dwellers and later a member of the BJP. Millions of rupees were then bagged and dispatched to Srinagar, there to be disbursed to enough National Conference members of the state legislative assembly to erode Farooq's majority. He was subsequently summoned by the new governor and without so much as a vote of no confidence relieved of the chief ministership. The unctuous Ghulam Mohammed Shah took over at the head of a coalition formed between his breakaway Awami National Conference and Congress.

Happily, Shah was never likely to turn into another Bhindranwale. But Gandhi's penchant for disastrous interventions seemed undiminished. The installation of Governor Jagmohan, a Hindu with an anti-Muslim record, boded ill for communal relations in Kashmir. Likewise, the toppling of another Abdullah was seen by Kashmiris as yet further evidence of Delhi's bad faith. This alienation of the valley's Muslims led inexorably to their radicalization. Some looked abroad: a Jammu and Kashmir Liberation Front had been founded in the United Kingdom by Amanullah Khan, a Pakistani citizen born in the Northern Areas who in 1984 had been held responsible for the kidnapping and murder of India's assistant high commissioner in Britain. Others looked nearer to home and to parties with an Islamist agenda, such as the Jamaat-e-Islami. When five years later a veritable intifada plunged Jammu and Kashmir state into its bloodiest crisis yet, this last of Indira Gandhi's ill-judged interventions would be remembered as the turning point.

As if to set the seal on her Kashmiri handiwork, on October 27, 1984, Mrs. Gandhi paid a flying visit to Srinagar. It had been four months since Operation Blue Star but just two weeks since Margaret Thatcher, a friend and fellow prime minister, had narrowly escaped death from an Irish Republican Army bomb in a Brighton hotel. Gandhi caught the valley at its autumnal best: the lakeside willows wept with gold and each giant plane tree stood rooted in a carpet of ruby-red leaves. Between briefings with Governor Jagmohan on the worsening security situation, she visited temples and consulted a holy man. The holy man sized up the moment. "He felt death very close to her," remembered one of her acolytes, not without the benefit of hindsight.[13]

Four days later, back in Delhi, Indira Gandhi bustled past the bougainvillea along the garden path between her residence and her office. It was just after nine on the morning of Halloween. At the garden gate she joined her hands in a *namaste* greeting to the duty guard. He too raised his hands, but to aim a revolver. Five shots rang out, followed by a stutter of machine-gun fire from another body-guard. The prime minister slumped to the ground, bleeding heavily. Despite the rush-hour traffic, she was bundled into a car and taken to the hospital. Sonia Gandhi, Rajiv's Italian-born wife, nursed her on the backseat, but she never recovered consciousness. That after-noon the doctors declared her dead.

Both the assassins were Sikhs and both had lately returned from Punjab. The job complete, they downed their weapons and accepted arrest. "I have done what I had to," said one. Whether or not they acted on their own account, there was no question that it was in retribution for Operation Blue Star. Many in Punjab were already celebrating. In New York some wealthy Sikhs were filmed toasting the killers in champagne; "in Vancouver, it was a party . . . with Halloween firecrackers, bhangra dances [and] sweets distribution."[14] When one of the assassins was shot in custody and the other hanged, they, like Bhindranwale, were hailed as "martyrs" by many Sikhs. And their dependents being obvious vote winners in Punjab, more than one of them was fast-tracked to electoral success and a seat in the Punjab state assembly.

If this was predictable, then so was the reaction of many non-Sikhs. Within minutes, grief over Indira's death found expression in a blood hunt for anyone sporting a beard and a tightly tied turban. The anti-Sikh pogrom swept through several cities, but nowhere did it rage more violently than in the capital itself. While Congress met in conclave to co-opt Rajiv as its leader and install him as Indira's un-contested successor, across town Hindus baying for revenge torched Sikh homes and businesses, massacred the people inside, and dese-crated Sikh shrines and gurdwaras. For three days the mobs raged un-checked by the authorities, indeed encouraged by them: "Often they were led and directed by Congress politicians: metropolitan coun-cillors, members of parliament, even Union [Government] ministers. The Congress leaders promised money and liquor to those willing to do the job; this in addition to whatever goods they could loot. The police looked on or actively aided the looting and murder."[15]

By the time a belated deployment of regular troops brought the situation under control, either 2,733 (the official figure) or 3,870 (that of the victims' legal team) men, women, and children of Delhi's Sikh community had perished horribly at the hands of their fellow citizens. Thousands more had found refuge in makeshift camps or fled the city. Yet in the midst of this mayhem, just twenty-six people had been arrested—and all of them were Sikhs. Worse still, a quarter of a century later, and despite interminable enquiries, those officials who were allegedly responsible for inciting and directing the mobs had yet to be prosecuted.[16] Instead, like the families of the prime minister's assassins, three of the four officials named as complicit in the atrocities were selected by Congress to contest the upcoming elections. All won handsome majorities.

Official connivance in sectarian violence was nothing new. Like the massacres themselves, it stirred memories of Partition and horrified not just Sikhs. But the government's reluctance to pass a vote of condolence for the victims and its failure to bring the culprits to justice rankled no less. The violence in Punjab was not about to end.

IN THE DECEMBER 1984 national elections Congress again swept the board. Not even Nehru or Indira Gandhi had won more than four hundred seats in the Lok Sabha. A combination of sympathy for Indira's bereaved family and deep concern over the plight of the nation had brought a closing of ranks. To some minds Congress still represented the democratic commitment and confessional neutrality of Pandit Nehru; to others its appeal lay in its recent stand against separatist dissent, especially in Punjab. Either way it posed as the only party whose nationwide roots could hold the country together. As its posters reminded the voter, his or her mark could make the difference between "unity and separation." Now led by the young and presentable Rajiv at the head of a team of managerially minded associates, it promised less confrontational tactics and more inclusive decision making.

True to this billing, within three years Rajiv had signed a string of conciliatory agreements. One of these accords was with the Asom Gana Parishad, the political wing of and successor to the All-Assam Students Union, which in the elections had bucked the national trend and won a majority in the Assam state assembly. Among the issues addressed in the accord was the critical question of the cutoff date in the registration of immigrants, after which their status could be challenged. Both sides settled on 1966. But the scrutiny process would prove a farce, the troubles were far from over, and the accord, signed in 1985, could just as well have been reached in 1982. Nellie need never have happened.

Another of the accords, signed in 1986, was with the warring parties in Sri Lanka. In addition to some constitutional concessions to the Tamils, Colombo accepted the offer of an Indian peacekeeping force to monitor a cease-fire agreement with the Tamil guerrillas. Since the guerrillas' stronghold in the north was currently under pressure from government forces, the accord pleased Tamils in India and was generally welcomed by both sides in Sri Lanka. Initially the peacekeepers numbered under seven thousand. Two years later they had grown to a hundred thousand, which was around half the size of the force that had liberated Bangladesh. Sucked into hostilities with the Tamil Tigers, the peacekeeping force had then fallen out with the government and was suffering heavy casualties. It was withdrawn amid much head-shaking in 1990. Fighting between the Colombo government and the Tamil guerrillas resumed almost immediately.

Just as promising and ultimately just as counterproductive was the Kashmir Accord. Rajiv had no personal animosity toward Farooq Abdullah. Both in their forties and both keen to make a new start, the two leaders thought they could work together. An opportunity arose in early 1986 when Mrs. Gandhi's unpopular minister G. M. Shah was dismissed after the army had to be called in to quell communal rioting. An interlude of direct rule under the hard-line Governor Jagmohan proved even more divisive and was ended by the accord. It provided for the installation of a coalition Congress–National Conference government with Farooq back as chief minister.

But this went down badly in Kashmir. Once again the state government had been changed without the electorate being consulted; it was a turnaround too many for most of the valley's Muslims. "Overnight, Farooq was transformed from hero to traitor," according to journalist Tavleen Singh. "People could not understand how a man who had been treated the way he had by Delhi . . . could now be crawling to it for accords and alliances."[17] In 1987 the new coalition did win a popular mandate, but the poll was marred by widespread accusations of vote rigging. "Voters were intimidated, opposition politicians were harassed, and ballot boxes were tampered [with]."[18] Incensed by the result, the Muslim United Front, which had been formed to contest the election, quickly disintegrated into warring factions, some demanding self-determination, others seeking secession, and nearly all in favor of a more central role for Islam.

By now Amanullah Khan, the Britain-based leader of the Jammu and Kashmir Liberation Front (JKLF), was back in South Asia. Though acquitted of murdering the Indian diplomat in the United Kingdom, he had nevertheless been deported to his native Pakistan. There as of 1987 his JKLF began training militant young Kashmiris and dispatching them across the Line of Control into Indian-held Kashmir. India accused General Zia ul-Haq's regime of arming and supporting them; Pakistan denied this and contended that such rumors were planted by the Indian intelligence agency.

Both sides had good reason to ratchet up the tension. India, anxious to demonstrate that the situation in Punjab had not left it vulnerable to a Pakistani attack, conducted maneuvers along the Pakistani border in 1986. Pakistan then responded with a show of force of its own. Meanwhile, along an undemarcated section at the eastern extremity of the Kashmir "line of control" (the former cease-fire line), troops from both sides exchanged fire whenever visibility permitted. This followed the preemptive Indian occupation of the Siachen Glacier in 1984. Forty-five miles of moraine and ice at a mean altitude of around twenty-one thousand feet, the Siachen Glacier was surely the most inhospitable and worthless battlefield ever contested. Yet the dispute over its status, like the glacier itself, would groan on indefinitely. Further icy skirmishes were recorded in 1990, 1995, 1996, and 1999. By the time a cease-fire was agreed to in 2003, an estimated two thousand lives had been lost in the contest for this "third pole," mostly from frostbite, pulmonary edema, and climbing accidents. Avalanches also took a heavy toll, one in 2012 burying 120 Pakistanis.

Against this background of hostilities in the mountains and maneuvers in the plains, the situation in the Kashmir Valley steadily worsened. Farooq Abdullah's motorcade was attacked in 1987, and the following year bombers targeted first Srinagar's combined telegraph and television station and then its police chief. Tourist numbers, a fair barometer of Kashmiri confidence, plummeted. As Victoria Schofield notes, anti-Indian sentiment in the valley was mirrored by a swell of support for Pakistan.[19] Instead of celebrating India's Independence Day on August 15, thousands turned out a day early, on Pakistan's Independence Day. The fortieth anniversary of the Indian takeover of the state on October 27 was mourned as "Occupation Day." Demonstrators carried Pakistani flags, vehicles were burned, and police were attacked.

India blamed the JKLF and its presumed Pakistani backers. The possibility that poor employment prospects, heavy-handed policing, widespread disillusionment with the democratic process, and its own obduracy had alienated a new generation of Kashmiris was loftily discounted. But the JKLF also faced competition from its supposed constituency. Its violent but essentially secular agenda of "liberating" the whole of what had once been the princely state of Jammu and Kashmir was in danger of being upstaged by a bewildering array of locally based groupings, many of them armed and abetted by elements of the radical Islamist resistance to the Soviet presence in Afghanistan.

The JKLF was therefore happy to claim responsibility for the highest-profile outrage to date: In December 1989, within days of the general election that had just ousted Rajiv Gandhi's Congress government, the daughter of the newly appointed home minister was kidnapped. A twenty-three-year-old Muslim, Rubaiya Sayeed had somewhat unwisely been serving her medical internship at a Srinagar hospital. Returning home after a shift, she was snatched from a vehicle.

Her captors immediately let it be known that they would negotiate: they would trade her freedom for that of five imprisoned JKLF militants. And since this demand was phoned to a local newspaper, the press were on to it from the start. For days Rubaiya's fate made headlines throughout India. While a refusal to negotiate would please hard-line Hindu opinion yet antagonize many Muslims and inflame the situation in Kashmir, capitulation would discredit the new government and also inflame the situation in Kashmir. Farooq advised against any deal, but by now confidence in his handling of the troubles was at rock bottom, just like his popularity. After five days the new government in Delhi caved in. The militants were released to a hero's reception, and two hours later Rubaiya Sayeed was freed.

This affair had unexpected consequences. The government responsible was that of Vishwanath Pratap Singh, formerly Rajiv's high-minded finance minister. To win the 1989 elections, Singh had formed a Janata-like National Front that relied on the support of the resurgent BJP. After the Rubaiya fiasco, this new administration urgently needed to redeem its reputation and placate its BJP partner. To that end, in early 1990 "it made the worst mistake it could have" by sending former governor Jagmohan back to Kashmir.[20] There were to be no more deals with the terrorists, no more concessions to Kashmiri exceptionalism. As of 1990 Rajiv's accord was a dead letter. Farooq resigned immediately. "The attempt to find a political solution to Kashmir's problem," writes Schofield, "was put aside in favour of a policy of repression."[21]

Within a couple of weeks, Governor Jagmohan's house-to-house searches and mass arrests had provoked the action that would define the Kashmir conflict for the next decade. In the heart of Srinagar a large unarmed demonstration against Jagmohan's crackdown converged on one of several bridges over the Jhelum River. When the crowd pushed forward onto the bridge, the police opened fire from all sides. Maybe a hundred died, some by drowning in the river, some from gunshot wounds.

The worst massacre in Kashmir's unhappy relationship with India brought thousands more onto the streets. Whatever support India still enjoyed in the valley was now lost. From the minarets the cry of "Allahu Akbar" was bracketed with shouts of "Azadi . . . azadi," "Freedom . . . freedom." Jagmohan replied with a curfew, the expulsion of foreign correspondents, and blithe indifference to appeals for an inquiry. The kidnappings, killings, and bombings resumed. So did the arrests, the "encounters" (often a euphemism for unprovoked killings by the police), and the interrogations (often under torture).

The vast encampments of the Central Police Reserve Force and the army, the latter's presence being in part a reaction to increased tension with Pakistan, left the visitor in no doubt that Kashmir was under occupation: by the end of 1990 one could see as many as eighty thousand uniformed Indians in the area.[22] While rarely described as a war, the new Kashmiri intifada would rank as one of the dirtiest non-wars on record.

AND THEN THERE WAS THE PUNJAB ACCORD. Back in 1985, this had been Rajiv's topmost priority, more urgent than Kashmir and much more menacing than Assam. The high-voltage tit-for-tat of the previous year—Bhindranwale's reign of terror, Operation Blue Star, the army mutinies, Indira Gandhi's assassination, and the Delhi massacres—had left the dangling wires of separatist sentiment in Punjab arcing against Hindu resentment elsewhere. Rajiv moved swiftly to defuse them. The restoration of the Golden Temple was meticulously conducted, the Akali Dal's leaders were released from detention, and the stalled talks on vexed issues such as Chandigarh resumed.

These talks were nearing a conclusion when on June 23, 1985, someone's suitcase exploded at Tokyo's international airport; two baggage handlers were killed and others were injured. Fifty-five minutes earlier but as yet unreported, on the other side of the world Air India Flight 182, with 307 passengers and 22 crew members, had disappeared off the radar as it entered Irish airspace in the eastern Atlantic. The two incidents were not immediately connected. Though hijackings were commonplace, the world was as yet unaccustomed to airliners being blown up in midair. No jumbo jet had been targeted in this way. Multipronged terrorist attacks that were globally coordinated were unknown.

Air India 182 had been en route from Montreal to London and Delhi. When it emerged that it had most likely been downed by the detonation of an onboard bomb, suspicion attached to Khalistan militants in Canada. Canada's police and intelligence had earlier been alerted to bomb-making activity by British Columbia's Bhindranwale sympathizers; indeed, several Sikh activists were under observation. But the enormity of what had been planned only emerged later. Baggage on the Montreal–Delhi flight was traced back to connecting flights from Toronto and Vancouver, and the exploding suitcase in Tokyo had also come off a flight originating in Vancouver. Moreover, the suitcase had blown up when being transferred from its incoming Canadian Pacific flight to another Air India flight, this time to Bangkok. Thus a second and simultaneous midair tragedy involving an Air India airliner had only narrowly been avoided when the bomb detonated prematurely in Tokyo.

Curiously, these appalling acts provoked less outrage in India than might have been expected. Of the 329 lives lost on Air India 182, only 24 had been those of Indian citizens, though the 268 Canadians included many of Indian descent. It was left to the Canadian authorities to investigate the crime and bring to justice those responsible for the worst mass murder in Canadian history. The investigation extended over many years. No group claimed responsibility, and the main culprits—those who had bought the tickets and checked the bags but not boarded the flights—were never identified with certainty. Only the bomb maker was tried and convicted. But the passenger manifests revealed that the no-shows on both flights had the name Singh, and the bookings had been made by other Singhs. Since nearly all Sikhs have the name Singh, this was taken as evidence that all those responsible were Sikhs and that they were not averse to being recognized as such. The likely organizer was thought to be a cousin of Bhindranwale's, and the main operative was supposedly Talwinder Singh Parmar, of the Babbar Khalsa, a militant group that was linked to the pro-Khalistan Sikh Students Association and had been responsible for several bombings in Punjab. Though a Canadian citizen, Talwinder Singh had been born in Punjab, and he soon died there: taken into police custody in 1992, he would allegedly confess to his part in the bombing and then be shot in a police "encounter."

Coordinated attacks on prestigious civilian targets would soon come to be reckoned the prerogative of well-financed Islamist groups such as al-Qaeda. That it was in fact diasporic Sikh militants who pioneered this form of horror has been largely forgotten. The protracted nature of the Canadian investigation left some uncertainty about the identity and motivation of the culprits until well into the 1990s. Meanwhile, the Indian government was determined that nothing should be allowed to derail its search for a lasting Punjab accord.

Nor was it. Some of those arrested after Operation Blue Star were released, the military were partially withdrawn from Punjab, and to address the state's employment shortage Rajiv announced the setting up of a railway carriage production facility with the promise of twenty thousand jobs. In July 1985, a month after the downing of Air India 182, Harcharan Singh Longowal, the Akali Dal leader who had been Bhindranwale's neighbor in the Golden Temple hostel, finally came to Delhi. There he signed on to the accord's eleven-point memorandum of understanding. Chandigarh was to go to Punjab in return for just one district being handed over to Haryana; the water dispute and other matters were to be referred to independent commissions. Once again the terms scarcely differed from those offered by Indira Gandhi in 1984.

This should have been the end of the matter. But a month later, while announcing the Punjab Accord, Harcharan Singh Longowal was shot dead. His killers claimed that the agreement betrayed the Sikh nation. In another sympathy vote, this time for Longowal, the Akali Dal was returned to power in state elections in September. Some of the party's divided leadership then reneged on the terms of the accord and renewed contacts with the Khalistan militants. The eminent Sikh writer and historian Khushwant Singh bemoaned the decline of a revered party into "a bunch of bearded buffoons bereft of the power of thinking and vision."[23] Terrorist attacks in 1986 were said to have claimed more lives than in 1984, and they spread beyond Punjab with bombs in Delhi and elsewhere.

In 1986 and in 1988 Khalistan militants once again had to be flushed out of Amritsar's Golden Temple. Code-named "Black Thunder," these two operations were conducted with a sensitivity that had been lacking in Blue Star and were reckoned a qualified success. Heavy policing, sterner direction, and more international cooperation in counterterrorism were finally paying off. With no thanks to the Akali Dal, which had been relieved of power in 1987, and at enormous cost in military deployment and lives lost (including those of more than 1,550 police in 1988–92), by 1993 Punjab could be considered virtually free of terrorist activity.[24]

Give or take the conflict in Kashmir, India had emerged intact from its worst decade to date. The economy was in tatters and Congress could no longer command an overall majority. Yet separatist dissent had been channeled back to the ballot box, and a plethora of local parties with caste-based agendas were breathing new life into the nation's electoral arithmetic. Above all, the democratic consensus had held. This was not something that could not be said of the rest of South Asia. Indeed, India's abiding commitment to electoral accountability was setting a norm for which the peoples of Pakistan, Bangladesh, and Nepal could not but be grateful. A hegemonist tendency, when wreathed in smiles of popular endorsement, was almost acceptable.

OUTSIDE
THE GATES

PADDING AROUND ONE OF ASIA'S MOST NOTORIOUS SLUMS
in pajamas and an old pair of running shoes was no guarantee
of anonymity for Dr. Akhtar Hameed Khan. He was too well
known, for one thing; for another, however he was attired, his pa-
trician mien and air of bespectacled purpose betrayed his Cambridge
degree and onetime membership in the vaunted Indian Civil Service.
Born in Agra in 1914, Khan had served under the British before
opting for Pakistan in 1950 and had then been posted to Comilla
in east Pakistan. There in the 1960s he had devised a model of rural
development that, while based on the cooperatives championed by
the pony-riding Malcolm Darling in the 1940s, carried an additional
incentive: the provision of small loans to those, especially women,
whose income-generating prospects were insufficiently creditworthy
to interest the banks.

Known as microfinance or microcredit, this pioneering initiative
had far-reaching consequences. In the aftermath of the Bangladesh
war, the practice of microcredit was adopted by the Bangladesh Rural
Advancement Committee (BRAC), a body that was soon to outgrow
its name and become "the world's largest non-governmental development agency." Then in the 1980s the principle of small-scale lending
to community-supported individuals was formally institutionalized

with the foundation in Chittagong by Professor Muhammad Yunus of the Grameen Bank. Grameen provided the blueprint for a host of other community-based credit agencies across the developing world and in 2006 was awarded a Nobel Peace Prize—the only financial institution ever to have been so honored. By 2010 Grameen had eight million borrowers and was active in every village in Bangladesh.[1] Together, BRAC and Grameen gained for unfancied Bangladesh the respect of international finance. More than any official initiatives, such self-help organizations contributed to that country's gradual shedding of its "basket case" image.

Yet little of this acclaim went to Khan. In 1971, just ahead of the Bangladesh war, he had returned to (west) Pakistan. An inspirational figure, bony, balding, and disarmingly modest, he held a succession of academic posts both there and in the United States before again deploying his community expertise, this time on behalf of the urban poor of Karachi. In what was to be as much a research project as a developmental offensive, Khan chose Orangi, Asia's most lawless bustee and the largest of the several hundred *katchi abadis,* or self-built slum townships, on the outskirts of Karachi. To Orangi's million-strong population of struggling squatters—*muhajirs* from India, Bihari refugees from Bangladesh, and Pathans, Balochis, Punjabis, and Sindis from the rest of Pakistan—Khan devoted the remainder of his life, living and working there from 1980 onward. As founder and director of the Orangi Pilot Project (OPP), he possibly did more for the alleviation of urban distress than any contemporary.

From a pioneering scheme to educate, organize, and support Orangi's residents in their efforts to lay sewer systems, the OPP branched out into self-help programs for house construction, health facilities, family planning, employment cooperatives, and of course micro-credit. By the time Khan died in 1999, the community-led principles of his OPP were being adopted throughout Pakistan and beyond. Deployed in the aftermath of the 2005 earthquake in Azad Kashmir and then in the wake of the 2010 Indus River floods, they lent to the task of rehabilitation a self-help dimension that was in marked contrast to the top-down interventions of governments, international aid agencies, and religious charities.

Khan had no illusions about Karachi. From a pre-Partition total of about four hundred thousand, the city's population soared toward ten to twelve million by the end of the century. Not only did the OPP have to contend with appalling levels of deprivation and corruption, but it had to do so under conditions tantamount to urban warfare as different ethnic and religious groups competed for living space, jobs. and a tenuous security. Quoting the British socialist Harold Laski, Khan saw the city as an arena in which the political process, "the counting of heads," was so discredited that "the cutting of heads" had come to represent the preferred means of communal assertion. The OPP was therefore as much about introducing some sense of shared purpose into the warring lanes of Orangi as it was about improving sanitation and services. It could scarcely redeem the city as a whole, however. "I fear terrible consequences within the next twenty years," said Khan in 1988.[2]

Initially the main conflict in Karachi had been between the incoming *muhajirs* and the native Sindis. Zulfikar Ali Bhutto's preferential treatment of his fellow Sindis had antagonized the Urdu-speaking *muhajirs,* who saw themselves as Jinnah's chosen people and the rightful heirs to his one-nation Pakistan. They looked to the political and military establishment in Pakistan's Punjab province to uphold their claim, and they had few regrets when Bhutto was toppled. Conversely, in the post-Bhutto era of General Zia ul-Haq, it was the Sindis who felt alienated and marginalized. In the early 1980s Sindi nationalists, with or without encouragement from India, mounted a campaign of lawlessness and secessionism throughout Sind. Three army divisions plus helicopter gunships were deployed to suppress it, yet the fighting spread to Karachi itself. There both sides fielded their own armed vigilantes and laid claim to large areas of the city.

This situation rapidly deteriorated—and was vastly complicated—as a result of the war in Afghanistan. Arms shipments to the US-backed *mujahidin* contesting the post-1979 Soviet occupation of Afghanistan passed through Karachi's docks in one direction; heroin from the poppy fields of Afghanistan and the NWFP passed through in the other. Consignments of both were easily sidetracked. According to Akhtar Hameed Khan, "half the arms that were supposed to go to the

Afghan *mujahidin* were distributed in Pakistan."[3] The profits to be made from the transport and distribution of such spoils spawned a black economy that allegedly dwarfed the official one. Meanwhile, triggered by the influx of some three million Afghan refugees, a population drift from the north and west of Pakistan augmented Karachi's ethnic mix with a sizable new infusion of Pathans and Balochis.

In 1984 second-generation *muhajirs,* many of them ex-students of Karachi University, met this new challenge to their job prospects and their community's demographic superiority by launching their own political organization, the Muttahida (originally Muhajir) Qaumi Mahaz (United National Movement) or MQM. Claiming to represent Pakistan's "fifth nationality," and with an eye to the creation of a *muhajir* "province" based on Karachi, the MQM demanded for *muhajirs* the same subnational status as Punjabis, Sindis, Pathans, or Balochis. By contesting elections the MQM sought the same consideration from the central government, and by enforcing rigid discipline it imposed a comparable solidarity on its members. When in 1985 a *muhajir* student was run over by a Pathan truck driver, intercommunal warfare brought the city to a standstill. Fifty-three died, a figure that was more than doubled a year later when Pathans armed with AK-47s gunned down *muhajirs* and were slaughtered in turn. "Mohajirs tied the hands of [Pathans] behind their backs and burnt them alive . . . at least 70 people died on the 15th [of December, 1986]. There was so much arson that a pall of thick black smoke covered the city."[4] "In scenes reminiscent of the [anti-Sikh] Delhi riots of 1984" non-Pathan homes and businesses were specifically targeted.[5]

By the 1990s it was estimated that between four hundred and six hundred political murders a year were being committed in the city.[6] Altaf Hussain, the leader of the main MQM faction, dodged the bullets plus a string of criminal charges only by emigrating to north London. From there, funded and abetted by *muhajir* sympathizers, he continued to direct operations in Pakistan while rallying supporters with a deluge of inflammatory audio and videocassettes, satellite TV appearances, and Internet appeals. Once again diasporic connections and the globalization of communications were facilitating the transnational assertion of an essentially subnational identity.

General Zia ul-Haq's 1985 restoration of civilian rule, albeit within the constraints of military supervision and an emasculated constitution, should have given the MQM its big chance. In the 1988 elections that followed Zia's unexplained death, the MQM won thirteen of Karachi's fifteen National Assembly seats to emerge as the country's third-largest party. It continued to repeat this feat in the 1990s, though to little effect. Pacts promising the redress of *muhajir* grievances, first with Benazir Bhutto's PPP, then with Nawaz Sharif's Muslim League, failed to deliver. Holding the balance of power in a hopelessly flawed democracy proved no guarantee of concessions. Rather, a demand for the admission of more Bihari refugees from Bangladesh—who could be expected to swell the ranks of the *muhajirs*—antagonized the Sindis and served to revive the earlier *muhajir*-Sindi hostilities. The shutdowns and the communal killings continued, discrediting elected governments and providing a constant pretext for curfews and military interventions. As a byword for a metropolis in the final stages of self-destruction, Karachi came to outrank Calcutta and trail only Beirut.

Mazar Ali Khan, the respected editor of the leftist journal *Viewpoint,* blamed the generals and the politicians: "Our rulers presented a parade of incompetence and dishonesty—a gallery of quick-change artists, pompous buffoons, naïve imbeciles, clever ignoramuses, and occasionally gangsters capable of every known crime. Whatever our people's sins, these governments they did not deserve."[7]

But in Orangi, Akhtar Hameed Khan detected an even more worrying trend. Pakistan had been predicated on the idea of a Muslim nation, yet Islam, instead of underwriting the nation's cohesion, was now tearing it apart. The call to arms was coming from the mosques, where weapons were being stockpiled and death squads trained. Though a ritual bond still existed among all Muslims, ethnic and doctrinal differences were being exaggerated and exploited by sectarian bigotry. Khan blamed "the religious schools which are being established with the help of [the Iranian ayatollah] Khomeini's funds or Saudi Arabian funds and the literature that's being taught there, most of it produced in the eighth and ninth centuries which in Islamic history were periods of civil war and great violence." The effect of this teaching on young and impressionable minds was what left Khan in fear of the future. His foreboding was justified. Through the madrassas of Orangi and elsewhere were passing recruits for the Afghan Taliban, and from the same madrassas would come the Pakistani Taliban and their suicide-belted foot soldiers.

This was all somewhat ironic given that Pakistan post-1977 had at last begun to live up to its billing as an Islamic state. No government had been more committed to Islamizing the nation than the eleven-year regime of Zia ul-Haq. Moreover, none of his elected successors would dare openly to reverse his ordinances. Personally devout, the general-cum-president had sincerely believed that Islamic rectitude held the key to Pakistan's problems. He even had some experience of Islamic polities, having previously been seconded to the Hashemite kingdom of Jordan in the wake of the "Black September" expulsion of its Palestinian refugees. As Zia saw it, privileging Islam would set Pakistan straight. It would reorient the nation's political *qibla* (literally "direction of prayer") toward Mecca, firmly aligning it with Muslim West Asia. In the eyes of the faithful, promoting Islamic values would also afford his unelected regime some much-needed validation.

Better still, events had obligingly played into Zia's hands; for Washington's determination to contain and contest the Soviet presence in Afghanistan had restored Pakistan to frontline status in what would prove to be the final phase of the Cold War. To ensure the flow of arms to the Afghan resistance and to provide its fighters with safe havens, training facilities, and funds, the Reagan administration had had to look no further than Zia's Pakistan. Human rights questions over the execution of Bhutto were brushed aside. So were antiproliferation concerns over Pakistan's nuclear program. To sustain the anti-Soviet war in Afghanistan, Reagan was happy to direct aid and investment Pakistan's way, reequip the country's armed forces, and give Zia carte blanche in his efforts to contain dissent by promoting Islam.

With everything to gain, Zia ul-Haq had consulted Islamic ideologues associated with the fundamentalist Jamaat-e-Islami and launched a program of what many regarded as regressive Islamization. Foreign-funded madrassas were encouraged as a means of educating a new generation of Pakistanis in Quranic teaching. These schools demonstrated in miniature "what an Islamic government is like," according to one maulana, and supplemented the pitiful education budget of the state.[8] More generally, the sale of alcohol was banned, all public performances required a license, strict blasphemy laws bore heavily on the heterodox, and donations to religious welfare organizations became obligatory. The financial system was purged in accordance with Islamic strictures against interest payments, ordinances other than those imposed by the military were subject to scrutiny by Islamic scholars, and, most notoriously, elements of sharia, or Islamic law, were enshrined in the legal system. If the evidence presented to them conformed to the rather elevated standards of proof required by sharia, religious courts were obliged to convict in accord with archaic notions of criminality, then mete out the draconian sentences—including floggings, stonings, and amputations—appropriate to the Middle Ages.[9]

But much judicial confusion over the validity and implementation of these reforms somewhat blunted their impact. As the federal and lower sharia courts jostled with the civil and military tribunals, "there were many courts but there was little justice," writes Ian Talbot.[10] Some laws were contested; others, like those concerning the observance of *namaz* (daily prayers), purdah, and the Ramadan fast, were never fully enforced. Pakistan did not undergo an Islamic revolution like that in Iran. Instead, the piecemeal and contested nature of the reforms stirred up a hornet's nest of self-righteous acrimony. Constitutional die-hards, women's groups, and liberals in general joined the Western-educated elite in trying to alleviate the impact of Zia's program. More crucially, many devout Muslims also found fault with it. Privileging the Jamaat-e-Islami's brand of orthodoxy alienated Sufi devotees, antagonized the large Shi'ite minority, and seldom satisfied all shades even of Sunni opinion. Seemingly the most that these groups could agree on was another wave of persecution directed at the supposedly heretical Ahmadis. In the absence of a universally relevant and accepted authority on the sunna, which relates the deeds and practices of the Prophet and the early caliphs, there was no consensus on the precepts to be adopted, let alone on how they could be turned into workable laws.

General Zia, with the slicked-back hair and waxed mustache of a matinee magician, waved his swagger stick like a magic wand; but what he conjured up was not Islamic solidarity but cutthroat Islamic contention. Akhtar Hameed Khan saw it as a reversion to medieval thuggery rather than an assertion of Islamic brotherhood. The failure of the political process and the license afforded to sectarian demagogues radicalized discontent, turning whole congregations into warring zealots. "People have come to believe that problems can only be solved by the gun, the junta of the gun; and from 1979 we have had no lack of guns," moaned Khan.[11] The "Kalashnikov culture" was transforming sectarian militants into sectarian paramilitaries. The result was what has been called "the Islamization of criminal activity and the criminalisation of segments of Islamism."[12]

Nor, insofar as martial law permitted, was there any lack of political activity. Like the various ethnic groups, the different shades of Islamic opinion were represented by a kaleidoscope of political groupings. Come elections, Pakistan's secularists would take heart from the poor showing of these *jamaats* (literally "gatherings" rather than political parties) and see it as evidence of Islamization's limited appeal. Perhaps they should have taken more account of the estimated one million who turned out to mourn the Islamizing Zia's death—and this despite his latter-day backtracking on the more divisive of his reforms. At any rate, electoral returns could be deceptive. The Islamist vote was fragmented among numerous Sunni and Shi'ite parties, ethnic organizations such as the MQM siphoned off many potential *jamaatis,* and religious opinion was further divided over whether political parties, or even democracy itself, were Quranically legitimate.

Given the constraints on Pakistan's post-Zia democracy, these doubters had a point. The military retained oversight of the political process; the defense budget was ring-fenced, and the conduct of foreign affairs was reserved to the generals and the Inter-Services Intelligence (ISI) agency. Meanwhile, the army's bureaucratic siblings pulled the electoral strings, stifled legislative initiatives, and clung to

Zia's Eighth Amendment, empowering the president summarily to dismiss any ministry. In short, mandated governments enjoyed little more freedom of movement after Zia than they had under him.

The problem was compounded by the fragile parliamentary majorities of the post-Zia decade. A veritable musical chairs saw Benazir Bhutto (1988–90), Nawaz Sharif (1990–93), then Bhutto again (1993–96) and Sharif again (1996–99) trooping through the prime ministerial residence. Both premiers were constrained by the need to form coalitions with minor parties, both failed to adjust to the idea of legitimate opposition, and both struggled with the weakening economy and the closer international scrutiny that followed Washington's loss of interest in Afghanistan after the 1989 Soviet withdrawal. Fending off one another's accusations of corruption was perhaps their most notable achievement. Bhutto championed populist causes and invoked the legacy of her father; Sharif favored Islam and fielded among his sponsors the wife and son of the dead Zia. But when in 1999 General Pervez Musharraf, the army's chief of staff, survived Sharif's quixotic attempt to replace him and then hit back by restoring martial rule, the game was over. Bhutto (and, after a spell in detention, her husband) bolted back to London; Sharif set up home in Saudi Arabia. Pakistan entered its third decade under military rule. And once again, according to the BBC's correspondent, "most Pakistanis were delighted."[13]

THE PATTERN OF PAKISTANI POLITICS under Zia ul-Haq and his successors so nicely mirrors that of Bangladesh under Ziaur Rahman and his successors that collusion might be suspected. Both Generals Zia had been brought up in what was now India (Haq in Punjab, Rahman in Calcutta); both when rising through the ranks of the Pakistani army had imbibed its authoritarian contempt for politicians; and both when in power turned to Islam to redefine their respective nations. Just as Zia ul-Haq favored the ultra-orthodox Jamaat-e-Islami in Pakistan, so did Ziaur Rahman favor its namesake in Bangladesh; as well as rehabilitating the Jamaat's leaders after their near-fatal support for Pakistan in the 1971 war, he introduced the use of religious phrasing in official parlance. In a further bid for legitimacy, both generals also strove to civilianize their regimes. In Zia's Bangladesh, as in the other Zia's Pakistan, elections were promised, political parties sponsored, referenda conducted, national assemblies reinstated, and polls eventually held—which in both cases yielded suspiciously large majorities for the Zia-backed contenders.

Personally, the two Zias were reckoned courteous, dedicated, and untainted by corruption. Each esteemed the example of Ayub Khan and genuinely believed that only a disciplined military could fend off national chaos. Despite taking thousands of political prisoners, neither was universally detested, and, if Zia ul-Haq's demise in a still-unexplained plane crash brought a million mourners onto the streets of Lahore, just so did Ziaur Rahman's death in a botched coup attempt bring as many onto the streets of Dhaka.

There were of course differences. The beady-eyed Zia ul-Haq managed a decade in power (1978–88), while the sunglasses-wearing Ziaur Rahman survived for little more than half as long (1975–81). But when the latter was gunned down in what was supposedly the twenty-first attempt on his life, it was not the end of military rule. In General Mohamed Ershad, he left a second-in-command who reimposed martial law within a matter of months and then clung to office for a further six years (1982–90). Ershad's greatest compliment to his predecessor's example was to follow it to the letter. He too favored a more central role for religion; indeed, he finally declared Islam the state creed and labeled Bangladesh an Islamic republic. Like the Zias, Ershad also formed his own political party and claimed to be readying the nation for a return to civilian rule that was repeatedly postponed. Though lacking Ziaur Rahman's charismatic record as a battlefield commander and the voice of Bangladeshi independence, the uninspiring Ershad was "something less than a villain" and, according to Lawrence Ziring, "his rule was more benign than ruthless."[14]

Ershad still dealt firmly with opponents, whether military rivals or civilian politicians. The latter he so antagonized that to Ershad belongs the distinction of driving Khaleda Zia, the widow of Ziaur Rahman and leader of his Bangladesh National Party, into a short-lived pro-democracy alliance with Sheikh Hasina Wajed, the daughter of Banglabandhu Mujibur Rahman and leader of Mujib's Awami League. Never again would the "two begums" make common cause. Rather, it was their detestation of each other that would dominate the Bangladesh political scene for the next quarter of a century.

Like Benazir Bhutto in Pakistan, both begums had challenged martial law and been detained under it. They too considered themselves champions of democracy and, like Benazir Bhutto, each claimed to be the sole legitimate heir to the foundational legacy of her "martyred" father or husband. Each thus felt uniquely qualified to speak for the people. But there the similarities ended. Hasina promoted the secular, socialist, and India-friendly policies associated with Mujib; Khaleda favored the more Islam-inclusive, free-market, and India-cautious policies associated with Zia. More fatally, each bore a personal grudge against the other. Hasina held Zia, and so his widow, guilty for failing to prosecute those responsible for the 1975 murder of her father and family, if not for the murder itself, and Khaleda retaliated by blaming Hasina for ambivalence over attempts to reinvestigate the 1981 murder of her own husband. This bitter personal vendetta cut to the heart of Bangladeshi identity. The bereaveds' demand for justice crowded out the normal business of government and would ensure that recriminatory moves over the events of 1971–81 remained front-page news for as long as the begums lasted.

In 1990 Ershad finally capitulated to a show of "people power" like those that four years earlier had toppled Ferdinand Marcos in the Philippines and were now convulsing the erstwhile Soviet-bloc countries of eastern Europe. Elections were duly called in which an alliance headed by Khaleda Zia's Bangladesh National Party confronted another headed by Hasina Wajed's Awami League. Both won around 30 percent of the vote, and thus began a back-and-forth struggle very like that between Benazir Bhutto and Nawaz Sharif. Khaleda formed the first government (1991–96), Hasina the second (1996–2001), Khaleda the third (2001–6), and after a two-year interlude of army-backed rule, Hasina the fourth (2009–). All lasted their full five-year term; democracy of a sort seemed to be taking root. But so slim were the begums' majorities, so disruptive their tactics, so confrontational their policies, and so negligible their achievements that many observers began to see either government as an irrelevance.

Instead, the business of actually running the country—evaluating needs, providing services, disbursing funds, protecting the vulnerable, engaging the masses, and managing the country's perennial natural disasters—was increasingly being shouldered by a concourse of over twenty thousand nongovernmental organizations (NGOs). These included not only indigenous giants such as BRAC and the Grameen Bank but a host of foreign or international aid and development agencies plus innumerable community-led local ventures, dozens of religious and charitable foundations, and not a few well-camouflaged scams. Many of them relied on foreign or government funding, though others aimed to be self-financing. According to a World Bank report of 2006, "some 20% to 35% of the country's population is believed to receive some services, usually credit, health or education, from an NGO."[15] Microcredit was the developmentalists' panacea, although it came with interest rates that were neither Islamic nor particularly cheap. Education ranged from universities such as that founded by BRAC to rural programs designed to increase civic awareness that might verge on the politically partisan. Even health was not wholly uncontroversial. A clash with the pharmaceutical giants resulted when an NGO called the People's Health Centre won the Ershad government's support for the domestic production of cheaper generic alternatives to some essential branded medicines.

The NGO trend was never without its critics. While some observers hailed it as evidence of an emerging civil society, others detected the incubation of a parallel state. They winced at the ranks of Land Rovers and Land Cruisers parked outside the expat watering holes of north Dhaka and wondered whether the NGO presence, in relieving the begums' elected governments of so many present responsibilities, was not in fact contributing to their obsession with past injustices. Noted one observer, "NGOs compete with government for donor resources and for wider legitimacy because successful NGO work can easily be perceived as governmental 'failure.'"[16] Conversely, military rulers had looked on the NGOs more benignly. As politically neutral organizations, they could be useful allies in a dictator's quest for credibility. Moreover, their achievements served to stifle opponents' criticism.

In Bangladesh, voluntary grassroots organizations already had a respectable pedigree. Among the new NGOs, indigenous initiative continued to play a major role and was widely applauded. Although hard to quantify, NGO activities appeared to raise educational and health standards, boost employment and land use, and improve the quality of the workforce. Women in particular benefited. Female literacy came to exceed that among males, while female participation in, for instance, the garment industry helped to transform the economy. The impact of environmental disasters, especially flooding, may have been blunted by NGO initiatives. Poverty in general, if not alleviated, was at least made more bearable.

But if the product of all this outsourcing to NGOs was an inert and paranoid government in Dhaka, it was a high price to pay. Grassroots activity was no substitute for state-level undertakings. Sweatshops went woefully unregulated; roads, bridges, and other essential infrastructure were slow to materialize. Bangladesh took thirty years to come to terms with the Farakka Dam, built by India across the Ganges on its own side of the border, and twenty years to begin similar negotiations over water sharing of the Teesta River following construction of another Indian dam. A third, at Tipaimukh in the Indian state of Manipur, was commenced in the 1980s but halted in the 1990s by a combination of environmental concerns and official objections; in 2012 work remained at a standstill. All these projects certainly had implications for downstream Bangladesh and merited careful study. But in a flood plain subject to often catastrophic inundation, the opportunity to manage the rivers and obtain a share of their hydroelectric potential ought to have been accorded the highest priority.

Other opportunities were also let slip. In 2004 the Bombay- (now Mumbai-) based Tata group of companies announced discussions that would make Bangladesh the largest-ever recipient of overseas Indian investment. Two and a half billion dollars were to be spent there constructing an industrial complex that included a colossal steel mill, a thermal power plant, an open-cast coal mine, and a urea fertilizer plant. Together they would have represented much the biggest direct foreign investment made in Bangladesh, doubling its industrial capacity overnight and creating some twenty-four thousand jobs.

But they never materialized. The negotiations dragged on until 2007. Dhaka recognized the value of the project and accepted the quid pro quo of giving India access to the gas expected from the offshore waters of the Bay of Bengal. But actually signing up for the project was more than successive Bangladeshi governments could agree on. Despite the obvious benefits, the politicians seem to have backed down lest they expose themselves to accusations of betraying the nation's sovereignty by kowtowing to Delhi and trading away a national asset. Delhi's patience was sorely tested.

SIMILAR CONCERNS DOGGED RELATIONS between the kingdom of Nepal and India, and for similar reasons. Impoverished countries with weak governments and a heavy dependency on foreign aid are not the easiest to deal with. In Nepal's case, the difficulty of exercising any kind of administrative control was a result of the switchback Himalayan terrain plus the ethnic, linguistic, and caste fragmentation of the population. The *panchayati* raj, a variant of Ayub Khan's bottom-up "basic democracy," was supposed to function well in this situation. Panchayats, village-based or district-based councils, were meant to encourage grassroots consensus by reflecting particularist interests and being locally accountable. But as in Bangladesh—where both Zia and Ershad introduced their own versions of decentralized government—devolving power proved in practice to be more about creating a personal constituency for an otherwise unrepresentative regime and so giving it a veneer of democratic legitimacy.

In the Nepal of the 1980s the regime had been that of King Birendra, whose officials had managed the panchayat system as a projection of his authority and patronage. The main beneficiaries were the landed local elites rather than the actual cultivators. But for the support of these middlemen, the court had to compete with politicians promising reform and still greater perks. In particular, leaders of the Nepali Congress Party "heartily embraced these local power brokers . . . [and] tried their level best to recruit former members of the monarchical *panchayat* system at the grass roots level." Come the restoration of parliamentary democracy, this policy would bear fruit. But in the process the politicians "unwittingly intervene[d] in favour of rural elites [and] against the rural poor, who had suffered under the same elites during the *panchayat* period."[17] Thus would be perpetuated governmental indifference to the removal of social iniquities, such as forced labor and various forms of caste and ethnic discrimination, that bore most heavily on the poorest minorities. This was especially true in the remote and sparsely administered midwestern districts of the country. There exploitation and neglect created a fertile ground for popular insurgency. It awaited only the dibbling in of revolutionary dogma by bandana-bedecked Maoists.

As in both Pakistan and Bangladesh, in Nepal 1990 brought long-awaited change. Here too democracy was restored, which meant reinstating the multiparty format that had been jettisoned back in 1951. Elsewhere in the world the wind of glasnost was fanning anti-authoritarian protest from Berlin to Beijing and had already ruffled Kathmandu. But the country also faced a crisis of its own. The king had recently brokered an arms purchase from China. India had objected and had retaliated by terminating the preferential trade and transit arrangements along the Indo-Nepali border. Hardship and shortages resulted, against which Nepali students and politicians protested with strikes, mass demonstrations, and violence that was amply repaid by the police. For fifty days Kathmandu had been paralyzed.

With the protesters focusing their ire not just on India but on the panchayat system and its royal sponsor, Birendra had opted for damage limitation. He reauthorized political parties and offered constitutional talks. These talks, though protracted enough, short-circuited the usually contentious workings of a Constituent Assembly. Instead, the participants simply agreed on a constitution in which Nepal was declared a "multi-ethnic, multi-lingual, democratic, independent, indivisible, sovereign, Hindu, constitutional monarchical kingdom." The catchall phrasing pointed up the deep divisions it was designed to accommodate. A parliamentary system was reinstated and elections scheduled, whereupon the short-lived consensus of protest dissolved into a seething mass of multiethnic, multilingual, independent, et cetera, contenders. Democratic freedoms did encourage wider participation in the political process and produced healthy election turnouts. But this was largely thanks to the politicizing of tribal and low-caste minorities who held the Hindu monarchical kingdom and its upper-caste bureaucracy responsible for their plight.

Over the next twelve years Nepal had twelve governments. A Nepali Congress ministry led by Girija Prasad Koirala managed three and a half turbulent years (1991–94), but at the cost of abandoning its more radical policies and operating within "the politics of patronage"; all the other ministries came and went in a matter of months. They included several coalitions led by the Communist Party of Nepal (United Marxist-Leninist), itself an amalgam of numerous ultra-leftist splinter groups. At a moment in history when the hammers and sickles were being tossed just about everywhere else, the ballot box victory of Marxist-Leninists under a monarchical dispensation looked to be another Himalayan anomaly.

It was also self-defeating. In power the Communists too "came to be viewed as the party of the establishment" and quickly alienated some of their grassroots cadres.[18] Nor did they fare much better out of power. Brutal police repression of revolutionary communes, ordered by the Nepal Congress government in 1995, further divided the Communist faithful and provoked much soul-searching as to the ideologically correct response. Some Communist groups stepped up their efforts to present a credible parliamentary challenge; others, led by Pushpa Kamal Dahal, alias "Comrade Prachanda," turned their backs on Kathmandu and opted for a "people's war" under the banner of the Communist Party of Nepal (Maoist). Weapons were acquired, study groups set up, and social betterment programs promoted. Among the minority peoples of the Rukun and Rolpa districts in the midwest, the insurgency took root.

The war began in earnest when in early 1996 a forty-point memorandum of Communist demands went unanswered by the government. The demands were designed to be as inclusive as possible. They called for a revision of the Indo-Nepal treaties by way of curtailing "Indian expansionism," the creation of a Constituent Assembly, and a radical redistribution of power aimed at ending royal control of the army, replacing the specifically Hindu complexion of the state with secular ideals, ensuring local autonomy, and introducing a predictable package of land reforms and social provisions. Nothing was said about overthrowing the monarchy. The revolutionary tactics that the Maoists were already employing in their "liberated areas" were barely mentioned, nor was the mix of indoctrination and intimidation that accompanied them.

From 1996 till 2001 the insurgents concentrated on eliminating such vestiges of the central administration as remained in these "liberated" districts—police posts were especially targeted—and replacing them with the apparatus of "people's governments." Operating through an elaborate chain of local cells, district politburos, and standing committees, the new governments were designed to widen support for the party by educating and empowering Dalits, tribal groups, bonded laborers, women in general, and other marginalized elements in society. Skills were taught, public health and education promoted, land redistributed. Female participation was especially impressive at every level, including the military. And though discipline was strict and taxation common, such things seemed a small price to pay for dedicated service to the common good.

In effect, the Maoists were constructing a parallel state of their own; and they were doing so partly by addressing grievances and promoting causes that elsewhere in Nepal were becoming the preserve of NGOs. Until the restoration of democracy in 1990, NGO activity had been restricted. Royal approval had been needed to set up any voluntary scheme and had mostly been withheld lest such schemes unsettle the panchayat system. After 1990, these constraints no longer applied. In fact, something of a free-for-all ensued. Government supervision now being minimal, competition between NGOs was fierce, and coordination suffered. Although the definition of an NGO was problematic—in Nepal it could be anything from a sports club to Oxfam—the number operating in the country suddenly grew from a few hundred to tens of thousands.

To cynics it looked like another case of the flies finding the sugar—of nongovernmental agencies being drawn to ungovernmental nations. But NGO activity could also be seen as a useful antidote to Maoist contagion. With aid accounting for around 20 percent of the nation's GDP, most NGOs relied on foreign or international funding. The preferred arrangement saw foreign donors, typically based in the United States, the United Kingdom, or India, working in tandem with Nepali-run NGOs and channeling funds through them. Thus NGO activity, besides redressing many social ills and filling the void left by government, served to alert the international community to the Maoist threat and to afford some reassurance to the Nepal government.

All of which was of course grist for the Maoists' mill. The government was blamed for betraying the people's trust by outsourcing its responsibilities to unaccountable foreign enterprises, many supposedly with neocolonial or neoconservative agendas. Aid workers were said to be overpaid parasites; official misappropriation was said to account for up to 90 percent of their funds. In particular, India and the United States were accused of using NGOs to subvert Nepali sovereignty.

But the Maoist propaganda was not indiscriminate; it seldom targeted individual aid workers, and it held the government to account rather than the sovereign. Indeed, the king, who had yet to be reconciled to his supposedly constitutional role, appeared just as keen to discredit the elected governments as were the Maoists. Hence the abolition of the monarchy and the creation of a republic, which should have been fundamental to the Maoist manifesto, were not pressed. Instead, all such constitutional issues were subsumed in the demand for a Constituent Assembly.

There is even evidence of an unholy alliance between the politburos and the palace. By 2001 the Maoists controlled about a quarter of the countryside. But the government, which was again that of the Nepal Congress, could tackle the insurgents only by deploying the police. For despite repeated requests, the Royal Nepalese Army remained in its barracks on the orders of its royal commander in chief. In other words, while castigating the government's failure to roll back the insurgency, King Birendra steadfastly declined to engage his own troops. Comrade Prachanda would himself later acknowledge his movement's gratitude for this forbearance. He applauded what he dubbed the king's "soft policy toward the Maoist People's War" and recalled Maoist hopes "that Birendra would play the role of [Prince] Sihanouk" (he being the Cambodian monarch who had thrown in his lot with the Khmer Rouge).[19]

It seems, then, highly improbable that the Maoists played any part in the imminent mass murder of Nepal's royal family. Nor does the Maoist charge that it was India and the United States that were behind the regicide seem any more probable. Around that scene of carnage, which would define Nepal's crisis to the wider world, conspiracy theories abound as wantonly as they do around the horrors of 9/11 three months later. The more improbable the outrage, the more outrageous the conjecture—indeed, so much so that the originally improbable becomes plausible.

The Kathmandu massacre occurred within the king's residence in the grounds of the Narayanhithi Palace. On the warm summer's evening of June 1, 2001, the royals had gathered for the customary monthly audience. Greetings were exchanged and drinks served as the formally attired guests emerged from the adjoining billiard room. According to later testimony, the proceedings were then interrupted when Crown Prince Dipendra made his entry dressed in military fatigues. Heavily armed, certainly drunk, and possibly drugged, the prince began shooting immediately. He then withdrew only to return for more of the same. By the time he reportedly turned one of his guns on himself, King Birendra and Queen Aishwarya lay dead, as did seven other princes and princesses. The survivors were few. They included the dead king's unpopular brother Gyanendra, who happened to be absent that day, Gyanendra's even more unloved son, who was only slightly wounded, and the demented Crown Prince Dipendra, whose attempt at suicide had left him in a deep coma but still breathing.

Hitherto an uncontroversial figure, the burly Dipendra is supposed to have been mentally deranged by his mother's refusal to let him marry the girl he loved. But assuming that he was indeed solely responsible for the massacre, it is hard to understand the sequence of events that followed. At first it was claimed that the whole affair had been accidental; a gun had gone off by mistake. Then, after several eyewitnesses had pinned the blame squarely on Dipendra, it emerged that none of them had actually seen the prince shooting himself. Moreover, the next day, while the regicidal Dipendra still lay comatose, he was officially recognized as king, with his uncle Gyanendra being appointed as temporary regent. Only when, three days later, Dipendra did indeed expire, presumably of his wounds, was Gyanendra elevated to the throne.

Meanwhile, the bodies of all the slain were cremated before autopsies could be conducted, King Gyanendra somehow failed to attend the obsequies, and a later inquiry, whose impartiality was itself questionable, only fueled the uncertainty by presenting self-contradictory findings. So much confusion argues strongly against the idea of premeditation. On the other hand, suspicion would inevitably attach to Gyanendra and his son—for surviving as much as for anything else. More certainly, after three kings in four days, Nepal's monarchy was looking decidedly shaky.

Gyanendra, a stern-faced sixty-three-year-old, was not one to shirk his new responsibilities. "The days of the monarchy being seen . . . but not heard" were, he declared, over.[20] Prime Minister G. P. Koirala promptly resigned. His replacement opened talks with the Maoists, and, when these failed, the new king suspended the political process and declared a state of emergency. Parliament was dismissed, the army finally emerged from its barracks, and on doubtful legal grounds Gyanendra formed a ministry of his own. A new crackdown backed by powers of summary arrest was justified on the grounds of combating terrorism, although the shootings and bombings continued. In the country at large the Maoists now fielded some fifteen thousand troops and the total death toll was approaching ten thousand.

In this worsening situation yet another cease-fire and more talks lasted through the first half of 2003. Gyanendra, though under both international and donor pressure to settle with the Maoists, first balked at their demand for an elected Constituent Assembly, which he rightly feared would lead to the abolition of the monarchy, then scuppered the cease-fire with an army operation in which "nearly nineteen Maoists" lost their lives.[21]

Mass protests by the political parties brought a short-lived restoration of democracy in 2004. Long-overdue elections were promised, although without Maoist approval they could scarcely be held. The politicians were easy prey for palace intrigue, and the stalemate, combined with the war's mounting death toll, emboldened Gyanendra to take a second bite at the cherry. In yet another royal coup, on February 1, 2005, a new state of emergency was declared. The king usurped all executive powers, imprisoned or detained many parliamentarians, and clamped down hard on the press. He also predicted defeat for the Maoists within six months. In what would prove to be the endgame for Nepal's embattled monarchy, Gyanendra had embraced the post-9/11 "war on terror."

As with General Musharraf in Pakistan, the conventional wisdom about failed states providing a haven and breeding ground for cross-national terrorists persuaded some foreign governments to overlook Gyanendra's constitutional shortcomings. The George W. Bush administration in the United States was at first sympathetic. So was a now notably un-Maoist China. And the Indian government, confronted by a revival of Maoist (or Naxalite) insurgency within its own borders, was positively supportive. But as the strength of Nepali opposition to the crackdown became clear, such sentiments cooled. Gyanendra's six months came and went with no letup in the war. The country teetered on the edge of complete collapse. Aid receipts fell, and some NGOs pulled out. "Tourism, the second largest foreign-exchange earner, on which 100,000 Nepalese depend, has dropped by 40%," reported the *Guardian* in early 2006, "and the economy—one of the poorest in Asia—is sinking under the weight of diminished revenues and increased military spending."[22]

Meanwhile, the political parties, with their backs against the wall, had rediscovered a common purpose in resisting the king's authoritarian rule. A Seven Party Alliance was formed to fight for a revival of parliament, and an appeal was issued to the Maoists to join it. This they did, but only after another cease-fire had come to nothing and only on the understanding that a revived parliament would convene a Constituent Assembly whose deliberations would result in a constitution that put an end to royal interventions. Evidently the new king's aggressive tactics had snuffed out Comrade Prachanda's soft spot for the monarchy.

Gyanendra responded to the multiparty challenge by announcing elections for February 2006. But the elections were to be at the municipal level only and were to be conducted under his emergency regime. This meant that the palace would have a veto on the candidates and an excellent chance of managing the results in its favor. Presumably Gyanendra reasoned that if the Maoists let the poll go ahead, he would be credited with having won a mandate, and, if they prevented it, he would be credited with having given democracy a try. What he didn't reckon on was universal condemnation. As never before, all sections of Nepali society—rural Maoists, urbane Congress men, students, intellectuals, traders, and minorities—united in decrying the elections as the cynical ploy they undoubtedly were. In a land where kings staged coups and Maoists made common cause with monarchists, a spokesman for the European Union detected a new anomaly: Elections would be "a backward step for democracy." The Indian government agreed. Despite its distaste for the Maoist presence at the barricades, it threw its weight behind the democratic movement and looked to its erstwhile allies in the Nepal Congress.

In Kathmandu the multiparty alliance called a general strike. It was met with erratic curfews and indiscriminate shooting by the army. When this claimed at least thirteen civilian lives, the whole country erupted in the greatest mass uprising in its history. "Hordes of Nepalese defy shoot-on-sight curfew orders and have brought the capital to a virtual standstill," reported a *New York Times* correspondent.[23] As transport backed up at the border, fuel supplies ran low and the price of tomatoes tripled. But the strike went on. The Maoists held their fire and the multiparty alliance held together. The king's ploy had spectacularly misfired. On April 22, 2006, faced with a threatened occupation of the capital's governmental district, an "ashen-faced" Gyanendra went on television to concede demands for the reinstatement of parliament. "Within minutes of his appearance the streets of Katmandu exploded in jubilation."[24]

It was not the end of the monarchy. That took another two years, during which the king was progressively stripped of his powers, his perquisites, and his palaces. He nevertheless stayed on as a private citizen with extensive business interests. Indeed, in 2012 he made it clear that he was still available. Claiming that the abolition of the monarchy had been unconstitutional, he pretended that his status as a constitutional ruler was still valid and might yet be reactivated.

Nor was this the end of the interminable search for political stability in the now Federal Democratic Republic of Nepal. With the Maoists having aligned themselves with the Seven Party Alliance in the mass uprising and agreed to participate in the subsequent political process, the ten-year war had effectively ended. An immediate cease-fire was followed by a peace agreement in late 2006. But contentious issues such as the disbandment of the people's governments, the disarmament of the Maoist guerrillas, and the release of prisoners had yet to be addressed. There was also the outstanding matter of a Constituent Assembly and the new constitution it would draft.

After Gyanendra backed down, G. P. Koirala had for the umpteenth time shouldered the burden of prime minister in the recalled lower house of parliament. Under his stewardship, and with the help of the United Nations Mission in Nepal (UNMIN), disarmament made some progress and a Constituent Assembly was elected. The election unexpectedly gave the Maoists a slim majority. Accordingly, in 2008 the new assembly formally abolished the monarchy and installed a president, to whom the now eighty-three-year-old Koirala tendered his resignation. Comrade Prachanda succeeded him. But Prachanda's term of office lasted only a year. He resigned in 2009 when the president countermanded his dismissal of the army's chief of staff. The latter, supposedly with encouragement from New Delhi, had refused to incorporate the Maoists' eighteen thousand fighters into the regular army.

This question of accommodating the guerrillas topped a growing agenda of contentious issues that soon threatened both the peace and the constitutional process. The setting up of a truth and reconciliation commission was repeatedly postponed; so was the deadline for agreement on the new constitution. Meanwhile, parliamentary business ground to a standstill as the Maoists backed up their demands by orchestrating strikes and walkouts. Disaffection and factionalism within both the main political parties further complicated matters.

A resolution of these problems looked no nearer in 2014 than it had six years earlier. Elections due in 2012 had twice been postponed. The Maoist guerrillas were still awaiting rehabilitation, human rights abuses dating back to the war had yet to be investigated, and the scale of compensation to be offered for the Maoists' land grabs had yet to be decided. The new republic remained without a constitution, and for all practical purposes the country remained without a government. The best that could be said was that all parties, including the Maoists, professed a commitment to the democratic process and were still gearing up for elections.

In a sign of more hopeful times, tourism—"the second biggest income-earner after remittances from Nepalese abroad," according to the BBC—began to pick up. No doubt it was boosted by the introduction in 2012 of the first "guerrilla treks." Offering tourists twenty-one days among the erstwhile cadres and their collectivized holdings in Rolpa and Rukun, guerrilla treks looked like Nepal's way of consigning the war to history.[25]

The tourists themselves were another sign of the changing times. Once mostly backpacking Westerners, they were now overwhelmingly free-spending Indians. From an airport enlivened by the liveries of Indian-owned budget airlines, the visitors were being bused into town in Indian-built vehicles past billboards advertising Indian-made furnishings. Kathmandu can have seemed no more exotic than Gangtok. Indeed, to outsiders, especially Pakistanis or Bangladeshis, Nepal appeared to be showcasing Indianization as the twenty-first century's riposte to Partition.

Just as sharing a subcontinent with the world's largest democracy enhanced the prospects of electoral accountability elsewhere in South Asia, so sharing it with one of the most dynamic of the world's emerging economies promised dividends of a different sort. Hitherto "dynamic" had been a word not readily associated with the Indian economy. The economic miracle had been a long time coming; it took many by surprise and was already faltering. But there was no doubt that, in the space of a couple of decades, India's prospects had been transformed. Rising living standards, however unevenly distributed, plus a more aspirational environment also served to quell dissent and draw the sting of protest. Communists could become IT entrepreneurs, "slumdogs" become millionaires. For South Asia as a whole there was much to be learned from a suddenly "shining India."

INDIA ASTIR

Y COMMON CONSENT THE 1980S HAD BEEN INDIA'S WORST decade to date. Predictions of an imminent economic lift-off had again proved hopelessly misplaced. By the end of the decade the national debt had risen to an unsustainable $70 billion, the growth rate and investment were sluggish, underemployment was endemic, and reserves of foreign currency were perilously low. Once projected as the "Japan of the 1980s," the country felt more like the China of the 1930s. Navigating it meant dodging sudden curfews and endless demonstrations. The roads were not for the fainthearted, and the extremities of the country were virtually no-go areas. Trains got blown up; rivers either stank or flooded. Although television had already reached some villages, audiences for the nation's state-run network were subject to the vagaries of the state-run power supply. Making a telephone call could take a morning, and buying an airline ticket or cashing a check took all day. Always unwieldy, India in the 1980s was feeling increasingly unmanageable.

Rajiv Gandhi's big idea as prime minister (1984–89) had been to wean the people off their reliance on the state and get them to take responsibility for their own lives. He liked computers and believed in self-empowerment. A paperless desk matched his peerless complexion, and when a lamp needed fixing he dug out a screwdriver. Instead of fielding endless petitions, he pleaded for local initiative. "If a road needs ditching, why don't they organise it themselves?" he said. "The people have become too dependent on the state providing every-thing."[1] He too favored bottom-up regeneration, but not because, as in Bangladesh and Nepal, there was a governmental vacuum; rather, because there was a governmental overload.

For in India it was decision making that had been moving up-ward. With the democratic process reduced to an electoral squabble, parliamentarians looked on office more as a reward than as a re-sponsibility. Between repeated adjournments for unruly conduct, the Lok Sabha continued to function, but it legislated little. State gov-ernments were no better; when not actually suspended, they lived in constant fear of being so. The courts, on the other hand, were busy; their backlog of cases stretched back a decade or more. Seemingly, litigation led where legislation feared to tread. Willy-nilly, everything non-actionable, from protest to dissent, found its way into the prime minister's office and from there onto the national agenda.

It was depressing fodder. In 1988, for a published collection of his recent journalism, the respected editor M. J. Akbar chose the title *Riot After Riot*. Two years later V. S. Naipaul subtitled the last of his three India books *A Million Mutinies Now*. The Jeremiahs were having a field day. Ramachandra Guha quotes from a 1985 edition of the Calcutta weekly *Sunday,* to which numerous distinguished journalists contributed gloom-laden observations: "tension and frus-tration everywhere—social, economic and political. . . . Acts of sab-otage, arson, killings and destruction are breaking out all over India like an ugly rash. . . . [F]ear is growing that we are moving beyond the point of no return . . . discontent seems to have reached a burst-ing point. . . . India finds itself at a crucial point in its history." Guha added the caveat that "every decade since Independence had been designated the 'most dangerous,'" but there was clearly not much to celebrate.[2] Hostilities of caste, class, creed, and ethnicity hogged the headlines. Forty years after independence, Indians were more divided among themselves—and more violently divided—than ever before. If the nation was going anywhere, it was not upward but backward.

Pakistan, on the other hand, was receiving comparatively favor-able ratings. Moderately progressive in 1967, by 1987 some found it even more so. Here was "a fast moving country," according to the

Economist's special report of that year. Pakistanis could look back on their first four decades with some satisfaction. Starting out with little in the way of industry or infrastructure, the economy was now powering ahead of India's. Cotton production had made up for the loss of East Bengal's jute. GDP per head stood at $390 compared with India's $260, and growth under Zia ul-Haq was averaging 7 percent against India's 4 percent. "It has better road, transport and telephone services than India. It has 450,000 cars compared with 1.5 m in India, which has eight times as many people. Color television is common in areas called slums. The people are bigger and healthier looking. You do not find the hopeless poverty of lethargic, underfed people that is still so common in India's backward areas."[3]

The *Economist* had its reservations, as always. The prosperity was down to "foreign money," notably the diaspora's remittances ($2–3 billion a year in the mid-1980s), US aid ($600 million a year and rising), and profits from the arms and heroin trade ("incalculable millions"). Businessmen were not complaining, but then neither were they investing. The political future was too uncertain. "A psychoanalyst would tell Pakistan that it . . . was stuck in a crisis-ridden adolescence." Democracy had stalled, and dictatorship was becoming addictive. Only 24 percent of the adult population was literate because education received a pitiful 1.5 percent of budgeted expenditure compared with the around 40 percent earmarked for the defense establishment. General Zia conjured up plenty of resentment. But compared with Zulfikar Ali Bhutto, the *Economist* reckoned his repression less arbitrary and less offensive. As of 1985, in which year Zia's regime had acquired a civilian veneer with the appointment of the mild-mannered Mohamed Khan Junejo as prime minister, "Pakistan was freer than it ever was under Bhutto."

Such comparisons only contributed to the gloom that enveloped India. Nor were reports from Karachi of the ethno-sectarian carnage there much consolation. For if the Islamizing of an avowedly Muslim Pakistan was proving highly divisive, then so was the Hinduizing of a proudly secular India. Nehru had embedded religious neutrality in the nationalist prospectus; his daughter, Indira, had pruned it back for electoral advantage; and then, for similar reasons, her son Rajiv seemed to have wrenched at its roots.

Rajiv was not alone in this, nor was he perhaps fully alert to its consequences. Nevertheless, when an excruciating legal issue had floated up to the prime ministerial desk in July 1985, his vacillation had done much to light the fuse of confessional strife. Known as the "Shah Bano affair," the case caused acute embarrassment at the time. Liberals wrung their hands in anguish and huddled in corners whispering over their whiskies late into the night. Foreign observers struggled to follow the intricacies of the case. Often they failed to appreciate its significance, as it made for labored copy. But the profound discomfort was real enough.

The issue at stake concerned the relationship between Indian civil law and Muslim customary law. A petition from an organization called the All India Muslim Personal Law Board (AIMPLB) had urged the prime minister to amend an article in the directive principles of the constitution that foresaw a uniform civil code applying to all Indian citizens regardless of their faith. In particular, the prime minister was asked to overrule a decision of the Supreme Court, which, anticipating this universal civil code, had just found against a plaintiff in the sensitive matter of a Muslim divorce settlement.

At the center of the affair was Shah Bano, a seventy-five-year-old Muslim woman from Indore in Madhya Pradesh. Divorced six years previously by her lawyer husband, Shah Bano had taken her case for indefinite maintenance as per the Indian Code of Criminal Procedure to a local court; and she had won. But her ex-husband had then contested this in the Supreme Court on the basis that Muslim personal law obliged him to pay maintenance for only three months. Thus in rejecting the appeal, the Supreme Court had found in favor of Shah Bano and the civil code. The court also somewhat gratuitously backed up its judgment by offering the view that Quranic jurisprudence could in fact be taken to favor maintenance payments for as long as the divorced wife's circumstances required.

In effect, the Supreme Court had not only upheld the primacy of the secular civil code but presumed to interpret Muslim family law. Orthodox Islamic opinion was incensed; vast Muslim crowds—one supposedly of 400,000 people in Bihar and another in Bombay of 300,000—demanded greater protection for Muslim rights.[4] Conversely, Hindu supremacists, already smarting over the erection of Saudi-funded mosques and a wave of Dalit conversions to Islam, heartily approved.

All of which was too much for the AIMPLB, which redoubled its lobbying of the prime minister; it was also too much for Shah Bano, who, vilified by fellow Muslims, eventually disclaimed her victory and announced that her ex-husband's princely allowance of Rs 179 a month (about $6) would be donated to charity. It was also too much for Rajiv Gandhi. Having just defeated a private member's bill to exempt Muslims from the offending section of the Criminal Procedures Code, in early 1986 he performed a political somersault. Muslim voters appeared to have deserted Congress in recent by-elections; to win them back, therefore, the code must after all be amended to exclude Muslim practice from its purview. Furthermore, a bill would be introduced to "protect" (i.e., enshrine) Muslim women's "rights" in the event of divorce—including the husband's option of terminating maintenance payments after three months. Congress MPs, who had just been whipped through the lobbies to vote down the private member's bill exempting Muslims, were now whipped through the lobbies in support of the Muslim exemption.

Naturally this about-face provoked varied reactions. Orthodox Muslims celebrated: their mass demonstrations had paid off, and they had repelled an assault on their religious autonomy. Liberal secularists, on the other hand, along with those Muslims anxious to shed their faith's reputation for gender discrimination, were acutely embarrassed. The exemption seemed to conflict with the equality of rights guaranteed in the constitution; worse still, it meant that enlightened members of the intelligentsia now found themselves lining up alongside the enraged champions of Hindu supremacism.

For to the BJP, the RSS, and their saffron-shirted associates on the Hindu right, the decision was a clear case of the government capitulating to "Muslim fundamentalism." "From now on, the underlying theme of all discussions among militant Hindus was that of 'Hindu society under siege.'"[5] Yet while stigmatizing Islam as an obscurantist and proselytizing menace, militant Hindus also saw fit to learn from it. They urged their co-religionists to rediscover their own culture, to promote it with pride, and to unite en masse for the purposes of political action. A Hindu backlash was looming. Meanwhile, "Rajiv's reputation as a peace-maker—won in brokering accords in Kashmir and Assam as well as Punjab—was shattered, his political honeymoon over."[6]

Along with the BJP as its main political wing and with the RSS providing a disciplined and motivated all-India network of activist volunteers, the so-called Sangh Parivar (the "Family Association" of patriotic Hindu organizations) comprised a host of other political, religious, and social groups. Among them was the Vishwa Hindu Parishad (VHP, or "World Hindu Council"). This body had long been engaged in trying to get the different sects within "the Hindu communion" to coalesce. Common objectives, such as cow protection and the abolition of untouchability, were promoted, and all manner of revered holy men (acharyas, saddhus, mahants, sants, pujaris, gurus, etc.) were encouraged to sink their sectarian differences in support of a Faith Council. In effect, through a nationwide program of conferences an attempt was being made to endow Hinduism with the authoritative guidance of what amounted to a clerical establishment, indeed an ecclesiastical hierarchy.

Such moves appealed strongly to those devout Hindus who were aware of their religion's doctrinal and organizational deficiencies when compared to other faiths. In particular, the VHP's Hindu ecumenism found influential supporters and donors among some of India's industrialists and mercantile magnates and among the Hindu diaspora in the United States and western Europe. The movement would not be short of funds.

To promote this Hindu "reformation," in 1983 the VHP had hit on the idea of organizing a nationwide *ekatmata yatra*, or "unity pilgrimage." Images of Mother India and Mother Ganga, both of whom were more national divinities than sect-specific ones, were mounted on trailers for motorized processions that converged on sites rich in Hindu associations. Water from India's holiest rivers was collected and distributed along the way, and devotions to the deities were performed before massive crowds led by distinguished Hindu leaders.

As an exercise in ethno-religious mobilization, the *yatra* "introduced a new ideological devotionalism" and was reckoned a sensational success.[7] A repetition of its explosive combination of ecstatic worship, mass organization, and political activism promised much to the Sangh Parivar. All that was lacking was the tighter focus that a single symbolic issue or a single emotive location would confer.

AYODHYA IS A SMALL, unfashionable city in western UP. Many Hindus believe it to be Ramjanmabhoomi, or the birthplace of Lord Ram, himself a reincarnation of Lord Vishnu and the hero of the *Ramayana* epic. Whether Lord Ram was in fact born in Ayodhya—indeed, whether he was born at all—is debatable. Some historians bow to tradition in the matter, others dismiss it; archaeologists too are divided. More certainly, a mosque was built there in the sixteenth century during the reign of the Mughal emperor Babur. In the belief that this three-domed *Baburi masjid,* or Babri mosque, was erected on the very spot where a temple commemorating Lord Ram's birth had once stood, some devout Hindus had been laying sporadic claim to the site ever since.

In 1949 a recitation of the *Ramayana* outside the mosque had attracted large crowds. It also occasioned visible hostility toward the Muslim community plus a minor miracle: a tinseltown image of the baby Ram materialized inside the mosque. Though the state authorities and then Nehru himself ordered the removal of the image, their instructions were stymied by the courts. Instead the whole site was fenced off and its gate locked, in effect shutting down the mosque.[8] Muslim plans for its restoration were put on hold; so were Hindu plans for replacing it with a temple. The only concession to Hindu opinion was occasional admission, plus permission to construct a platform outside the fence from which Hindu worship of the Ram image could be performed, albeit at long range.

No one was happy with this arrangement. Muslim groups formed a committee for the defense of the mosque even as Hindu groups agitated for its demolition. In the *Ramayana* Lord Ram, a quintessential god-child, grows up to become the epitome of Hindu kingship; thus the idea of his "miraculous" image being imprisoned within a mosque was deeply offensive to devout opinion. Posters and wheeled floats depicting the young god behind bars also served as a powerful metaphor for the supposed plight of contemporary Hindus. The message was obvious: a pseudo-secular state intent on appeasing its Muslim minority was forcibly constraining its Hindu majority and depriving them of their rights.

Although "liberating" Ayodhya's Ramjanmabhoomi had earlier featured among the VHP's demands, as of 1985 it became the central plank. New processional cavalcades began converging on the city from different parts of the country, overseas Hindus were alerted to the need for funds and endorsement through conferences and the formation of local chapters, and a petition was filed with the district court for the (re-)opening of the site for Hindu worship.

When the petition was unexpectedly granted, it was assumed that this could only have been the result of prime ministerial intervention: "It was said that Rajiv Gandhi opened the locks on the advice of his colleague Arun Nehru, who thought the Congress now needed to compensate the [Hindu] chauvinists [for defeat in the Shah Bano affair]."[9] To Rajiv the gesture may have been one of even-handedness. But to the extended Sangh Parivar it was the green light: the VHP took it as vindication of its efforts to unite Hindus, the RSS saw it as evidence of its long-sought awakening of Hindu national pride, and the BJP scented a substantial electoral dividend. Additionally, although implementation of the order was again frustrated by the courts, all saw it as proof that no vote-conscious government cared to defy such a display of concerted action.

At this point, as if to fan the sparks of Hindu resurgence, in January 1987 all India plunged into a prolonged orgy of Rama-mania. Sunday after Sunday for eighteen months the nation immersed itself in the televisual screening of a spectacular seventy-eight-episode dramatization of the *Ramayana*. For an hour each week traffic fell silent and the streets emptied. The audience figures were among the highest ever recorded. Commissioned by the state network at enormous expense—and apparently without any prompting—it was certainly a triumph for television. Set ownership rocketed; the small screen had stolen a march on Bollywood and the channel responsible basked in unwonted applause. A ninety-one-episode version of the *Mahabharata,* the other great Hindu epic, was immediately commissioned and proved equally popular. For all of four years, two of which included national elections, Indians wallowed in the high-minded sentiments, low intrigues, and convoluted story lines of divine soap opera.

In some households the act of watching became one of worship. For the appointed hour, sets were garlanded, lamps lit, and incense burned. Family and friends gathered; refreshments might follow. With an estimated 91 percent of the nation's televisions tuning in, any load shedding of the power supply was out of the question. The gods took priority. Although there exist numerous different rescensions of the *Ramayana,* the one favored by the TV producers was naturally that richest in heroic endeavor and romantic entanglements. Lord Ram was promoted as preeminent among all India's deities, "co-extensive with all beliefs," and epitomizing everything that was noblest and most admirable in Hinduism.[10] Bolstered by the viewing figures, this television version won universal acceptance and was accorded near-canonical status. For once, Hindus of whatever sect sank their differences and subscribed to a single glamorized presentation of the epic. Moreover, in immersing themselves in it simultaneously, they experienced a new sense of congregation that was both compelling and quasi-national. Thanks to the TV schedulers, India's confessional majority emerged from each Sunday screening as charged and uplifted as churchgoers from a Sunday service.

How this devotional confidence would play out at the polling booths was uncertain. But already the elections due in 1989—five years after Rajiv had won a massive mandate in the aftermath of his mother's assassination—did not bode well for Congress. Naipaul's "million mutinies" were happening now. As noted, the accords brokered over Kashmir, Punjab, and Assam had unraveled; violence in all three states had revived, and in none could a Congress or Congress-friendly majority be confidently expected. Other insurgencies troubled the northeastern states in particular. The continued influx of immigrants and settlers from Bangladesh had sparked a reign of terror by nationalists in the state of Tripura and another by the indigenous Bodo people of Assam. Meanwhile, the Nagas' irredentist struggle was affecting not just Nagaland but neighboring states with a large Naga minority, such as Manipur. Even West Bengal only remained intact thanks to concessions to a Gorkha National Liberation Front demanding greater autonomy for Nepali settlers in the state's hill districts.

Elsewhere in the country the catastrophic harvests of 1985 and 1987 had reawakened the specter of famine. Five in every ten Indians still lived below what most indices considered the poverty line. Additionally, the government was mired in a scandal over the payment of bribes by the Swedish Bofors company in connection with a Defense Ministry arms purchase. Rajiv's reputation as Mr. Clean was as tarnished as his standing as a peacemaker.

The debacle in Sri Lanka looked like the final straw. Some now spoke of that island as "India's Vietnam." A thousand members of the Indian peacekeeping force had been killed there, yet a settlement was more remote than ever. In retrospect the situation looked like an early case of what Afghanistan watchers would call "blowback." New Delhi's attempt to relieve the Tamil Tigers of the arms and safe havens that it had once made freely available to them had backfired. Instead of bolstering the Sri Lankan Tamils' prospects of autonomy, the Indian troops found themselves targeted by the Tigers and so fighting Colombo's war against Tamil autonomy. This suited the Sri Lankan government, which could deploy its own forces against an uprising in the south of the island. But once that was taken care of, growing Sinhala resentment of the Indian presence was, if anything, gratified by the vicious Tamil attacks on the Indians. Unpopular with all Sri Lankans, whether Tamil-speaking or Sinhala-speaking, by 1989 the Indian peacekeeping force was in the early stages of an ignominious withdrawal.

For the most part these setbacks affected India's peripheral states. But it was in the populous core regions of north, central, and western India that elections were traditionally decided, and it was there that the Sangh Parivar was most active. In the run-up to the 1989 elections, the VHP organized a repeat of its *ekatmata yatra*, this time with the focus on Ayodhya. To build a massive new temple at what some were now calling the "Hindu Bethlehem," the faithful were urged to bake bricks. These were then consecrated in elaborate ceremonies before being taken on the road in mobile tableaux accompanied by armies of slogan-chanting followers. Violence often marked their progress. Muslim districts responded to the challenge of anti-Islamic taunts with brickbats; police roadblocks were attacked. In the communal riots that accompanied the *shilapujans* (brick ceremonies) for Ram, hundreds died and property was looted or burned from Rajasthan and Madhya Pradesh to UP and Bihar. The death toll in the Ganges town of Bhagalpur alone was officially put at 538 and unofficially at over 1,000.

The victims being disproportionately Muslims, newspapers in Bangladesh and Pakistan afforded generous coverage of the mayhem. In a rare show of unanimity, Pakistanis met every twist in the Ayodhya assault on Muslim sensibilities by taking to the streets to demand vengeance. Muslim Bangladeshis simply turned again on Hindu Bangladeshis. Thousands of the latter, who had somehow weathered the Partition of 1947, the anti-Hindu riots of the 1950s and 1960s, and the birth pangs of Bangladesh in the 1970s, finally gave up. They trailed across the unpoliceable border into Indian territory.

In October 1989 the VHP tested its strength by issuing a directive to Hindus worldwide. At precisely 1:35 P.M. on November 10, all were enjoined to put down their tools, face in the direction of Ayodhya, and make an offering of flowers. That was the moment at which, on a piece of disputed ground near the Babri mosque, the foundation-laying ceremonies for the new temple would be reaching their climax. "There the principal symbol was the heap of 167,093 *Ram Shilas* [Ram bricks] collected throughout India and in the Hindu diaspora, which had then been transported to Ayodhya."[11] Despite the vast crowds, prominent among whom were many of the BJP's electoral candidates, these ceremonies went off peacefully. The government made no attempt to interfere, for fear of a threatened backlash. Instead Rajiv Gandhi expressed satisfaction over their orderly conduct.

The elections that followed later the same month were arguably the most significant in India's history. Rajiv's Congress was humiliated.

It lost more than two hundred seats and could no longer claim a majority. In fact, for the first time ever, no single party had a majority. A new pattern was being set in which cross-party alliances would be crucial and coalition governments would become the norm. More obviously, the BJP had made its long-awaited breakthrough as a power broker. From just two seats in the previous Lok Sabha, its tally had shot up to eighty-six, mostly from constituencies that had witnessed Ayodhya-related activity. With BJP support and that of the Communist Party (Marxist), a government was formed. It was headed by Vishwanath Pratap Singh, Rajiv's former finance minister and an ex-rajah of doughty integrity. Based on a left-leaning coalition of anti-Congress interests, Singh's National Front government had much in common with the Janata government cobbled together under J. P. Narayan's banner in the aftermath of Indira Gandhi's Emergency.

Nor did the new National Front government fare any better or last any longer than its Janata predecessor. Within eighteen months it had lost the support of the BJP, lost the leadership of the respected V. P. Singh, and lost its parliamentary majority. Like his mother in 1981, Rajiv thus found himself making a swift return to the hustings at the head of a resurgent Congress. While campaigning for these second elections in two years, in May 1991 he went to Sriperumbudur in Tamil Nadu. There, as with his mother seven years earlier, Nemesis caught up with him. He too was assassinated, in this case blown to bits along with eighteen others by a lady who wore a belt of explosives beneath her sari.

Suicide bombings, although not unknown in the Middle East, had by now become the hallmark of the Tamil Tigers. Though conspiracy theorists would have a heyday, there seems no reason to doubt the findings of two subsequent inquiries that Rajiv's assassin and her accomplices were part of a well-planned LTTE plot. But while the LTTE's involvement seems certain, its motivation is less so. Possibly it was in revenge for Rajiv's role in sending the Indian peacekeeping force to Sri Lanka in the first place; possibly it was to preempt his recent threat to do the same again; and just possibly Indian Tamil militants were somehow complicit. Blowback is by its nature imprecise.

Come polling day, a sympathy vote, this time for Rajiv's widow, Sonia, and their children, again proved decisive. It helped return another Congress government, albeit after heavy losses in the northern states and in alliance with lesser parties to make up a majority. Sonia Gandhi, handicapped by her Italian birth, her poor Hindi, and her inexperience, declined the prime ministership. She did, though, lend her name and image to Congress publicity and would later be persuaded to take on the leadership of the party. Instead the prime ministerial office went to Narasimha Rao, a fragile-looking but experienced Congress minister with an unexpectedly open mind on the economy.

But the BJP had done well too, increasing its representation from 86 MPs to 120. An also-ran in 1984, in 1991 the political wing of the Sangh Parivar was now second only to Congress in the Lok Sabha and controlled several states, including the largest, UP. And again it had done so on the back of one of the Sangh Parivar's Ayodhya spectaculars.

Having gotten the bricks for the new temple, the VHP had still faced the problem of how to secure possession of the site. Various legal approaches were explored, but, when these failed, the idea of simply commandeering the site and then removing the mosque found much support. If allowed to go ahead, this would be a blatant sacrilege in Muslim eyes as well as the most flagrant betrayal imaginable of India's secular pretensions.

Undeterred, in 1990 the VHP had launched another *yatra*. The centerpiece this time was a *rath* (or temple chariot) like those familiar to viewers of the TV epics—and, like them, in fact a Toyota pickup suitably customized, bedecked in saffron, and adorned with Hindu symbols, including the lotus of the BJP. In its air-conditioned cab rode Lal Krishna Advani. A former member of the RSS and now the fiery-tongued and silver-mustachioed president of the BJP, Advani was feted by relays of party activists, some wearing monkey masks to identify them as followers of Lord Hanuman, the leader of Lord Ram's simian army in the *Ramayana*. Setting off from Somnath, a place on the Gujarat coast where a gleaming new temple had already replaced one destroyed by Muslims in the eleventh century, the cavalcade had for weeks wound its way east and south as far as Hyderabad. Then it headed north for Delhi and Ayodhya.

The *rath yatra* had a dual purpose, which was often summed up as "Mandal and *mandir*." On one hand, it was undertaken as a protest against Prime Minister V. P. Singh's adoption of the so-called Mandal report. This had been prepared ten years earlier at the request of the Janata government. Justice B. P. Mandal had been asked to look into the question of whether the affirmative action opportunities— principally reserved educational places and government jobs—that were already available to the lowest scheduled castes should be extended to castes equally disadvantaged but not quite so low in the pecking order. Mandal thought it should. In fact, since these other backward castes accounted for around half the total population he recommended even more reserved places for the backward castes than for the scheduled castes. But the report had found no favor with the subsequent Congress governments and had been shelved.

When resurrected by V. P. Singh in 1990, it met with the condemnation that Congress had feared. This came from the higher castes. Mindful of their own chances in a career market drastically reduced by the reservation of more than 50 percent of all educational and governmental places, the less well-off members of the upper castes protested vehemently. Some schools and colleges were forced to close, sixty protesters were killed in battles with the police, and hundreds of Brahmin youths set fire to themselves. Implementing a report aimed at redressing one example of social inequality simply stirred up another. Although supposedly anathema in independent India, caste was in effect being written into law. Moreover, intercaste competition would intensify as a result: decidedly unbackward castes would begin mobilizing to have themselves downgraded, so qualifying for backward-caste status and the opportunities it promised.

All of this posed a quandary for the BJP. The party was dominated by the higher castes; moreover, the Mandal recommendations were clearly divisive and therefore objectionable to anyone committed to uniting the "Hindu nation." Yet the BJP could hardly risk alienating the half of the nation that stood to gain if listed as backward castes. The trick in 1990 had therefore been to disguise the party's opposition to Mandal by a dramatic reassertion of its commitment to *mandir*. *Mandir* is the Hindi word for "temple," the *mandir* in question being of course that planned for Ayodhya. As the *rath yatra* sped north, Advani appealed for *karsevaks,* or volunteers, with the strength and dedication to tear down the Babri mosque and begin the erection of a Ram *mandir* worthy of what some now saw as the future "Hindu Vatican."

Accordingly, once arrived in Delhi, Advani had challenged V. P. Singh to put aside the contentious Mandal and concentrate on the glorious *mandir*. The suggestion had been declined, which was the signal for the BJP to withdraw its support for the Singh government. The 1991 midterm elections—those that proved so fatal to Rajiv—followed in May, and the hot potato that was Mandal thus passed to Narasimha Rao's Congress ministry. Since Congress had fared dismally in states such as UP, where the anti-Mandal agitation was most intense, Rao jumped at a chance to reestablish his party's fortunes by endorsing Mandal. With a few amendments, the report finally passed into law.

Meanwhile, the *rath yatra* had run into trouble. Entering UP in October 1990, it had been stopped by the state government, whose ruling party was part of the National Front coalition in Delhi and whose chief minister was himself a member of a backward caste. Advani was arrested along with thirty thousand supporters, whereupon "violence affected most of the country."[12] The nationwide demonstrations led to Hindu-Muslim riots as far away as Karnataka. Hundreds of deaths were reported, and, in UP, to keep Ayodhya volunteers at bay, whole trains were turned back at the state border. The final total of those detained within this one state was reported by the *Indian Express* to be around 150,000.

Some forty thousand *karsevaks* nevertheless reached Ayodhya, and of these a hard core forced their way through to the Babri mosque. The gates were broken open and the mosque was stormed, a saffron flag raised above it. Further damage was prevented by the police, whose tactics resulted in the deaths of dozens more. Like Mother Ganga's holy water and Lord Ram's bricks, the ashes of these "martyrs" were then trundled round the countryside for mass veneration. The new temple remained unbuilt and the old mosque still stood, but the VHP and its allies in the Sangh Parivar were far from cowed.

JUST OVER A YEAR LATER, at a dinner in New Delhi's embassy quarter early in 1993, the United Kingdom's high commissioner (i.e., ambassador) rose from his seat at the head of the table, requested silence with a ringing tap on a wineglass, and announced that he was about to break with diplomatic protocol. The situation was so "concerning," he said, that he was sure the assembled company of some twenty mainly Indian luminaries would understand. Starting on his left, then, he would ask each guest in turn to share his or her thoughts on the crisis. The speakers could be as candid as they liked. Their impromptu contributions were to follow the port decanter round the table.

No one demurred; no one even disputed that there was a crisis. Sadly, and with little in the way of after-dinner pleasantries, each held forth on what one described as "the greatest threat to the nation since independence." Memories of Partition were dredged up. Scenarios dire and less dire were painted. For once the perennial platitudes about "tolerant India," "unity in diversity," and "this non-violent nation" went unmentioned. Instead someone suggested that an India now so catastrophically divided might be described as tolerant only of a quite appalling level of violence. The usual reference to a foreign hand behind the recent troubles was also missing, and no one thought to reflect on how these troubles might appear to India's neighbors. As if faced with a purely personal tragedy, grief and shame made the usually ebullient company look inward.

Elsewhere in the subcontinent, the democrats—Benazir Bhutto in Islamabad, G. P. Koirala in Kathmandu, and Khaleda Zia in Dhaka— were currently in the ascendant. Moreover, for once no superpower was exercising undue pressure in the region. Washington's interest in South Asia had cooled following the Soviet withdrawal from Afghanistan, Moscow was no longer a global contender, and Beijing was busy trumpeting growth rates to drown out the memories of

Tiananmen Square. Why, then, was it New Delhi, with the proudest of democratic records and a natural preference for an unaligned South Asia, that found itself plunged into an existential crisis? No one around the table asked this. No one reflected on how Mandal and *mandir* had impeccably Indian pedigrees, and, though both demands enjoyed enormous popular support, no one suggested that democracy itself might in some way be to blame. Perhaps the pain of the moment was too great, the prognoses of what might follow too grim.

The televised news footage had been showing scenes that did indeed recall the Great Partition. In the space of a week (December 6–13, 1992) at least twelve hundred Indian citizens had been horribly slaughtered by their fellow countrymen. As many again were now dying in Hindu-Muslim battles in Mumbai and elsewhere. Tens of thousands had lost their homes; girls were being raped and babies butchered. Advani and the other leaders in the Sangh Parivar were not directly involved; they were in jail and the UP government had been dismissed. But it was all too little too late. As in 1947, the pogroms had acquired a momentum of their own. "Like the three domes that crowned the 464-year-old Babri mosque," ran an apocalyptic piece in *Time* magazine, "the three pillars of the Indian state—democracy, secularism and the rule of law—are now at risk from the fury of religious nationalism."[13] In short, Ayodhya had finally erupted. Though democracy and the rule of law would eventually prove robust enough, India's cherished reputation for religious neutrality lay strewn among the ruins of Babur's mosque.

The decisive factor had been the victory of the BJP in the 1991 state elections in UP. State governments had extensive powers within their own borders and could exercise considerable discretion in implementing directives from Delhi. With the new BJP government in UP committed to the Sangh Parivar's policies on promoting *hindutva* (Hinduness), the opportunity to press ahead with the Ayodhya temple had seemed too good to miss. On the other hand, state governments were also responsible for law and order and could be dismissed for not enforcing them. The BJP government in the state capital of Lucknow had therefore to tread carefully. Hotheads who saw Ayodhya as just the prelude to reclaiming sites in Mathura and Varanasi, both also in UP and both with mosques built on what may have been temple foundations, were brushed aside. In power, a government had to act responsibly. Even in the case of Ayodhya, legal sanction was desirable; failing that, any impromptu action must not be seen as directly attributable to the government.

This official ambivalence in Lucknow had partially reassured Narasimha Rao's government in New Delhi. But it antagonized gung-ho members of the Sangh Parivar and brought a challenge from the VHP. To revive the momentum of the *rath yatra,* the VHP had declared December 6, 1992, to be the astrologically ordained day for recommencing construction of the Ram *mandir.*

Once again thousands of volunteers immediately headed for Ayodhya. Far from being stopped, this time they were fed and welcomed by the state government. Advani set off to join them. He left Delhi, where he was now leader of the parliamentary opposition, with an ominous statement: "All I know is that we are going to perform *karseva.*"[14] Literally the term meant "work-service," but figuratively it is something more like "physical labor." As a precaution, the Rao government ordered out twenty thousand paramilitaries. But the number of *karsevaks* now in the vicinity of Ayodhya was put at over a hundred thousand. Some had brought along archaic tridents or bows and arrows, the accoutrements of the Hindu heroes on television; others had obtained access to pickaxes, sledgehammers, and crowbars.

If, as they claimed, the BJP leaders were unaware that the *karsevaks* intended to demolish the mosque, on the night of December 5 they appear to have been alerted. At a top-level meeting in Lucknow plans were concerted and objections overcome. From there Atal Bihari Vajpayee, the BJP's political supremo, headed straight for Delhi, while Advani drove through the night to Ayodhya. "Something wasn't as they had expected," noted Prashant Panjiar. A photographer working for *India Today,* Panjiar wondered whether Advani was in control of the situation. The BJP leader had even mistaken Panjiar for a member of his own press corps and now gave him a ride to Ayodhya.[15]

Next morning the Sangh's leaders, plus Panjiar, assembled on an illegally erected dais to watch the dedication ceremonies (*pujas*) for the new temple. Panjiar recalled that "Advani and Seshadri [of the RSS] looked nervous. The pujas began; so did the speeches. At around 11.30 some *karsevaks* started climbing the domes [of the mosque]. . . . Through the [camera] lens I could see men with iron rods. . . . There was laughter on the stage. Suddenly a larger group appeared on top of the dome and it looked like the beginnings of a serious attack."[16]

Advani now evinced—or possibly feigned—a look of horror. His companions ignored his protests and egged on the demolition squads. One by one the domes of the mosque crashed to the floor. "A cloud of dust rose to fill the air. The sight of [the last] dome, tilted in mid-air, about to fall, remains a striking image. There was complete jubilation on the stage. Soon I saw the city's horizon pierced with spirals of smoke. An *acharya* said into the mike, 'Look at these Muslims. They are burning their own homes to malign us.' The *karsewaks* went berserk. The killing began. The sky was all on fire."[17]

Muslims in Ayodhya, and then across India, vented their anger by attacking Hindus, but they were just as often attacked, and surely they never resorted to self-inflicted incendiarism. Meanwhile, the police stood by, and the state government signally failed to authorize the intervention of the waiting troops. In the weeks and months of communal killings, burnings, and bombings that followed, this pattern would be repeated, and, of the many thousands who died, often unspeakably, the majority were Muslims. Later, isolated Christian communities and missionaries would be picked off by elements of the Sangh Parivar, but it was against the 10 percent of all Indians who adhered to Islam that the Sangh directed its venom.

Nor was this venom easily contained or assuaged. In January 1993, at the height of the Ayodhya riots, Indian troops in Kashmir launched "the largest reprisal attack by the security forces" in the whole ongoing insurgency there. The town of Sopore was set alight by members of the Border Security Force, who then allegedly "prevented fire fighters from putting out the blaze."[18] Around fifty civilians, all Muslims, were burned to death in their homes. In the preceding years virtually all of Kashmir's Hindu community had fled the valley following targeted attacks of the utmost ferocity by the

Pakistan-backed Hizbul Mujahidin. The Sangh Parivar had rushed to condemn this "Islamic terrorism" and may in fact have encouraged the exodus for its own purposes. Kashmir's agony was being compounded by the Hindu-Muslim hostility generated by Ayodhya.

And so it went on. In 2001 thirty-eight people died when the state assembly building in Srinagar was attacked. In December of the same year the parliament building in New Delhi was stormed. The latter assault was as surprising as it was murky. Just the day before, the prime minister himself had warned that Parliament might be attacked. Yet a group of armed men dressed in military fatigues—there were either four, five, or six of them—were able to drive unchecked through the gates in a white car packed with explosives and attempt "what looked like an astonishingly incompetent terrorist strike."[19] Most of the explosives were never detonated, and the assailants all perished in a firefight with the police. The government blamed the usual suspects: the Pakistan-based Lashkar-e-Taiba and Jaish-e-Mohamed. But apart from a confession to that effect by Mohamed Afzal, a one-time terrorist who had turned counterintelligence informant, the evidence was circumstantial. Afzal's statement would later be rejected by the Supreme Court. His involvement in organizing the attack was not disputed, but it remained far from clear on whose behalf he acted and whether or not he had done so under compulsion. In 2013, when he was finally hanged after twelve years on death row, these questions remained unanswered.

A year after the 2001 attacks, flames tore through a railway carriage near Godhra in Gujarat. It was full of *karsevaks* returning to their home state after yet more dedication rituals for the still-unbuilt Ramjanmabhoomi temple. Fifty-eight died, all of them Hindus. Though the cause of the fire was uncertain, the blame for it readily attached to some Muslim platform vendors at Godhra station who had been reviled by the *karsevaks*.

In retaliation for this train burning, Hindu mobs ran riot throughout Gujarat. For days the two main cities of Ahmedabad and Vadodara (Baroda) witnessed scenes of unprecedently savage destruction and carnage. The death toll among Muslims reached over two thousand, and at least fifty times that many lost their homes.[20]

The police and even some ministers in the state government—it was another BJP government, led in this case by Narendra Modi, another former RSS commander—were accused of failing to protect the victims and even of colluding with the perpetrators. Modi was unmoved. He would never admit any responsibility or express any regret. Actions brought against the officials responsible got nowhere; Gujarat continued as a BJP stronghold.

Six years on, in a state room of the Taj Mahal Hotel in Bombay (Mumbai), one of several bandana-masked gunmen was asked by one of his hostages why he wanted to kill them. According to the filmed testimony of a survivor, "He replied, 'Have you not heard of Babri Masjid? Have you not heard of Vadodara?' Then he opened fire."[21] This 2008 commando-style attack on several of Bombay's landmarks claimed 164 lives and was watched live on television across the world. It followed a 2006 bombing of the city's suburban railway that claimed around two hundred lives. Both attacks were attributed to Lashkar-e-Taiba, one of several militant Islamic organizations based in Pakistan, all of them subject to frequent name changes and all with close links to Pakistan's Inter-Services Intelligence (ISI) agency. Islamic zealotry, however divisive within Pakistan itself, became Islamic solidarity when it straddled borders. Every Hindu assault on Muslims, whether in Kashmir, Assam, Ayodhya, or Mumbai, inflamed opinion in both Bangladesh and Pakistan and swelled the ranks of the *jihadist* Lashkars.

After the Ayodhya massacres of 1992–93, as after those in Gujarat in 2002, the need in India was for rehabilitation and trust-building initiatives. Some voluntary bodies rose to the challenge, but there was no official truth and reconciliation program. Many Indian Muslim communities continued to live in fear for their livelihoods and lives; many Hindus, when pressed, evinced either indifference to the Muslims' plight or a quiet sense of satisfaction. The baleful catalogue of transnational atrocities by militant Islamic terror groups in the Middle East, East Africa, Afghanistan, and the West merely reinforced such attitudes.

As for the Sangh Parivar, far from being disgraced by Ayodhya and its aftermath, its saffron star shone more brightly than ever. Four years later, in the general election of 1996, the BJP increased its tally of seats yet again. With 161 MPs to Congress's 140, it was now the largest party in the Lok Sabha and duly set about forming a national government. It proved a false start. Atal Bihari Vajpayee's first tenure as prime minister lasted just a fortnight, after which a Congress-backed coalition took over for the rest of 1996 and was followed by another in 1997. Still inching its way to power, in the elections called for 1998 the BJP hit back by taking 183 seats. It now formed a new ruling coalition, the National Democratic Alliance (NDA), which increased its tally further in 1999. The BJP would remain in power for the next five years.

"IT APPEARS," BEMOANED THE PRO-CONGRESS authors of *India After Independence,* published in 1999, "that the millennium will be ushered in by a government led by a party that for years seemed to be more interested in reviving and avenging the past than in heralding the future; . . . the indomitable Indian people deserve better."[22] Others put it more bluntly. One scholar drew parallels with Germany in the 1930s: the Sangh Parivar was orchestrating "a multiplicity of localized *Kristallnachts*" prior to a quasi-fascist takeover.[23] Another analyst foresaw an exodus of persecuted Muslims to Pakistan and of disaffected Hindus to the United States. The former never materialized, and the exodus of mainly Hindu Indians to the United States had more to do with career advancement than with dodging bigotry. Many headed for Silicon Valley, among them both supporters and opponents of the Sangh.

The fact was that in the late 1990s the BJP was the party that the "indomitable Indian people" did deserve. It best articulated the national mood and it therefore attracted the most votes. Rao's Congress government had turned the economy around, but it was the BJP's promise to make India a "great power" that resonated with the nation.

To this end, within a few weeks of assuming office, the government of the BJP-led National Democratic Alliance ordered a Richter-scale explosion in the Rajasthan desert. Known as Pokharan II

(Pokharan I being Indira Gandhi's "peaceful" nuclear test of 1974), it announced in unambiguous terms that India was now a member of the nuclear-armed fraternity. Three devices had been detonated; a temperature about that of the sun had been generated, and an area the size of a soccer field had been gouged out of the desert. Anti-proliferationists, headed by the United States and including most of the international community, were aghast. As one, they condemned the test in the strongest possible terms and imposed debilitating sanctions.

In India the response was equally unconstrained. Thousands celebrated in the streets. One paper called the test an "explosion of self-esteem," another a "moment of pride." Congress being the party responsible for the bomb's development, it too jumped aboard the bandwagon; so did most of the other opposition parties. The BJP government called for a program of national celebrations, and the VHP promised to build a new temple at the test site; by way of preparation, its followers were invited to scoop up handfuls of sand from the vicinity and have them blessed for nationwide distribution. Acquiring the ability to incinerate millions seemed to count as a greater national triumph than conquering Everest, winning a test match, or doubling the economy's growth rate.

In testing its bomb, India was giving notice not just to old enemies such as Pakistan and China but also to the United States. Without formally committing itself to the Comprehensive Test Ban Treaty, it now angled for recognition of its great-power status in the form of a permanent seat on the UN Security Council and, once the sanctions and the sniping had subsided, a closer relationship with the world's one remaining superpower. This looked to be a tall order, especially for a government headed by sectarian chauvinists with neo-Nazi supporters. Yet it turned out quite otherwise. Circumstances would play into India's hands, and the BJP, once in power, would prove a lot more pragmatic and conciliatory than either its critics or its supporters had expected.

Within a matter of weeks, the chances of India reaping a reward for flouting international conventions became somewhat less improbable. In May 1998 Pakistan responded to Pokharan II by test-firing its own nuclear deterrent in the Balochistan desert. India consoled itself by claiming that this "Islamic bomb" vindicated the apprehensions that had prompted its own test; Pakistan, amid more delirious celebrations, claimed that the threat of the "Hindu bomb" had been neutralized and a parity of sorts restored. Intense US pressure, sweetened in this case with offers of conventional weaponry, debt write-offs, and new borrowing, had failed to dissuade Nawaz Sharif's administration from going ahead with the test. Washington, though mortified, was not surprised. Once India had publicly gone nuclear, it was a certainty that Pakistan would follow suit.[24]

More worrying were the circumstances surrounding the Pakistani tests. (Both countries had immediately followed their first tests with a second.) Unlike the Rajasthan tests, those in Balochistan had supposedly been prompted by reports of an imminent attack. A strike force of Indian and Israeli aircraft was said to be preparing to enter Pakistan airspace, its mission being a preemptive bombing of A. Q. Khan's nuclear research facility at Kahuta and of the Balochistan test site. This story was almost certainly a fabrication; the Israelis had been implicated simply because they had once dealt in similar fashion with a nuclear facility in Baghdad. But it raised the question of who had concocted the story and why. A likely answer was that Pakistan's ISI had dreamed it up in order to persuade Nawaz Sharif and reluctant elements in the military of the necessity of an immediate response. But if the bomb could be tested on such spurious grounds, many outside Pakistan worried that it might be delivered on spurious grounds. They wondered who precisely was in control of "Bhutto's bomb" in what they were now calling a "military democracy," and what safeguards were in place to protect it from dissident attack or unauthorized use.

Concerns about an incidental armageddon were matched by those about an accidental armageddon. In early December 1984, soon after Indira Gandhi's assassination, a greater tragedy than the subsequent Sikh massacres in Delhi had struck the Madhya Pradesh capital, Bhopal. Following an escape of highly toxic gas from Union Carbide's ill-maintained and possibly sabotaged pesticide plant, the city of Bhopal had awoken to scenes of human devastation not witnessed since

Hiroshima and Nagasaki. Eight thousand either lay dead or would die within the first seventy-two hours. As many as another twelve thousand would later succumb to the effects of contamination. Subsequent generations would see miscarriages, abnormal births, and deformed babies. It was—and still is—the worst industrial accident ever recorded.[25] Thirty years later, responsibility for the leakage was still being disputed and the survivors were still seeking justice.

Pakistan suffered something similar in April 1988. At a place called Ojhri, an underground arsenal in which US ordnance was being stored prior to shipment to Afghanistan exploded. As the bombs blew up, the missiles rained down, and the fires raged out of control, residents in the nearby cities of Islamabad and Rawalpindi supposed they were under attack, presumably by India. Hundreds were killed, thousands wounded. Like General Zia ul-Haq's death in an air crash four months later, it could have been an accident or it could have been sabotage. Either way, Bhopal and then Ojhri had raised serious questions about the competence of South Asian governments in ensuring the security, supervision, and regulation of volatile technologies, whether conventional or nuclear.

With such concerns in mind, US condemnation of the Indian and Pakistani tests soon gave way to engagement. The priority was to get the nuclear newcomers to sign President Clinton's Comprehensive Test Ban Treaty and submit to its regime of self-denial, international monitoring, and regional peace building. Neither New Delhi nor Islamabad was enthusiastic. Both played for time and demanded the prior lifting of sanctions. In the case of New Delhi, crucial support came from the diaspora in the United States. In the previous twenty years the number of Indians resident in North America had soared to over 1.2 million. Most were highly educated, and many "had formed professional associations and political organizations that wielded impressive clout." During the 1990s the Indian community's financial contributions to US congressional candidates had doubled to the point where "more than a quarter of the entire House of Representatives" belonged to a pro-India caucus.[26] Thanks in large part to this constituency, in the end it was the US Congress that failed to approve Clinton's test ban treaty, so letting India off the hook.

Perhaps a greater surprise was the willingness of the BJP-led government to accommodate American concerns. Instead of pitching India into another military confrontation with its neighbor, as was generally feared, Prime Minister Vajpayee responded to US promptings for a normalization of Indo-Pak relations with a veritable charm offensive. Specifically, he made the first symbolic overture in over a decade to mend—or in this case, open—fences with Pakistan.

The gesture took the form of a bus ride. Following amicable encounters with Nawaz Sharif in Colombo and New York, in February 1999 Vajpayee boarded the inaugural run of a cross-border bus service, the first in the living memory of most South Asians. In Lahore, Sharif was on hand to greet and host the visit. It included an improbable excursion to the Eiffel-esque Pakistan Tower. There, at the spot on which Jinnah had first voiced the demand for a Muslim homeland, respects were paid by the champion of a Hindu homeland. Fifty years after Partition, an Indian prime minister was endorsing the "two-nation" theory. Memoranda were signed about closer consultation over nuclear security, communications, and other confidence-building matters. And both leaders pledged to increase their efforts to resolve outstanding differences, "including the issue of Jammu and Kashmir." Optimists might reasonably have concluded that where all else had failed, the bomb was succeeding.

The euphoria lasted barely two months. In early May 1999 reports reached New Delhi from Kashmir of an infiltration from the Pakistan side of the line of control. Numerous Indian positions in the mountains overlooking Kargil, which had been vacated for the Himalayan winter, had been captured. A pit-stop town of diesel spillages and tire vulcanizing, Kargil straddled the vital Srinagar-Leh highway to Ladakh. The highway itself was coming under attack; the "Kargil war" had begun.

Pakistan claimed that the infiltrators were Kashmiri freedom fighters, though it later conceded that regular troops and artillery were also involved. To dislodge them, India sent in the air force and ordered up reinforcements. As per Bhutto's war of 1965, an Indian diversionary advance looked likely, either elsewhere across the line of control or across the Indo-Pak frontier in the Punjab. In preparation for just such a development Pakistan was reported to be deploying missiles with nuclear warheads. By June, an obscure cross-border incursion was being portrayed as the greatest current threat to world peace.

Yet by mid-July the crisis was over. Indian forces had retaken their lost eyries. Meanwhile, Washington, in no doubt as to Pakistani responsibility, had been pressing Sharif to withdraw and Vajpayee to withstand demands for escalation. Each leader also faced domestic criticism. There had been failures of intelligence on both sides and around a thousand lives had been lost with little to show for them. Benazir Bhutto called the whole affair "the worst blunder in Pakistan's history." For Vajpayee there was at least the consolation of having restored the status quo. Less plausibly, Sharif claimed ignorance. When the pretense that the infiltrators were Kashmiri dissidents fell through, he accused his new chief of staff, Pervez Musharraf, of authorizing the infiltration without consulting him. Musharraf denied this, and it was this blame game that led to Sharif's ham-handed attempt to replace his chief of staff, followed by the retaliatory military coup that brought Musharraf to power for the next eight years (1999–2007).

Another military, and possibly nuclear, confrontation loomed following the 2001 attack on the Indian Parliament. Occurring within weeks of America's 9/11, it brought an Indian endorsement of the "war on terror," calls for instant retaliation, and a massive buildup of troops along the line of control and the Indo-Pak frontier. US analysts likened the danger of an international conflagration to that over Cuba in 1962. In Nepal, a country that was itself reeling from the mass assassination of its royal family, all South Asia was described as "poised on the cusp of the war."[27]

Happily, the BJP-led government in Delhi did nothing rash. State elections due in Kashmir in 2002 went ahead as planned and saw a gratifying turnout. There the tit-for-tat of outrage and retaliation continued, as did governmental threats and counterthreats. But the security forces in Kashmir showed a little more restraint and tourists trickled back to the valley. Over in Pakistan, Musharraf, now president, responded to international pressure: Lashkar-e-Taiba and Jaish-e-Mohamed were banned (albeit temporarily), and Pakistani backing for Islamist fighters in Kashmir was curtailed. When in 2003 Musharraf survived a couple of assassination attempts, he was reportedly "appalled to discover that some of those responsible belonged to Pakistan-based Kashmiri militant organizations."[28] The Kashmiris themselves also seemed to have had enough of the Islamist militants. Twelve years of brutal strife had brought a solution no nearer, and the attractions of joining Pakistan had waned. A glance at the economic indicators left no doubt that Kashmir was potentially far better off under India than under Pakistan.

With these considerations in mind, dialogue between Islamabad and New Delhi resumed. The cross-border bus and train links were reinstated. Indeed, in 2005 another was added—a carefully monitored bus shuttle across the line of control between Srinagar in Indian Kashmir and Muzaffarabad in Azad Kashmir. Trade links, an important consideration for both governments, followed. At the Wagah checkpoint on the Punjab border, queues of carriers from Haryana emblazoned with the slogan "Jai Hind" jousted with garishly painted hauliers from the mecca of truck art in Peshawar. By 2006 this bilateral trade was valued at $1 billion a year.

Meanwhile, Musharraf had announced a unilateral cease-fire along the line of control, which Vajpayee had reciprocated. In 2004 the two leaders met once again in Islamabad. An agreement on further confidence-building measures was signed, and though Vajpayee's National Democratic Alliance was promptly defeated at the polls, its successor, a Congress-led United Progressive Alliance led by Manmohan Singh, continued the so-called composite dialogue. Musharraf now seemed willing to go the distance in seeking a Kashmir solution. Kashmiri training camps in Pakistan were being turned into resettlement camps; instead of being armed and funded to fight, the militants received cash payments not to fight. "They got $800 for stopping their fight and another $800 for settling into civilian life by getting married."[29]

A long-term settlement of the Kashmir dispute was still far in the future. But by 2007 Musharraf was airing the possibility that Pakistan might abandon its preference for UN involvement along with its concomitant insistence on a plebiscite. Instead, a bilateral program of demilitarization, abolition of the line of control, joint administration in some areas, and greater autonomy overall was discussed. This looked promising. Reconciling public opinion to it, however, did not. The UPA government in Delhi seemed to get cold feet, and in 2008 Musharraf himself was forced into exile following elections marred by the assassination of Benazir Bhutto. In Pakistan, no government, least of all a PPP one led by Benazir's husband, could afford to be seen abandoning a sixty-year claim to a state without which, in Zulfikar Ali Bhutto's words, Pakistan remained "headless."

Even if Benazir, and then her husband, Asif Ali Zardari, personally favored pursuing the negotiations, neither could count on the support of the military or the ISI, let alone the Islamists, any or all of whom would construe such a move as justifying extraconstitutional intervention. In Pakistan, as in India, movement on Kashmir remained hostage to the dictates of electocratic politics and the irredentism of the bureaucratic-military establishments.

As well as some progress on Kashmir, in 2003 Vajpayee made a weeklong visit to China. It was the first by an Indian prime minister in a decade. Contentious issues, such as the still disputed boundaries in Ladakh and the northeast, were left open, but bilateral trade was promoted and Indian recognition of Chinese sovereignty in Tibet was reaffirmed in return for de facto Chinese recognition of Indian sovereignty in Sikkim. The veneer of accord between the world's two most populous nations was reassuring.

Domestically too, the BJP-led government picked its way with caution. To scholarly disapproval, India's schoolroom histories were radically rewritten to reflect Hindu nationalist contentions. On the other hand, the Sangh Parivar's temple-building expectations at Ayodhya and elsewhere were judged too provocative to be championed. Besides triggering further communal unrest, they would alienate the BJP's partners in government, many of whom had local caste or ethnic affiliations that conflicted with the Sangh's prioritizing of an all-embracing Hinduness. The moderating influence exercised by these lesser parties and their so-called identity agendas would prove as inimical to ideological rigidity as to dictatorial leadership. Coalition politics in India, far from ushering in an era of instability, could be seen as evidence of a new maturity.

This did not make for electoral certainty, however. With no party likely to command an overall majority, and, in the absence of an incumbent scion of the Nehru-Gandhi dynasty, the composition of upcoming governments could be hard to predict. The Congress-led UPA government, which won India's 2004 elections and then repeated the feat in 2009, was a case in point. A victory for the BJP had been confidently predicted in 2004. Instead Congress surprised itself and was able to form a ruling coalition with help from caste-based parties in UP and Bihar and leftist parties elsewhere. No less surprising, the new government was for the first time headed by a technocrat. Sonia Gandhi, Rajiv's Italian-born widow, had again declined the post, only to award it to someone who was almost as much an outsider as she.

Though already in his seventies, Dr. Manmohan Singh was seen as a political neophyte. He had been plucked from the upper house of the Indian parliament and had never contested an election; indeed, after a distinguished career as an academic and bureaucrat, he had entered the political fray when his contemporaries were retiring. He had no obvious base of support within the party and little experience of the horse-trading necessary to acquire one. He was also a Sikh, a stranger to charisma, soft-spoken, self-effacing, and apparently incorruptible. Indian politics had rarely seen his like.

His one claim to fame and preferment rested on a stint as finance minister in the Narasimha Rao government of the early 1990s. When invited to join that ministry, he had been as surprised as anyone. "I didn't take it seriously," he told the BBC's Mark Tully. Rao, however, had persisted, and Singh had eventually obliged. He donned a high-collared suit, wrapped on his turban, and "that's how I got started in politics."[30]

The summer of 1991 had not been a good moment to be taking charge of the nation's finances. Iraq's invasion of Kuwait had again inflated the price of oil, leaving India's national debt at an unprecedented $70 billion. The fiscal deficit stood at 8 percent of GDP and revenue from direct taxes contributed only a pitiful 19 percent. Foreign currency reserves had dwindled till they sufficed for just two weeks' imports. A loan from the International Monetary Fund was unavoidable, and, to obtain it, part of the nation's gold reserves would have to be pledged as collateral.

None of this was popular. The crisis might well have brought down the government before it had even started. But Narasimha Rao admired Singh's writings on the drawbacks of statist regulation and shared his faith in the power of the markets. Where Thatcher, Reagan, and the "tiger economies" of Southeast and East Asia had led, India would follow. Four decades of centralized economic management would be reversed in twenty-four months. It had been a case of back to square one for the Indian economy, then forward into the global unknown.

The rupee had promptly been devalued by 20 percent, encouraging exports and negating the need for export subsidies. Import quotas and licenses were likewise eased, customs duties reduced, and foreign direct investment welcomed. Instead of erecting a protectionist wall designed to support indigenous production and repel the hostile forces of capitalist imperialism, India's doors had suddenly opened for business. Internally, the permit raj and the state purchasing agencies were steadily dismantled. Markets in almost everything from cars to cough mixture were thrown open to all. Privately owned industries could expand without restriction, while state-owned industries, though not privatized, had their spending curbed. Competition in the service and construction industries followed, with easier entry into banking, insurance, aviation, road building, and telecommunications.

Tax rates came down in expectation of overall receipts rising, which they did. Within two years the fiscal deficit had fallen substantially and the foreign exchange reserve had risen dramatically, to $20 billion from $1 billion in 1991.[31] Inflation had halved, foreign investment was doubling every year, and the economy began growing by 6–8 percent. Rao's gamble and Singh's arithmetic had paid off. Indians would toast the new millennium as the new "billennium." In 2000 the country's population passed the billion mark just as the number of rupee billionaires passed the hundred mark. With occasional setbacks and a lot of grousing over the protection extended to still-reserved sectors of the economy, the growth continued. It peaked in 2010 at around 10 percent, by which point the billionaires numbered in their thousands.

Manmohan Singh deserved much of the credit for all this and would eventually receive it. But in the early 1990s his bombshell had barely registered outside financial circles. Even there it encountered opposition. A group of major industrialists formed a "Bombay Club" to plead for caution in exposing them to global competition. "Thankfully the government of the day did not respond to all that high-powered and slightly hysterical lobbying."[32]

The reforms had not been entirely new either. In the 1980s, while refusing to open domestic markets to competition, let alone to foreign competition, both Indira Gandhi and Rajiv Gandhi had made it slightly easier for existing businesses to expand. Dhirubhai Ambani, founder of Reliance Industries, had progressed from trading in synthetic fabrics to producing the polymers for them in the 1980s. Come the 1990s, Reliance turned to petrochemicals and by 2010 was one of the largest conglomerates in India, with more than 2.5 million satisfied shareholders. Other companies were less successful. Vayudoot, the first low-cost domestic airline, had taken to the skies in 1981. It was to serve routes that its state-owned parent companies regarded as hazardous or commercially unattractive. So they proved; Vayudoot had lost both money and friends before civil aviation was deregulated and a host of brightly colored competitors made off with its passengers.

Rajiv had overseen other changes. The success of domestically produced pharmaceuticals had been acknowledged and encouraged in the 1980s. Also in that decade, every roadside village had acquired, among the mud huts and the haystacks, a bright yellow booth advertising various telephone and fax services. Thanks to new switching gear, fiber-optic cables, metered handsets, and a pioneering entrepreneur called Sam Pitroda, India was suddenly swamped with telephones that actually worked. But Rajiv's greatest contribution had probably been his advocacy of digital technology. From 135 percent, import duties on computer hardware had been reduced to 60 percent. Then in 1987 a Texas Instruments experiment in outsourcing chip design to Bangalore had led to the first direct satellite link with the United States. This "changed the rules of the game."[33] Instead of migrating to Silicon Valley, computer-savvy Indians found opportunities at home. Companies such as Infosys thrived as much because of the revolution in globalized IT as because of the 1990s' economic liberalization. Started with just $600 in 1981, by early 2000 Infosys was worth $15 billion.[34]

Yet, overshadowed by Ayodhya and its aftermath, the reforms introduced by Narasimha Rao and finance minister Manmohan Singh in the early 1990s had not proved sufficiently popular to ensure re-election. Defeated in 1996, Rao's government had made way for the BJP-led National Democratic Alliance in 1998. Prime Minister Atal Bihari Vajpayee had then conducted Pokharan II and made his bid for great-power status. To the confidence and excitement generated by the bomb was added that of the takeoff in the economy. Sacrificing such tangible gains for confessional extravaganzas was not in the interests of the BJP and its business supporters. The *mandir* would have to wait and the Ram bricks take their chance in the Indian climate. The BJP and its National Democratic Alliance stuck with liberalization.

In fact, it was Vajpayee who highlighted the crying need for better infrastructure if Indian production was to compete internationally. Specifically, he focused on the atrocious state of India's road network by, in 1999, launching construction of a thirty-seven-hundred-mile "Golden Quadrilateral." A multilane highway, the Quadrilateral linked Delhi, Calcutta (Kolkata), Madras (Chennai), and Bombay (Mumbai), plus numerous cities in between (such as Bangalore and Pune). Completed on time and under budget in 2012–13, the network was a revelation. Freight logjams were eased and Indians explored the culture, if not the driving conventions, of life in the fast lane. No one wanted to be reminded that the $12 billion over eight years spent on the Quadrilateral was in China being spent on new roads every year.

Returning to power in 2004, the Congress-led United Progressive Alliance under Manmohan Singh progressed less certainly. Growth remained buoyant but telecom scandals revealed the seedier side of private enterprise, while sectors such as retailing and finance were still subject to some protection. Walmart and Ikea, for instance, were kept waiting while the government endeavored to convince its coalition partners that votes lost by endangering the livelihoods of shopkeeping supporters could be replaced by those of the grateful shelf stackers signed up by the multinationals.

The debate, as so often, was conducted in the context of the growing and largely urban middle classes. It was of no relevance to the rural poor, who still made up the majority of the population. Their share of every scheme designed to improve their lot was probably no better than the 15 percent allowed by Rajiv Gandhi's estimate that 85 percent of all development funds was pocketed by corrupt officials.

The Unique Identification Scheme launched by Manmohan Singh in 2009 is designed to eliminate this "wastage." Every one of India's 1.2 billion citizens is being issued a biometric ID card to ensure that any benefits to which he or she is entitled actually reaches that person. The scheme, though fraught with teething problems, is not beyond the number-crunching capacity of an IT-confident people accustomed to conducting the world's largest electoral count. And by reducing administrative costs and distributive wastage, it could make existing programs for poverty alleviation much more cost-effective.

One such program guarantees to every person of working age a hundred days paid employment per year; another provides heavily subsidized foodstuffs to the poorest. A new version of the latter is intended to benefit over two-thirds of the entire population. Rolled out in 2013, it is not without its critics. Some see the cheap food as a vote-catching ploy ahead of the 2014 elections; others think its cost of Rs 1.3 trillion (about $26 billion) an extravagance that India's no longer buoyant economy can ill afford. All, however, anticipate a bonanza for the wholesalers and retailers who, in time-honored fashion, will sell top-quality subsidized cereals on the open market while so adulterating the substandard remainder as to make much of it inedible. But if the ID cards help in tracking this munificence through the dealers and the "fair price" shops to the shopping bags of the eight hundred million entitled to it, a mighty obstacle to all schemes of relief and betterment will have been overcome. Armed with their unique ID cards, the next generation of Midnight's Descendants should be in line for all the maternity, health, educational, and training opportunities on offer. Such leveling up might have reconciled even Pandit Nehru to the rampant consumerism of "shining India."

Better still, the ID scheme strikes at that most basic of contradictions identified by the constitution-drafting Ambedkar and the political scientist Sunil Khilnani: that the Indian constitution and the bloc voting it encourages reinforces community solidarity to the detriment of individual rights and a sense of shared citizenship based on them.

On the face of it, community identities seem more entrenched than ever. In 2012 Ms. Mayawati, a fifty-six-year-old Dalit teacher who had become leader of the Bahujan Samaj Party (BSP), completed five years in office as chief minister of the largest state in India. *Bahujan* being another euphemism for Dalit, the BSP relies entirely on Uttar Pradesh's Dalit vote. Mayawati repays this loyalty by combining a relentless promotion of Dalit identity with dazzling displays of personal wealth and a passion for Dalit-related statuary and public spectacles. The effect is to promote individual empowerment as much as community betterment. According to her biographer, Mayawati is revered above all as "a woman belonging to the most crushed community known to mankind [who] has risen through the heat and dust of elections to rule two hundred million people."[35] The message is obvious: Even for a Dalit, anything is possible in today's India. The public celebrity of the few—in politics as in sport, business, or the movies—nurtures personal aspirations among the many. By enshrining the entitlement rights of each and every citizen regardless of age, gender, family, or community, the ID card should confirm this growing sense of individual identity.

As a result, the pattern of Indian politics could get even more fragmented and parochial. That may not be a bad thing. The pattern of politics over the last six decades has not endeared itself to everyone. Many in India now argue that domestic instability could best be contained by constitutional reform at the top, and many outside India argue that regional stability could usefully be promoted by some genuine engagement among all the states of South Asia. New, even hopeful, perspectives are opening.

EPILOGUE

I N June 2013 the *Katmandu Post* carried a report about Nepal's Ministry of Foreign Affairs placing an order for assorted vehicles: "twenty-one Mercedes including eight super-luxury bullet-proof ones, . . . eight medium luxurious cars, ten small cars and seven vans." What made the matter newsworthy was not the purchase but its purpose, for according to the paper, such an order could only mean that the country's interim government had "seriously started preparing" for the Eighteenth Summit Conference of the South Asian Association for Regional Co-Operation (SAARC). Already much postponed by Nepal's delayed elections and constitutional uncertainties, the conference would "likely be held" in February 2014, that month's "pleasant weather" being an important consideration, said the paper. A venue for the heads of state to meet had already been chosen, and plans would soon be unveiled for "a trade fair, a junket for spouses of VVIPs and VIPs, and SAARC-related exhibitions and promotions." The total cost was put at 750 million rupees, a third of which would be needed to buy the cars.[1]

So far so good. By the time this book is published, the twenty-one Mercedes should be gliding around Kathmandu's much-contested thoroughfares. Nepal's delayed elections should have been held, a new constitution should be in the offing, and the Eighteenth SAARC Summit Conference should be getting underway. Alternatively none of these things will have come to pass, in which case the least regretted is likely to be the SAARC Summit.

Regional cooperation has a rather depressing record in South Asia. In a subcontinent with so much in the way of shared culture, common history, mutual traditions of exchange, and matching experience of poverty and displacement, the logic of collaboration has long been recognized. SAARC was officially set up on the initiative of President Ziaur Rahman of Bangladesh in 1985. As well as recognizing the potential for developmental cooperation, Zia saw the organization as a way of offsetting the influential role accorded to India by his predecessor Mujibur Rahman. Pakistan, Sri Lanka, and Nepal sympathized, and so, for similar reasons, did Bhutan and the Maldives. Not without misgivings, India also went along with the idea, and thus came into being the seven-member SAARC (later increased to eight members with the admission of Afghanistan, hence the eight bulletproof limousines).

The association was—and nearly thirty years later, still is— sometimes hailed as a potential counterpart of ASEAN or even the European Union. Joint initiatives on everything from tourism and counterterrorism to tuberculosis prevention and visa exemption have been explored. Scrupulously fair in distributing its favors, SAARC has awarded its chamber of commerce to Islamabad, its cultural center to Colombo, its meteorological center to Dhaka, and its disaster management center to Delhi. The secretariat is in Kathmandu. Film and literary festivals are held and various awards are doled out. Under SAARC's auspices a South Asian Free Trade Area (SAFTA) was launched in 2006 and a South Asian University in 2010. Although the association has no political role, informal contact among SAARC members is credited with providing a channel for feelers over contentious issues such as Kashmir; similarly, summits help break the ice between hostile heads of state. On the face of it, SAARC is doing more to heal the divisions created by Partition and half a century of mutual suspicion than any other organization.

Yet much of this is often written off as the window dressing to be expected of a debating club. Mutual distrust along with instability in one or more of the member states cripples almost every initiative.

Laudable in its intent, the visa exemption scheme applies to such a privileged few and is so bureaucratically encumbered that the vast majority of cross-border travel remains of the illegal variety. Likewise, SAFTA, once seen as the preliminary to a South Asian customs union and a single common currency, has become bogged down in tariff reduction targets and interminable lists of the items to be excluded from them. The festivals are often a farce and the summits notoriously unproductive. SAARC remains a good idea whose moment is still to come.

The second decade of the twenty-first century could prove to be just such a moment. At last the guns have mostly fallen silent and accountable government prevails. As of 2006 Kathmandu ceased to be engaged in war with the Maoists, and as of 2009 Colombo could claim to have defeated the Tamil Tigers. The fallout from these conflicts continues. Nepal awaits a settlement that will permit elections and the formation of a government, and the Sri Lankan regime of President Mahinda Rajapakse and his family has yet to deal convincingly with accusations of war crimes, let alone the roots of Tamil alienation. Nevertheless, normality of a sort has been restored. The integrity of Nepal and Sri Lanka are no longer under threat. Tourism and inward investment, much of it from China, are picking up in both countries. Relations with India are generally good.

So too is the outlook for democracy in the region. Barring postponements, Pakistan, Bangladesh, the Maldives, India, Nepal, and even Afghanistan will all have newly elected governments by the end of 2014. Meanwhile, the only coup of recent date, that in the Maldives in 2012, is said not to have been a coup at all. Given a choice between protest and progress, South Asians seem increasingly inclined to put their own interests ahead of those of the communal hotheads. In cities heaving under the weight of ten to twenty million people, more take the metro to the local mall than take to the streets with sticks. Bombings—dare one say it?—are rarer; they may have peaked even in Pakistan. Outside Pakistan the same holds true for communal massacres. Shootouts along the line of control in Kashmir, which might once have threatened all-out war, are now played down by both Delhi and Islamabad as the work of extremist elements keen to derail any Indo-Pak rapprochement. By mutual agreement the gladiatorial choreography of the daily flag-lowering ceremony at the Wagah border crossing on the Indo-Pak frontier has been toned down; the partisan crowds bused in by both sides to abet the nonsense no longer rate the spectacle worth the journey. In the east, a train a day links Calcutta and Dhaka, as do several bus services and airlines. Visitors are at last being freely admitted to India's northeastern states, and newsrooms are no longer taxed by that area's proliferation of National or United Liberation Fronts. Everywhere cross-border trade has increased dramatically, although still only a fraction of its potential.

It all amounts to what could be the most significant lull yet in the fraught affairs of Midnight's Descendants. After a decade and a half of nation building, followed by similar periods of populist posturing, assertive confessionalism, and then frantic globalization, the region has a chance to draw breath and take stock. For SAARC, the Eighteenth Summit could be a turning point. With US and NATO forces poised to withdraw from Afghanistan, superpower involvement in South Asia's constituent states has reached a low ebb and the region has an unusually free hand in determining its future. The worldwide recession may actually have helped. A relapse in India's growth rate from around 10 percent in 2010 to around 5 percent in 2013 has had a sobering effect. The "miracle" of the previous decade may, it is said, have been just a "spurt," a "bubble," even. Bullish projections about India as an emerging rival to China have been revised, and the disparity between Delhi's economic performance and that of its immediate neighbors looks less unbridgeable. As salaries rise in Bangalore and Gurgaon, outsourcing by international companies is increasingly benefiting Dhaka and Colombo. Incredibly, in 2013 Mumbai's stock exchange was being outperformed by Karachi's. Inflation in India remained in double digits and the value of its rupee had slipped by 27 percent in as many months. Another spike in oil prices, plus South Asians' traditional recourse in uncertain times of buying gold, was creating havoc with the balance of trade. Meanwhile, inward foreign investment was declining as outward Indian investment to low-tax destinations such as Dubai, Singapore, and Mauritius was increasing.

Global collaboration at the corporate level, having long sidelined re-gional cooperation at the governmental level, could yet give SAARC a new relevance.

BREATHING LIFE INTO THE BODIES POLITIC may be more problem-atic. The shortcomings of Westminster-style democracy as practiced in South Asia have long been conceded, yet incumbent governments, having successfully mastered its dark arts, are not keen to change it. Given constituencies containing up to a quarter of a million voters, many of them illiterate and readily swayed by modest inducements, the trade in bloc votes is probably inevitable. Likewise, personal at-tributes such as caste, wealth, and popular image will continue to count for more in the choice of candidates than policies, principles, or even party allegiance. The caliber of those elected suffers as a result. Many assembly members aspire merely to retain their seats while angling for lucrative governmental posts that they often are un-qualified to hold. Government MPs see their primary task as provid-ing loyal lobby fodder; "opposition members feel that the best way to show the strength of their feelings is to disrupt the law-making rather than debate the law."[2] In this endeavor fists may fly as freely as insults and missiles. On one occasion a vituperative but stickless Raj Narain—he who dogged Indira Gandhi's first decade in power—had to be lifted bodily and borne shouting from the chamber.

Legislative business suffers accordingly. In its 2010–11 session, the Indian Lok Sabha was so often adjourned, usually as a result of unparliamentary behavior, that it sat for little over half its allotted hours; two-thirds of bills pending at the beginning of the year were still pending at the end of the year. The legislatures of Bangladesh and Nepal have an even worse record; boycotts and suspensions are there the norm, with sittings being the exception. In a three-year period in the early 1990s, Bangladesh's opposition parties walked out of parliament or boycotted sessions on a total of fifty-seven oc-casions.[3] When an Assembly is actually sitting, procedural wrangles often edge out constructive debate, which may be as poorly attended as it is infrequent. Little wonder, then, that governments throughout the region, however ostensibly "democratic," often feel obliged to bypass parliament and legislate by presidential ordinance.

In India it has been suggested that a solution to this state of affairs may lie in the adoption of a formally presidential constitution. Naturally the preferred models are said to be those of France or the United States rather than Sri Lanka or Pakistan. Under such a dispensation, parliament's democratic credentials as a directly elected assembly would not be affected. They would simply be counterbalanced by a directly elected president whose equally democratic credentials would be rewarded with supreme executive power plus the option of choosing his ministers from outside parliament. Thus law making and policy making would be disentangled, the legislature and the executive separated. Presidents accountable to the nation rather than to parliament would enjoy guaranteed terms of office during which they should be able to provide the stable direction and speedy execution that necessarily eludes prime ministers beholden to some unwieldy coalition of disparate parties. China's rapid transformation into a superpower has often been linked to the discipline imposed by an authoritarian Communist Party at the helm of a command economy. It is supposed that a presidential constitution in India, while retaining democratic accountability, might have something of the same effect.

None of this, though, is likely to happen. Thanks as much to Indira Gandhi's Emergency as to the dictatorial examples of Pakistan and Bangladesh, any constitutional add-on in which might lurk the germs of autocratic rule is out of the question. But the existing machinery could be reconditioned. In the 1960s, state governments in India were commonly formed or felled by assembly members being bribed to change their party allegiance. This floor-crossing reached epidemic proportions, with at least one politician changing sides nine times in a couple of decades. The practice infected the national parliament in the 1970s and was in part responsible for the quick collapse of the post-Emergency Janata government. But in 1985, amid the closing of ranks that followed Mrs. Gandhi's assassination, an anti-defection bill finally made it into the statute books. Individuals defecting from one party to another could now expect disqualification.

Unfortunately, nothing was said at the time about whole parties defecting, a threat that in the context of today's coalition governments is all too common and makes for inertia and instability. But, like the endless parliamentary adjournments and the unseemly conduct of members, this too could surely be rectified, if not by Parliament itself then by the existing provision for presidential ordinances.

Given the current lull in protest and dissent, another long overdue reform might also be undertaken. On November 3, 2000, Sharmila Irom, a young would-be poet and activist from Manipur in India's far northeast, ate her last meal. Twelve and a half years later, when flown from hospital detention in Manipur to appear before a Delhi magistrate on a charge of attempted suicide (an offense under India's Civil Code), Irom had still not taken either food or drink. A feeding tube trailed from her nose as she was helped into court, and her hair looked in need of a brushing. Some forty-five hundred days of forced feeding had also taken a toll on her constitution. Not, though, on her resolve. She duly denied the accusation of suicide, as she has at countless other hearings, and said she wanted to live. As to her fast, which by any standards is "the longest hunger strike anywhere by anyone," she said she would happily end it there and then; all she asked was that the Indian government first repeal AFSPA.

Otherwise the Armed Forces (Special Powers) Act, AFSPA dates from 1958 and affords legal immunity to members of the Indian security forces operating within areas that have first been designated as "disturbed." Troops in such areas may, on suspicion of hostile intent, detain or shoot any individual and enter, search, and destroy any premises, all without risk of prosecution. Imposed in the face of the Naga insurgency and originally applicable only in the northeastern states, the act was subsequently extended to Punjab in the 1980s and to Kashmir in 1990.

Sharmila Irom became aware of it when in 2000 a local newspaper printed photographs of ten Manipuri civilians, one of them an elderly woman, who had been shot dead at a bus stop in a place called Malom. The killers were members of the paramilitary Assam Rifles, and they presumably had their reasons. But because AFSPA affords them blanket protection, the circumstances can never be known for sure. No case can be brought and no impartial investigation under-taken. Such, it is said, is the price that a liberal democracy must pay to guarantee the security of its citizens.

Irom disagreed then, and she still does. So do many other In-dians and countless human rights organizations, including that of the United Nations. AFSPA's condoning of state violence may have served a purpose at the height of the Naga revolt, but it is now wholly counterproductive. Instead of deterring insurgents, it induces the climate of fear and resentment that sustains them. Without it, the northeast might be claimed as a success story. In 2013 Nagaland, along with other northeastern states, held elections. Turnouts were high and disruption minimal. Nagas and Manipuris have done well out of "shining India." Subsidies have poured into the region and young northeasterners have poured out. Their missionary-taught English is put to remunerative effect in the call centers of Bangalore and the cabin-crew training schools of Mumbai. Give or take occa-sional resentment of these un-Indian-looking and largely Christian northeasterners, integration is working. The fragmentation of the northeast's insurgent militias is a sign not of escalation but of their frustration and disarray. AFSPA has become an anachronism that the army could manage without. To end it, and with it Irom's long agony, all that is required is a little common sense and some legisla-tive compassion.

The same could be said with respect to Kashmir. There AFSPA is still being readily invoked and is even more resented. Under its pro-visions, supposed militants are shot on sight while suspects emerge from summary detention, if they emerge at all, with gruesome ev-idence of mistreatment and torture. The army claims that AFSPA is essential to dealing with a situation in which Pakistani-backed guerrillas expect sanctuary from a sullen population. They eagerly credit the act with having reduced the number of "terrorist incidents" while citing any new incidents, including those directly attributable to AFSPA, as proof that it nevertheless remains indispensable. Others argue that its draconian provisions and the injustices it condones discredit the liberal secular values that India stands for. Kashmir, they claim, can never be reconciled to Indian rule while the act remains in force. Repeal is urged and revision discussed, but the solution of simply declaring all but the immediate border region as no longer a "disturbed area" seems a step too far.

For at least twenty years New Delhi and Islamabad have professedly been committed to normalizing their relationship. By easing contacts, building confidence, and sharing concerns, bilateral tensions have been reduced and the Kashmir issue temporarily sidelined. But tacitly it is agreed that resolving the Kashmir conundrum remains the key to Indo-Pak rapprochement.

The current lull affords an opportunity to reconsider this assumption. Instead of deeming the normalization of Indo-Pak relations as hostage to a solution of the Kashmir issue, the equation might be reversed: Kashmir might be seen as hostage to the abnormality of Indo-Pak relations. Kashmiris have long been saying as much, and they may be right. Afghans too are becoming aware of their exposure to this regional rivalry. The plight of Kashmir, and arguably of Afghanistan, may be symptomatic of the hostility between their nuclear neighbors; it is not, though, the cause of it. That lies far from dormant in the legacy of Partition and the troubled adolescence of both of South Asia's sibling states, especially Pakistan.

JUDGED BY ITS APPALLING RECORD of sectarian bombings, Islamist outrages, and political murders, today's Pakistan has earned its pariah status. In Akhtar Hamid Khan's phrasing, the "cutting of heads" still rivals the "counting of heads" as a means of expressing dissent. In 2013 the security forces were grappling with a new wave of insurgency in Balochistan, the ongoing ethnosectarian strife in Karachi, an indigenous Taliban based in the Federally Administered Tribal Areas (FATA), numerous militias and terror cells in Punjab and the Frontier Province, and the devastating spillover from the war in Afghanistan. And all this in an Islamic republic buffeted by the wider Muslim world's expectations of its second-most-populous nation and the only one with a proven nuclear capability.

Data compiled by the Delhi-based Pakistan Terrorism Portal indicate that in the two-year period 2011–12 some 12,500 civilians, insurgents, and security personnel lost their lives, as against over 19,000 in the period 2009–10. Catastrophic flooding by the Indus River as a result of 2010's excessive rains claimed another 18,000 lives and displaced an estimated 14 million people—nearly as many the Great Partition of 1947. The UN estimated the humanitarian crisis occasioned by the floods as worse than the combined effects of the 2002 Asian tsunami, the 2005 earthquake in Azad Kashmir, and the 2010 earthquake in Haiti. In devising a tragedy commensurate with those already afflicting Pakistan, fate had shown the country no favors.

Yet, contrary to expectations, South Asia's "failing state" resolutely fails to fail. In May 2011 the most wanted man in the universe was found to have spent the past five years living with his extended family in a large and conspicuously cloistered residence within a short stroll of Pakistan's premier military academy. The government had claimed Osama bin Laden was still in Afghanistan; the Inter-Services Intelligence agency, elements of which may have known otherwise, were wise neither to the CIA's ploy to locate him nor to the US special forces' plan to get rid of him; and a surveillance-conscious military somehow failed to detect, let alone intercept, the airborne raid that duly did so. For a nation shamed on all fronts by its superpower ally, this fiasco could have been the last straw. Azif Ali Zardari's PPP government might reasonably have leaped at the opportunity to discredit the generals and rein in the intelligence service. The generals must have been tempted to get rid of a civilian government that, already mired in scandal and at loggerheads with the judiciary, was now revealed as the dupe of its US backers. And the Islamist militiamen must have stroked their beards and thanked Allah for a wave of anti-American sentiment beyond their wildest dreams.

But in fact, though accusations flew, nothing untoward followed. The Zardari government served out its term of office; then in 2013 Pakistan went to the polls. By targeting candidates tainted with secularist sympathies, the Pakistan Taliban threatened to dictate the result. Yet the PPP probably would have lost anyway, and the highest-profile casualty proved to be Imran Khan, the cricketer turned politician whose party was one of those approved by the Taliban. Khan's injuries were accidental; he toppled backward off a forklift truck while being raised to the rostrum, then conducted the rest of his campaign from a hospital bed and still did creditably. Victory nevertheless went to Nawaz Sharif and his Pakistan Muslim League–N (PML-N). With an overall majority and a new line in conciliation—of militant Islamists, ISI mavericks, and the military's top brass (excluding his bête noir, ex-president Pervez Musharraf)—Sharif embarked on his third term. The only thing abnormal about the changeover was that, for the first time ever and without any obvious military interference, an elected Pakistani government had lasted its full term, honored the result of the subsequent election, and ceded power to another elected government.

This was no small achievement. Zardari and Sharif, both of them businessmen whose managerial skills have attracted a string of corruption charges, deserve full credit. Nor was the transfer of power their only achievement. In a vital move to underpin democratic practice, Zardari, while in temporary alliance with Sharif's PML-N in 2010, had repealed Zia ul-Haq's Thirty-Eighth Amendment to the constitution, under which the president might arbitrarily dismiss the prime minister and dissolve the National Assembly. Zardari also mollified ethnic sentiment by endorsing a move to rename the North-West Frontier Province as Khyber-Pakhtunwa Province and by according to the once Kashmir-controlled Northern Areas a de facto provincial status as Gilgit-Baltistan.

Sharif's credentials are more pro-Islamic and economic. His government offers to talk with the Pakistan Taliban instead of fighting them and to end collusion with the United States over cross-border drone attacks. With the benefit of hindsight he claims that it was his efforts to open up Pakistan's economy in the 1990s and attract foreign investment that alerted India to the benefits of liberalization. He promises the same again. The parlous state of the Pakistan economy is to be redeemed by securing international loans, reassuring investors, and addressing the chronic power shortages that condemn Pakistanis to an un-air-conditioned hell for much of every summer.

None of this will solve the country's long-term problems. With a population fast approaching two hundred million and with literacy and female empowerment lagging well behind even those in Bangladesh, the state needs to slash military expenditure, create a tax base to which more than the current 0.57 percent of the population contributes, and pour more funds into education, health, and job creation. Politics needs to rid itself of its patriarchal traditions and open up to more newcomers such as Imran Khan. Infrastructure too cries out for investment, and the environment, both urban and riparian, for regeneration and safeguards. Corruption, as ever, needs to be contained. But perhaps that most contentious question about the nature of Pakistani identity needs to be left unaddressed. Academia may agonize over it, but an answer is best consigned to the benign passage of time.

Less remarked than the smoothness of the governmental changeover in 2013 was the near absence of India and Kashmir as electoral issues. Instead of talking up the threat from across the border in time-honored fashion, both Zardari and Sharif pledged themselves to improving Indo-Pak relations and seeking a peaceful solution in Kashmir—in that order. The latter is no longer necessarily contingent on the former.

India should be reassured. Pakistani incursions across the Kashmir line of control nowadays bring condemnation from Islamabad as well as Delhi. Suspicions of Indian support for Balochistan's separatists receive scant publicity, and the Pakistani nightmare of India being accorded a prominent role in Afghanistan surely will be discounted once the Taliban secure a share in the latter country's government.

If Sharif's prime ministership lasts as long as Zardari's, and if the 2014 government in India proves as pragmatic as Atal Bihari Vajpayee's at the turn of the century, real progress could be made in repairing the divisive legacy of Partition. The sibling rivalry could be subdued and the most estranged of Midnight's Descendants sufficiently reconciled to direct their genius for global engagement on improving the lot of a sixth of mankind.

August 2013

AUTHOR'S NOTE

I WAS SIX IN 1947, WHEN what was then British India won its independence. I vaguely recall the pomp and ceremony of the Delhi celebrations as filmed for Pathé News but have no recollection of seeing any coverage of the horrors of the Great Partition that followed. Pakistan I came across only in the classroom; it was not till nineteen years after independence that I first visited what is now called South Asia.

Midnight's Descendants is nevertheless a contemporary history. It spans my lifetime and has revived as many memories as questions. Since that first visit in 1966 I have been returning almost annually— as a journalist, documentary maker, lecturer, writer of many books, and taker of many holidays. In the process I have learned enough to know just how presumptuous this book is.

Contemporary history is itself fraught with pitfalls. It is, of course, a contradiction in terms: By definition, what's contemporary can't be history. No record of the current can aspire to the detachment expected when writing of the past. Memory proves dangerously unreliable; impressions muddy the facts. A ready-made consensus does not exist with respect to many crucial developments, and access to the documentation on which later histories may be based is still embargoed. This book probably will be challenged and certainly will be superseded.

So why write it? The answer is simply that—both despite Partition and because of it—South Asia remains as distinct and crisis prone a global entity as the Middle East (or "West Asia" to South Asians). With a population greater than China's, it is already the world's largest market, and it may well host the world's next superpower. In sixty-five years it has also staged at least five nasty wars and more than once taken the world to the brink of nuclear conflagration. Yet its problems remain poorly understood and its influence easily underrated. Studies of the region as a whole are surprisingly few. Visa restrictions limit travel and inhibit mutual exchange, much as prejudice limits mutual understanding. The outsider has a slight advantage here, which is my excuse for undertaking the book.

Over the years literally hundreds of friends and contacts have contributed to *Midnight's Descendants*. It would be invidious to attempt to list them, but one and all, I thank them. Sam Miller in Delhi and Philip Bowring in Hong Kong kindly read an early draft of the book. For their comments and encouragement I am enormously grateful and have enjoyed returning the compliment with respect to their own books. More immediately, I want to record my debt to editors Lara Heimert and Sue Warga at Basic Books and Robert Lacey and Martin Redfern at William Collins. This is not by way of an authorial convention. Creative editors are a rare breed; so are patient ones. I have been blessed with four of the finest and most forbearing, and I thank them all most sincerely. For her still greater patience and unstinting support, and for her love, I am indebted to Amanda. But in her case thanks would be inappropriate and hopelessly inadequate. So I say no more.

John Keay
Argyll, 2013

NOTES

INTRODUCTION

1. Van Schendel, "Stateless in South Asia."
2. Chatterjee, "All Disquiet."
3. PTI, "Indo-Bangla Border."
4. Baruah, *Durable Disorder,* 5.
5. Kaku Iralu at National Seminar on Resolving Ethnic Conflicts, Guwahati, 2002, quoted in Glancey, *Nagaland,* 96–97.
6. Van Schendel, *Bengal Borderland,* 4.
7. Chatterji, "The Fashioning of a Frontier," 190.
8. Sinha-Kerkhoff, *Tyranny of Partition,* 135.

CHAPTER 1 CASTING THE DIE

1. Mansergh and Moon, eds., *Cabinet Mission,* 582–85.
2. Peck, *Delhi,* 274.
3. Moore, *Escape from Empire,* 78.
4. Mansergh and Moon, eds., *Cabinet Mission,* 598–99.
5. Azad, *India Wins Freedom,* 164–65.
6. Jinnah, quoted in Moon, *Divide and Quit,* 57.
7. *People's Age,* August 26, 1946, reproduced in Sarkar, ed., *Towards Freedom,* 1:676–80.
8. Dalton, "Gandhi During Partition," 228.
9. Darling, *At Freedom's Door,* 55.
10. Sarkar, ed., *Towards Freedom,* 423–24.
11. Darling, *At Freedom's Door,* 56–57.
12. Ibid., 86.
13. Ibid., 302.
14. Ibid., 76–77.
15. Mayaram, *Resisting Regimes,* passim.
16. Darling, *At Freedom's Door,* 11, 22.
17. Ibid., 200.
18. Mayaram, *Resisting Regimes,* 172–75.

19. Copland, *Princes of India,* 354.
20. Ibid., 8.

CHAPTER 2 COUNTING THE COST
1. See especially Jalal, *Sole Spokesman.*
2. Nehru, "Speech on the Granting of Independence."
3. Jinnah, "Presidential Address to the Constituent Assembly of Pakistan."
4. Osman, "The Viceroy's Verdict."
5. Jalal, *Sole Spokesman,* 292.
6. Quoted in Chopra, *Partition, Jihad and Peace,* 166.
7. Jawaharlal Nehru, quoted in von Tunzelmann, *Indian Summer,* 165.
8. Jalal, *Sole Spokesman,* 292–93.
9. Moon, *Divide and Quit,* 114–15.
10. Quoted in Collins and Lapierre, *Freedom at Midnight,* 278.
11. Von Tunzelmann, *Indian Summer,* 209.
12. Aiyar, "'August Anarchy,'" 18–19.
13. Moon, *Divide and Quit,* 116.
14. Ibid., 111, 110.
15. Khan, *Great Partition,* 129.
16. Moon, *Divide and Quit,* 134–35.
17. Khan, *Great Partition,* 131.
18. Moon, *Divide and Quit,* 248.
19. Pandey, *Remembering Partition,* 36.
20. Moon, *Divide and Quit,* 269, 233.
21. Pandey, "India and Pakistan, 1947–2002," 8.
22. Symonds, *In the Margins of Independence,* 52, 56.
23. Khosla, *Stern Reckoning.*
24. Tuker, *While Memory Serves,* 121.
25. Ibid., 415.
26. Ayub Khan, *Friends Not Masters,* 22.
27. Quoted in Chatterji, *Spoils of Partition,* 130 n. 71.
28. Roy, "And Still They Come," 80–81.
29. Zinkin, *Reporting India,* 47.
30. Khan, *Great Partition,* 130.
31. Zakir Hussain, quoted in ibid., 144.
32. Symonds, *In the Margins of Independence,* 34.
33. Ibid., 33–34.
34. Zinkin, *Reporting India.*
35. Kudaisya, "Divided Landscapes, Fragmented Identities," 114.
36. Ibid., 122.

CHAPTER 3 "WHO HAS NOT HEARD OF THE VALE OF CASHMERE?"
1. Copland, "Integration of the Princely States," 154.
2. Ziegler, *Mountbatten,* 410.

3. Guha, *India After Gandhi*, 42.

4. Jawaharlal Nehru, quoted in Ziegler, *Mountbatten*, 445.

5. Ziegler, *Mountbatten*, 409.

6. Keay, *India*, 512.

7. Lamb, *Incomplete Partition*, 98, 101.

8. Nehru letter to Sri Prakasa, November 25, 1947, quoted in Brown, *Nehru*, 178.

9. Symonds, *In the Margins of Independence*, 68.

10. Schofield, *Kashmir in Conflict*, 41.

11. Lamb, *Incomplete Partition*, 130–31.

12. Quoted in Whitehead, *A Mission in Kashmir*, 102.

13. See especially Lamb, *Incomplete Partition*, 150–60.

14. Schofield, *Kashmir in Conflict*, 60.

15. Ziegler, *Mountbatten*, 446.

16. Trench, *Frontier Scouts*, 275–76.

17. Lamb, *Incomplete Partition*, 194.

18. Quoted in Lamb, *Incomplete Partition*, 202.

19. Lamb, *Incomplete Partition*, 227.

20. Quoted in Schofield, *Kashmir in Conflict*, 68.

21. Quoted in Chandra, Mukherjee, and Mukherjee, *India After Independence*, 79.

22. Whitehead, *A Mission in Kashmir*, 208.

CHAPTER 4 PAST CONDITIONAL

1. Shaikh, *Making Sense of Pakistan*, 5.

2. Mazar Ali Khan, interviewed in 1988.

3. Keay, *India*, 519.

4. Shaikh, *Making Sense of Pakistan*, 6.

5. Ibid., 8, 12.

6. Malik, *State and Civil Society in Pakistan*, 27.

7. Keay, *India*, 539.

8. Zinkin, *Reporting India*, 29.

9. Ibid., 37.

10. Jalal, *The State of Martial Rule*, 159.

11. Keay, *India*, 541–42.

12. Ayub Khan, *Friends Not Masters*, 52.

13. Ibid., 54.

14. Ibid., 70.

15. Cohen, *The Idea of Pakistan*, 60.

16. Keay, *India*, 544.

17. Cohen, *The Idea of Pakistan*, 2.

18. Ibid., 296.

19. Guha, *India After Gandhi*, 103.

20. Quoted in ibid.

21. Khilnani, *The Idea of India*, 37.

22. Guha, *India After Gandhi*, 273.

23. Keay, *India*, 527.

24. Kothari, *Politics in India*, 114.

25. Chandra, Mukherjee, and Mukherjee, *India After Independence*, 348–49.

26. Zinkin, *Reporting India*, 150.

27. Ibid., 157

28. Ibid., 167.

29. Ibid., 171.

CHAPTER 5 REALITY CHECK

1. Quoted in Avedon, *In Exile from the Land of Snows*, 36.

2. *Jawaharlal Nehru's Speeches*, vol. 3, *March 1953–August 1957* (New Delhi: Government of India, Ministry of Information and Broadcasting, 1958), p. 253.

3. Myrdal, *Asia Drama*, 185.

4. Maxwell, *India's China War*, 104.

5. *Times of India*, August 31, 1959, quoted in Maxwell, *India's China War*, 111.

6. Nehru, *Prime Minister on Sino-Indian Relations*, quoted in Maxwell, *India's China War*, 118.

7. Maxwell, *India's China War*, 340.

8. Guha, *India After Gandhi*, 332.

9. Naipaul, *An Area of Darkness*, 248.

10. Ibid.

11. Ayub Khan, *Friends Not Masters*, 128.

12. Schofield, *Kashmir in Conflict*, 102.

13. Ziring, *Pakistan in the Twentieth Century*, 280–81.

14. Ballard, "Kashmir Crisis: View from Mirpur," *Economic and Political Weekly* 26, nos. 9/10 (March 2–9, 1991).

15. Ibid., 514.

16. Keay, *India*, 545.

17. Ziring, *Pakistan in the Twentieth Century*, 254.

18. Talbot, *Pakistan*, 161.

19. Quoted in Ziring, *Pakistan in the Twentieth Century*, 281.

20. Talbot, *Pakistan*, 178.

21. Ibid., 179.

CHAPTER 6 POWER TO THE PEOPLE

1. Naipaul, *An Area of Darkness*, 266.

2. Frank, *Indira*, 324.

3. Quoted in Guha, *India After Gandhi*, 416–17.

4. Segal, *The Crisis of India*, 14.

5. Keay, *India*, 551.

6. P. N. Haksar, quoted in Guha, *India After Gandhi*, 437.

7. Khilnani, *The Idea of India*, 48.

8. Ziring, *Pakistan in the Twentieth Century*, 308.

9. Jahan, *Pakistan*, 168–69.

10. Ziring, *Bangladesh*, 50.

11. Bennett-Jones, *Pakistan*, 152.

12. Bhutto, *Myth of Independence*, 180–81.

13. Ziring, *Pakistan in the Twentieth Century*, 329.

14. Library of Congress, "Emerging Discontent, 1966–70," *Bangladesh Country Study*.

15. Keay, *India*, 555.

16. Mascarenhas, *The Rape of Bangladesh*, 91.

17. Jahanara Imam, *Of Blood and Fire: The Untold Story of Bangladesh's War of Independence*, quoted in Van Schendel, *A History of Bangladesh*, 163.

18. Sisson and Rose, *War and Secession*, 148, 152.

19. Ibid., 189–90.

20. Frank, *Indira*, 335–36.

21. Sisson and Rose, *War and Secession*.

22. A. M. Malik to Yahya Khan, 7–9 December 1971, quoted in Ali, *Understanding Bangladesh*, 85–86.

CHAPTER 7 AN ILL-STARRED CONJUNCTION

1. Ziring, *Bangladesh*, 94.

2. Ibid., 83.

3. Van Schendel, *A History of Bangladesh*, 178.

4. Lewis, *Bangladesh*, 80.

5. Quoted in Lifschultz, *Bangladesh*, 141.

6. Ziring, *Bangladesh*, 102–3.

7. Ziring, *Pakistan in the Twentieth Century*, 377.

8. Ahsan, *The Indus Saga and the Making of Pakistan*, xv.

9. Ibid., 136.

10. Talbot, *Pakistan*, 229.

11. Ibid., 224.

12. Quoted in Perkovich, *India's Nuclear Bomb*, 108; quoted in Bennett-Jones, *Pakistan*, 338.

13. Bhutto, *If I Am Assassinated*, 137.

14. Ibid., 25.

15. Cohen, *The Idea of Pakistan*, 140.

16. Durrani, *My Feudal Lord*, 6–7.

17. Bhutto, *If I Am Assassinated*, 193.

18. Durrani, *My Feudal Lord*, 243.

19. Jagdish Bhagwati, quoted in Guha, *India After Gandhi*, 469.

20. Guha, *India After Gandhi*, 473.

21. Datta-Ray, *Smash and Grab*, 71.

22. Ibid., 73.

23. Ibid., 149.

24. Singh, *Himalayan Triangle*, 271.

25. Datta-Ray, *Smash and Grab*, 230.

26. "A Merger Is Arranged," *Hindustan Times*, April 10, 1975, quoted in Datta-Ray, *Smash and Grab*, 309.

27. Singh, *Himalayan Triangle*, 276.

28. Quoted in Moraes, *Mrs. Indira Gandhi*, 220.

29. Quoted in Wolpert, *Zulfi Bhutto of Pakistan*, 254.

30. Naipaul, *India*, 134.

31. Frank, *Indira*, 389.

32. Ibid., 406.

Chapter 8 Two-Way Tickets, Double Standards

1. Naipaul, *India: A Wounded Civilisation*, 140.

2. La Brack, "The New Patrons," 263.

3. Kazi, "Domestic Impact of Overseas Migration: Pakistan," 181–82.

4. Ibid., 193–94.

5. Nair, "Incidence, Impact and Implications of Migration to the Middle East from Kerala," 344.

6. Helweg, "Sikh Politics in India," 310.

7. Akbar, *India: The Siege Within*, 103.

8. Helweg, "Sikh Politics in India," 309.

9. Keay, *India*, 589.

10. Jaffrelot, *The Hindu Nationalist Movement*, 255–81.

11. Chandra, Mukherjee, and Mukherjee, *India After Independence*, 260.

12. Guha, *India After Gandhi*, 527.

13. Chandra, Mukherjee, and Mukherjess, *India After Independence*, 262.

14. Guha, *India After Gandhi*, 548.

15. Chandra, Mukherjee, and Mukherjee, *India After Independence*, 266.

16. K. R. Malkarni, "Updating Hind Swaraj," quoted in Jaffrelot, *The Hindu Nationalist Movement in India*, 329.

17. De Silva, *Sri Lanka's Troubled Inheritance*, 228.

18. Wickramasinghe, *Sri Lanka in the Modern Age*, 272.

19. Ibid., 279.

20. Quoted in ibid., 280.

21. De Silva, *Sri Lanka's Troubled Inheritance*, 247.

22. Bullion, *India, Sri Lanka and the Tamil Crisis*, 51.

23. Wickramasinghe, *Sri Lanka in the Modern Age*, 287.

24. De Silva, *Sri Lanka's Troubled Inheritance*, 253.

25. Jean Alphonse-Bernard, quoted in Bullion, *India, Sri Lanka and*

the Tamil Crisis, 50; also Bullion's own analysis, 51.

26. Quoted in Bullion, *India, Sri Lanka and the Tamil Crisis,* 53.

CHAPTER 9 THINGS FALL APART

1. Hazarika, *Rites of Passage,* 29.

2. Hussain, "Bangladeshi Migrants in India," 128.

3. Hazarika, *Rites of Passage,* 31.

4. Rehman, "Nellie Revisited."

5. Helweg, "Sikh Politics in India," 317.

6. Tully and Jacob, *Amritsar,* 58.

7. Ibid., 71.

8. Ibid., 91.

9. Chandra, Mukherjee, and Mukherjee, *India After Independence,* 334.

10. Tully and Jacob, *Amritsar,* 194.

11. Quoted in Frank, *Indira,* 487, 490.

12. Guha, *India After Gandhi,* 570.

13. Pupul Jayakar, quoted in Frank, *Indira,* 489.

14. Helweg, "Sikh Politics in India," 318.

15. Guha, *India After Gandhi,* 571.

16. Keay, *India,* 580.

17. Tavleen Singh, quoted in Schofield, *Kashmir in Conflict,* 136.

18. Ganguly, *Conflict Unending,* 90,

19. Schofield, *Kashmir in Conflict,* 140.

20. Tavleen Singh, quoted in Schofield, *Kashmir in Conflict,* 131.

21. Schofield, *Kashmir in Conflict,* 147.

22. Guha, *India After Gandhi,* 623.

23. Singh, *Truth, Love and a Little Malice,* 345.

24. Chandra, Mukherjee, and Mukherjee, *India After Independence,* 337.

CHAPTER 10 OUTSIDE THE GATES

1. Muhammad Yunus, quoted in Lewis, *Bangladesh,* 115.

2. Author interview, February 1988.

3. Ibid.

4. Bennett-Jones, *Pakistan,* 58.

5. Talbot, *Pakistan,* 265.

6. Cohen, *The Idea of Pakistan,* 208.

7. Mazar Ali Khan, in *Viewpoint,* August 13, 1981, reprinted in *Pakistan: The Barren Years 1975–1992,* 26.

8. Maulana Rafi Usmani, quoted in Shaikh, *Making Sense of Pakistan,* 140–41.

9. Keay, *India,* 590–91.

10. Talbot, *Pakistan,* 274.

11. Author interview, February 1988.

12. Ahmed Rashid, quoted in Shaikh, *Making Sense of Pakistan,* 173.

13. Bennett-Jones, *Pakistan,* 297.

14. Ziring, *Bangladesh,* 171.

15. Quoted in Lewis, *Bangladesh,* 110.

16. Lewis, *Bangladesh,* 121.

17. Rias and Basu, *Paradise Lost?* 130.

18. Ibid., 126.

19. Ibid., 150–51.

20. BBC, "Profile: Nepal's Ex-King Gyanendra."

21. Rias and Basu, *Paradise Lost?* 63.

22. Hilton, "When a King's Looking-Glass World Is Paid for in Blood."

23. Sengupta, "In a Retreat, Nepal's King Says He Will Reinstate Parliament."

24. Ibid.

25. Anbarasan, "Nepal Seeks to Attract More Tourists from Asian Nations."

CHAPTER 11 INDIA ASTIR

1. Rajiv Gandhi, author interview, April 1985.

2. *Sunday,* June 16–22, 1985, quoted in Guha, *India After Gandhi,* 599–601.

3. Emma Duncan in the *Economist* Special Report on Pakistan, January 17, 1987, 3.

4. Jaffrelot, *The Hindu Nationalist Movement and Indian Politics, 1925–1990s,* 335.

5. Ibid., 342.

6. Keay, *India,* 589.

7. Jaffrelot, *The Hindu Nationalist Movement and Indian Politics, 1925–1990s,* 361.

8. Chandhoke, "The Tragedy of Ayodhya."

9. Guha, *India After Gandhi,* 583.

10. Jaffrelot, *The Hindu Nationalist Movement and Indian Politics, 1925–1990s,* 390.

11. Ibid., 399–400.

12. Ibid., 420.

13. Serill, "India: The Holy War."

14. Quoted in Guha, *India After Gandhi,* 638.

15. Panjiar, "Advani Looked Disturbed . . . Mouth Gaping Open."

16. Ibid.

17. Ibid.

18. Schofield, *Kashmir in Conflict,* 158.

19. Roy, "Introduction: Breaking the News," ix.

20. Guha, *India After Gandhi,* 656–57.

21. Keay, *India,* 599–600.

22. Chandra, Mukherjee, and Mukherjee, *India After Independence,* 292.

23. Paul R. Brass, quoted in Guha, *India After Gandhi,* 659.

24. Talbott, *Engaging India,* 70.

25. Keay, *India,* 584.

26. Talbott, *Engaging India,* 16.

27. Guha, *India After Gandhi,* 679.

28. Bennett-Jones, *Pakistan,* 132.

29. Ibid., 135.

30. Tully, "Architect of the New India."

31. Das, *India Unbound,* 220.

32. Rajadhyaksha, *The Rise of India,* 92.

33. Ibid., 75.

34. Das, *India Unbound,* 246.

35. Bose, *Behenji,* 11–12.

EPILOGUE

1. Giri, "SAARC Summit Preparations."

2. Tharoor, "Shall We Call the President."

3. Ali, *Understanding Bangladesh,* 196.

BIBLIOGRAPHY

Ahmed, Abu Nasar Saied. *Fundamentalism in Bangladesh: Its Impact on India*. New Delhi: Akansha, 2008.

Ahmed, Imtiaz, A. Dasgupta, and K. Sinha-Kerkhoff, eds. *State, Society and Displaced People in South Asia*. Dhaka: Dhaka University Press, 2004.

Ahmed, Ishtiaq. *State, Nation and Ethnicity in Contemporary South Asia*. London: Pinter, 1996.

Ahsan, Aitzaz. *Indus Saga and the Making of Pakistan*. Karachi: Oxford University Press, 1996.

Aiyar, Mani Shankar. *Pakistan Papers*. Delhi: UBS, 1994.

Aiyar, Swarna. "'August Anarchy': The Partition Massacres in Punjab, 1947." In D. A. Low and Howard Brasted, eds., *Freedom, Trauma, Continuities: Northern India and Independence*. New Delhi: Sage, 1998.

Akbar, M. J. *India: The Siege Within*. Delhi: UBS, 1996.

Ali, S. Mahmud. *Understanding Bangladesh*. London: Hurst, 2010.

Amjad, Rashid, ed. *To the Gulf and Back: Studies on the Economic Impact of Asian Labour Migration*. Geneva: UNDP, 1989.

Anbarasan, Ethirajan. "Nepal Seeks to Attract More Tourists from Asian Nations." BBC News. March 28, 2013. http://www.bbc.co.uk/news/business-21826181.

Ansari, S. *Life After Partition: Migration, Community and Strife in Sind 1947–62*. Karachi: Oxford University Press, 2005.

Avedon, John F. *In Exile from the Land of Snows*. London: Michael Joseph, 1984.

Ayub Khan, Mohammad. *Friends Not Masters: A Political Biography*. London: Oxford University Press, 1967.

Azad, Maulana Abul Kalam. *India Wins Freedom*. Hyderabad: Orient Longman, 1988.

Azad, Salam. *Contribution of India in the War of Liberation in Bangladesh*. New Delhi: Bookwell, 2006.

Aziz, K. K. *Rahmat Ali: A Biography*. Lahore: Vanguard Books, 1987.

Bagchi, Jasodhara, and Subhoranjan Dasgupta, eds. *The Trauma and the Triumph: Gender and Partition in Eastern India.* Kolkata: Stree, 2003.

Bahadur Singh, I. J., ed. *The Other India: Overseas Indians and Their Relationship with India.* New Delhi: Arnold-Heinemann, 1979.

Ballard, Roger. "Kashmir Crisis: View from Mirpur." *Economic and Political Weekly* 26, nos. 9/10 (March 2–9, 1991).

Ballard, Roger, and Marcus Banks, eds. *Desh Pardesh: The South Asian Presence in Britain.* London: Hurst, 1994.

Baral, Lok Raj. *The Regional Paradox: Essays in Nepali and South Asian Affairs.* New Delhi: Adroit, 2000.

Barrier, N. G., and V. A. Dusenberry. *The Sikh Diaspora: Migration and the Experience Beyond Punjab.* New Delhi: Chanakya, 1989.

Baruah, Sanjib. *Beyond Counter Insurgency: Breaking the Impasse in the North East.* New Delhi: Oxford University Press, 2009.

———. *Durable Disorder: Understanding the Politics of Northeast India.* New Delhi: Oxford University Press, 2007.

BBC. "Profile: Nepal's Ex-King Gyanendra." June 11, 2008. Available at: http://news.bbc.co.uk/2/hi/south_asia/4225171.stm.

Bennett-Jones, Owen. *Pakistan: Eye of the Storm.* New Haven: Yale University Press, 2002.

Bhuttto, Benazir. *Daughter of the East.* London: Hamish Hamilton, 1998.

Bhutto, Z. A. *If I Am Assassinated.* New Delhi: Vikas, 1979.

———. *The Myth of Independence.* London: Oxford University Press, 1969.

Bose, Ajoy. *Behenji: A Political Biography of Mayawati.* New Delhi: Penguin Viking, 2008.

Brass, Paul. *The Politics of India Since Independence.* New Cambridge History of India, part 4, volume 1. Cambridge: Cambridge University Press, 1990.

Brown, J., and R. Foot. *Migration: The Asian Experience.* New York: St Martin's, 1994.

Brown, Judith M. *Nehru: A Political Biography.* New Haven: Yale University Press, 2003.

Bullion, Alan. *India, Sri Lanka and the Tamil Crisis.* London: Pinter, 1995.

Burki, Shaheed Javed, and Craig Baxter. *Pakistan Under the Military: Eleven Years of Zia ul-Haq.* Boulder, CO: Westview, 1991.

Butalia, U. *The Other Side of Silence: Voices from the Partition of India.* London: Hurst, 2000.

Chandhoke, Neera. "The Tragedy of Ayodhya." *Frontline* 17, no. 3 (June 24–July 7, 2000).

Chandra, Bipan, M. Mukherjee, and A. Mukherjee. *India After Independence 1947–2000.* New Delhi: Penguin, 1999.

Chari, P. R., et al., eds. *Missing Boundaries: Refugees, Migrants, Stateless and Internally Displaced Persons in South Asia*. New Delhi: Manohar, 2003.

Chatterjee, Partha, ed. *State and Politics in India*. Delhi: Oxford University Press, 1998.

Chatterjee, Shib Shankar. "All Disquiet in North-East India." *News Blaze*, November 6, 2009.

Chatterji, Joya. *Bengal Divided: Hindu Communalism and Partition, 1932–1947*. Cambridge: Cambridge University Press, 1994.

———. "The Fashioning of a Frontier: The Radcliffe Line and Bengal's Border Landscape 1947–52." *Modern Asian Studies* 33, no. 1 (1999).

———. *The Spoils of Partition: Bengal and India, 1947–1967*. Cambridge: Cambridge University Press, 2007.

Chopra, Subhash. *Partition, Jihad and Peace: South Asia After Bin Laden*. Northolt: Asian Affairs, 2009.

Clarke, C., C. Peach, and S. Vertovec, eds. *South Asians Overseas: Migration and Ethnicity*. Cambridge: CUP, 1990.

Cohen, S. P. *The Idea of Pakistan*. New Delhi: Oxford University Press, 2004.

Collins, Larry, and Dominique Lapierre. *Freedom at Midnight*. London: Collins, 1975.

Copland, Ian. "The Integration of the Princely States: A Bloodless Revolution." In D. A. Low and Howard Brasted, eds., *Freedom, Trauma Continuities: Northern India and Independence*. Walnut Creek, CA: Altamira, 1998.

———. *The Princes of India and the Endgame of Empire, 1917–1947*. Cambridge: Cambridge University Press, 1997.

Dalton, D. G. "Gandhi During Partition." In C. H. Philips and Doreen Wainwright, eds., *The Partition of India: Policies and Perspectives 1935–47*, 227–30. London: Allen and Unwin, 1970.

Darling, M. *At Freedom's Door: The Story of a Ride Across Northern India in the Winter of 1946–7*. London: Oxford University Press, 1949.

Das, Gurcharan. *India Unbound: From Independence to the Global Information Age*. London: Profile, 2002.

Datta-Ray, Sunanda K. *Smash and Grab: Annexation of Sikkim*. New Delhi: Vikas, 1984.

De Silva, K. M. *Sri Lanka's Troubled Inheritance*. Kandy: International Centre for Ethnic Studies, 2007.

Deschaumes, Ghislaine, and Rada Ivekovich, eds. *Divided Countries, Separated Cities: The Modern Legacy of Partition*. New Delhi: Oxford University Press, 2003.

Durrani, Tehmina. *My Feudal Lord*. Lahore: Durrani, 1991.

Frank, Katherine. *Indira: The Life of Indira Nehru Gandhi*. London: HarperCollins, 2001.

Fraser, Bashabi, ed. *Bengal Partition Stories: An Unclosed Chapter*. London: Anthem, 2006.

Ganguly, Sumit. *Conflict Unending: India-Pakistan Tensions Since 1947*. New York: Columbia University Press, 2001.

Ghosh, Papiya. *Partition and the South Asian Diaspora: Extending the Subcontinent*. London: Routledge, 2007.

Ghosh, Partha S. *Co-Operation and Conflict in South Asia*. New Delhi: Manohar, 1995.

———. *Unwanted and Uprooted: A Political Study of Migrants, Refugees, Stateless and Displaced of South Asia*. New Delhi: Sanskriti, 2004.

Giri, Anil. "SAARC Summit Preparations: MoFA Seeks Cash, to Import 21 Mercedes Cars for VIPs," *Kathmandu Post*, June 3, 2013.

Glancey, Jonathan. *Nagaland: A Journey to India's Forgotten Frontier*. London: Faber, 2011.

Gopal, S., ed. *Anatomy of a Confrontation: The Babri Masjid/Ram Janmabhumi Issue*. New Delhi: Penguin, 1991.

Guha, Ramachandra. *India After Gandhi: The History of the World's Largest Democracy*. London: Macmillan, 2007.

Harrison, Selig, et al., eds. *India and Pakistan: The First Fifty Years*. Cambridge: Cambridge University Press, 1998.

Hasan, Mushirul. *India's Partition: Process, Strategy, Motivation*. Delhi: Oxford University Press, 1993.

———. *The Legacy of a Divided Nation: India's Muslims Since Independence*. London: Hurst, 1997.

Hazarika, Sanjoy. *Rites of Passage: Border Crossings, Imagined Homelands: India's East and Bangladesh*. New Delhi: Penguin, 2000.

Helweg, Arthur W. "Sikh Politics in India: The Emigrant Factor." In N. G. Barrier and V. A. Dusenberry, eds., *The Sikh Diaspora: Migration and the Experience Beyond Punjab*. New Delhi: Chanakya, 1989.

Hilton, Isobel. "When a King's Looking-Glass World Is Paid for in Blood." *Guardian*, February 1, 2006.

Hussain, Wasbir. "Bangladeshi Migrants in India: Towards a Practical Solution—A View from the North-Eastern Frontier." In P. R. Chari et al., eds., *Missing Boundaries: Refugees, Migrants, Stateless and Internally Displaced Persons in South Asia*. New Delhi: Manohar, 2003.

Jaffrelot, Christophe. *The Hindu Nationalist Movement and Indian Politics, 1925–the 1990s*. New York: Columbia University Press, 1996.

———. *Pakistan: Nationalism Without a Nation*. London: Zed, 2002.

Jahan, Rounaq, ed. *Bangladesh: Promise and Performance*. London: Zed, 2000.

———. *Pakistan: Failure in National Integration*. New York: Columbia University Press, 1972.

Jalal, Ayesha. *Democracy and Authoritarianism in South Asia: A Comparative and Historical Perspective*. Cambridge: Cambridge University Press, 1995.

———. *Partisans of Allah: Jihad in South Asia*. Cambridge, MA: Harvard University Press, 2008.

———. *The Sole Spokesman: Jinnah, the Muslim League and the Demand for Pakistan*. Cambridge: Cambridge University Press, 1985.

———. *The State of Martial Rule: The Origins of Pakistan's Political Economy of Defence*. Lahore: Vanguard, 1991.

Jalal, Ayesha, and Sugata Bose. *Modern South Asia: History, Culture, Political Economy*. London: Routledge, 1998.

Jinnah, M. A. "Presidential Address to the Constituent Assembly of Pakistan." August 11, 1947. Reproduced in *Dawn,* Independence Day supplement, August 14, 1999.

Joshi, Shashi. *The Last Durbar*. New Delhi: Oxford University Press, 2006.

Kaul, S., ed. *The Partitions of Memory: The Afterlife of the Division of India*. Delhi: Permanent Black, 2001.

Kazi, Shahnaz. "Domestic Impact of Overseas Migration: Pakistan." In Rashid Amjad, ed., *To the Gulf and Back: Studies on the Economic Impact of Asian Labour Migration*. Geneva: UNDP, 1989.

Keay, John. *India: A History*. 2nd edition. London: HarperCollins, 2010.

Khan, Mazar Ali. *Pakistan: The Barren Years 1975–1992*. Karachi: Oxford University Press, 1998.

Khan, Yasmin. *The Great Partition: The Making of India and Pakistan*. New Haven: Yale University Press, 2007.

Khilnani, Sunil. *The Idea of India*. London: Hamish Hamilton, 1997.

Khosla, Gopal Das. *Stern Reckoning: A Survey of Events Leadng Up to and Following the Partition of India*. In David Page, Anita Inder Singh, Penderel Moon, and G. D. Khosla. *The Partition Omnibus*, 322–49. London: Oxford University Press, 2006.

Kothari, Rajni. *Politics in India*. New Delhi: Orient Longman, 1994.

Kudaisya, G. "Divided Landscapes, Fragmented Identities: East Bengal Refugees and Their Rehabilitation in India, 1947–79." In D. A. Low and Howard Brasted, eds., *Freedom, Trauma, Continuities: Northern India and Independence*. Walnut Creek, CA: Altamira, 1998.

Kudaisya, G., and Tai Yong Tan. *The Aftermath of Partition in South Asia*. London: Routledge, 2000.

Kumar, Radha. *Making Peace with Partition*. New Delhi: Penguin, 2005.

La Brack, Bruce. "The New Patrons: Sikhs Overseas." In N. G. Barrier and V. A. Dusenberry, eds., *The Sikh Diaspora: Migration and the Experience Beyond Punjab*. New Delhi: Chanakya, 1989.

Lall, M. C. *India's Missed Opportunity: India's Relationship with Non Resident Indians*. Aldershot: Ashgate, 2001.

Lamb, Alastair. *The Birth of a Tragedy: Kashmir 1947*. Hertingfordbury: Roxford, 1994.

———. *Incomplete Partition: The Genesis of the Kashmir Dispute 1947–8*. Hertingfordbury: Roxford, 1997.

Lamb, Christina. *Waiting for Allah: Pakistan's Struggle for Democracy*. London: Hamish Hamilton, 1991.

Lewis, David. *Bangladesh: Politics, Economy and Civil Society*. New York: Cambridge University Press, 2011.

Lifschultz, Lawrence. *Bangladesh: The Unfinished Revolution*. London: Zed, 1979.

Louis, William Roger, *Ends of British Imperialism: The Scramble for Empire, Suez and Decolonisation*. New York: Tauris, 2000.

Low, D. A., ed. *The Political Inheritance of Pakistan*. London: Macmillan, 1991.

Low, D. A., and H. Brasted, eds. *Freedom, Trauma, Continuities: Northern India and Independence*. Delhi: Sage, 1998.

Luce, Edward. *In Spite of the Gods: The Strange Rise of Modern India*. London: Little, Brown, 2006.

Malik, Iftikar H. *The History of Pakistan*. Westport, CT: Greenwood, 2008.

———. *Jihad, Hindutva and the Taliban: South Asia at the Crossroads*. Karachi: Oxford University Press, 2005.

———. *State and Civil Society in Pakistan: The Politics of Authority, Ideology, and Ethnicity*, Basingstoke: Macmillan, 1997.

Mansergh, Nicholas, and Penderel Moon. *The Cabinet Mission 23 March–29 June 1946*. Volume 7 of *Constitutional Relations Between Britain and India*. London: HMSO, 1977.

Mascarenhas, A. *The Rape of Bangladesh*. Delhi: Vikas, 1971.

Maxwell, Neville. *India's China War*. London: Cape, 1970.

Mayaram, Shail. *Resisting Regimes: Myth, Memory and the Shaping of a Muslim Identity*. New Delhi: Oxford University Press, 1997.

Menon, V. P. *The Transfer of Power in India*. Princeton, NJ: Princeton University Press, 1957.

Moon, P. *Divide and Quit: An Eyewitness Account of the Partition of India*. Delhi: Oxford University Press, 1998 [1961].

Moore, R. J. *Escape from Empire: The Attlee Government and the Indian Problem*. Oxford: Clarendon, 1983.

Moraes, Dom. *Mrs. Indira Gandhi*. London: Cape, 1980.

More, J. B. P. *Partition of India: Players and Partners*. Nirmalagiri: Institute for Research in Social Sciences and Humanities, 2008.

Myrdal, Gunnar. *Asia Drama: An Enquiry into the Poverty of Nations.* London: Allen Lane, 1972.

Naipaul, V. S. *An Area of Darkness.* London: André Deutsch, 1964.

———. *India: A Million Mutinies Now.* London: Heineman, 1990.

———. *India: A Wounded Civilisation.* London: André Deutsch, 1977.

Nair, Gopinath. "Incidence, Impact and Implications of Migration to the Middle East from Kerala." In Rashid Amjad, ed., *To the Gulf and Back: Studies on the Economic Impact of Asian Labour Migration.* Geneva: UNDP, 1989.

Nayar, Kamala E. *The Sikh Diaspora In Vancouver: Three Generations amid Tradition, Modernity and Multiculturalism.* Toronto: University of Toronto Press, 2004.

Nehru, Jawaharlal. "Speech on the Granting of Independence, 14 August 1947." In Brian MacArthur, ed., *Penguin Book of Twentieth Century Speeches,* 234–37. London: Viking, 1992.

Osman, John. "The Viceroy's Verdict." Letter to the *Spectator,* September 4, 2004.

Page, David, Anita Inder Singh, Penderel Moon, and G. D. Khosla. *The Partition Omnibus.* London: Oxford University Press, 2006.

Pandey, Gyanendra. "India and Pakistan, 1947–2002." *Economic and Political Weekly,* March 16, 2002.

———. *Remembering Partition: Violence, Nationalism and History in India.* Cambridge: Cambridge University Press, 2001.

Panjiar, Prashant. "Advani Looked Disturbed . . . Mouth Gaping Open." *Tehelka* 6, no. 27 (July 11, 2009).

Peck, Lucy. *Delhi: A Thousand Years of Building.* New Delhi: Roli Books, 2005.

Pethick, Lawrence. "The Final Years." In H. S. L. Polak, ed., *Mahatma Gandhi.* London: Odhams, 1949.

Philips, C. H., and Doreen Wainwright, eds. *The Partition of India: Policies and Perspectives 1935–47.* London: Allen and Unwin, 1970.

PTI. "Indo-Bangla Border: Fencing Forces Thousands in No Man's Land." *Hindustan Times,* January 31, 2010.

Rajadhyaksha, Niranjan. *The Rise of India: Its Transformation from Poverty to Prosperity.* Singapore: Wiley and Sons, 2007.

Rashid, Ahmed. *Descent into Chaos,* London: Penguin, 2008.

Rashid, Harun-ur. *Indo-Bangladesh Relations: An Insider's View.* New Delhi: Haranand, 2002.

Rehman, Teresa. "Nellie Revisited: The Horror's Nagging Shadow." *Tehelka,* September 30, 2006.

Rias, Ali, and Subho Basu. *Paradise Lost? State Failure in Nepal.* Lanham, MD: Lexington Books, 2007.

Roy, Arundhati. "Introduction: Breaking the News." In *13 December: A Reader: The Strange Case of the Attack on the Indian Parliament.* New Delhi: Penguin, 2006.

Roy, Renuka. "And Still They Come." In Jasodhara Bagchi and Sub-horanjan Dasgupta, eds., *The Trauma and the Triumph: Gender and Partition in Eastern India*. Kolkata: Stree, 2009.

Rustomji, Nari. *Enchanted Frontiers: Sikkim, Bhutan, and India's Northeastern Borderlands*. Calcutta: Oxford University Press, 1973.

Samad, Yunas. *Nation in Turmoil: Nationalism and Ethnicity in Pakistan, 1935–58*. New Delhi: Sage, 1995.

Samaddar, Ranabir. *The Marginal Nation: Transborder Migration from Bangladesh to West Bengal*. New Delhi: Sage, 1999.

———. *Reflections on Partition in the East*. Calcutta: Calcutta Research Group, 1997.

Sarkar, Sumit, ed. *Towards Freedom: Documents on the Movement for Independence in India 1946*. Oxford: Oxford University Press, 2007.

Schofield, Victoria. *Kashmir in Conflict: India, Pakistan and the Unfinished War*. London: Tauris, 2000.

Segal, Ronald. *The Crisis of India*. Harmondsworth: Penguin, 1965.

Sengupta, Somini. "In a Retreat, Nepal's King Says He Will Reinstate Parliament." *New York Times,* April 25, 2006.

Serill, Michael S. "India: The Holy War." *Time*, December 21, 1992.

Shaikh, Farzana. *Making Sense of Pakistan*. London: Hurst, 2009.

Singh, Amar Kaur Jasbir. *Himalayan Triangle: A Historical Survey of British India's Relations with Tibet, Sikkim and Bhutan 1765–1950*. London: British Library, 1988.

Singh, Anita Inder. *The Origins of the Partition of India 1936–47*. Delhi: Oxford University Press, 1987.

Singh, Gurharpal, and Ian Talbot. *The Partition of India*. Cambridge: Cambridge University Press, 2009.

Singh, Khushwant. *Truth, Love and a Little Malice: An Autobiography*. New Delhi: Ravi Dayal/Penguin, 2002.

Sinha-Kerkhoff, K. *Tyranny of Partition. Hindus in Bangladesh and Muslims in India*. New Delhi: Gyan, 2006.

Sisson, Richard, and Leo E. Rose. *War and Secession: Pakistan, India and the Creation of Bangla Desh*. Berkeley: University of California Press, 1990.

Symonds, Richard. *In the Margins of Independence: A Relief Worker in India and Pakistan (1942–49)*. Karachi: Oxford University Press, 2001.

Talbot, Ian. *Pakistan: A Modern History*. New York: St Martin's, 1998.

———. *Pakistan: A New History*. London: Hurst, 2012.

Talbott, Strobe. *Engaging India: Diplomacy, Democracy and the Bomb*. Washington, DC: Brookings Institution Press, 2004.

Tan, T. Y., and Gyanesh Kudaisya. *The Aftermath of Partition in South Asia*. London: Routledge, 2000.

———, eds. *Partition and Post-Colonial South Asia: A Reader*. 2 volumes. Abingdon: Routledge, 2008.

Tharoor, Shashi. *India from Midnight to the Millennium*. New Delhi: Viking, 1997.

———. "Shall We Call the President." *Tehelka* 8, no. 50 (December 17, 2011).

Trench, Charles Chenevix. *The Frontier Scouts*. London: Cape, 1985.

Tuker, Francis. *While Memory Serves*. London: Cassell, 1960.

Tully, Mark. "Architect of the New India." *Cambridge Alumni Magazine*, Michaelmas 2005.

Tully, Mark, and Satish Jacob. *Amritsar: Mrs. Gandhi's Last Battle*. London: v Cape, 1985.

Van der Veer, Peter. *Religious Nationalism: Hindus and Muslims in India*. Berkeley, CA: University of California Press, 1994.

Van Schendel, W. *The Bengal Borderland: Beyond State and Nation in South Asia*. London: Anthem, 2005.

———. *A History of Bangladesh*. Cambridge: Cambridge University Press, 2009.

———. "Stateless in South Asia: The Making of the India-Bangladesh Enclaves." *Journal of Asian Studies* 61, no. 1 (February 2002): 115–47.

Varma, Sushma J., and Radhika Seshan. *Fractured Identity: The Indian Diaspora in Canada*. Jaipur: Rawat, 2003.

Von Tunzelmann, Alex. *Indian Summer: The Secret History of the End of an Empire*. New York: Henry Holt, 2007.

Whitehead, Andrew. *A Mission in Kashmir*. New Delhi: Viking Penguin, 2007.

Wickramasinghe, Nira. *Sri Lanka in the Modern Age: A History of Contested Identities*. London: Hurst, 2006.

Wilson, A. Jayaratnam. *Sri Lankan Tamil Nationalism: Its Origins and Development in the Nineteenth and Twentieth Centuries*. London: Hurst, 2000.

Wirsing, Robert. *India, Pakistan and the Kashmir Dispute: On Regional Conflict and Its Resolution*. New York: St Martin's, 1994.

Wolpert, Stanley. *Zulfi Bhutto of Pakistan*. New York: Oxford University Press, 1993.

Zamindar, Vazira Fazila-Yacoobali. *The Long Partition and the Making of Modern South Asia: Refugees, Boundaries, Histories*. New York: Columbia University Press, 2007.

Ziegler, Philip. *Mountbatten: The Official Biography*. London: Collins, 1985.

Zinkin, Taya. *Reporting India*. London: Chatto and Windus, 1962.

Ziring, Lawrence. *Bangladesh: From Mujib to Ershad, an Interpretive Study*. Karachi: Oxford University Press, 1992.

———. *Pakistan in the Twentieth Century: A Political History*. Karachi: Oxford University Press, 1997.

INDEX

AASU. *See* All-Assam Students
Union

Abdullah, Farooq, 238, 239,
263–265, 268–271

Abdullah, Sheikh Mohamed, 65,
78–79, 84, 85–86, 91, 93,
97–99, 100, 138, 155, 164,
194, 233, 238, 239, 264

Accession of Princely States, 24,
27, 39, 67–74, 81, 83–88,
90–92, 95, 97–100, 120, 173

Advani, Lal Krishna, 315, 317,
319–321

Affirmative Action, 118, 242, 316

Afghanistan, xxvi, 5, 68, 75, 82,
340

democracy in, 341

Kashmir problem and, 75

SAARC and, 340

Soviet occupation of, xxxiii,
207, 223, 270, 279–280, 282,
285, 318

Taliban in, 282, 350

terrorism and, 323, 348

United States and, 285, 318, 342

Africa, xxix, 112, 141, 225, 323

AFSPA. *See* Armed Forces (Special
Powers) Act

Afzal, Mohamed, 322

Agartala Conspiracy, 177

Agriculture, farming, 62, 109,
118, 140, 156, 195, 206, 228,
230, 234, 237, 256, 323

Ahmadis, 109, 257, 283

Ahmed, Tajuddin, 196

Ahom Gana Parishad (AGP), 253

See also All-Assam Students
Union (AASU)

Ahsan, Aitzaz, 199–200

AIADMK, 235, 243, 245, 246

AIMPLB. *See* All India Muslim
Personal Law Board

Air India Flight 182, 272–273

Aishwarya, Queen of Nepal, 295

Akali Dal, 119–120, 231, 235,
255–261, 272, 274

Akbar, M. J., 304

Akhal Takht, 259–260

Aksai Chin, 143–144, 145, 146,
147, 149, 150, 151, 152, 153

Alexander, Albert Victor, 2, 4

Ali, Bagh, 47

Ali, Nizam Mir Usman, 72–73

Ali, Tariq, 105

All India Muslim Personal Law
Board (AIMPLB), 306, 307

All-Assam Students Union
(AASU), 250–253, 267

See also Ahom Gana Parishad
(AGP)

Ambani, Dhirubhai, 334
Ambedkar, B. R., xxx, 118, 337
Amin, Nurul, 56–57
Amritsar, India, 42, 230, 232,
    257, 258, 262, 263, 274
Anandpur Sahib Resolution, 231,
    255, 256, 260
Anglo-Nepal war of 1814–1816,
    135
Arab-Israeli War (1973), 196
An Area of Darkness (Naipaul),
    66, 172
Armed Forces (Special Powers)
    Act (AFSPA), 345–347
Asian Employment Programme
    of the International Labour
    Organization, 227–228
Assam, xxi, 47, 120, 151, 159,
    189, 212, 224, 234, 248, 258,
    267, 272, 320, 323
  accord in, 308, 311, 312
  deletion of names from electoral
    registers and, 250–251
  Gandhi, Indira intervention in,
    251–254
  Muslims in, 55–57
  population of, 249–250
  princely states, accession of
    and, 71
Assam Rifles, 121, 345
Assamese, 249
Assamese (language), 249
Assamese (people), xxxiii, 151,
    250–255
Ataturk, Mustafa Kemal,
    160–161
Atomic Energy Commission
    (Pakistan), 202
Attlee, Clement, 1, 37, 38, 90
Authoritarianism, xxvii, xxxiv,
    117, 119, 194, 197, 201, 235,
    285, 291, 297, 344
Autocracy, autocrats, xxvii, xxxiii,
    72, 115, 137, 198, 219, 344
Autonomy, xxiii–xxiv, xxiv, 17,
    27, 76, 77, 79, 82, 98, 107,

114, 120, 136, 167, 176, 180,
    183, 200, 214, 231, 242, 254,
    293, 312, 331
Awami League, 111–113, 176–
    177, 180–182, 185, 187–188,
    190, 195–198, 226, 231, 287
Awami National Conference, 265
Ayodhya, India, xxxi, 56, 309–
    323, 331, 335
Azad, Maulana, 6, 7
Azad Kashmir, xxix, 81–83, 86,
    88–89, 97, 99, 100, 152,
    158–160, 226, 278, 330, 348

Babri Mosque, Ayodhya, India,
    xxxi, 56, 309, 313, 317, 319,
    323
Baghdad Pact, 142
Bahawalpur, Pakistan, 21, 43–45,
    47–59
Bahujan Samaj Party (BSP), 337
BAKSAL. *See* Bangladesh Peasants
    and Workers Awami League
Balochis, 60, 278, 280
Balochistan, xxvi, xxxii–xxxiii,
    40, 50, 109, 114, 115, 201,
    326, 347, 350
Baltistan, 77, 89, 349
Bandaranaike, Sirimavo, 171,
    243, 244, 246
Bangalore, 335, 342, 346
Bangladesh, 75, 172
  birth of, 56, 184
  China and, xxxiv
  constitution making in, 233
  democracy in, xxxiii, 193, 287
  economy in, xxv, 195, 196, 289
  famine in, 196
  foreign aid and, 196, 289–290
  government-in-exile of, 192, 195
  Gulf migration and, 226, 227
  identity and, 233, 287
  independence and, 185
  Islam and, xxv, xxvi, 233, 286
  microfinance (microcredit) in,
    277–278, 288

military coup (1975) in, 56
NGO government of, 288–289
Partition and, xvii
population of, 240
poverty in, 289
Rahman, Mujibur government in, xxxiii, 217
secularism and, 233
war in East Bengal (1971) and, 185–187
Ziaur Rahman government in, xxxiii, 198, 285–286
See also East Pakistan
Bangladesh Peasants and Workers Awami League (BAKSAL), 197
Bangladesh Rural Advancement Committee (BRAC), 277–278, 288
Baramula, India, 83, 84
Basic Objectives Resolution, 107
Basu, Jyoti, 132
BBC. *See* British Broadcasting Corporation
Bengal
   Direct Action Day (August 16, 1946) in, 9–12
   economy of, 57
   famine in, 15, 57
   Hindu-Muslim animosity in, 15–16, 19
   migration and, 54–63
   Muslim League in, 15–16, 52
   Operation Searchlight and, 185–186
   Partition and, 32, 33, 45, 46, 52–63, 112, 156
   See also East Bengal; West Pakistan
Bengali, xxi, 61, 111, 250
Bengalis, xxviii, 9, 53–55, 61–63, 109–113, 115, 159, 178, 181–187, 191, 195, 200, 249, 251
Bharatiya Janata Party (BJP), xxxiii, 234–238, 244, 255,

256, 264, 313–320, 323–325, 328–332, 335, 344
Bharatpur, India, 22, 23, 45
Bhashani, Abdul Hamid Khan "Maulana," 181, 182
Bhindranwale, Sant Jarnail Singh, 256–266, 272–274
Bhopal, India, 60, 67, 69, 202, 326, 327
Bhutto, Benazir, 21, 281, 285, 287, 318, 329, 331
Bhutto, Zulfikar Ali, xxxiii, 115, 154–156, 164–167, 169–170, 178–184, 192–194, 197–207, 211, 217–218, 222, 226, 279, 282, 305, 328, 331
Bhutto's war (1965), 170, 176, 178, 182, 202, 208, 251, 328
Bihar, 11, 16, 19, 31, 61, 110, 121, 172, 210–211, 215, 262, 307, 313, 332
Biharis, xxviii, 56, 186, 259, 278, 281
Bin Laden, Osama, 257, 348
Birendra, King of Nepal, 138, 215, 291, 294, 295
BJP. *See* Bharatiya Janata Party
Bombay (Mumbai), 107, 124–126, 148, 207, 215, 307, 323, 325
BRAC. *See* Bangladesh Rural Advancement Committee
Brezhnev doctrine, xxv, 188
Britain
   Cabinet Mission (1946) and, 1–6
   Direct Action Day (August 16, 1946) and, 11
   imperialism and, 10
   imperialism of, 15
   India and, xvii
   Pakistani migration to, 158–160
   Partition and, xvi, xvii
   reconstruction crisis in, 1
   See also Bangladesh; United Kingdom

British Broadcasting Corporation (BBC), 37, 256, 262, 285, 300, 332
British Columbia, xxxix, 225, 255, 272–273
Brohi, A. K., 105
Brown, William, 87–88
BSP. *See* Bahujan Samaj Party
Buddhism, Buddhists, 77, 171, 186, 212, 213, 241, 242, 243
Burma (Myanmar), xxi, 5, 68, 136, 141, 147
Bush, George W., 297

Cabinet Mission (1946), 1–6, 7–8, 17–18, 23–29, 32, 79, 231
Calcutta, India, xxviii, 39, 53, 55, 57–58, 61, 63, 110, 124, 151, 281
    Calcutta Killings, 9–13, 15–16, 31, 52, 53, 56, 245
Canada, xxxi, 202, 229, 241, 247, 255, 272
Capitalism, 15, 128, 131, 141, 208, 333
Carter, Jimmy, 236
CENTO. *See* Central Treaty Organization
Central Intelligence Agency (CIA), 164, 348
Central Treaty Organization (CENTO), 142, 164
Ceylon, 4, 41, 140, 141, 171–172, 184, 189, 240
    See also Sri Lanka
Chandigarh, India, 231, 256, 260, 272, 274
Chatterji, Joya, xxiv
Chauhan, Jagjit Singh, 255–256, 263
Chelvanayakam, S. J. V., 243
China, xxvi, xxxii, xxxiv, 126–127, 291, 303, 318–319, 331, 344
    authoritarianism of, xxxiv
    Bangladesh and, xxxiv

Cultural Revolution and, 167
    Everest, conquest of and, 134–135
    Goa, seizure of and, 148–149
    Indian relations with, 136, 140, 143–152, 182, 212
    Indo-Pakistan relations and, 191
    Kashmir issue and, 178–179
    Nepal and, xxxiv, 149
    nuclear weapons and, xxvi, 202
    Pakistan and, xxxiv, 178–179, 188, 203
    People's Liberation Army (PLA) of, 135, 136, 144, 147, 150
    Soviet Union and, 131
    Sri Lanka and, xxxiv
    Thala Ridge and, 149–150
    Tibet and, 77, 134, 136–137, 139, 140, 144
Chinese Communist Party, 212
Chittagong Hill Tracts, 38, 47, 185, 186, 191, 278
Chogyal, 212–217
Chou Enlai, 127
Churchill, Winston, 35, 37, 133
CIA. *See* Central Intelligence Agency
Clinton, Bill, 327
Cohen, Stephen Philip, 116
Cold War, 92, 126, 141
Colombo, Sri Lanka. *See* Sri Lanka
Communalism, 23, 155, 232, 238
Communism, Communists, 15, 23, 53, 62, 142, 150, 164, 172, 174, 189
    in China, 136, 139, 203, 212, 344
    in India, 62, 125–132, 314
    in Nepal, 292
Communist Party (Marxist) (CPM), 131, 314
Communist Party Marxist-Leninist (CPM-L), 132
Communist Party of India (CPI), 62, 128–130, 132

Communist Party of Nepal
    (Maoist), 292
Communist Party of Nepal
    (United Marxist-Leninist),
    292
Congress Party, xxxiii, 22, 67,
    106, 128, 130, 220, 258, 290
    Bengal and, 15–16, 62
    Cabinet Mission (1946) and,
        4–8
    Calcutta Killings and, 9–12
    Direct Action Day (August 16,
        1946) and, 9–11
    Gandhi, Indira and, 131
    Kashmir and, 69, 71–74, 78,
        79, 93
    Muslim League and, 20
    Nehru, Jawaharlal and, 108,
        117–118, 120, 124–126
    Nepal and, 136–138, 217
    Partition and, 32–34, 37–41,
        46, 54
    princely states, accession of
        and, 26–28
    Syndicate of, 171, 173–174,
        175, 230
Cooke, Hope, 213, 214
Counterterrorism, 340
CPI. See Communist Party of
    India
CPM. See Communist Party
    (Marxist)
CPM-L. See Communist Party
    Marxist-Leninist
Cripps, Sir Stafford, 2, 4, 6, 26
The Crisis of India (Segal), 172

Dahal, Pushpa Kamal, 292,
    294–295, 299
Dalai Lama, 134, 136, 144
Dalits (harijans or untouchables),
    118, 232, 293, 307, 337
Dandakaranya, India, 62–63, 132
Darling, Malcolm Lyall, 12–17,
    17–23, 25, 27, 36, 277
Datta-Ray, Sunanda, 213, 214

De Silva, K. M., 240, 244, 246
Delhi, India
    See India
Delhi massacres, 272, 280, 326
Democracy, xxvii
    basic, 138, 162, 163, 178, 180,
        290
    military, 326
    parliamentary, 142, 180, 200,
        290–291, 344
    See also individual countries
Desai, Morarji, 173, 178, 208,
    215, 217, 218, 234, 235
Dhaka, Bangladesh, xxx, 9, 11,
    42, 55, 57, 110, 111–112,
    114, 158, 176, 183, 186, 188,
    192, 196, 286, 342
Dipendra, Crown Prince, 295–296
Direct Action Day (August 16,
    1946), 8–12, 15
DMK. See Dravida Munetra
    Kazagham
Dong, Pham Van, 141
Dravida Munetra Kazagham
    (DMK), 123, 171, 172, 189,
    243

East Bengal, 42, 53, 56, 57,
    61–62, 107
    autonomy and, 176
    Constituent Assembly in,
        112–114
    constitutional crisis in, 112–114
    elections in, 112
    Hindus in, 110
    Islam and, 178
    jute industry in, 109
    language riots in, 111–112, 123
    Muslim League in, 54, 112
    Pakistan and, 109–115,
        181–183
    Pakistan-Bangladesh war in,
        185–187
    Partition and, 47
    population of, 109
    See also Bengal; West Bengal

East Pakistan, xxix, xxxviii, 121,
    202, 244, 250, 251, 277, 312
  autonomy and, 167, 176
  Bengalis of, 55
  constitution making and, 163
  Indus Water Treaty and, 157,
    159
  Kashmir and, 155
  one-unit scheme and, 113
  poverty in, 161
  rebirth as Bangladesh of, 179
  See also Bangladesh
East Timor, 148
Economist, 207, 305
Economy
  in Bangladesh, xxv, 195, 196
  migration and, 224
  in Pakistan, xxv, 201, 204
  remittances and, 224–229
  "tiger economies" and, xxvii
Eelam Revolutionary
    Organisation of Students
    (EROS), 244
Eighteenth Summit Conference of
    SAARC (2013), 339–343
Enclaves, xviii–xix, xix, xxiii, 47,
    56
English (language), xxvi, 66, 122,
    123, 171, 242
EROS. See Eelam Revolutionary
    Organisation of Students
Ershad, Mohamed, 226, 233,
    286–288
EU. See European Union
European Union (EU), 297, 340

Far Eastern Economic Review,
    196
Farming, farmers. See Agriculture,
    farming
FATA. See Federally Administered
    Tribal Areas (FATA)
Federal Party (Sri Lankan Tamils),
    243
Federal Security Force (FSF), 201,
    204, 205

Federalism, 119, 126, 200
Federally Administered Tribal
    Areas (FATA), 347
Five Principles of Peaceful
    Coexistence, 140–141
Fokker Friendship, 184
France, 69, 140–141, 167, 202
FSF. See Federal Security Force
Fundamentalism, 232, 282, 307

Gagarin, Yuri, 133
Gandhi, Indira, 55, 131, 141, 178,
    182, 184, 192, 229
  Assam, intervention in of, 249,
    251–253
  assassination of, xxxiii, 206,
    265–267, 272, 311, 326,
    344
  authoritarianism of, 194
  Bangladesh and, 193, 207, 208,
    214
  bank nationalization and, 173,
    174
  Bhutto, Zulfikar Ali and, 197,
    218–219
  Emergency and, 194, 219–222,
    224, 233, 235, 236, 314, 344
  Janata Party and, xxxiii, 217,
    234–238, 244, 264
  JP Movement and, 210–211,
    233
  Kashmir and, 263–265
  Last Battle of, 231–232
  nonintervention and, 249
  nuclear weapons and, 214, 325
  Operation Blue Star and,
    231–232
  Punjab and, 230, 231, 255–256,
    258, 259–260, 272–275
  Rae Bareilly election (1971)
    and, 170, 210, 217–218
  religious neutrality and,
    305–306
  secularism and, 233, 249
  Sikkim annexation and, 217
  Sri Lanka and, 241, 254

Gandhi, Mahatma, xxx, 13, 71, 99, 117, 120, 130, 216, 219, 233
　assassination of, xxxii, 94, 234
　Cabinet Mission (1946) and, 5, 7, 8
　Calcutta Killings and, 10, 11
　fasting of, 92–93
　Indian constitution and, 6
　Kashmir and, 75, 84, 92–93, 100
　Muslims and, 234
　national identity and, xxii
　nuclear weapons and, 202
　Pakistan, break up of and, 188
　Partition and, 52–53, 54
　war in East Bengal (1971) and, 189
Gandhi, Rajiv, 247
　Assam accord and, 308
　assassination of, xxxiii, 314–315
　Babri Mosque demolition and, 310
　digital technology and, 334–335
　Gandhi, Indira assassination of and, 266
　Kashmir and, 264, 267–272, 308
　as peacemaker, 312, 314
　as prime minister (1984–89), 303–304
　Punjab and, 258, 308
　religious neutrality and, 306
Gandhi, Sanjay, 209–210, 218, 220–221, 237–238, 259, 264
　death of, 247
　forced sterilization program of, 235, 264
　Khalistan movement and, 256
　population control and, 221–222
　slum clearances of, 235
Gandhi, Sonia, 315, 332
Gauhati, India, 151, 250, 252
George VI, King, 37, 43

Gilgit, Pakistan, 77, 79, 87, 88–89, 349
Gilgit Scouts, 87–89
Globalization, xxvii, xxx, xxxii, xxxiii, 127–128, 222, 280, 342
GNLF. See Gorkha National Liberation Front
Goa, India, 69, 141, 148, 149, 163, 189, 211
Godhra, India, 322
Godse, Nathuram, 94, 234
Golden Temple, Amritsar, India, 230, 232, 258–263, 272, 274
Gorkha National Liberation Front (GNLF), xx–xxi, 312
Gorkhali, xx, xxi
Government of India Act of 1935, 112
Grameen Bank, 278, 288
Grassroots organizations, 289
Great Calcutta Killings, 9–13, 15–16, 31, 52, 56, 245
Great Partition. See Partition
Green revolution, 208, 229, 230
Guha, Ramachandra, 67, 95, 117, 123, 149, 210, 219, 236, 238, 304
Guinness Book of World Records, 133
Gujarat, 24, 67, 70, 120, 124–126, 210, 215, 217, 315, 322–323
Gulf states, xxix, 224–228, 247
Gurkhas, 60, 89, 135, 139, 149, 159
Gyanendra, King of Nepal, 295–299

Helweg, Arthur, 228, 229
High Commissioner for Refugees (UNHCR), 190
Hijackings, 184, 188, 272–273
Hillary, Edmund, 133, 137
Hindi, 66, 122–123, 125, 126, 145, 171, 230, 231, 243, 315, 317

Hinduism, xxiii, 234, 308, 311
Hinduization, 305–309
Hinduness, 251, 319, 331
Hindus, xvi, xxii, xxiii–xxiv,
    xxxiii, 130, 155, 313
  Babri Mosque and, 309–311
  Bengali, 110, 112, 119, 186–
    188, 251
  Calcutta Killings and, 9–12, 15
  Gandhi, Indira and, 238, 266
  Kashmir and, 75, 93
  Khalistan movement and, 259
  Muslim conflict with, 17–23,
    321–324
  Nepal and, 135
  Pakistan and, 104
  Partition and, 31, 33, 36, 42,
    47, 48, 51, 53–57, 60, 61
  Shah Bano affair and, 307–308
  Sri Lankan Tamils and, 171
Hindustan, 18, 38, 40
Hindustan Times, 216, 217
Hindustani, 122
Huq, Fazul, 112
Hussein, Altaf, 204, 280
Hyderabad, India, 25, 27, 63,
    68–70, 72–74, 84, 95–97,
    120, 125, 136, 189, 316

The Idea of Pakistan (Cohen), 116
ICS. *See* Indian Civil Service
    (ICS)
Immigration. *See* Migration
Imperialism, 10, 15, 141
Independence Day (August 14/15,
    1947), 43, 215, 270
India
  Bangladesh and, xv–xvi, xviii–
    xx, xxi, 193–194, 285–290
  Cabinet Mission (1946) and,
    1–6, 17–18
  China and, 136, 140, 143–145,
    145–152, 182, 212
  Communists in, 126–132
  constitution making and, 4–5,
    117–119, 210

democracy in, xxxiii, 116,
    116–118, 128, 142, 172, 175,
    194, 218, 275, 300–301,
    318–319
economy in, 119, 139–140,
    142, 208–209, 219
Emergency in, 170, 194,
    219–222, 224, 233, 235, 236,
    314, 344
Gulf migration and, 227
Hinduization of, 305–309
identity and, 17, 41, 116
independence and, 31, 37
Indus Water Treaty and,
    156–158
Islam and, xxvi, 12
Janata government in, 235–238,
    314, 316, 344
JP Movement in, 210–211, 215,
    219
Kashmir and, 153–156, 179,
    346–347, 350
language debate in, xx–xxi,
    121–124, 124–126, 142, 171,
    239–243
National Front government in,
    314, 317
Nehru, Jawaharlal, government
    in, 103, 116, 119, 139–145
Nepal and, xx–xxi, 136,
    138–139, 290–301
nuclear program of, xxvi, 202,
    211, 324–327
Pakistan and, 24, 72, 152–158,
    170, 176, 178, 182,
    187–189, 202, 208, 251,
    326–328
population of, xxv, 7, 221–222,
    240
press in, 254
princely states, accession of
    and, xxxii, 23–29, 33, 65–75,
    120
Punjab and, 272–275
Rae Bareilly election in, 169,
    174, 175, 210, 215

Rao government in, 332–334, 335
secularism in, 155, 194, 233, 319
Shah Bano affair in, 306–309, 310
Sikkim, annexation of by, 212
Soviet Union and, 187–188
Sri Lanka and, 240–248
United States and, 235–236
UPA government in, 331–332
war in East Bengal (1971) and, 186–187, 188
India Today, 248, 320
India-China War (1962), 149–151, 182
Indian Civil Service (ICS), 13, 21, 41, 50, 277
Indian National Congress, 179
Cabinet Mission (1946) and, 3–5, 7, 8
Direct Action Day (August 16, 1946) and, 10
Muslim League and, 15–16, 20, 28
North-West Frontier Province and, 16
Partition and, 40
princely states, accession of and, 26, 27, 28–29, 74
Punjab, Sikhs in and, 256
in West Bengal, 54
See also Congress Party
Indo-Pak war (1965), 166, 170, 176, 178, 182, 202, 208, 251, 328
Indo-Soviet Treaty of Peace, Friendship and Cooperation, 187–188
Indus River floods, 278, 348
The Indus Saga and the Making of Pakistan (Ahsan), 199
Indus Water Treaty, 156–158, 230
Instruments of Accession, 28, 67, 69, 73, 74, 83–85, 95, 212
International Monetary Fund, 333

Inter-Services Intelligence (ISI), 82, 284, 323, 348
Iran, 207, 223
Iraq, xxvi, 332
Irish Republican Army, 265
Irom, Sharmila, 345–346
ISI. *See* Inter-Services Intelligence
Islam, 45, 66, 182, 231, 269
Bangladesh and, xxv, xxvi, 286
conversion to, 19
divisions of, xxiii
East Bengal and, 178
India and, xxvi, 12
migration and, 232
nationalism and, 105–106
orthodoxy and, 181
Pakistan and, xxv, xxvi, 36–37, 116, 180, 181, 281–285
religious identity and, 232–233
sharia and, 21–22, 105
Shi'ite, xxiii, 283
Sufi, xxiii, 283
Sunni, xxiii, 200
Wahhabi, 232
Islamabad, Pakistan, xxx, 160, 183, 235, 327
Israel, 58, 223

Jagmohan Malhotra, 221, 264, 265, 268
Jaipur, India, 20
Jalal, Ayesha, 40
Jamaat-e-Islami, xxiii, 105–106, 265, 282–283, 285
Jammu and Kashmir. *See* Kashmir
Jammu and Kashmir Liberation Front (JKLF), xxxi, 160, 265, 269–270
Jan Sangh, 99, 117, 119–120, 123, 234–238
Janata Party. *See* Bharatiya Janata Party (BJP)
Japan, 1, 34, 223, 303
Jatistan, 22, 23
Jats, 12, 19, 20, 22–23, 53
Jayawardene, J. R., 244–248

Jihad, xxiv, 82
Jinnah, Mahomed Ali, xxx, 15,
    26, 96, 111, 117, 232, 279
  Cabinet Mission (1946) and,
    3, 5–8
  death of, 96–97
  Kashmir and, 82, 86, 90–91
  Kashmir problem and, 75
  Muslim homeland and, 328
  Pakistan government and, 12,
    32–34, 38, 39, 42, 104–106
  princely states, accession of
    and, 27, 71
JKLF. See Jammu and Kashmir
    Liberation Front
JP Movement, 211, 214, 215,
    219, 233–234
Junagadh, India, 70–73, 91, 115,
    126
Junejo, Mohamed Khan, 305

Karachi, Pakistan, xxviii, 42, 44,
    60, 63, 116, 204, 278–280
Kargil war, 328–329
Kashmir, xxvi, 50, 57, 63, 65–75,
    68, 70, 189, 350
  accession of, 86–90, 90–97,
    97–99, 120
  Bhutto, Zulfikar Ali and, 167
  exceptionalism of, 270
  Farooq Abdullah
    administration in, 263–265
  Hindu-Muslim animosity in,
    322
  Indo-Pak relations and, 72,
    74–75, 153–156, 163–166,
    346–347
  Kashmir Accord and, 267–272
  Khan, Ayub, and, 179
  language and, 66
  liberation of, xxxiii
  Muslims and, 56, 265
  Pakistan and, 160, 329–330
  Partition and, xxiv, 47, 65–101,
    75–83
  Poonch and, 76–77

princely states, accession of
    and, 25, 72, 84–86
  regions of, 75–77
  registration of immigrants in,
    268
  Sino-Pakistan relations and,
    178–179
  tourism in, 270
  United States and, 164
Kennedy, John F., 94, 150
Kerala, 122, 125, 126, 128–131,
    172, 228
Khalistan movement, xxxi–
    xxxiii, 18, 22, 255–263,
    272–274
Khan, Abdul Qadeer, 202–203,
    326
Khan, Akhtar Hameed, 277–279,
    279–280, 281–282, 284,
    347
Khan, Amanullah, 265, 269
Khan, Ayub, 53, 108, 113–115,
    116, 130, 152–158, 161–166,
    175–180, 187, 190, 191, 205,
    286, 290
Khan, Imran, 348–349, 350
Khan, Khan Abdul Wali, 204
Khan, Liaquat Ali, 40, 54–55, 82,
    90, 91, 97, 107, 108, 117
Khan, Mazar Ali, 105, 281
Khan, Yahya, 178, 179–180,
    180–181, 183–184, 192,
    197, 202
Khan, Yasmin, 49
Khar, Mustafa, 206
Khilnani, Sunil, 116, 118, 127,
    175, 337
Khomeini, Ayatollah, 281
Khosla, Gopal Das, 50–51, 52
Khrushchev, Nikita, 127
Kissinger, Henry, 187, 190–191
Koirala, B. P., 137–138, 217
Koirala, Girija Prasad, 292, 296,
    299, 318
Kongka, 146
Kotharj, Rajni, 126

Ladakh, Jammu and Kashmir, 77, 79, 89, 143, 145, 146, 149, 150–151, 212, 328, 331

Lahore, Pakistan, xxviii, 9, 18, 42, 43, 44, 53, 58, 60, 184, 204

Lamb, Alastair, 78, 81, 88, 92

Lashkar-e-Taiba, 322, 323, 329

Laski, Harold, 279

Left Front government, 62

Legal Framework Order (Pakistan), 180, 181

Leh, India, 89–90, 156, 328

Liberation Tigers of Tamil Eelam (LTTE) (Tamil Tigers), xxxi, 244, 246, 247, 255, 268, 312, 314

Line of Control, Kashmir, 194, 269, 341

Literacy, 25, 138, 208, 220, 289, 349–350

Liu Shaoqi, 212

Lok Sabha, 126, 169, 174, 267, 304, 314, 315, 324, 343

London *Times*, 149, 172

Longowal, Harcharan Singh, 259, 274

LTTE. *See* Liberation Tigers of Tamil Eelam (Tamil Tigers)

Lucknow, India, 60, 319, 320

Madras (Chennai), 15, 60, 73, 124, 125, 140, 243, 245, 335

Madrassas, xxxi, 282, 283

Mahasbha, xxiii, 94, 99, 110, 117, 125

Mahendra, King of Nepal, 137, 138, 162

Maintenance of Internal Security Act (MISA), 210, 218, 219

Makarios, Archbishop, 141

Manchester Guardian, 110

Mandal, B. P., 316, 319

Manipur, India, 68, 70, 289, 312, 345, 346

Mandir, 317–320, 335; *See also* Babri Mosque

Mao Zedong, 132, 145, 178

Maoist revolutionaries (Naxalites), xxxii, 63, 132, 138, 259, 297

Marcos, Ferdinand, 287

Maxwell, Neville, 149, 172

Mayaram, Shail, 20, 22

Mayawati, Ms., 337

McMahon Line, 145, 146, 147, 149, 150, 151

Menon, Krishna, 145, 146, 148, 150

Menon, V. P., 28, 40, 67, 68, 84

Meoistan, 22

Meos, 19–20, 22–23, 39, 45, 49, 58–59

Mewat, India, 19–20, 22, 49

Microfinance (microcredit), 277–278, 288

Midnight's Descendants, xxxii, xxxiii, 75, 124, 337, 342, 350

Migration
  Bengal and, 54–63
  economic impact of, 224
  education and, 225
  to Gulf States, 224–228
  identity and, xxix
  independence and, xxix
  involuntary, xix–xx, 48
  Islam and, 232
  labor and, xxix
  language and, xx–xxi
  mass, 32
  Partition and, 32, 47–48, 54–56
  patterns of, xvii
  remittances and, xxix, 159–160, 224–229
  war in East Bengal (1971) and, 186–187, 189–190

Mirpur, Jammu and Kashmir, 81, 158–160

Mirza, Iskander, 112, 113, 114, 115, 130, 180

MISA. *See* Maintenance of Internal Security Act

Modi, Narendra, 323

Mohamed, Ghulam, 65–66, 72, 78, 82, 85

Monarchy, 25, 74, 136, 137, 213, 293, 294, 296–299

Monroe doctrine, xxv, 247

Mookherjee, Shyama Prasad, 99–100

Moon, Penderel, 43, 44–45, 46, 47, 49, 50, 51, 52

Moore, Thomas, 68

Mount Everest, 133–135, 137, 147

Mountbatten, Lady Edwina, 38, 43, 44

Mountbatten, Lord Louis, 3, 27–29, 34, 37–40, 43–44, 46, 52, 66–71, 73–74, 79, 84–85, 90–92, 95, 120, 161, 212, 215

MQM. *See* Muttahida (Muhajir) Qaumi Mahaz (United National Movement)

Muhajirs, xxviii, xxxii, 60, 63, 111, 186, 202, 204, 226, 278, 279–281

Mujibnagar, Bangladesh, 188, 192, 196

Mukti Bahini, 189–190, 191, 196, 260

Mumbai. *See* Bombay (Mumbai)

Musharraf, Pervez, 285, 297, 329–330, 331, 349

Muslim Conference (Kashmir), 78, 79

Muslim League, 128, 195, 281
  Bengal and, 15–16, 111–114
  Cabinet Mission (1946) and, 1–6
  Calcutta Killings and, 9–12
  Congress Party and, 20
  Kashmir and, 71–73, 78, 94
  Pakistan and, 106–108, 163, 174
  Partition and, 32–33, 37–40, 46, 52–54
  princely states, accession of and, 24, 26–28

Muslims, xvi–xvii, xxvi–xxviii, xxxi
  Cabinet Mission (1946) and, 5–7
  Hindu conflict with, 16–20
  Kashmir and, 78–82, 92–96
  Pakistan and, 104–106, 154–155
  Partition and, 44–45, 47, 49, 56–60

Muttahida Qaumi Movement (MQM), xxxii, 63, 204, 284

Muttahida (Muhajir) Qaumi Mahaz (United National Movement) (MQM), 280–281

Myanmar. *See* Burma (Myanmar)

Myrdal, Gunnar, 143

Nagaland, xxi, xxvi, xxxi, 148, 163, 189, 230, 250, 254, 312

Nagas, xxi–xxii, 120–121, 312, 345, 346

Naipaul, V. S., 66, 169, 170, 172, 219, 224, 304

Namboodiripad, E. M. S., 129

Narain, Raj, 169–171, 174, 175, 210, 215, 217, 218, 219, 234, 235, 343

Narayan, J. P., 210, 215, 217, 218, 219, 233–234, 235, 237

Nasser, Gamal, 141

National Conference (Kashmir), 78, 99, 238, 264

National Council of Khalistan, 255

National Democratic Alliance (NDA), 324, 329, 335

National Front, 270, 314, 317

National Panchayat (Nepal), 138

National Planning Commission, 127

Nationalization, 171, 174, 178, 200, 201, 209, 220

NATO. *See* North Atlantic Treaty Organization

Natural disasters, xix, xxxii, 57,
    181–182, 195, 278, 289,
    348
Naxalites (Maoist revolutionaries),
    xxxii, 63, 132, 138, 259, 297
Nazimuddin, Khwaja, 109, 111
NDA. *See* National Democratic
    Alliance
NEFA. *See* North-East Frontier
    Agency
Nehru, Arun, 310
Nehru, B. K., 264
Nehru, Jawaharlal, 2, 13, 15,
    211–212, 216, 249
    Cabinet Mission (1946) and, 3,
        6–7, 8
    Communism and, 127
    Communist Party and, 130–131
    constitution making and, 8
    death of, 152, 156, 164
    Gandhi, Mahatma and, 94
    Great Calcutta Killing and, 10,
        11
    identity and, 232
    India, government of and, 103,
        116, 119, 139–145
    Indo-Chinese relations and,
        143–145, 145–152
    Indo-Pakistan hostility and,
        153, 155
    Jammu and Kashmir accession
        and, 90
    Kashmir and, 68, 78, 79, 85,
        86, 97–99, 100
    language and, 121–124, 125
    nonalignment and, 141–142
    Pakistan and, 33
    Partition and, 32, 33, 34, 35,
        38–39, 39–40, 41, 43–44, 49,
        54–55, 59
    princely states, accession of
        and, 27, 68, 73–74, 85, 86
    Punjab and, 230
    religious neutrality and, 305
    secularism of, 36, 93, 119, 142,
        233
    socialism and, 173
    Tibet and, 144–145, 189
Nellie, Assam, massacre of, 252,
    253, 254, 268
Nepal, 69, 75, 131
    autonomy and, 312
    bureaucracy in, 292
    China and, xxxiv
    Chinese alliance with, 149
    civil wars in, xxv
    Congress government in, 292
    constitution making in, 137
    democracy in, xxxiii, 137–138,
        290–291
    economy in, 137
    elections in, 137
    Everest, conquest of and,
        134–135, 136–137
    foreign aid and, 294
    Gulf migration and, 227
    identity and, 138–139
    India and, xx–xxi, 136, 138–
        139, 290–301
    Kathmandu massacre in,
        295–296
    literacy in, 138
    NGO government of, 293–294
    panchayat government in, 138,
        290–293
    Partition and, xx
    population of, xx–xxi
    Rana family in, 135, 136
    Seven Party Alliance in, 297, 299
    sovereignty and, 135, 294
    terrorism in, 296
    Tibet and, 139
    UN and, 139
New Delhi, India. *See* India
New York Times, 298
New Zealand, 225
Newsweek, 170
Nirankaris, 257
Nixon, Richard, 187, 190, 191, 223
Nongovernmental agencies
    (NGOs), xxxi, 288–289, 293
Norgay, Tenzing, 133–134, 137

North Atlantic Treaty
    Organization (NATO), 342
North-East Frontier Agency
    (NEFA), 143, 145, 146, 149,
    150, 151
Northern Areas, Pakistan, 89, 97,
    100, 114, 134, 143, 152, 154,
    265, 349
North-West Frontier Province
    (NWFP), xxxiii, 16, 21, 53,
    71–72, 81–82, 87, 107, 179,
    204, 279, 349
Nuclear weapons
    China and, xxvi
    Comprehensive Test Ban Treaty
        and, 325, 327
    India and, xxvi, 202, 211, 214,
        324–327
    Pakistan and, xxvi, 202–203,
        207, 211, 282, 325–327, 329
    United States and, 327
NWFP. *See* North-West Frontier
    Province

October War (1973), 223
Official Language Act (1956),
    239–243
Oil, 196, 208, 223–224, 227, 237
Ojhri, Pakistan, 327
Operation Blue Star, 231–232,
    261–262, 265, 272, 274
Operation Searchlight, 184,
    185–186
OPP. *See* Orangi Pilot Project
Orangi, Pakistan, 278–279,
    281–282
Orangi Pilot Project (OPP),
    278–279
Organization of the Islamic
    Conference, 193
Osman, John, 37

Padmanabhan, Mannathu, 130
Pakistan, 26, 304–305
    Agartala Conspiracy and, 177
    Ahmadis in, 257

autonomy in, 180
Bengal and, 131
Bhutto, Benazir government in,
    285, 287
Bhutto, Zulfikar Ali
    government in, xxxiii, 167,
    193–198, 198–207
birth of, 34–39
break up of, 187–189
bureaucracy in, 177, 201
Cabinet Mission (1946) and, 3,
    7, 8, 9
China and, xxxiv, 188, 203
Communism and, 142
Constituent Assembly of, 32,
    106, 107–108
constitution making and,
    162–163, 179, 180, 183, 203,
    205
corruption in, 22, 180
democracy in, xxxiii, 114–115,
    116–117, 162–163, 167,
    175, 178, 180, 193, 284–
    285, 305
East Bengal and, 109–115
economy in, xxv, 159–160, 167,
    180, 201, 204, 227–228
education and, 177
elections in, 180–182, 203
elites in, 177
employment in, 180
India and, 24, 152–158,
    326–328
Indo-Pak war (1965) and, 170,
    176, 178, 182, 202, 208, 251,
    328
Indus Water Treaty and,
    156–158
inflation in, 177
Islam and, xxvi, 36–37, 116,
    180, 181
as Islamic republic, 114, 200,
    281–285
Jinnah, Mahomed Ali and,
    32–34, 38, 39, 42, 104–106
Kargil war and, 328–329

Kashmir and, xxxiii, 68–69,
    106, 153–156, 160, 178–179,
    264, 329–330, 346–347, 350
Khan, Ayub government in,
    103, 108, 116, 152–158,
    175–179
Khan, Yahya government in,
    180–181
language and, 111–112, 122
Legal Framework Order in,
    180
martial law in, xxv, 176–177,
    179–180, 192, 200, 204, 284
as Muslim homeland, 3, 5, 8,
    12–13, 105–106, 199
Muslim League and, 27, 32–33,
    106–107, 181
Muslims in, xxii, xxvii, 199,
    226
nation building and, xxxii–
    xxxiii
National Assembly in, 180, 183
Nehru, Jawaharlal and, 33
nuclear program of, xxvi,
    202–203, 207, 282, 329
Partition and, xvi, xvii, xxiv, 31,
    32–42, 55
political parties in, 115, 163
political profile of, xxv
population of, 240
Rann of Kutch affair in, 165
religious identity and, 233
remittances to, 227–228
sovereignty and, 3, 5
Taliban in, xxxii, 282, 349
United States and, 163–164,
    179, 246
war in East Bengal (1971) and,
    185–187
Zia ul-Haq government of,
    xxxiii, 279–285, 285–286,
    305
Pakistan Muslim League-N
    (PML-N), 349
Pakistan National Alliance, 203,
    204

Pakistan People's Party (PPP),
    167, 178, 179, 183, 198,
    200–201, 203, 204, 205, 226,
    281
Pakistan Terrorism Portal,
    347–348
Palestine, xxiii, xxvi
Panchayats, 138, 162, 290, 291,
    293
Panjiar, Prashant, 320–321
Partition
    aftermath of, 3, 10
    Assam and, 251
    Bangladesh and, xvi, xvii
    Bengal and, 45, 52–63, 112, 156
    borders and, xv–xvi, xviii–xx
    Britain and, xvi, xvii
    Gandhi, Mahatma and, 52–53,
        54
    implementation of, 39–42,
        42–52
    independence and, xvi–xvii,
        xxv, 3
    India and, xvi, xvii, 31
    Indo-Bangladesh border and,
        xv–xvi, xviii–xx
    Jinnah, Mahomed Ali and, 32,
        32–34, 35–36, 38, 39, 39–40
    Kashmir problem and, 75–83
    landholding patterns and, xviii
    legacy of, xxiv–xxxiv
    massacres of, 182
    migration and, 32, 47–48,
        54–56
    Mountbatten, Lord Louis and,
        34, 34–39, 39–40, 43–44,
        46, 52
    Muslim League and, 38–39, 40
    Nehru, Jawaharlal and, 32, 33,
        34, 35, 38–39, 39–40, 41,
        43–44, 49, 59
    Nepal and, xx
    Pakistan and, xvi, xvii, 31,
        32–34, 34–39, 39–42, 55
    princely states, accession of
        and, 32, 38–39, 65–75, 116

Partition *(continued)*
  Punjab and, 45, 48, 49, 50,
    52–56, 79–80, 156
  Sovereignty and, 32, 33
  strategic contiguity and, xvi
  territory allocation and, 31
  twin principles of, 46–47, 70, 86
Patel, Sardar, xxx, 40, 67, 68,
    70–71, 73–74, 79, 92, 94, 95,
    98, 117, 120
Pathans, 12, 21, 53, 60, 81, 82,
    86, 89, 226, 278, 280
People's Age, 9, 10
People's Liberation Army (PLA),
    135, 136, 144, 147, 149, 150
People's Republic of China. *See*
    China
Peshawar, Pakistan, 12, 82, 161,
    330
Pethick-Lawrence, Lord, 2, 4
Phizo, Angami Zapu, xxxi-xxxii,
    121, 233
Pitroda, Sam, 334
PLA. *See* People's Liberation Army
Pokharan I, 324–326
Pokharan II, 335
Poonch, Jammu and Kashmir,
    76–83, 88, 89–90, 159
Pondicherry, India, 69, 140, 141,
    211
Portugal, 69, 141, 148
Poverty, xxxii, 161, 172, 174,
    178, 208, 221, 289, 305, 312,
    336, 340
Powers, Gary, 164
PPP. *See* Pakistan People's Party
Prabhakaran, Velupillai, 244, 246,
    255
Prachanda, Comrade. *See* Dahal,
    Pushpa Kamal
Princely states, 65
  accession of, 24, 28–29, 33,
    65–75, 79, 84–86, 86–90,
    120
  Cabinet Mission (1946) and,
    23–29

government of, 25
  Partition and, 32, 38–39, 116
Provisional Government of
    the People's Republic of
    Bangladesh, 192
Punjab, xxvii, 9, 12, 43, 125, 148
  accord in, 311
  Kashmir and, 179
  Khalistan movement in,
    254–261
  migration and, 55
  Muslim League and, 107
  Muslim League in, 16
  Operation Blue Star in,
    261–262
  Pakistan and, 16
  Partition and, 32, 33, 45, 46,
    47, 48, 49, 50, 52–56, 79–80,
    156
  Punjab Accord and, 272–275
  remittances to, 228–229
  separatism in, 272
  Sikhs and, 17–19, 230–231,
    254–261, 261–263
Punjab Legislative Assembly, 47
Punjabi, 111, 125
Punjabis, 12, 16, 18, 47, 53, 54,
    58, 61, 159, 182–183, 226,
    229–231, 278, 280

Quit India Movement, 8, 79
Quit Kashmir movement, 79
Quran, 105, 106, 200, 283, 306
Qureshi Muslims, 12–14, 21

Radcliffe, Sir Cyril, 45–47, 55, 76,
    156
Rae Bareilly election (1971), 169,
    174, 175, 210, 215, 217–218,
    235
Rahman, Mujibur, 113, 180, 181,
    208, 287, 340
  assassination of, 198, 206, 219,
    226
  Bangladesh and, 193–198, 217
  Gulf migration and, 226

identity and, 232
Indo-Bangladeshi relations and, 193–194
military overthrow of, xxxiii
Pakistan elections and, 182, 183–184
Rakhi Bahini of, 196, 201
six point program of, 176–178, 180, 183, 231
trial for treason of, 177–178
war in East Bengal (1971) and, 185
Rajapakse, Mahinda, 341
Rajputs, 12, 19
Ramchandran, M. G., 245
Rao, Narasimha, 315, 317, 320, 324, 332–334, 335
Rashtrapati Bhawan, 3, 41, 58, 218
Rashtriya Swayamsevak Sangh (RSS), xxxi, 93–95, 234, 237, 251, 253, 308, 310
Rawalpindi, Pakistan, 82, 108, 114, 155, 160, 161, 164, 202, 216, 327
Reagan, Ronald, 282, 333
Rehman, Teresa, 253
Remittances, xxix, 139, 159–160, 224–229
Republic of India, xx–xxi, xxv, xxx, 3, 40, 118, 133, 143
See also India
Riot After Riot (Akbar), 304
Rose, L. E., 190–191
Roy, B. C., 57
RSS. See Rashtriya Swayamsevak Sangh
Rubaiya Sayeed, 270–271

SAARC. See South Asian Association for Regional Co-operation
SAFTA. See South Asian Free Trade Area
Saikia, Hiteswar, 251
Salazar, Antonio, 141, 148

Sangh Parivar, 308, 309, 312, 318, 319, 320, 321, 322, 323, 324, 331
Saudi Arabia, 226, 232, 281, 285
Saurashtra (Gujarat), 67
Schofield, Victoria, 81, 270
SEATO. See Southeast Asia Treaty Organization
Second World War, 1, 34, 81, 134, 136
Secularism, 15, 36, 93, 107, 119, 142, 155, 194, 232, 233, 319
Segal, Ronald, 172
Separatism, xxiii, 243, 259, 272
September 11, 2001, 295, 329
Seven Party Alliance (Nepal), 297, 299
Shah, Ghulam Mohamed, 264–265, 268
Shah Bano affair, 306–309, 310
Shaikh, Farzana, 105–106, 106
Sharif, Nawaz, 281, 285, 287, 326, 328, 329, 349, 350
Shastri, Lal Bahadur, 156, 164, 165, 166, 170, 241
Shi'ite Islam, xxiii, 283
Shiv Sena, xxxi
Siachen Glacier, 269
Sihanouk, Prince, 141
Sikh Student Association, 273
Sikhism, 257
Sikhs, xxxiii, 12, 17–19, 44, 51, 125, 230
autonomy and, 254
Bengal and, 33, 58
Cabinet Mission (1946) and, 5
Constituent Assembly and, 5
foreign earnings and, 224–225
Gandhi, Indira assassination of and, 265–267
identity and, 254
Khalistan movement and, xxxi, xxxii, 18–19, 254–261, 261–263, 272–273
migration of, 159, 228–229
Partition and, 18, 31, 53

Sikhs *(continued)*
  Punjab and, 33, 230–231,
    254–261, 261–263
  separatism and, 259
Sikkim, xxxii, 69, 211–217, 250
Simla, India, 4, 43, 45, 194
Sind and Sindis, xxviii, 60, 111,
    226, 278, 279–281
Singh, Amar Kaur Jasbir, 217
Singh, Brijendra, 22
Singh, Karan, 98, 99
Singh, Khushwant, 274
Singh, Maharajah Hari, 79, 98,
    100
Singh, Manmohan, 63, 329, 332,
    333–334, 335–337
Singh, Shahbeg (Shubeg), 260
Singh, Tavleen, 268
Singh, Vishwanath Pratap, 270,
    314, 316, 317
Singh, Zail, 256, 257, 259, 262
Sinha, Jagmohanlal, 215
Sinhala, 242, 243, 245–246
Sinhalese, 242, 249
Sisson, Richard, 190
Six Points of Awami League, 180
Socialism, 2, 78, 127, 173, 193,
    208
Socialist Party (India), 169, 174
South Asian Association for
    Regional Co-operation
    (SAARC), 339–343
South Asian Free Trade Area
    (SAFTA), 340–341
Southeast Asia Treaty
    Organization (SEATO), 142,
    164
Sovereignty, xxxii
  autonomy and, xxiv
  Cabinet Mission (1946) and, 5
  ethnicity and, xxi
  identity and, xviii, xxii
  Nepal and, 135, 294
  Pakistan and, 3, 5
  Partition and, 32, 33
  territorial, xxii, xxiv

Soviet Union, xxxiv, 68, 108
  Afghanistan, occupation of
    by, xxxiii, 207, 223, 270,
    279–280, 282, 285, 318
  Bangladesh and, 196
  China and, 131
  Indo-Pakistan hostility and, 166
  Indo-Soviet relations and,
    187–188
  Sino-Indian war and, 151
Sri Lanka, xxv, 4, 41, 75, 131, 184,
    189, 240–241, 245–246, 268
  China and, xxxiv
  economy of, xxvii
  education in, 242
  Gulf migration and, 227
  Jayawardene government in,
    245–247
  language debate in, xxi, 239–243
  population of, 240
  Tamil Tigers in, xxxi, 244–247,
    253, 255, 268, 312, 314, 341
  Tamils in, xxxi, 123, 171–172,
    241–246, 254, 268; 312
  See also Ceylon
Srinagar, Jammu and Kashmir, 65,
    66, 71, 74, 76, 79, 83, 84, 87,
    89, 90, 99, 100, 154, 184,
    264, 265, 270, 271, 322, 328,
    330
Sriramulu, Potti, 125
Stern Reckoning (Khosla), 51
Stevenson, Adlai, 100
Suharto, General, 148
Suhrawardy, Husayn Shaheed,
    52–53, 56, 109, 113, 176
Suicide bombings, xxxii, 282, 314
Sukarno, President of Indonesia,
    141
Sundarbans, xv–xvi, xvii, xxiv, 62
Sunday, 304
Sunderlal Report, 95
Swat, 21–22, 25
Symonds, Richard, 51, 58–59, 80
Syndicate, 171, 173–174, 175,
    230

Talbot, Ian, 163, 200
Taliban, xxxii, 21, 282, 347, 349
Tamil, xxi, 242
Tamil Nadu, 122, 125, 171, 172,
    189, 232, 242, 243, 245,
    246–247
Tamil Students' Federation, 244
Tamil Tigers. See Liberation
    Tigers of Tamil Eelam (LTTE)
Tamil United Liberation Front
    (TULF), 244, 246, 247
Tamils, xxxii, 171–172, 240–248,
    249, 268, 312
Tashkent Declaration, 166, 167,
    170, 176, 178, 179
Terrorism, terrorists, xvii, xx,
    xxiv, xxxii, 157, 177, 206,
    245, 246, 260, 261, 271,
    272–275, 296, 297, 322, 340,
    346
Tezpur, India, 151
Thagla Ridge, 149, 150
Thatcher, Margaret, 263, 265,
    333
Tibet, xxxiv, 68, 77, 134–137,
    139, 140, 144, 189
Time magazine, 319
Times of India, 43, 146
Toddy Tappers, 128–130
Tokyo airport bombing (1985),
    272–273
Treaty of Friendship, Alliance and
    Mutual Assistance, 141–142
Treaty of Peace and Friendship
    (1950), 136, 213–214
Tribhuvan, King of Nepal, 135,
    136
Tripura, xxi, 52, 56, 177, 250
Trivandrum, India, 131
TULF. See Tamil United
    Liberation Front
Tully, Mark, 256, 258, 262, 332

ULFA. See United Liberation
    Front of Assam
UN. See United Nations

UN Commission for India and
    Pakistan (UNCIP), 92, 97
UNHCR. See High Commissioner
    for Refugees
United Front, 131, 243, 269
United Kingdom, xxix, 93, 108,
    225, 265
  diaspora in, 255
  foreign aid and, 294
  Kashmir issue and, 153
  Pakistan elections and, 182
  Sino-Indian war and, 150
  South Asian migration to, 224,
    229
  Sylheti community in, 226
  Tamil diaspora in, 241, 247
  See also Britain
United Liberation Front of Assam
    (ULFA), 253–254
United Nations Military
    Observer Group in India and
    Pakistan (UNMOGIP), 66,
    97, 100
United Nations Mission in Nepal
    (UNMIN), 299
United Nations Security Council,
    325
United Nations (UN), 25, 91–92,
    95, 98, 133, 136, 139, 166,
    196, 240, 256, 329
United Progressive Alliance, 329,
    335–336
United Provinces/Uttar Pradesh
    (UP), 16, 17, 32, 107, 169,
    319–320
United States, xxxiv, 40
  Afghanistan and, 285, 318,
    342
  Bangladesh and, 196
  diaspora in, 255
  foreign aid and, 294
  Indo-Pak relations and, 166,
    178, 235–236
  Kashmir issue and, 153, 164
  Khan, Ayub and, 163–164, 187
  nuclear weapons and, 202, 327

United States *(continued)*
  Pakistan and, 163–164, 179,
    182, 246
  Sino-Indian war and, 150, 151,
    152
  South Asian migration to, 229
  Soviet occupation of
    Afghanistan and, 282
  Tamil diaspora in, 247
  Vietnam War and, 167
  war in East Bengal (1971) and,
    187, 190
UNMIN. *See* United Nations
    Mission in Nepal
UNMOGIP. *See* United Nations
    Military Observer Group in
    India and Pakistan
UP. *See* United Provinces/Uttar
    Pradesh
Urdu, 66, 111, 122, 125, 279
Uri, Jammu and Kashmir, 83
Usmanistan. *See* Hyderabad

Vajpayee, Atal Bihari, 235, 320,
    324, 328, 329, 331, 335,
    350
Van Schendel, Willem, xviii, xix,
    195
VHP. *See* Vishwa Hindu Parishad
Viewpoint, 281
Vishwa Hindu Parishad (VHP),
    308–309, 312–313, 315, 318,
    320, 325

Wajed, Sheikh Hasina, 286–287
War on Terror, 297
Wavell, Lord, 2, 7, 11–12, 13,
    27–28, 161
West Bengal, xvii, xx–xxi, xxvii,
    47, 54–58, 61–62, 110,
    131–133, 172, 181–182, 189,
    195, 213, 312
    See also Bengal; East Bengal
West Pakistan, 72, 109, 113,
    114, 162, 176, 180, 181,
    182, 183
Whitehead, Andrew, 100
Wickramasinghe, Nira, 246
World Bank, 158, 196, 227, 288
World War I, 225, 255
World War II, 1, 81, 134, 136

Yunus, Muhammad, 278

Zardari, Asif Ali, 331, 348–350
Zhou Enlai, 141, 144, 147, 150,
    164
Zia, Khaleda, 286–287, 318
Zia ul-Haq, xxxiii, 105, 203,
    204–207, 226, 233, 269,
    279–286, 305, 327, 349
Ziaur Rahman, xxxiii, 185, 198,
    226, 233, 285–286, 340
Zinkin, Taya, 59, 128, 129–130,
    131
Ziring, Lawrence, 177, 195, 197,
    198, 286